DAILY LIFE IN
CIVIL WAR
AMERICA

Recent Titles in
The Greenwood Press "Daily Life Through History" Series

Daily Life in Elizabethan England
Jeffrey L. Singman

Daily Life in Chaucer's England
Jeffrey L. Singman and Will McLean

Daily Life in the Inca Empire
Michael A. Malpass

Daily Life in Maya Civilization
Robert J. Sharer

Daily Life in Victorian England
Sally Mitchell

Daily Life in the United States, 1960–1990: Decades of Discord
Myron A. Marty

Daily Life of the Aztecs: People of the Sun and Earth
David Carrasco with Scott Sessions

Daily Life in Ancient Mesopotamia
Karen Rhea Nemet-Nejat

Daily Life of the Ancient Greeks
Robert Garland

Daily Life During the Holocaust
Eve Nussbaum Soumerai and Carol D. Schulz

DAILY LIFE IN

CIVIL WAR AMERICA

DOROTHY DENNEEN VOLO
AND JAMES M. VOLO

The Greenwood Press "Daily Life Through History" Series

GREENWOOD PRESS
Westport, Connecticut • London

Library of Congress Cataloging-in-Publication Data

Volo, Dorothy Denneen, 1949–
    Daily life in Civil War America / Dorothy Denneen Volo and James
M. Volo.
       p. cm.—(The Greenwood Press "Daily life through history"
series, ISSN 1080–4749)
    Includes bibliographical references (p.) and index.
    ISBN 0–313–30516–1 (alk. paper)
    1. United States—History—Civil War, 1861–1865—Social aspects.
2. United States—Social life and customs—1783–1865. I. Volo,
James M., 1947– . II. Title. III. Series.
E468.9.V6   1998
973.1'1—DC21   98–17486

British Library Cataloguing in Publication Data is available.

Library of Congress Catalog Card Number: 98–17486
ISBN: 0–313–30516–1
ISSN: 1080–4749

First published in 1998

Greenwood Press, 88 Post Road West, Westport, CT 06881
An imprint of Greenwood Publishing Group, Inc.

Printed in the United States of America

The paper used in this book complies with the
Permanent Paper Standard issued by the National
Information Standards Organization (Z39.48–1984).

10 9 8 7 6 5 4 3 2 1

Contents

Introduction   xi

Chronology   xv

Part I
History, Politics, and Slavery

1. The Historians' War   3
   Nineteenth-Century America   3
   Sowing the Seeds of Conflict   6
   A Divided Economy   8
   Modernization   9
   Politics as Usual   12

2. Politics: The National Hobby   15
   The Politics of Division   15
   The Election of 1860   19
   Secession   22
   Fire-eaters   22
   The Southern Radical Press   24
   The Act of Disunion   25

3. The American Zion   31

    The American Zion   31

    Growing Government   33

    Urbanization   35

    Religion   38

    Reform Movements   40

4. On Behalf of Southern Independence   49

    Southern Nationalism   49

    Reestablishing the American Revolution   53

    Blockade Runners   57

    The Bread Riots   58

5. The Peculiar Institution: Slavery   61

    The Slave Trade   61

    Plantation Slavery   65

    Slave Clothing   68

    Slave Work Week   68

    Slave Food   69

    Slave Entertainment   70

    Legal Rights for Slaves and Discipline   70

    Draft Riots   72

    Black Churches   73

    The Slave Family   74

    Miscegenation   75

6. Abolition   81

    The Anti-slavery Movement   81

    Abolitionists   85

    Black Anti-slavery Activists   88

    Slaveowners   89

    Slavery and the Courts   91

    Mutiny on the _Amistad_   91

    The Lemmon Case   92

    The Dred Scott Decision   93

Part II
Soldiers' Lives

7. Billy Yank and Johnny Reb 97
   Common Soldiers 97
   Boys in War 106
   Partisan Warfare 108
   Conscription 108
   Prisoners of War 111
   Disbanding the Armies 111

8. Hardtack and Coffee 115
   Supplying the Army with Grub 115
   Army Food 116
   Cookware 116
   The Commissary 117
   Foodstuffs 118

9. Tenting Tonight: The Soldier's Life 133
   Shelter 133
   Equipment 139
   Uniforms 144
   Camp Life and Recreation 145

10. Tactics and Strategy 149
    Strategy 149
    Geography 151
    Raiders 154
    Railroads 155
    Roads 158
    Military Organization 160
    Armies 162
    Corps and Divisions 163
    Tactics 165
    Ancillary Units 165
    Moral Awakening 169
    Women at War 170

11. Seeing the Elephant: The Realities of Life in Battle 173

Part III:
Civilians' Lives

12. Be It Ever So Humble   191
         The Front Hall   191
         The Parlor   193
         The Library   199
         The Dining Room   200
         The Kitchen   200
         The Bedrooms   201
         The Nursery   201
         The Necessary   202

13. Leisure Time   203
         Literature   203
         Newspapers   211
         Availability of Reading Material   214
         Women Writers   215
         Photography   216
         Optical Novelties   218
         Cultural Institutions   219
         Reading Clubs   219
         Lectures   219
         Games   220
         Ladies' Crafts   221

14. Feast or Famine: Food and Cooking   225
         Storage   225
         Modern Advancement   226
         Food Attitudes   228
         Common Foods   228
         Food Prices   229
         The War's Effect   230
         Shortages   230
         Supplementing the Troops   235

15. The Look: Fashion and Women's Clothing   237
         Women's Clothing   238
         The Dress   238
         Undergarments   245

	Outerwear	247
	Headgear	248
	Ancillary Clothing	249
	Footwear	250
	Accessories	250
	Jewelry	251
	Hairstyles	252
16.	Dressed for the Part: Men's, Children's, and Slaves' Clothing	257
	Men's Clothing	257
	Children's Clothing	262
	Slaves' Clothing	267
17.	Elevating and Expanding the Young Mind	271
18.	Till the Mournful Night Is Gone: Death and Dying	283
	Bibliography	301
	Index	309

Introduction

The federal capital at Washington was highly valued as a symbol by nineteenth-century Americans. Carefully laid out in a district allocated from within the boundaries of Maryland in order to salve the pride of the South, the nation's capital city had been under construction since the turn of the century. Americans pointed proudly to the imposing structure of the Capitol building, as well as the General Post Office, the Bureau of the Treasury, the Smithsonian Institution, and the Executive Mansion, as representative of a vigorous young nation preparing to take its place among the leading countries of the world.

Unfortunately, Washington was also symbolic of other things. The plans for the city, like the basic founding concepts of the nation itself, were as pretentious as they were visionary, and in 1860 both lay unfulfilled and disordered. Sprawling along the banks of the Potomac with the "Old City" of Alexandria, Virginia, across the water, the great buildings of the new capital remained incomplete even after the expenditure of vast sums of money and six decades of effort. The Capitol building lay unfinished with its original dome removed—a scaffolding and a towering crane representative of restructuring and rethinking. The wings of the building were "stretched bare and unfinished, devoid even of steps." The imposing obelisk of the Washington Monument lay as a mere foundation. Blocks of marble, lumber, cast iron plates, and the tools of workmen strewn about the district gave quiet testimony to the fact that the plan for the nation's first city, like the social and political plan for the American nation itself, was incomplete and open to revision.[1]

At the head of the James River, one hundred miles south of Washington and in sharp contrast to it, was Richmond, Virginia. As the third largest city in the South, Richmond had proven an elegant state capital with fine buildings and traditional architecture. Although the city was cultivated and cosmopolitan, it was also the center of Virginia's economy, with mills, railways, and trading establishments. In 1861 Richmond was the finest city in the South and one of the better places in which to live in the entire country. Within a few months of secession, though, Richmond had been made the capital of the new Confederate nation, and its tenor changed dramatically. The city teemed with soldiers, wagons, and government officials. Defenses in the form of artillery emplacements, trenches, and earthworks rimmed its suburbs. The South's only major foundry, the Tredegar Iron Works, turned out cannon, rails, and plates for gunboats. But in a mere four years the once stately city would be a ruin comparable to the broken hulk of Berlin at the end of World War II. Its people would be described as looking "hungry, gaunt, ghastly, and yellow." Even the young were so pale and thin that it was "pitiful to see."[2]

The War of Southern Secession, a civil war, had come to America. It would be one of the most tragic events in the nation's history, resulting from a dispute among its citizens over just what the new country should look like. For four years the country passed through a traumatic military and social upheaval that touched the lives of its people in many ways. More than 600,000 soldiers died from wounds and disease, and an incalculable number of civilian lives were permanently disrupted by war. Such matters have sent historians delving in the depths of old newspaper columns, official records, letters, and memoirs to unearth the details of constitutional pressures, agricultural and industrial production, social development, and political evolution, thereby producing over the intervening decades an enormous and ever-growing body of printed work. More than 100,000 volumes have been written about the American Civil War.

No event in American history has had so much written about it, but much of the research has dealt with battles, operations, commanders, and military personalities. When a nation is at war it is not just the soldiers whose lives are changed. The lives of the civilians who remain behind, whether they are joined to the battle by the ties of love or not, are altered just as irrevocably. This book is designed to dovetail with other texts that focus on the widespread activities of armies and states in conflict while it attends to the events of daily life. It is hoped that the work will integrate into the body of military knowledge the details of the lifestyles of the people who populated the great northern cities or lived amid the ruins of the South through almost fifteen hundred days of conflict.

Of great weight, and equal importance, are the details of soldier life in the camps and on campaign. Nonetheless, the devotees of warfare will find this work almost devoid of descriptions of specific battles except insofar as they provide a chronology of events. The vagaries and hazards of military life are reported as the soldiers would have experienced them in their own microcosm rather than in a giant overview. The chapter on the ordeals of combat is drawn almost solely from firsthand accounts of the actual experiences of the soldiers who fought.

The research for the sections of this book dealing with politics, clothing, mourning, amusements, religion, and the household has led to untold diaries, letters, journals, maps, tracts, and old newspapers as well as to museums, historic places, antique shops, and old bookstores. The authors—devoted historians and teachers for close to three decades— hope that they have extricated the germ of truth from these and other sources without distorting a genuine picture of daily life in Civil War America.

NOTES

1. Margaret Leech, *Reveille in Washington* (New York: Harper & Brothers, 1941), 5–6.

2. James H. Croushore, ed., *A Volunteer's Adventure*, by Captain John W. De Forest (New Haven: Yale University Press, 1949), 35.

Chronology

March 1820
:   The Missouri Compromise admits Maine and Missouri as free and slave states, respectively, and prohibits slavery in the territories north of 36°30' north latitude.

May 1822
:   Denmark Vesey is executed for plotting a slave uprising.

December 1828
:   First nullification crisis. South Carolina nullifies the Tariff of 1828.

January 1831
:   William Lloyd Garrison begins publishing *The Liberator*.

August 1831
:   Nat Turner, a radical slave preacher, is killed as he leads a bloody slave revolt in Virginia.

November 1832
:   South Carolina nullifies the Tariff of 1832. President Jackson utilizes the Force Bill against South Carolina, but Henry Clay provides a compromise.

December 1833
:   The American Anti-Slavery Society is organized.

August 1839
:   The Cuban slave ship *Amistad* is brought into New Haven, Connecticut, by a U.S. naval vessel.

March 1841
:   The Africans from the *Amistad* are freed by the Supreme Court to return to Africa.

July 1845	The Republic of Texas formally agrees to annexation to the United States.
May 1846–February 1848	The Mexican-American War. General Winfield Scott marches victoriously into Mexico City. The Treaty of Guadalupe Hidalgo ends the war by giving a half million square miles of the West to the United States.
September 1850	The Compromise of 1850 extends the bounds of legal slavery and strengthens the Fugitive Slave Act.
June 1851–March 1852	Harriet Beecher Stowe's *Uncle Tom's Cabin* appears first as a serial and finally as a complete novel.
January 1854	The Kansas-Nebraska Act, which would repeal the Compromise of 1850 and substitute the concept of popular sovereignty, is endorsed by Northern Democrats.
February 1854	Anti-slavery proponents form the Republican Party in reaction to the Kansas-Nebraska Act.
May 1854	The Kansas-Nebraska Act is passed by Congress and signed by President Pierce.
December 1855	A virtual civil war over slavery exists along the border between Kansas and Missouri.
May 1856	Senator Charles Sumner is beaten with a cane by Rep. Preston Brooks of South Carolina in the Senate Chamber of the Capitol. Fiery abolitionist John Brown kills five pro-slavery men at Pottawotamie Creek in Kansas.
March 1857	The Supreme Court hands down its decision against Dred Scott and declares the Missouri Compromise of 1820 unconstitutional.
June 1858	In Illinois, the Republican Party chooses Abraham Lincoln to run for the Senate against Stephen Douglas. Lincoln gives his famous "House Divided" speech.
October 1859	John Brown is seized by federal troops led by Col. Robert E. Lee at Harper's Ferry. By December he is tried, convicted of treason, and hanged.

May 1860	The Republican Party nominates Lincoln for president.
November 1860	Lincoln wins election in a four-way race.
December 1860	South Carolina votes to secede from the Union, beginning a rush by some Southern states to form the Confederacy.
April 1861	With the bombardment of Fort Sumter, Lincoln calls for 75,000 volunteers to defend the Union. Virginia joins the Confederate States, followed by Arkansas, North Carolina, and Tennessee. The American Civil War has begun.
April–June 1861	West Virginia supports the Union. Although federal soldiers are killed in Baltimore, Maryland repudiates secession. Col. Thomas J. Jackson seizes the federal arsenal at Harper's Ferry. Missouri and much of Kentucky come under federal control.
July 1861	Battle of First Manassas, or First Bull Run, in Virginia. After the surprising defeat of the federal forces only minor skirmishing takes place for several months between the opponents on either side of the Potomac, in Missouri, and in Kentucky.
October 1861	Gen. Winfield Scott passes command of the federal forces to Gen. George McClellan.
November– December 1861	The *Trent* Affair. Possible war looms between the federal government and Great Britain over the seizure of Confederate diplomats from a British vessel. The crisis is averted when the men are released at year's end.
February 1862	Forts Henry and Donelson fall to Gen. Ulysses S. Grant. Grant demands "unconditional and immediate surrender."
March 1862	Gen. Thomas "Stonewall" Jackson begins a three-month campaign in the Shenandoah Valley against three federal armies that will become a model of tactics and strategy for students of military science. The CSS *Virginia* and USS *Monitor* battle in Hampton Roads, Virginia.

April 1862	The Battle of Shiloh in Tennessee is the bloodiest of the war to this point, but New Orleans falls to federal naval forces and troops with little opposition.
June and July 1862	The Seven Days Battles begin McClellan's failed Peninsular campaign.
September 1862	Battle of Second Manassas or Second Bull Run. Battle of Antietam. Lincoln drafts the Emancipation Proclamation.
December 1862	Battle of Murfreesboro, Tennessee, or Stones River. Battle of Fredericksburg.
January 1863	Emancipation Proclamation takes effect.
April 1863	Richmond Bread Riot.
May 1863	Battle of Chancellorsville.
July 1863	Battle of Gettysburg. Fall of Vicksburg.
September 1863	Battle of Chickamauga.
November 1863	Battle of Chattanooga.
March 1864	Gen. U. S. Grant becomes commander of federal forces.
May 1864	Battle of the Wilderness. Battle of Spotsylvania Courthouse. While May is the bloodiest month of the war, in June 1864, 7,000 men fall in twenty minutes at the Battle of Cold Harbor.
June–July 1864	The campaign leading to the fall of Atlanta begins. The siege of Petersburg begins.
November 1864	Lincoln defeats McClellan in the presidential election.
January 1865	Lincoln begins his second term with Andrew Johnson of Tennessee as vice-president.
April 1865	Lee surrenders at Appomattox Courthouse. Lincoln is assassinated by John Wilkes Booth.
June 1865	The last of the Confederate forces under Gen. Stand Wati formally surrender.

Part I

History, Politics, and Slavery

1

The Historians' War

"An irrepressible conflict between opposing and enduring forces."
—William H. Seward

At the outbreak of the war, all but the most astute observers thought that the question of national unity would be settled in a single afternoon of combat. But in the first great battle of the war, the intrinsic drama of Americans locked in mortal combat diverted everyone's attention from the fact that indecisiveness had crept into warfare over the centuries. From 1861 to 1865 Yankees were "bushwhacked" in western Virginia and Rebels "sniped at" near Washington. Federal "Red Legs" and Confederate "Partisans" mauled one another across the plains of Kansas and Missouri and were held in contempt by the politicians on both sides.

Simultaneously, giant armies trudged across Northern Virginia, Louisiana, and middle Tennessee in efforts to either defend or dismantle the Old South and its characteristic lifestyle. The war policies of both governments so extended into the lives of the local populations that people came to look seriously upon the result as "the hard hand of war." Meanwhile, the terrible cost of war, measured in thousands of lives, afflicted the North with such a palpable weariness that Abraham Lincoln despaired of winning reelection in 1864. He began to lay plans for turning the federal government over to a successor who would end the war by simply declaring it finished.[1]

The Battle of Gettysburg, the bloodiest ever fought on the North American continent, has long been a focal point of Civil War historians. Taken with the simultaneous fall of Vicksburg, the Confederate stronghold on the Mississippi, the federal victory at Gettysburg should have been one of the most decisive military actions in history. Yet the internecine struggle continued, seemingly powered by the undiminished will of the Southern people to prevail. "We shall not give up the contest," said one Confederate officer after the fall of the Southern stronghold at Port Hudson, "and I think we shall tire you out at last." From the rousing partisan raids of cavalier clad horsemen in Tennessee to the dreary siege warfare of the Petersburg trenches, the obstinate refusal of the ragged troops to be forced from a thousand battlefields left the issue of what constituted the American nation undecided for four long years. Yet only about a dozen engagements of the war are considered worthy of general interest in today's classrooms and lecture halls.[2]

Immediately after the war, the public was swamped with war stories, journals, memoirs, and battle descriptions. Former army commanders renewed wartime arguments about tactics and strategies in print—the pen and the printing press their only weapons. Battlefield opponents, and sometimes former comrades, aired the dirty laundry of their respective commands before an awaiting public. Southern apologists, particularly, tried to rationalize their lost cause by finding unexploited opportunities, scapegoats, excuses, and martyrs. For quite some time—in fact for almost as long as the veterans of the war lived—this was the stuff of Civil War history.

However, in the 1940s and 1950s historians became mesmerized by the idea of identifying the reasons for the conflict, setting off a new wave of printing. Yet the causes proved so lost in a maze of interrelated factors and so obscured by the hidden agendas of those who wrote, or rewrote, history that there was no possibility of identifying all of them. Historians found that more than two years before the outbreak of hostilities, Americans had already identified, to their satisfaction at least, a very powerful cause for the bloody struggle that loomed between the increasingly antagonistic sections of their country. "It is an irrepressible conflict between opposing and enduring forces," declared William H. Seward. Some modern historians still agree with this outspoken anti-slavery Republican, but others disagree, believing the war could have been avoided by compromise. Nonetheless, it seems certain, from the distance of generations, that some form of civil upheaval was inevitable.[3]

A more meaningful debate has centered in recent years around the people who found themselves caught in undercurrents of history so strong and compelling that they were unable to avoid conflict. This discussion has sparked several interesting lines of research into the nature

The Hard Hand of War: Sketch artist Henry Lovie's view of the condition of refugee families driven from their homes in the border states as printed in *Leslie's Illustrated Magazine*.

of American society before and during the conflict, and historians have studied constitutional theory, politics, economics, geography, and society in an attempt to understand the wartime generation. Research in these areas has been particularly helpful in producing a mass of documentary evidence concerning the lives of the people of the Civil War era.

This research has made it clear that secession, and not slavery, was the precipitating controversy of the war. Although anti-slavery was a prominent reform movement of the period, other causes, such as temperance, women's rights, religious revival, public education, concerns for the poor, and prison reform, were as zealously pursued by activists. Of these only slavery and disunion became politically charged issues in the antebellum period; and as the middle ground of compromise on such issues was eroded, only the extreme positions became viable, until disunion brought on armed conflict. Universal abolition, never an overall war aim of the North, was not even recognized by the proclamation of emancipation of 1863. As expressed by one abolitionist, the prominence of secession as a cause of the war becomes obvious: "Who cares now about slavery. Secession, and the Oligarchy built upon it, have crowded it out."[4]

The case for secession had flourished for more than seven decades, and it would seem, from an unbiased reading of the record, that the secessionists had at least an arguable case on their side. By comparison, the case for a perpetual union was a recent product of the sectional conflicts of the 1850s. Moreover, its fundamental legal principles were far from perfect, and the logic behind its arguments was fraught with ambiguity. Unfortunately the specific legal status of secession was never adjudicated by a court due to the haste with which both North and South resorted to armed conflict.

Sowing the Seeds of Conflict How did the nation come to such an impasse? Historians have long held that part of the answer may lie in the questions about the nature of the American nation that had been left undecided by the Founding Fathers. Of these questions, the continuation of slavery and the political relationship between the state and national governments had resisted resolution. The crux of the slavery issue revolved around the question of whether the United States had been founded as a free republic that allowed slavery or as a slaveholding republic with pockets of freedom. The question of "states' rights" held at issue whether the state or the national government was ultimately sovereign. Since both situations had existed simultaneously for decades, which was the aberration?

The Founders produced a loose-knit union of sovereign states under the Articles of Confederation which had resulted from their dedication to the historic concepts of personal, political, and property rights. The limitations of the Articles became almost immediately apparent, however, and the Constitutional Convention of 1787 was called to amend them. The delegates chose, instead, to write a totally new underpinning document.

To provide for free and open discussion, no minutes of the deliberations were taken. If not for the personal notes taken by the delegates, nothing of the constitutional debates would be known today. The lack of explicit and indisputable records from the convention created a problem during the antebellum political wrangling. Advocates of one position or another tended to use self-serving and selective excerpts from the writings of the Founding Fathers. Those who supported abolition, for instance, invoked Jefferson's phrase, "All men are created equal," while those who opposed it were quick to point out that Jefferson had also written that "blacks . . . are inferior to the whites in the endowments both of body and mind."[5]

Free from the intensity of the debate that was prevalent in the 1850s, it is clear today that the primary desire of the framers of the Constitution was to design a government that would possess only those powers necessary to carry out the common needs of the thirteen states and relieve the obvious weaknesses in the Articles. There was considerable disagreement about the exact limits of the relationship among the new federal government, the older states, and the individual citizen. In this regard, the delegates invoked the concept of state sovereignty; but republicanism, social pluralism, and constitutionalism were deemed the primary characteristics for a new government by the majority. Slavery and the possibility of future disunion were considered secondary issues. Few observers at the time thought that the questions raised about the fundamentals of American society and government would come to be "settled only at the cannon's mouth."[6]

The idea of limited federal power was much older than the slavery debates of the nineteenth century and was recognized as an unresolved issue at the time. Would the *united states*, melted down into one nation, be practicable or consistent with freedom? Thomas Jefferson warned that if the federal government was allowed to define the limits of its own powers, the result would be "not short of despotism." The anxiety over the exact extent of federal authority was serious enough to require the addition of a separate Bill of Rights defining the limits of governmental power alluded to in the principal document. Without a Bill of Rights it was deemed impossible to achieve the adoption of the Constitution by the delegates or to ensure its ratification by the states. Nonetheless, even a radical politician like Patrick Henry refused to sanction the new Constitution, saying, "I smell a rat!"[7]

It is important in this discussion to emphasize the contrast between "rights" and "powers." Ironically, many strong reservations about "powers" came from the Northern states during the ratification debates. The Massachusetts legislature expressed a fear that the Constitution might be interpreted so as to extend the powers of Congress, and Rhode Island proposed a remarkable statement of states' rights similar in sentiment to that used by Southern secessionists two generations later. Even New England politicians resorted to their rights and threatened secession if their demands were not met. Among the Southern states, the people of Virginia required that the powers granted the national government under the Constitution "be resumed by the states, whensoever the same shall be perverted to their injury or oppression."[8] Both Thomas Jefferson and James Madison believed that the states were "not united on the principle of unlimited submission to their general government" but reserved "each State to itself, the . . . right to their own self-government."[9]

The concept of states' rights was clearly a separate issue from that of slavery in the minds of the Founding Fathers. Although Southerners frequently invoked states' rights as a symbol in their turmoil over slavery, the concept was first elaborated in the tariff nullification crises of the 1820s and 1830s. Nonetheless, states' rights advocates seem to have been able to keep the two questions of sovereignty and slavery distinct. In much of the North, however, the questions of states' rights and the continuation of slavery became a single issue on which it was impossible to have divergent views.

The Constitution clearly recognized and protected the right of a citizen to own slaves. Only by the most tortured of legal arguments could slavery have been considered illegal under the original founding document. Moreover, the Tenth Amendment explicitly forbade the federal government to intervene in state affairs. For this reason alone, the South proclaimed that the federal government had no justification in law to interfere with slavery. The Supreme Court, often top-heavy with Southern justices, had generally sided with the South on these questions, and Southerners had prevented any changes in law by maintaining control of the Senate. Historians feel that when the South perceived a possible loss of this legislative and judicial advantage, it resorted to secession as a remedy.

A Divided Economy

A favorite area of study by the historians of the 1970s was economics. On the surface, at least, the Southern section of the country was doing well in 1850. The South shared with the rest of the country a common language, an identification with many basic legal principles, and a growing body of literature, music, and history. Indeed, both cultures were basically moral, righteous, and eminently Protestant. Each side viewed itself as truly patriotic and dedicated to the Constitution. But the economies of the industrialized North and the agrarian South were becoming increasingly difficult to reconcile. Southern nationalists, in particular, deplored the increasing dependence of their economy on Northern manufacturing and shipping. By the 1850s, canal and railroad construction had strengthened the economic position of the northeastern cities to the detriment of Southern ports. Farmers in the Northwest were now able to bypass traditional Southern trading outlets and ship directly to the East Coast. Consequently the political allegiance of the Northwest had also shifted and upset the traditional political balance of the government in favor of the North.

The South's importance as a comprehensive producer of agricultural products was also waning in this period, being replaced by the farms of Michigan, Iowa, Kansas, and Missouri. Tobacco remained an important crop in North Carolina and Kentucky, but the tobacco plantations of Virginia and Maryland were feeling the effects of depressed prices and depleted soils. The largest Southern crop was corn, which was consumed locally by man and beast. Rice was a valuable export item, and the rice plantations of South Carolina and Georgia were still prosperous in the 1850s.

Southern cotton production had originated along the coast and moved into the back country of South Carolina and Georgia by the end of the eighteenth century, but it quickly spread into all the states that were to become members of the Confederacy. The significance of cotton in the money-conscious nineteenth century resulted primarily from the fact that it was a cash crop. By mid-century more than 5 million bales were being produced annually, causing cotton to be termed the "king" of agricultural exports. The Southern cities, particularly New Orleans, Mobile, Savannah, and Charleston, continued to flourish because of their dedication to the export of cotton. In 1853 New Orleans was described in a child's geography text as "remarkable for the number of ships and steamboats that crowd its levee, or [land] along the river."[10] Yet on the eve of the war, New York was exporting more cotton to Europe than Charleston, much of it transshipped from other Southern ports including New Orleans. Seventy-five percent of all cotton came from plantations, as did almost all of the rice, sugar, and tobacco. The success of the plantation economy, and of the cotton plantations in particular, therefore, was vital to the continuation of the genteel Southern lifestyle.

Cultural and social changes were sweeping the North in the 1840s and 1850s. Industry and urbanization had **Modernization** moved the North toward a more modern society with an unprecedented set of novel social values, while the South had essentially lagged behind, clinging to the traditions of the eighteenth century.

Historians have noted that the differences between the folk culture of the South and the modern culture of the North certainly fueled the broad-based reform movements of mid-century and may have ignited the turmoil over state sovereignty and slavery. The debate surrounding these questions, driven by an intensely partisan press, "not only aroused feelings of jealousy, honor, and regional pride, but raised fundamental questions about the future direction of the American society."[11]

The most obvious modern element in the North was the rapid growth of its urban centers as more and more people flocked to the cities to find work in the factories. Although the class structure was still dominated by the old social elite, a new middle class was striving to become socially acceptable; and it was becoming increasingly difficult for the community to distinguish between the two. Unfortunately, the distinctions between these and the urban lower classes continued to be characterized by sharp contrasts in wealth, ethnic origin, and religion.

The lower classes of the North were exceedingly poor and were composed largely of immigrants. Many of the poorest immigrants were Irish Catholics. The Irish were the first truly urban group in America, living in crowded slums rife with crime and disease, and experiencing severe religious prejudice at the hands of the Protestant majority. "Help wanted" advertisements often stated, "Irish need not apply." One of the ironic characteristics of the new modernism in Northern society was the simultaneous existence of anti-slavery sentiment and severe ethnic prejudice among upper-class Protestants. This is especially surprising in view of the prominence of social reform movements in the North.

The South was a structured society tied to tradition and continuity rather than to progress and change. Southerners strove to maintain a romanticized version of the old aristocratic order as it was before the American Revolution. They were remarkably intolerant of social reform and disdainful of activism; yet they thought of themselves as well mannered, chivalrous to women and children, religious, and protective of all that was still fundamentally good in America. They lionized the stratified, but benevolent, social order portrayed in the nineteenth-century romance novel. To paraphrase the immensely popular Sir Walter Scott, the lower classes retained enough "insolence" to tell the aristocrats that any breach of proper formality between them was dishonorable to both. At all levels of Southern society individual liberty, manliness, and respect for authority and position were held in such high esteem that one put his life and personal honor on the line to protect them.[12]

The vast majority of Southern citizens were small farmers who planned their lives around rural activities and seasonal chores such as barn raising, quilting bees, planting, haying, and harvesting. Their concept of time was based on sunrise, noon, spring, or summer, and they set their appointments or ended the workday by this standard. Free white laborers and artisans were paid at the completion of a task, and rarely by the clock or calendar. The system provided continuity in the work relationship between employer and employee, and it was not unusual for one family to be employed by another in the same capacity for several generations. Family members usually cooperated in completing chores. This togetherness was thought to foster feelings of kinship and traditional family values. Fathers and mothers worked beside their children and grandchildren in an idyllic, if not a mechanically efficient, simplicity.

While many Northerners were still farmers, a growing segment of the population was becoming tied to the cities and factories. Middle-class men who had grown up in the first half of the century could remember a childhood spent living in a family working environment, either on the farm, in a cottage at the mill, or in a room behind the family shop. But as the century progressed men's work increasingly took place in the special atmosphere of business premises such as the factory or office. Fathers commonly left the home to work for ten to fourteen hours, and their children rarely saw them during daylight hours. A father's work and workplace became foreign to his children. This tendency to "go to work," rather than to work at home, led to the virtual removal of men from the home environment, leaving it the sole province of the female. The modern nineteenth-century home increasingly came to focus almost solely on the wife and children. The evolution to a female-dominated household may help to explain the growing formalism and rigid authoritarianism that Victorian fathers demanded when they were present.[13]

With the general availability of the pocket watch, these men increasingly lived their lives by the clock. They valued these timepieces as heirlooms. The last significant act of many Civil War soldiers was to ensure that their pocket watches were passed on to their sons. Factory workers were expected to work in shifts dictated by the public clocks that came to be prominently displayed on towers, in the streets, and on the factory walls. In 1847 John A. Thayer of Stoughton, Massachusetts, published one of the first books of tables for the calculation of wages "at various prices, either by the day, week, or month, for different lengths of time." The idea of being "on time" represented a significant change in the lifestyle of most city dwellers; and since the North was the most urbanized section of the country, being on time became characteristic of Northern life.[14]

Conversely, Southerners, who had no need to work by the clock, were often viewed as shiftless and lazy. Southern laborers feared the development of the unprecedented "work for wage" economy of the cities, and they saw Northern wage earners as degraded and enslaved persons. The city worker sold himself into economic bondage for a wage, and the expansion of a similar work for wage system was dreaded by Southerners almost as much as abolitionists dreaded the expansion of slavery. Southern whites were clearly anxious to maintain their status as freemen, even if this required that they be very poor freemen. Many in the laboring class believed that the North was determined to enslave them to the factory system or counting house. The modern egalitarian society of the North was viewed with disdain and seen as degenerate and immoral. Rising crime rates in the cities, flagrant and open prostitution, and the squalid conditions of the urban lower classes were proffered as proof of Northern inferiority.

The unmodernized South was led by a privileged planter class whose elite lifestyle was maintained at the expense of the rest of society. This planter aristocracy relied on its kinship network and social status as means to personal success. Southern culture and institutions were seen by outsiders as backward, inefficient, and harmful to the American nation as a whole. Nonetheless, the Southern elite voluntarily assumed the role of benefactor and knight errant to all other levels of their society. Like cavaliers on a quest, Southern men felt obliged to counsel and defend not only their own families, but all females and minor children placed under their protection. This obligation was extended to their slaves in an ambiguous, but serious, way. Many Southerners were genuinely concerned for the physical and moral welfare of their slaves, but only in terms of continued racial separation and subjugation.

Failing to acknowledge the good in Southern society because it was tied to slavery, Northern reformers made no attempt to hide their universal disapproval of all things Southern. They became increasingly acrimonious, alienating, and violent in their rhetoric as the war approached. These social reformers were widely viewed as interventionists, fanatics, anarchists, or worse by the Southern population.

Politics as Usual   The most modern element in American life in the first half of the century was a vigorous interest in politics. Politics became a great national pastime, almost a hobby, shared by both the North and the South. This interest crossed many of the old social and economic lines to engage devotees from many classes, with sharp debates resulting on an almost daily basis. Unfortunately, restraint was conspicuously absent from the political process of the 1850s.

Historians have observed that this widespread participation almost certainly added to the furor for war. Antagonists on all sides assailed their opponents with arguments taken from the law, the Bible, literature, pamphlets, election speeches, and the press. When unprepared to rebut these arguments on an equal footing, the opponents often resorted to ridiculous remarks and unsupported allegations. A Southern observer wrote of the period: "The hot headed politician and preacher seemed to be molding public opinion without any regard to the country as a whole. Both North and South proving, from their point of view, the righteousness of their positions by resorting to both the Bible and the Constitution."[15]

Politics became increasingly characterized by intemperate and abusive language, or even fisticuffs, especially when the subject turned to inflammatory issues such as slavery. When Senator Charles Sumner, a man of "wicked tongue" and "intemperate language" with regard to slavery, was beaten with a cane by Congressman Preston Brooks in the Senate, the blows were struck not only in the halls of Congress, but in the barbershops, parlors, and taverns of every small town and city.[16]

The great flaw in the work of historians of the antebellum period was that they could not explain how the geographic sections of the nation could share so many important cultural and political characteristics and still be mutually antagonistic to the point of shedding blood. The actual causes of the war are complex and multidimensional, and any discussion along these lines inevitably remains totally academic. It is clear that the nation did not go to war simply because of slavery any more than it did over disputes involving temperance, urbanization, poverty, politics, or economics. Possibly historians should look to the cumulative effect of all the various disputes as a cause of the war. Nonetheless, the work done by these researchers has proved helpful in documenting the characteristics of daily life in this period.

NOTES

1. See Virgil Carrington Jones, *Gray Ghosts and Rebel Raiders* (New York: Galahad, 1956), 45–46, 166; Russell F. Weigley, *The Age of Battles: The Quest for Decisive Warfare from Breitenfeld to Waterloo* (Bloomington: Indiana University Press, 1991), xii–xiii; Mark Grimsley, *The Hard Hand of War: Union Military Policy Toward Southern Civilians, 1861–1865* (Cambridge: Cambridge University Press, 1995), 5; and Thomas A. Lewis, *The Guns of Cedar Creek* (New York: Bantam, 1991), 25.

2. Croushore, 146; Joseph B. Mitchell, *Decisive Battles of the Civil War* (New York: Fawcett, 1955). A short list of these might include First Manassas/Bull Run (July 1861), Shiloh (April 1862), the Seven Days Battles (June and July 1862), Second Manassas/Second Bull Run (September 1862), Antietam (September 1862), Murfreesboro/Stones River (December 1862), Fredericksburg (December 1862), Chancellorsville (May 1863), Chickamauga (September 1863), Chattanooga (November 1863), the Wilderness (May 1864), Spotsylvania (May 1864), Atlanta (July 1864), and Petersburg (July 1864).

3. William H. Seward, from a speech given in Rochester, New York, on October 25, 1858, as quoted in David Donald, *The Civil War and Reconstruction* (Boston: Heath, 1961), 124. This speech provides the basis for the irrepressible conflict theory of Civil War causation.

4. Lewis, 163, quoting federal Col. Charles Russell Lowell in March 1861.

5. Emory M. Thomas, *The Confederacy as a Revolutionary Experience* (Columbia: University of South Carolina Press, 1991), 11.

6. Calvin Colton, ed., *The Private Correspondence of Henry Clay* (Cincinnati: N.p., 1856), 313. From a letter written by former president John Quincy Adams to Clay.

7. James R. Kennedy and Walter D. Kennedy, *The South Was Right* (Gretna, LA: Pelican, 1995), 164.

8. Ibid., 162.

9. Ibid., 164–165.

10. S. Augustus Mitchell, *An Easy Introduction to the Study of Geography* (Philadelphia: Thomas, Cowperthwait & Co., 1853), 49.

11. Richard H. Sewell, *A House Divided: Sectionalism and the Civil War, 1848–1865* (Baltimore: Johns Hopkins University Press, 1988), xi.

12. Sir Walter Scott, *The Fair Maid of Perth* (New York: Harper, 1831), 9. The actual quote reads: "Yes—respect; and who pays any respect to me?" said the haughty young lord. "A miserable artisan and his daughter, too much honored by my slightest notice, have the insolence to tell me that my notice dishonors them."

13. John Tosh, "New Men? The Bourgeois Cult of Home," *History Today* 46 (December 1996): 9–15.

14. John A. Thayer, *The Practical Expedite or Time-Book Companion* (Stoughton, MA: Privately published, 1847).

15. William A. Fletcher, *Rebel Private: Front and Rear* (1908; reprint, New York: Meridian, 1997), 2.

16. John S. Bowman, ed., *The Civil War Almanac* (New York: Bison Books, 1983), 383–384.

2

Politics: The National Hobby

"Both North and South seemed to be swayed by the demagogue."
—Confederate Private William Fletcher

In the 1940s a group of historians suggested that the Civil War was caused by the blundering of a generation of politicians and social agitators. Certainly some of what they said was true. Compromise had proven suc-

The Politics of Division

cessful in keeping the various sections of the country together for eight decades, and a modicum of moderation on both sides might have prevented bloodshed. These "blundering generation" theorists were very helpful in explaining how the war came to be.

During the 1840s, the Whigs and Democrats, the two oldest political parties in the United States, had reached agreement on several issues that had plagued the early republic. The tariff, the National Bank, and the regulation of internal commerce rank high among these divisive issues. Americans celebrated their limited form of federal government and considered any of its remaining weakness essential to the safeguarding of personal and political freedom.

The next decade was one of rapid economic and social change in America; and politics was gaining a more general audience than at any time since the Revolution. The Whigs and Democrats were searching for new issues that would mobilize the voters behind the old party structure. This attempt to underscore the meaning of the old parties was to have far-reaching consequences as political and social agendas began driving forward proposals that required strong federal action. One unforeseen consequence of trying to bolster the parties was that, ironically, it eventually led to the virtual dissolution of both.

In the 1850s the Democratic Party became divided over the issue of the extension of slavery. The Northern branch of the party favored "popular sovereignty," wherein the voters decided for or against the extension of slavery to new states or territories; the Southern branch preferred an unequivocal assertion that the Constitution absolutely protected the practice of slavery. Stephen A. Douglas became the leader of the Northern group, while Jefferson Davis led the Southern position. When Congress voted to ease the tensions over slavery with the passage of the Compromise of 1850, Davis voted against every provision of the bill except that which strengthened the Fugitive Slave Law. When Davis introduced legislation that would have condemned Northern interference in Southern "domestic institutions," the Douglas faction refused to support their own party.

An example of this political realignment can be seen in the reaction to the passage of the Kansas-Nebraska Act in 1854. A product of the optimism of the Northern Democrats and Stephen Douglas, the Kansas-Nebraska Act seemingly sabotaged the political compromises that had characterized the previous decades of American politics. The measure was popular among Northern Democrats, and the Southern Democrats gave it support, but its passage ultimately caused a split in the party. Moderates in the North felt betrayed. Outraged by the act, Northern voters began to speak of the existence of a "slave power conspiracy." In response, moderates in the South began to harden their position and seriously consider disunion.

While the Northern Democrats were hurt by the response to the act, the Whigs were devastated by it. The Southern wing of the Whig Party, sympathetic to compromise on the slavery issue, bolted, thereafter aligning themselves with the Southern Democrats; and the Whig Party, already weak after years of deterioration, was left in disarray and all but destroyed. A serious misreading of the temper of the voters had taken place, and they were left simmering in anger at the old parties. Significantly, this political upheaval came at a time when the old party system was already suffering from weakening voter support and poor party discipline. Yet in the wake of the disaster that followed the Kansas-Nebraska Act, interest in politics and political discussions increased, and several new parties moved in to fill the void.

Among these, two major new parties stood out, the Nativists and the Republicans. The Nativist, or American, Party rose very rapidly in popularity but failed in carrying its agenda to the national scene. The Republicans, after a false start in 1856, managed to win the White House in 1860, a victory that brought the country to civil war.

Nativist propaganda was widely promulgated throughout the nation, and even those who disagreed with Nativist positions were well aware of them. Nativists were solidly Protestant and radically anti-Catholic in their rhetoric. For support they tapped into the growing fear and resentment that paralleled the rapid changes taking place in American society. Nativist rhetoric portrayed Catholics, and especially the Catholic immigrants, as crime-ridden and intemperate, a drag on the economy, and a danger to the fabric of society. They viewed the acceptance of Catholics by the Northern wing of the Democratic Party as proof that the old political system would fail to support traditional American values. By tapping into a growing sense of resentment of politics as usual, out of touch with the pulse of the people and dedicated only to entrenched interests, the Nativists found an agenda designed to ensure the defeat of the old parties.

The Nativists were deeply immersed in the evangelical movement, and they were strongly supported by some of the finest established families of the North. Politically, they made some gains at the state level, especially in Massachusetts, only to have the party collapse after a few years because it failed to generate enough voter support nationally. Nativists were particularly embarrassed by their inability to bring about the passage of more stringent immigration laws. They did poorly with Southerners, who were more accepting of immigrants and more tolerant of Catholicism than many in the North. More generally, the Nativists failed because of their lack of political experience, their association with several prominent old party Whigs, and their violent anti-Catholic rhetoric, which bothered many politically active Protestants.

The Republican Party benefited from the collapse of the Nativists; developing more slowly, it avoided a similar meteoric rise and fall. While Nativists generally identified with social and cultural ideals, the motivations of the Republicans were purely those of political ambition. Even early Republicans were astute politicians. The party agenda called for a restructuring and expansion of government on all levels. The positions taken on abolition, urbanization, extension of the vote, and free labor were all carefully crafted to foster a positive public impression of the party and to increase its power and prestige.

Free labor seems to have been the most fundamental element of the Republican belief system and identity. It embodied the ideals of a classless, socially mobile society within the framework of a harmonic and expansive economic system, all deeply rooted in personal prosperity and capitalism. While Northern Democrats espoused many of these same principles, Republicans were more optimistic about the future of a highly industrialized America and were certain that the new society and culture of the North would ultimately supplant that of the South to the betterment of the nation as a whole.

The Republican Party benefited greatly from the rising tide of sectional resentment. The Kansas-Nebraska Act was a godsend for the Republican Party. They used the passage of the act and the subsequent decision of the courts in the Dred Scott case as symbols verifying the existence of a slave power conspiracy. Not only was such a conspiracy dangerous in itself, but it was clear evidence that the old powers wished to spread slavery to every corner of the land. The Republicans were in the unique position of being able to stand as the defenders of an idealized Northern culture, untainted, as were the Democrats, by former associations with the South.

An important part of the Republican arsenal of ideals was its characterization of the Southern planter class as the "slave aristocracy," viciously suppressing the mass of the Southern white population and all blacks, and denying them the benefits of true political democracy. The Republicans were able to transform the fears of papistry, slave power, and the unrestrained expansion of slavery into issues that could be blamed on the Democrats, North and South.

The Northern Democrats also used the symbols of progress, opportunity, and mobility to considerable effect. However, they had to defend their party's historic position on slavery. Southern planters were portrayed by the Democrats as favoring progress and opportunity, but only for whites; and some movement was made in the Southern states toward the expansion of the vote for white males. But the Democratic Party was often viewed as part of the problem, deeply involved in the political corruption of the day and supporting a widespread system of patronage. Voters were generally disenchanted with the party's "politics as usual" agenda, and many viewed the Democratic toleration of Catholics as self-serving and insincere. The Northern Democrats, although considerably weakened, were able to remain a political force until the outbreak of the war. The Southern branch maintained itself by championing the resistance to outside intervention in Southern lifestyle and culture, which were inexorably linked to slavery.

The 1856 election proved to be the death knell of the old two-party system. In the presidential race the Republicans championed the slogan "Free Speech, Free Press, Free Soil, Free Men, Fremont and Victory." John C. Fremont may have been made a national hero for his role in mapping and exploring the West, but he was an unacceptable presidential candidate in the South. Governor John Wise warned that if Fremont won the 1856 election, Virginia would secede. Consequently, the Democrats, fearing to incur the wrath of the Northern voter by nominating Stephen A. Douglas, the author of the Kansas-Nebraska Act, decided to run James Buchanan of Pennsylvania. Buchanan won the election against Fremont due to the entry into the race of a weak candidate from the American Party, a coalition of Nativists and Know-Nothings. This third party candidate was former president Millard Fillmore. Buchanan received only a minority of the popular votes for president, yet he handily won the electoral college.

As a new party, the Republicans had not had time to organize an electoral victory behind Fremont. Nonetheless, by the end of the decade the Republican Party had become the foremost instrument of anti-slavery sentiment in the country. Its condemnation of the slave power forces, coupled with the Kansas-Nebraska Act and the Dred Scott decision, brought it adherents. The events, both real and fabricated, taking place in "Bleeding Kansas" and the schemes of fanatical abolitionists like John Brown to forcibly liberate slaves and promote slave insurrections tended to radicalize even the most moderate politicians.

Northern office seekers, with their sights set on 1860, began calling for an assault on the traditions and honor of the South with all the enthusiasm that their rhetoric could convey. Such attacks fueled Southern indignation, created a desire for vindictive satisfaction, and led Southern moderates to retrench their positions. Southern radicals began to call for disunion as the best means of protecting sectional interests. "Both North and South seemed to be swayed by the demagogue," observed William Fletcher, who would go on to fight as a Rebel private.[1] Under the perceived weight of "accumulated wrongs and indignities," the South was swept up in a reckless euphoria for secession and the establishment of the Confederacy.[2]

James Buchanan's legacy as the fifteenth president of the United States was to follow, rather than to lead, the country to the brink of civil war. Buchanan entered office knowing that he was unpopular with most of America. **The Election of 1860** He was seemingly unwilling or powerless to control the radicals of either the North or the South. He had an honest desire for peace; but he was a pro-Southern unionist and as such was willing to make concessions to the South to maintain at least the semblance of national unity. Nevertheless, pro-Southern forces thought his concessions too harsh, while Northerners found him weak and pusillanimous. Buchanan was saddled with a cabinet divided by controversy over the same issues that split the country, and his vacillating policies did little but engender both social and political turmoil.

The rising star of national politics in the 1850s was a young former Whig politician from Illinois. Abraham Lincoln had not rushed to join the first groups that formed the Republican Party; but in 1854, in a speech in Peoria, Illinois, he began to speak out against the Kansas-Nebraska Act. The deep crusading tenor of this speech was closely linked to Lincoln's ambition for office. Instead of casting his fortunes with the Republicans, who were expounding on the issue of expanding slavery into the territories, he mistakenly continued to identify himself with the nearly defunct Whig Party. Viewed as an old party candidate, he lost the 1854 Senate election in a close race.

Immediately thereafter, he transferred his allegiance to the Republicans and helped to organize the party in Illinois. It was no surprise when Lincoln was chosen by the Republicans to face Stephen A. Douglas in the 1858 race for the Senate. Lincoln began his campaign with his famous "House Divided Against Itself" speech. In this address Lincoln gave the most radical speech of his entire life, calling for the country to become all free or all slave. Never again did he express such radical views. His words were widely interpreted as a declaration of war on Southern institutions. In a highly publicized series of debates, Douglas carefully pointed out that the country had been split for quite some time on the issue of slavery and could continue to be so indefinitely if the hotheads on both sides would leave well enough alone. By espousing moderation Douglas narrowly won the race, but Lincoln's stance had catapulted the young lawyer into a position of leadership in the Republican Party. By aligning himself with the influential radical wing of the party, he went on to engineer the Republican national convention in 1860 and received the party's presidential nomination instead of William H. Seward, a moderate on the slavery issue.

The radicals who joined the Republican Party did so largely because of the slavery issue. They generally came from the agricultural areas of the North or the cosmopolitan urban centers of the Northeast. The latter seemed especially absorbed by the concept of the immediate abolition of slavery and the granting of full civil rights to blacks. They saw no room for compromise in these matters and were willing to destroy the party if necessary to attain their goals. If the Union did not stand for liberty, it too was expendable.

While Lincoln had used the radicals to gain the nomination, he immediately began to modify his radical image to make himself more acceptable to other factions of the party. The moderates made up the majority, but there was a wider variety in their beliefs than among the radicals. The moderates tried to control the party by holding a balance of power. They emphasized that slavery was a territorial issue and were willing to leave slavery alone in areas of the South where it had long been established. Many believed in gradual emancipation and foreign colonization efforts by black freemen. By failing to center himself within the party spectrum, Lincoln essentially drove moderate Republicans toward the radical position. Certainly this is the light in which the South viewed the Republicans and Lincoln during the election. Southerners began to preach of "Black Republicanism" as a counterpoint to the charges of a "slave power conspiracy."

Lincoln probably would not have won the presidency in 1860 had the election not become a four-way race. The Democratic Party split between two candidates: pro-slavery John C. Breckinridge, a former vice-president of the United States; and Stephen A. Douglas, a moderate, who attempted to reprise his defeat of Lincoln in 1858. The fourth candidate, on the ticket of the new Constitutional Union Party, composed of former Whigs and Nativists, was John Bell of Tennessee. Tariffs, homesteads, railroads, immigrants, and political corruption all figured in the campaign, but slavery and the fear of disunion remained the pivotal questions. When it became obvious to the candidates, based on the results of gubernatorial elections in Pennsylvania and Indiana, that Lincoln was going to win, Bell and Breckinridge proclaimed dedication to immediate disunion; but Douglas, to his credit, disavowed any ideas of secession, saying, "If Lincoln is elected, he must be inaugurated."[3]

Lincoln won the election with just under 40 percent of the popular vote and 59 percent of the electoral votes. He carried eighteen states; yet, with the exception of coastal California, not one of them was below the Mason-Dixon line. This result reinforced his position as a sectional leader rather than a national one. Significantly, Douglas, who beat both Breckinridge and Bell with 30 percent of the popular vote, represented the views of at least some of the electorate in all parts of the country; but he received a mere 4 percent of the electoral votes. Besides Mississippi, the only other state won by Douglas was New Jersey. This seemingly strange pairing effectively ended the influence of Douglas and the Northern Democrats. Breckinridge, with 18 percent of the popular vote, carried every state that would come to be in the Confederacy except Mississippi and Virginia. The former vice-president also carried Maryland and Delaware. Bell captured the states of Kentucky, Tennessee, and Virginia and received 13 percent of the popular vote. Notwithstanding this result, 70 percent of the voters had shown support for at least a moderate stand against slavery, but they almost all resided in the North.

A group of moderate Virginia residents declared that "the election of a sectional president even with odious and dangerous sentiment" would not of itself be sufficient cause for secession. Yet they saw the election result as "an alarming indication" of the ripening schemes of abolitionists to "plunder" and "outrage" the Southern way of life with their growing fanaticism. The abolitionists exacerbated the seriousness of the situation by taunting Virginia as a "Plunderer of Cradles—she who has grown fat by selling her own children in the slave shambles: Virginia! Butcher—Pirate—Kidnapper—Slavocrat—the murderer of John Brown and his gallant band—at last, will meet her just doom." Secessionists warned that Virginia could soon expect an invasion of armed abolitionists and would become, as it subsequently did, the primary theater of the military campaign to eradicate slavery.[4]

Secession

In light of subsequent events it seems certain that the election of Lincoln in 1860 was the precipitating event that led to secession and ultimately to the Civil War. Lincoln, following the generally unpopular Buchanan, was the second minority president elected in succession, which suggests a growing lack of faith in the national government. But the question of secession had appeared much earlier than 1860, and from many quarters. The most serious confrontation between the federal government and the states had come in the nullification crisis of the 1830s. The question had been a political issue in the national elections in both 1852 and 1856. Virginia had threatened secession in 1856, and South Carolina had threatened to secede in both these years.

While the concept of state nullification was a moderate position compared to secession, its logical conclusion would have rendered the federal government impotent. John C. Calhoun, a brilliant legal mind, realized that, even in a democracy, 49 percent of the people could be tyrannized by the other 51 percent if the majority were well organized behind a single issue. Therefore, if the majority was to rule, the minority must be willing to assert its rights. In this case the right was that of state nullification. The administration of Andrew Jackson had reacted to nullification with the passage of a Force Bill authorizing the president to send troops to South Carolina if the state persisted in its refusal to allow the collection of the tariff and in its marshalling of an armed force in the form of a state militia. The crisis was averted by the passage of a compromise federal tariff acceptable to South Carolina, and the nullification of the Force Bill by the state. While disunion was averted by this face-saving device, the entire scenario would be played out again in 1860 with very different results.

In the nullification crisis the South found a new weapon with which to enforce its will on the national government. The threat of secession thereafter dominated the rhetoric of Southern politicians. The radical politicians of the South raised the concept of states' rights to the level of political gospel during the decade of the 1850s. Many Southern leaders espoused secession only sporadically, and usually only during an election campaign. Those who did otherwise did not achieve lasting prominence. However, with the help of the Southern radicals called "fire-eaters," what had started as an intriguing political device soon got out of hand.

Fire-eaters

Although there were numerous radicals actively pursuing disunion in all the Southern states, some fire-eaters are worthy of separate consideration, as they were conspicuously in the forefront of the clamor for secession and served as consistent and effective proponents of disunion.

Edmund Ruffin was an aged Virginian who had taken up the torch of secession in mid-life and allowed his quest to become an obsession. Ruffin devoted twenty years to the espousal of secessionist doctrine. He became a professional fire-eater, traveling widely, speaking to public gatherings, and writing prolifically on this sole theme. Ruffin was in his mid-sixties by the time secession became a reality; but he was still active in the cause and had the honor of firing the first shot on Fort Sumter.

Robert B. Rhett was from South Carolina, and as early as 1828 he was urging resistance to the rule of the federal government. Rhett was one of the earliest and most outspoken of the fire-eaters. He introduced amendments to the Constitution to protect Southern rights, and in 1844 he led an abortive tariff nullification movement. Rhett used his Charleston-based newspaper, the *Mercury*, to plead with the Southern states to secede en masse in defense of states' rights and Southern culture. When these supplications fell on deaf ears, he urged South Carolina to set an example and secede alone, believing that the rest of the South would follow. His long dedication to the cause earned him the appellation "Father of Secession."

William L. Yancey of Alabama was one of the best spoken of the disunion apologists. Yancey had lived as a youth in the North and never tired of using his personal experiences to reinforce the perception of its moral and cultural degradation. In the 1830s he became convinced that the South could no longer protect itself from the degrading Northern influences that seemed to be gaining control of Congress. When the Democrats refused to include a pro-slavery plank in their 1848 election platform, he became an ardent and unapologetic secessionist, urging immediate disunion. He hammered relentlessly on the themes of Southern unity of action and immediate disunion. The Southern states, he said, "all united may yet produce spirit enough to lead us forward, to call forth a Lexington, to fight a Bunker's Hill, to drive the foe from the city of our rights." It was Yancey, in the spring of 1860, who engineered the split in the Democratic convention that all but ensured the election of an anti-slavery Republican.[5]

Of the prominent fire-eaters, few went on to serve in battle, choosing rather to remain in politics. William Barkesdale of Mississippi, however, was a notable exception. Barkesdale, a true fire-eater, had been a vociferous and effective proponent of secession. The Southern war office made him a brigadier general, and he proved one of the most effective political commanders in the war. The tenacity with which his Mississippi regiments opposed the river crossing of federal troops during the Battle of Fredericksburg won him great renown. During the Battle of Gettysburg, Barkesdale was killed as he fought in the peach orchard.

In calling for secession, the fire-eaters were aided by a
The Southern highly partisan and radical press. Public orations, de-
Radical Press bates, and harangues were a popular instrument of the
fire-eaters and were well attended. Yet these forums
addressed only those who could be present, producing a somewhat tran-
sient enthusiasm for the particular topic of discussion. Therefore, the
nineteenth-century citizen favored the newspaper as a more individ-
ualized form of communication. Newspapers gained influence steadily
during the first half of the century. An amazingly large number of local
publications appeared. Speeches were printed in their entirety within a
few days of being given. Printed political arguments, essays, letters to
the editor, and discussions among dedicated readers—both genuine and
planted for effect—flowed in the wake of every issue.

People read alone or in small groups, with the leisure to reread and
analyze what was printed. The power of the press to influence a wider
audience than could be assembled at any one place and time was not to
be underestimated. Some papers tried to remain neutral, but others
sought out political alliances either because of the agenda of the editors,
or, more commonly, in order to attract a lucrative trade in political advertising and public printing. Neutrality on any topic of public interest
often doomed a newspaper to failure. "We have perfect unanimity in
the press," wrote one Southern observer. Local newspapers commonly
filled their pages with reprinted articles and speeches reported in other
journals from around the country, often with biting editorial preambles.[6]

Besides Rhett's Charleston *Mercury*, several newspapers were actively
stressing Southern independence. *DeBow's Review*, a monthly commercial
publication located in New Orleans, urged the South to diversify its
economy and to build railroads, factories, and canals, thereby freeing
itself from dependence on the North. By mid-century *DeBow's* was increasingly seen as a vehicle for secessionist propaganda. The Richmond
South, edited by Roger A. Pryor, and its sister paper, the *Enquirer*, edited
by Henry A. Wise, both stressed secessionist themes. The Richmond *Examiner* was described as firing "shot and shell" at those moderate on
secession. The *Whig* went "into the secession movement with all its
might." The *Dispatch*, once neutral and conservative, threw "all its powers, with its large circulation, into the cause" by 1860.[7] Southern nationalism was hawked by the respected *Southern Literary Messenger*, once
edited by Edgar Allan Poe, and even the *Southern Quarterly Review* was
pleading the cause of disunion.

Secessionist sentiment pervaded the churches, the shops, and even the
schools. Pro-secession radicals smashed unfriendly presses, banned
books, and fought duels with Unionists. The fire-eaters turned every
news article, pamphlet, sermon, and play into a propaganda piece for
secession. Even minor confrontations with the Unionists, or with the ab-

olitionists, were declared a crisis upon whose immediate resolution rested the very survival of the South. Warfare in Kansas, the publication of *Uncle Tom's Cabin*, and the anti-slavery raid of John Brown at Harper's Ferry gave credence to the tales of the fire-eaters. When there was no crisis, the radicals were fully capable of fabricating one. Southern leaders in Congress proposed the reopening of the transatlantic slave trade in 1859 without hope of the question being resolved in their favor so that the radicals might use the issue to good effect as propaganda.

Secessionists proclaimed South Carolina the leader of disunion, and it remained the natural home of secession **The Act of** throughout the period. This view was held by both the **Disunion** North and the South and was one of the few things that evoked widespread unanimity. The nullification crisis had all but eliminated any pro-Union feeling in the state. Radicals claimed that if South Carolina were to act for itself, the secession of the entire South would be "three-fourths finished." Many in the Deep South thought that the border states—Virginia, Maryland, Kentucky, and Tennessee among them—would ultimately join a new confederacy in their own time.[8]

The Palmetto State had renewed its threat to secede in 1859 by inviting its sister slaveholding states to consider a course of concerted action. Nonetheless, a positive decision was deferred pending the outcome of the 1860 election. It is not clear what result a Lincoln defeat or a Breckinridge, Douglas, or Bell victory would have meant to the secession movement. But in its declaration the Secession Convention listed as one of the reasons for its secession "the election of a man to the high office of President of the United States whose opinions and purposes are hostile to slavery." Certainly, a Republican victory had been a signal for action.

Some secessionists, including William Yancey, began the movement toward disunion on the eve of the presidential election by calling for part, if not all, of the South to make an immediate break with the North. These men were willing to leave Virginia and the other border states, thought to be soft on the question of slavery, in the Union in order to save the rest of the South from further Northern degradation. A border composed of states in the Union, yet amicable to slavery, might prove more effective to a new confederacy than confederated states that were lukewarm to disunion. The new nation would thereby have a border free of hostile abolitionists; and it was thought that neutral border states might be unwilling to allow the predicted Northern invasion to be marshaled in their territory.

On the afternoon of December 20, 1860, the South Carolina Convention passed an Ordinance of Secession. Five additional Southern states quickly followed its example: Mississippi, Florida, Alabama, Georgia, and Louisiana. In February, Texas came on board. At first it appeared

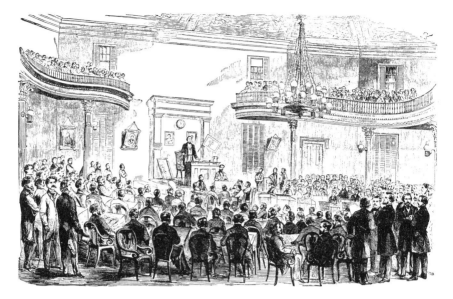

The Secession Congress: On December 20, 1860, South Carolina voted to dissolve the Union.

that only these seven states would secede, and early Confederate flags sported only seven stars. However, in April, after the bombardment of Fort Sumter and Lincoln's call for 75,000 volunteers to defend the Union, Virginia joined its sisters. A Confederate officer's teenage wife wrote in her journal, "Dear Old Virginia, long did she strive to keep her place in the Union, but trampled rights, a broken Constitution, and a dishonorable Government compelled her to join her sister states in a new Confederacy." This news was followed in May and June by the secession of Arkansas, North Carolina, and Tennessee.[9]

Secessionist sentiment in Missouri and Kentucky was somewhat split. As large areas of these states were quickly brought under federal control, actual secession was impractical. Eleven states had actually seceded; nonetheless, when the new Confederate battle flag was designed, it sported thirteen stars, the last two representing the fiction that Missouri and Kentucky were willing but unable to join their sisters. The use of thirteen stars was thought to reinforce the symbolic connections between the infant Confederacy and the American Revolution.

Although the radicals and fire-eaters had set secession in motion, they soon lost control of the new Southern nation. Few fire-eaters served successfully for any time in the new government. More moderate heads prevailed. Jeff Davis, the first president of the Confederacy, had been a strong advocate of states' rights, but he was far from being considered a radical. Alexander Stephens, a recent convert to disunion, was chosen to serve as the Confederate vice-president. Other moderates like Judah P. Benjamin and Robert E. Lee would lead the prosecution of the war.

Nonetheless, disunion was very popular in the South, not only among the social and political elite, but also with the average white Southerner. "The unanimity of the people was simply marvelous. So long as the question of secession was under discussion opinions were both various and violent. The moment secession was finally determined upon, a revolution was wrought. There was no longer anything to discuss, and so discussion ceased. Men got ready for war, and delicate women with equal spirit sent them off with smiling faces."[10] In 1861, after Lincoln's call for a Northern mobilization of 75,000 men, a clerk from the Confederate War Department noted, "From the ardor of the [Southern] volunteers . . . they might sweep the whole Abolition concern beyond the Susquehanna, and afterwards keep them there."[11] All seemed to understand the consequences if the cause of secession did not succeed. Southerners could not, without a complete sacrifice of their honor, do anything else but fight on to victory or utter defeat. "This is the irrevocable blow! Every reflecting mind here should know that the only alternatives now are successful revolution or abject subjugation."[12]

The function of honor, as an important component in the Southern rationale that led to secession and war should not be minimized. While no one can exactly define the reason for which each Confederate soldier fought, their diaries and letters suggest that the defense of Southern honor, which had been disparaged by Northern fanatics, was high on the list. Rebel private Carlton McCarthy noted, "When one section of the country oppresses and insults another, the result is . . . war!"[13] With respect to the secession of Virginia, General Robert E. Lee wrote, "We could have pursued no other course without dishonor. And sad as the results have been, if it had to be done over again, we should be compelled to act in precisely the same manner."[14]

Northerners responded to the act of disunion in a variety of ways. A young woman wrote, "The storm has broken over us. . . . How strange and awful it seems." In the North the stock markets fell and banks began to call in their loans. Many businessmen, forgetful of their recent enthusiasm for abolition, panicked at the specter of near bankruptcy. Yet initially the majority of the people celebrated the coming of the storm with fervor and enthusiasm. "We have flags on our papers and envelopes, and have all our stationery bordered with red, white and blue. We wear little flag pins for badges and tie our hair with red, white and blue ribbons and have pins and earrings made of the buttons the soldiers gave us." Women gathered to sew uniforms and made up "scrap lint and roll up bandages" in the churches and the local courthouses.[15]

Troops paraded through the streets of large cities and small towns. "It seemed," wrote Theodore Winthrop, "as if all the able-bodied men in

An artist's conception of the parade of the 7th New York Volunteers through the streets of New York—a scene repeated in many cities and small towns in the North (*Leslie's*).

the country were moving, on the first of May, with all their property on their backs, to agreeable, but dusty lodgings on the Potomac." Soldiers in gray and blue, and in the garish uniforms of Zouaves, Chasseurs, and Dragoons, carried their regimental flags past the White House. Six regiments from three different states arrived in Washington in such close succession that their separate parades formed "a continuous procession." The War Department could not provide for all the volunteers arriving in the capital, and placed them in warehouses and markets to sleep until proper camps could be arranged on the ring of hills around the city. Like irresponsible children, some soldiers joined the gaily dressed and carefree crowds that roamed the city, even to the grounds of the Executive Mansion, waving flags to the strains of patriotic songs such as "Yankee Doodle," "The Girl I Left Behind Me," and "Columbia, the Gem of the Ocean." Lincoln's call for volunteers had been answered with a vengeance.[16]

NOTES

1. Fletcher, 2.

2. Carlton McCarthy, *Detailed Minutiae of Soldier Life in the Army of Northern Virginia, 1861–1865* (1882; reprint, Lincoln: University of Nebraska Press, 1993), 3. Originally printed in 1882, this is one of the most readable Confederate ac-

counts of the daily life of the soldier. For a more detailed discussion of the disunion debate in the South, see Sewell, 68–78.

3. Sewell, 76.

4. Ervin L. Jordan, Jr., *Black Confederates and Afro-Yankees in Civil War Virginia* (Charlottesville: University Press of Virginia, 1995), 16. Attributed to the Charlottesville *Review*, March 15, 1861, as reported in the Winchester *Republican*, March 22, 1861.

5. Thomas, 28.

6. Earl Schenck Miers, ed., *A Rebel War Clerk's Diary, by John B. Jones, 1861–1865* (New York: Sagamore Press, 1958), 14.

7. Ibid.

8. Thomas, 30.

9. *Civil War Times Illustrated*, March–April 1991, 12.

10. George, C. Eggleston, *A Rebel's Recollections* (1874; reprint, Bloomington: Indiana University Press, 1959).

11. Miers, 8.

12. Ibid., 1.

13. McCarthy, 2.

14. Kennedy and Kennedy, 155.

15. Caroline C. Richards, *Village Life in America, 1852–1872* (Gansevoort, NY: Corner Book, 1997), 130–131.

16. Leech, 66–77.

3

The American Zion

"Boston rules Massachusetts, Massachusetts rules New England, and
New England rules the nation."

—William Lloyd Garrison

From the opening of the nineteenth century Northerners
persisted in an effort to portray the American Republic
in idealistic terms that reflected openness, unpretentious-
ness, and ease of ascent. Even though the reality was far
from the ideal, America continued to be viewed as a Zion for the world,
and the nonutopian inconsistencies, most evident in Northern urban life,
were excused as temporary problems with which the nation would come
to terms in time. Socially conscious Northerners declared that America
was the archetype of the perfect nation, with its expansive borders, rich
and prolific soil, abundant raw materials, citizens blessed with industry
and enterprise, and institutions and forms of government more free and
equal than any in Europe.

This view was periodically bolstered throughout the prewar period by
advances on many fronts. The nation had doubled in size with the Louisiana Purchase of 1803. Texas had been annexed, and California had
been added. In 1853 the Gadsden Purchase from Mexico filled out the
familiar continental boundaries of the United States. The nation had accomplished its Manifest Destiny by stretching from sea to sea in less than
three-quarters of a century. American industry was becoming the ideal

of the world, and American clipper ships were masters of the seas. The major cities of the North were connected either by rail, canal, or steamship, and the modern marvel of telegraphy crisscrossed the eastern half of the country by 1850.

Even in the face of severe social, political, and economic problems, Northerners sang the praises of their unique American way of life and soft-pedaled the traditional life of the South with its rural ways and race-based slavery. However, social inequities were not confined to the South. In the cities of the Northeast the disparities between the immigrant and the native born, the wealthy and the impoverished, and the educated and the ignorant were growing. Urbanization brought crowding and disease. Technological advancement led not only to labor-saving devices and better systems of transportation and communications, but also to derailments, steamboat explosions, and factory disasters. Increasing industrialization exploited white labor on a level that seemingly rivaled the evils of slavery.

Concerned Americans looked for remedies to a national government unfamiliar with dealing with social problems. The Founding Fathers had predicted that the republic could not meet all the imponderable requirements of an expanding society without modification. For this reason they had provided for amendments to the federal Constitution. Yet basic changes in the role of government were found to be unacceptable to many citizens; therefore, a quiet attempt began to perfect the American system incrementally rather than radically. As many problems were predominantly local in nature, nineteenth-century Americans began by tinkering with their state governments. Each state had its own constitution reflecting a regional consciousness generally more accepting of amendment than the founding federal document, which required a greater unity of the national mind.

During the first half of the century the political deficiencies that threatened the national utopia had become highlighted. Many voters came to a personal reappraisal of the traditional system of American self-government. Rapidly changing social circumstances fueled this dissatisfaction. Growing political partisanship was the natural outgrowth of these efforts to correct the situation with a minimum of turbulence. A growing lack of consideration among politicians for the public good underscored the need for leaders independent of partisan politics to decide on the new direction of the nation. The decision to change the basic character of the state to conform with visionary social principles quickly became a moral imperative to be pursued regardless of the consequences.

In a reactionary effort permanently to shield the new American utopia from the reach of later partisan politicians, legislatures in a few Northern states amended their constitutions in ways better left to well-thought-out and specific legislation. Politicians were pressed by reformers to pre-

sent amendments affecting the most minute details of daily life. Requirements for officeholding, taxation, and enfranchisement were changed,
and limits on police power, legislative prerogatives, and judicial authority were enacted. By mid-century most state and local offices had been
made elective instead of appointive. This feature of local government
allowed the electorate to replace those officials with whom they became
displeased and had the effect of further democratizing the process. By
mid-century adult white males could vote in every state in the Union,
and election turnouts often rose above 70 percent of the eligible voters.

In the Northern states the rise of urbanization, immigration, and manufacturing led to changes in property qualifications for officeholding and
voting. Often masked as an attempt to protect the rising middle classes,
such efforts were often designed to limit the influence of large employers
to control the votes of their workers. Officeholding became a good deal
more widespread than previously was the case, and "rotation in office"
came to be viewed as a leading principle of a republican form of government. It was seen as a way of enlarging the ranks of public servants
to include those outside the sphere of the landed gentry or the socially
elite.[1]

By contrast, the South had moved to ensure and perpetuate the influence of the planter class. Reformers generally discounted the views of
the planter class as being particularly detrimental to the national good
because of their support of slavery. Nonetheless, the old aristocratic
Southern families had a firm hold on the structure of local and state
government, and resisted any attempts at change. The mass of Southern
voters generally applauded this restraint, choosing to support their leaders in a defense of the traditional American way of life. Although small
farmers and shopkeepers found their way into government, the big
planters continued to control a disproportionate share of the public offices.[2]

In 1821 Thomas Jefferson had expressed concern over
the increasing presence of government at all levels of
American life, and many of his worst fears came to be **Growing Government**
realized. As a consequence of political and social tinkering,
the number of public offices on the local and state levels of government
began multiplying at an alarming rate. Government's expansion into areas of life heretofore untouched by bureaucracy was disheartening to
many. Local government, particularly, came to control a wide range of
economic activity in a given region. Local regulations governed inn-
keeping, markets, bakeries, port fees, and hauling rates, and the growth
of trade and manufacturing opened additional areas to control. The state
acted in the licensing of trades and professions, the setting of standards,
and the inspection of products. In the absence of strong federal policies,

regulating banking and credit and providing for a system of uniform taxation and revenue collection became major concerns of the state authorities. Strangely, the composition and implementation of such sweeping regulatory changes were left largely in the hands of people from outside the upper classes of society.

Personal aggrandizement and financial enhancement threatened to dictate much of the new governmental regulation. As most Northern voters were not influential or prosperous men, state legislatures began bestowing privileges on small groups of well-heeled political supporters. These privileges often took the form of charters for banks and corporations, rights of way for turnpikes and railways, lucrative monopolies for the construction and operation of canals, and favorable regulatory legislation. By means of bounties, exemptions, and subsidies, government officials were becoming increasingly involved in business. "The state governments regulated business, promoted business, and engaged in business," wrote one observer.[3]

By mid-century there were signs that the people were finding the unceasing intervention by government in their daily affairs tiresome. Political opponents were refused charters or licenses and were hounded by the minions of the controlling party until their taxes were paid, while the delinquencies of political allies were often overlooked. At the same time that state funds were stretched to the limit and local credit was less readily available, many state-supported enterprises were poorly run or did not live up to expectations. Governments began spending beyond the level of revenue, and the public debt increased everywhere.

The control of state politics gradually shifted and, in many cases, came to reside in unexpected hands. The petty politician was suddenly faced with unexpected opportunities in municipal government. Day-to-day politics became the domain of the man who had a hand on the pulse of local opinion. Political neophytes were attracted to positions as selectmen, sheriffs, justices, collectors, inspectors, and deputies of all kinds. Positions in the state capital or county seat often attracted lawyers who were there to enact other business. Sometimes the caliber of these officeholders was questionable. Genius, dedication to the commonwealth, and talent often lay neglected as offices were increasingly filled by the ambitious, the reprobate, the dishonest, or those who could barely read and write.[4]

The most influential officeholders operated from an ever-growing urban base. Established families in the North clutched at the reins of power, but the new class of municipal officeholders successfully manipulated the ever-changing social structure in the cities by rallying the population to one cause or another. A European observer of the American political system noted, "To gain votes, one must descend to maneuvers that disgust men of distinction. One must haunt the taverns, drink and argue with the mob; that is what is called Electioneering in America."[5]

In an effort to garner wider public support for their agendas, politicians consciously moved the decisionmaking process from the gatherings of a few influential individuals to the open conventions of political parties. Although the smoke-filled back room still played its role, the politicians recognized a need to develop a following in the electorate and a political platform from which to launch their schemes. Inevitably these tactics led to the benefits of an extended franchise and the removal of property qualifications for officeholding. As the process expanded to include persons never before allowed to participate in politics, many were attracted to socially acceptable outlets for their newfound zeal. As the traditional emphasis on sin and salvation in many New England churches came to be replaced by the more secularized obligations of social justice and humanitarianism, the great cities of the North, and Boston in particular, became hotbeds of political activism.

The American people appear to have had an unlimited faith in their ability to perfect the human condition and provide a model social setting for all. This optimism, somewhat misplaced in light of future events, placed a heavy burden on the social elite to ease the sharpening contrasts between the ideal American society and the realities of social misery that were becoming more visible in the city streets.

The influence of these social and moral pressures on the attitudes of the middle and upper classes should not be underestimated. Discontent and frustration with the inertia of the political process induced many Americans to join and support a number of reform movements. The perpetuation of social ills was ascribed to a lack of public will in implementing the appropriate cures. Reformers were absolute in their belief in the efficacy of these cures and demanded their immediate implementation. "A new type of despotism" emerged from the imperative to reform. Although it was based on intellectual and emotional forces rather than on physical compulsion, the reform movement, in many of its guises, was willing to suppress personal liberty, tradition, and even constitutional principles to correct the social ills in America.[6]

While there remained a strong belief in American individualism, personal strength of character, and the ability of a man to overcome the handicaps of his environment, such concepts were identified more and more with conservative resistance to social reform. Some Northerners and many in the South, unconvinced that poverty and disease among the lowest level of the social order posed a menace to their communities, were also distressed by the radical way social activists approached their task. Opposition forces found many of the reform proposals unrealistic, grandiose, sanctimonious, and antagonistic to traditional American concepts of personal rights and freedoms.

In 1800 the entire United States was essentially a rural country. Less than 6 percent of its population of 5 million **Urbanization** lived in towns with populations larger than 2,500. Only

Philadelphia and New York had populations greater than 25,000. The settlement of the Mississippi Valley and the Northwest during the first half of the nineteenth century had contributed to a vast internal migration. By 1850 the country had 23 million inhabitants, and more than 30 percent of the population lived in towns with more than 2,500 persons. Although two-thirds of the population was still involved in agriculture, the expansion of commerce and industry had drawn a large number of people into towns that were both old and new. The urban population became the fastest growing segment of the population.

Cities as distinct as Providence and Chicago were experiencing similar rates of growth due to their importance in trade. A number of small coastal towns became booming cities by mid-century in response to America's rise to maritime greatness in the clipper ship era. Boston, Salem, Portland, and New Haven, for example, were all active coastal trading cities in 1850. Boston alone was the terminus for no fewer than seven railroads. Westward expansion and the successful navigation of the western rivers by steamboats made a number of inland ports equally important. These included Pittsburgh, Cincinnati, Louisville, Memphis, Natchez, and St. Louis. The number of towns having more than 10,000 people increased from six to more than sixty in less than half a century.

The cities that had been the largest at the turn of the century remained so and experienced the greatest rates of population growth. By 1850 New York City boasted a population of more than half a million. Philadelphia, Boston, Newport, Baltimore, New Orleans, and Charleston had grown to hold hundreds of thousands of persons. Nonetheless, Southern cities had attracted less than 10 percent of the population of the region. The physical size of the American city also increased, from a radius of less than a mile to four or five miles. Northern cities were characterized by a well defined and established business district, socially and ethnically segregated residential areas, and the beginnings of the suburb.

The Southern cities grew along the perimeter of the region's heartland and tended to materialize after the surrounding area was well settled. These cities grew as planters and farmers came in from their outlying and relatively isolated holdings to take advantage of the social and cultural benefits cities offered. Coastal and river cities in the South also had a large itinerant population of traders, bargemen, and clerks, but Southern cities tended to avoid the development of slums and ghettos. Outside of the almost self-sufficient plantations, small towns in the rural South offered a few amenities such as a doctor, a tradesman, or a small store or two, but nothing more. Consequently, Southern towns often appeared shabby and run-down to visitors unfamiliar with rural life.

Immigration from abroad outstripped the physical expansion of the cities and stressed their infrastructure to the limit. This remarkable influx of foreigners had an incalculable effect on the nature of Northern culture.

Poverty, disease, crime, and ignorance became concentrated in the slum districts of Northern cities as immigrants drew together in the security of their own communities. Antebellum immigration reached its peak between 1845 and 1855. More than 3 million immigrants, ten times as many as had come to America since the founding of the republic, entered the country. Most congregated in the cities of the North. One had only to walk through an ethnic ghetto to discover the overwhelming atmosphere of social decay and moral degeneration—a condition Southerners quickly pointed to as evidence of the failure of Northern culture. Even the reformers believed that the standard of living among these immigrants had to be improved if the squalor of the cities was not to become a permanent feature of Northern society. Their predictions were borne out by the history of subsequent decades of urban poverty.

Many Americans could not escape the view that the decay and degeneracy were due to the immigrants themselves. Immigrant populations seemed to tolerate—if not frequent—taverns, beer halls, saloons, dance halls, gambling establishments, and houses of ill repute with amazing disregard for traditional American standards of conduct. A tone of condescension and disdain even entered the rhetoric of the reform movements. Many reformers attributed widespread social nonconformity among immigrants to social degradation rather than differences in ethnic character. They therefore misguidedly directed their reform campaigns against the foreign born instead of toward the correction of social injustice in the American system. By mid-century a strong ultra-Americanism had coalesced in the form of "American Only" organizations such as the Nativist Party.

There were three major countries of origin for the immigrants that entered America at this time. These were, in descending order of their proportion in the immigrant population, Ireland, Germany, and Great Britain. Together, they provided about 85 percent of all immigrants to the United States up to the beginning of the Civil War. The influx of Italians, Jews, and eastern Europeans would not become significant until late in the century. With the exception of the Germans, the majority of immigrants spoke English. There was therefore little in the way of a language barrier to frustrate economic success or attract prejudice. Immigrants from Great Britain assimilated fairly well into surroundings dominated by an American upper class that had strong English origins.

The Irish, who also spoke English, had an unfortunate history of poor relations with their cousins in Great Britain that followed them to the New World. The Irish were the first truly urban immigrants in American history, banding together in inner-city neighborhoods that quickly took on all of the outward appearances of slums. Many established Americans saw this development only in prejudicial terms and blamed the slumlike conditions on the Irish themselves, ignoring the anti-Irish bigotry of em-

ployers and landlords. In addition to being the victims of social prejudice, the Irish were also accused of voting illegally, of selling their votes
to unscrupulous politicians, and of engendering crime and immorality.

The Germans were generally ignored by the social observers of the
nineteenth century. They tended to separate themselves from traditional
America by moving away from the cities into more rural agricultural
areas in Pennsylvania and the upper Midwest. By this means they
avoided becoming targets of overwhelming prejudice and achieved a far
greater social solidarity than any other group of immigrants up to that
time. Nonetheless, they did not completely escape intolerance. As they
generally followed a European Sabbath tradition, Germans hurried home
from their religious observances to a convivial afternoon in music halls
and beer gardens that violated the more sober American concept of
proper conduct on the Lord's Day. This behavior was perfectly acceptable in their homeland, but it was perceived as a blasphemous public
exhibition of drunkenness and immorality worthy of censure by the
more sober-minded Americans. In this way German immigrants became
the particular target of Sabbatarian and temperance crusaders.

Religion A matter of primary concern influencing this bias was the
difference in religious background among immigrants. The
United States had been predominantly Protestant and Christian from its inception. Although the population was mainly Episcopal
(Anglican or Church of England) in colonial times, the American Revolution had shed many of the country's links with the established Church
in England. The Founding Fathers had almost all been Protestants, but
this Protestantism had been essentially related to Puritanism as represented by the Congregational churches. In the colonial period Scotch-
Irish immigrants had added an element of Presbyterianism, and later the
Baptist Church became popular. Both of these were largely within the
same religious tradition. Protestantism remained the dominant mode
of religious affiliation into the nineteenth century, with the Episcopal
Church remaining strong in the South. The predominantly Lutheran Germans and Scandinavians were the first to introduce a new element to
the religious mix. Nonetheless, their churches were essentially Protestant,
and they were assimilated with little fuss into the American social fabric.

At the time the nation was founded, Jews made up such a small proportion of the population that their presence was mathematically insig-
nificant. However, in 1845 a European economic depression caused
many Jews to immigrate to North America. German Jews made up the
largest portion of this wave of immigration, with the majority clustering
in the urban centers of America. For example, the Lower East Side of
Manhattan—famous for its tenement houses, neighborhood groceries,
and clothing stores—became an enclave of Judaism. Between 1850 and
1860, the number of American Jews tripled, to 150,000—a significant

number, but still less than one-half of 1 percent of a population of 32 million Americans.

The German Jews brought with them to America the idea of Reform Judaism. In their synagogues, they introduced innovations in the ritual, used both German and English, and allowed men and women to be seated together. Nonetheless, most still observed the traditional dietary laws in their homes. Apparently, Jews experienced little overt anti-Semitism. This may have been due to their isolation and their small number. A significant number of Jewish individuals played important roles as government officials and army officers in the war.[7]

However, it was the Christian religious revival at the beginning of the century that most affected American society. Evangelism, with its strong emotional appeal, was particularly influential among nineteenth-century Americans. By the 1830s Methodist and Baptist churches had become the two largest denominations in the country. Methodism, in particular, offered a new view of theology. The tenets of Methodism were more comforting and humanitarian than the stern predestination and selective salvation of the Puritans. The older denominations, which stressed the total depravity of man, seemed to be at odds with the democratic spirit of America. By mid-century most American Protestants had come to believe in their free will to choose a path to salvation by placing themselves in a position to receive God's grace if they were worthy of it. This belief was to have a profound effect on the way soldiers faced death in battle as they strove to be worthy of God's protection by exhibiting courage and steadiness under fire.

The newer religions stressed repentance, individual awakening, and conversion, and reflected the same trends in secular society. Unitarians and Disciples of Christ broke away from established churches, while Mormons and Adventists sprang from the soil of America itself. Mormons were so feared and hated in America that they were driven to isolation in the West in the prewar years.

Only the Quaker sect, one of the oldest in America, seems to have had a unanimous position on the questions of the war—renouncing violence and supporting abolition. Both the Baptists and the Methodists split along sectional lines in the 1840s over doctrinal and organizational controversies exacerbated by the issue of slavery. The other church sects equally lacked a strong spirit of fellowship. There was an increased tension in religious circles between social activism and private religious expression. Some of the community's leaders opted for positions in secular organizations rather than religious ones in an attempt to effect social change. Ordinary people, however, remained more interested in matters of spirituality.[8]

Added to this confusion were the new immigrants, particularly the Irish, who were predominantly Catholic. In the 1830s the Roman Catholic

Church was possibly the only religion in America not divided over doctrine. The Church was intolerant of criticism, unapologetically authoritarian, resolute, and unalterable in its structure. It was the oldest religion in the Western world, and it demanded the unquestioned obedience of its members to the will of the Pope. It was the Catholic Church that grew fastest because of the mass immigration of the 1840s and 1850s.

The Catholics were prospering. They established an educational system that still exists as well as colleges and seminaries that provided some of the best higher education available in the country at the time. A European touring the United States in 1831 said of the Catholic colleges in Maryland: "These colleges are full of Protestants. There is perhaps no young man in Maryland who has received a good education who has not been brought up by Catholics."[9]

A "Protestant crusade" to stem the growing influence of the Catholics in America began in the 1820s and grew in proportion to the increase in Catholic immigration. This movement, truly reactionary and discriminatory, was rooted in a traditional abhorrence of the Roman church and was aimed at the recent Catholic American immigrant. Americans feared the power of the Catholic Church. Even in the South, where concern over immigration and papal absolutism was marginal, due in large part to a significant minority population of French and Spanish ancestry, the authoritarian structure of the Catholic Church was viewed as incompatible with American principles and capable of marshaling Catholic immigrants against traditional American institutions.[10]

Reform Movements
The majority of reform movements initiated prior to the Civil War were essentially benevolent. Philanthropic reforms focused almost solely on the visibly degraded elements of society whose condition proved an embarrassment to the nation. These included paupers, drunkards, orphans, illiterates, Indians, slaves, prostitutes, and prisoners. Reform activities were popular primarily with the middle and upper classes, and were characterized by a laudable "urge to remedy visible social ills, alleviate suffering and discourage behavior that was considered immoral."[11] Although reform movements were common to urban areas generally, the home of reform was Boston. Many social reformers agreed that "Boston rules Massachusetts, Massachusetts rules New England, and New England rules the nation."[12]

Many different types of people were drawn into these reform movements. Some community leaders opted for positions in these highly visible secular organizations solely to improve their social standing.[13] Some obviously enjoyed the work because it satisfied their own aspirations and salved their feelings of frustration. Others crossed the lines between reform movements, working on one social ill and then another. William Lloyd Garrison, for example, began as a temperance advocate in 1828, founded the American Anti-Slavery Society in 1833, and took up the causes of feminism and radical pacifism in the 1840s.

Much of the resistance to reform was based in a natural social inertia, but some of it was caused by the inability of the activists to articulate the scope and righteousness of their agenda to the public. The activists proved most controversial in their insistence on immediate and total reform and in their unwillingness to compromise. This was particularly true of the radical abolitionists. Moreover, reformers demanded that the government supplement intellectual persuasion with legal coercion in many areas. Nonetheless, the majority of social reformers were motivated by a genuine sense of moral obligation and national pride.[14]

The Temperance Movement. The growing popularity of the temperance movement can serve as an example in this regard. From colonial times, a moderate use of strong drink was considered acceptable by all but the most radical portions of the population. The colonial population, magistrates, and clergy, in the absence of potable water, had consumed alcohol in prodigious quantities. Nonetheless, alcohol quickly became a target of nineteenth-century social reformers. When Secretary of War Jefferson Davis criticized the use of a statue of the Goddess of Liberty to adorn the top of the United States Capitol in 1850, one of the proffered recommendations for a substitute was a statue of the Goddess of Temperance. While the proposal was dismissed by the officials in Washington, the temperance crusaders, undaunted by the rebuff, put their movement into high gear. The failed campaign nonetheless produced a good deal of positive propaganda. Newspapers ran stories of drunken street brawls and bitter domestic scenes brought on by alcoholic consumption. Illustrations portrayed the general doom of the drunkard in its many guises in the shadow of the unfinished Capitol.

Immigrant families, following European custom, often used alcohol as a cultural prerogative, giving beer, light wines, and rum to children to "strengthen the blood" and prevent disease. Nonetheless, the dangers of immoderate drinking were real, and alcoholism could end in disaster. Many men actually drank away their wages, leaving their wives and children destitute. For the alcoholic, suicide became a cliché. Strong drink was often cited as the cause for eternal damnation and earthly licentiousness, as well as spouse abuse and rape.

In fact, the temperance movement was very closely allied with women's issues and may have mirrored a rising tide of women's discontent with their place in the social order. Women took up the temperance struggle by forming prayer groups and railing against saloons with their bottles, mirrors, and portraits of reclining nudes. A melodramatic scene printed on the cover of *Harper's Weekly* in 1858 showed a young wife and children, the alcoholic head of the family missing, turned out of their tenement into the cold. Whether the mother was widowed or

A copy of the *Temperance Recorder* of August 1834.
From the authors' collection.

abandoned—there was no suggestion of waywardness or immoral propensities in her appearance—the picture emphasized, once again, the message of a close connection between women's issues and social activism on many fronts.[15]

Alcohol was viewed as both the cause and the balm of the economic despair found among the poor in the urban slums. As the root cause of their problems, regular appearances in the local tavern with "jolly companions" were considered the "ultimate attainment of the confirmed drunkard." Conversely, temperance was equated with love, purity, truth, fidelity, marital stability, economic prosperity, social position, and religious salvation.[16]

The temperance movement was set back for a time by the defection of activists to the abolitionist cause and the exigencies of living in a war-torn nation. Yet the temperance reformers increased the stakes of their game and insisted on total abstinence from alcohol in any quantity or strength and supplemented their demands with calls for its legal prohibition. Temperance forces succeeded in passing prohibition legislation in a half dozen Northern states, but many of these laws were subsequently found to be unconstitutional. Not until the twentieth century did temperance legislation find solid ground in an amendment to the federal constitution. This shift from moderate and sometimes symbolic goals to conclusive ones, carved into the legal fabric of the nation, was typical of many of the reform movements of the nineteenth century.

The Society for the Prevention of Pauperism. One of the earliest reform organizations was the Society for the Prevention of Pauperism. In a country supposedly blessed with economic abundance, it was difficult to understand the causes and conditions that led to poverty among a large segment of the population. Americans in colonial times had adopted a calm and complacent cure for poverty. Disinclined to design large programs to relieve poverty, and reluctant to lay blame upon the poor for their condition, the colonials quickly and without tedious investigation simply provided support for the destitute. This support often took the form of financial aid, food, firewood, or clothing brought to the homes of the needy. If the recipients were disabled or suffering from extreme age, the support was funneled through the households of relatives or friends.

Traditional American culture, still in vogue in the South, exhibited a broader acceptance of the poor than was found in industrialized and urbanized areas in the North. Eighteenth-century Americans, in sharp contrast to nineteenth-century reformers, viewed a well-ordered society as hierarchical, with each social level enjoying its own special privileges and obligations. Unfortunately this conception made the poor a permanent fixture of the social order. If the poor were "always with us," asserted the Founding Fathers, using a biblical reference to justify the continued presence of the unfortunate in a supposedly enlightened social order, then "let God be praised" for the opportunity to help them.

Southern attitudes in the nineteenth century continued to reflect much the same perspective. The black slave was visibly marked by God to show his natural place in the social order. The place of the laborer or the artisan in Southern society was part of the natural order, not a demeaning or disparaging imposition from which one sought to escape. Moreover, the leadership of society was equally well established in the leading families of the South as a natural consequence of God's will. Of course, the needy were much less conspicuous and more sparsely concentrated in the largely rural areas of the South in the nineteenth century, much as they had been in colonial America, and the task of providing for their support under trying circumstances was thereby made less onerous.

Beginning in the 1820s, poverty came to be seen as unnatural in a bountiful America. Moreover, an implicit faith in the perfection of Amer-

A period illustration of poor boys shoveling snow for the rich in hope of
receiving a tip.

ica left many among the socially conscious with the notion that poverty
was capable of eradication if the systematic roadblocks and reluctance
to change in the old order were removed.

Nonetheless, if colonials had made little effort to eliminate poverty, at
least they did not punish and seek to isolate the poor. Colonial compla-
cency quickly gave way in the nineteenth century to a heightened sus-
picion of the poor themselves. "Surely the poor were partly to blame for
their own misery, having succumbed to the vice of idleness or intemperance. Yet . . . they were not inherently depraved but rather were the
victims of the numerous temptations set before them by society." As
religious thought became increasingly secular, God's will and the rav-
ages of original sin no longer seemed satisfactory explanations for the
condition of the poor.[17]

Reform advocates railed against towns that licensed grog shops and
saloons. They defamed politicians who allowed gambling halls and dens
of iniquity to flourish. Moreover, they castigated the poor themselves.
New York's Society for the Prevention of Pauperism found that most of
the poor of the city required support because they were so "depraved
and vicious." The poor were increasingly viewed as human raw material

"to be acted upon, to be improved, manipulated, elevated and re-formed."[18]

Of course, none of the reformers thought to ask the poor what they felt were the primary causes of their condition. The poor may have listed unfair labor practices, ethnic or religious bias, and unscrupulous land-lords as causes of their plight; but they were generally quiet on the subject. The reform movement of the nineteenth century was characterized as one of activism of the "haves" for the "have nots" rather than a demand for reform from those who were oppressed. This form of personal protest would not become popular until late in the century.

Activists formed a sort of reform elite that not only had the conceit to decide what areas of society needed reformation but also attempted to differentiate between the worthy poor, whose lot was due to misfortune, and the corrupted and unworthy idlers. Widows with small children were almost universally viewed as worthy of public assistance. An investigatory committee in 1827 unhesitatingly reported that the vice found in large eastern cities was attributable in large part to the actions of the poor themselves. The reformers concluded that eliminating the stain of poverty from the fabric of American society would require the isolation of the poor from their sources of temptation and the instruction, by force if necessary, of the destitute in the habits of industry and labor. This grandiose plan resulted in the institution of a series of almshouses. The poor, regardless of the particular circumstances of their plight, would receive aid only while confined within the almshouse. Once inside, they would be taught order, discipline, and responsibility.

A group of New England philanthropists was assured in 1843 that the almshouse was "a place where the tempted are removed from the means of their sin, and where the indolent, while he is usefully and industriously employed . . . is prepared for a better career."[19] Notwithstanding these assurances, the almshouses failed to relieve the problem of prolonged poverty or its symptoms. The truly depraved and corrupted among the poor avoided such institutions. Almshouses became filled to overcrowding with the helpless, the decrepit, the abandoned, and the very young. The emphasis on rehabilitation and personal reformation, initially a primary goal of the antipoverty reformers, quickly became irrelevant as the most heart-rending members of the poor community were hidden behind brick walls. A committee in New York reported in 1857 that the general conditions found in such institutions had degenerated into a cruel and punitive system of custodial care.

Social conservatives, North and South, particularly deplored the development of free public schools that admitted children from many class, ethnic, and family backgrounds, and inculcated in them a set of novel values that stressed social equality. The development of the public schools was paralleled by the institution of a Catholic school system in the immigrant-filled cities of the North. Such notions were seen as a threat to traditional fundamental values and represented a clear danger to the status quo, to be avoided at all costs.[20] The dimensions of the schemes put forth by the reformers of the nineteenth century were exceeded only by the depth of their failure. The poor remained in their crime-ridden environment, alcohol flowed freely until the twentieth century, and the freed slaves remained on the bottom rung of social and economic life. Yet, despite the incongruity between the utopian ideals of the reformers and the consequences of reality, mindless social tinkering and disgraceful forms of public altruism persisted and proliferated until well after the Civil War. Only the uncompromising conviction of the reform activists of the correctness of their self-proclaimed solutions to America's social ills, and their unrelenting hounding of public officials, could have kept such failed social experiments in existence.

NOTES

1. This is similar to the effort to set term limits in the 1990s.

2. Sewell, 3.

3. Don E. Fehrenbacher, *The Era of Expansion, 1800–1848* (New York: John Wiley & Sons, 1969), 76.

4. Oscar Handlin and Lilian Handlin, *Liberty and Expansion, 1760–1850* (New York: Harper & Row, 1989), 123.

5. J. P. Mayer, ed., *Journey to America*, by Alexis de Tocqueville. Translated by George Lawrence (New Haven: Yale University Press, 1960), 254.

6. Fehrenbacher, 98.

7. Frank L. Byrne and Jean Powers Soman, eds., *A Jewish Colonel in the Civil War: Marcus M. Spiegel of the Ohio Volunteers* (Lincoln: University of Nebraska Press, 1994), 2–3.

8. Anne C. Rose, *Victorian America and the Civil War* (Cambridge: Cambridge University Press, 1994), 54–60.

9. Mayer, 78.

10. It was not until the election of John F. Kennedy in 1960 that the Catholic taboo was broken.

11. Fehrenbacher, 111.

12. George M. Frederickson, ed., *Great Lives Observed: William Lloyd Garrison* (Englewood Cliffs: Prentice-Hall, 1968), 148.

13. Rose, 54–60.

14. Similar attitudes are prevalent in the United States of the late twentieth century.

15. David J. Rothman, "Our Brother's Keepers," *American Heritage*, December 1972, 39.

16. Ibid., 39–40.

17. See ibid., 38–42, 100–105.

18. Ibid., 41.

19. Attributed to Dr. Walter Channing. As quoted in ibid., 42.

20. These views were widely compared to the views of the seventeenth-century radicals of the English Civil Wars known as Levelers.

4

On Behalf of Southern Independence

"We have changed our constituent parts, but not the system of our government."

—Confederate President Jefferson Davis

Patriotism and nationalism were powerful motivations in Civil War America. A growing Southern nationalism accompanied the development of the Confederate States of America. Nationalism was on the rise throughout Europe in the nineteenth-century, and Confederates were quick to draw parallels between their struggle to found a Southern nation with those of the Dutch Republic and the Portuguese against Spain; the Italian revolutions in Sicily and Naples led by Garibaldi; the Polish rebellion against the power of Russian imperialism; and the ongoing Piedmontese struggle against Austria. Confederate diplomats held forth these examples to the world in the hope of gaining international support and recognition for their fledgling country.

Southern Nationalism

The North had similar nationalistic views, but they were more capitalistic and utopian than those of its Southern counterpart. The Northern nation was dedicated to physical liberty, freeing the slave from his bonds, separating the poor from their circumstances, and relieving the alcoholic from his dependence on liquor. By contrast the Southern nation was more dedicated to an abstract liberty defined by traditional political ideology and personal freedom of action unrestricted by governmental intervention. As the two cultures diverged during the first half of the nineteenth century, their separate concepts of which social, political, and cultural characteristics should be indicative of America's ideal national identity diverged also.

Several of the competing characteristics came to be mutually exclusive and served as focal points for controversy. These included questions of slavery or abolition; economies dedicated to the growth of agriculture or industry; social elitism or social mobility; limited suffrage or democratization; personal religion or societal morality; patriarchy or matriarchy; personal responsibility or governmental action; and conservative or progressive politics. Forces representing different opinions on these questions were in almost continual conflict by mid-century.

Although the questions of slavery or abolition stood out at the time, Southern nationalism was fueled not only by the endorsement of continued slavery, but also by a growing contrast between a conservative Southern culture and a progressive Northern industrial society increasingly in favor of popular suffrage, a changing role for women, widening democracy, and social reform.

The creation of Southern nationalism and the establishment of a national identity separate from that of the North came to be viewed as necessary for the survival of the Southern culture, with or without the challenge of war. Many historians have continued to view the nationalist trappings of the Confederacy as a kind of mask for the Southern defense of slavery. Nonetheless, Southerners were strikingly self-conscious about the need to explain themselves and publicly define their position on this question. Slavery was an embarrassment to some Southern apologists; yet, at the time, slavery and national identity may have been truly inseparable in the minds of most Southerners.

Historically, the South had been neither democratic nor purely aristocratic. Instead, Southern politics had reached a balance much closer to the classical Roman concept of the republic, a public order in which the power rested with an elite group of people who ruled for the good of all. When the war began, the South was a distinct political entity with a fully operational government, at least at the state and local levels. Confederate nationalism, although novel as a collective entity, had deep roots in a distinctive antebellum Southern ideology. The "plantation aristocracy" had successfully dominated Southern society for many years by applying their wealth and political influence to the wheels of government. Their numbers were so small that no more than 50,000 persons— men, women, and children—in a population of several million qualified as part of this class. Economic security, once the hallmark of plantations, which stood like agricultural city-states, was no longer a certainty. The historic political power of the planter class had largely been conveyed during the decades after the Revolution to a new moneyed aristocracy vested in industry, commerce, banking, and railroads.

Small farmers had so worn out their land that they looked to cast their lot with the expansionists who were moving into the territories. Many middle-class Southerners migrated with their manners and culture to other states: Kentucky and Southern Ohio, Mississippi and Southern Indiana, and Texas. Planters with modest holdings were able to maintain their gracious style of living by establishing subsidiaries to their planting operations. Sawmills, gristmills, distilleries, and even country stores were run on plantations. The sons of these planters turned to new professions such as law and medicine. Some went into the city to deal in tobacco-related industries, and some turned to the military as an honorable profession in keeping with the traditions of the aristocrat. This may help to explain the large number of Southern gentlemen who received their education at military academies such as West Point or Virginia Military Institute.

Southerners willingly tried all expedients to support their culture, even though the system had long ago become economically archaic. The large landowners hoped, at the very least, to maintain their social status under such conditions. As the traditional prerogatives faded from the landed families, they were replaced by a defense of a lifestyle that was increasingly becoming a social anachronism.

This distinctiveness provided a rather warped view of the South, but many Americans accepted it as a valid interpretation of Southern culture and acted accordingly upon it. No one would have cared how archaic the plantation system was becoming, but slavery was the one anachronism that many concerned Americans could not accept. Although the aristocratic Southern way of life was practiced by a small minority of the population, the lifestyle of the planter class came under attack by the forces of democratization, industrialization, and abolition. The very intensity of the attack, endured for several decades by the planter aristocracy, helped to define a narrow set of characteristic social customs as particularly "Southern."[1]

With the increasing likelihood of secession, the large planters moved quickly to ensure that Southern nationalism reflected their particular interests and strove to protect their cherished way of life under the new government. However, the planters clearly understood that they could not act alone effectively. Practical considerations made them more dependent than ever before on the white masses. Conservative and elitist tendencies were altered by this need to create a popular consensus. Politicians, journalists, and clergymen undertook, therefore, to enlist the support of the small slaveholders and the non-slaveowning white majority in the establishment of a new nation. They used an astonishing mix of political and religious language in an attempt to excite an ardent and enduring enthusiasm across the entire population for the Confederate government and its institutions. However, they carefully avoided presenting secession ordinances and state constitutions to the masses for ratification lest their plans fail the test of public support.[2]

Ordinary citizens quickly recognized that their support was needed for secession and that their physical assistance would be required on the battlefield. They sought to trade their support for reforms in taxation, governmental structure, and social and political access under the new government which had been denied to them in former years. However, it was the political, social, and religious elite who most effectively interjected their concerns into the new Southern nation, and they were successful in exporting their ideals beyond the battlefield soldier to the mass of the Southern people.

"If the Confederate experience did nothing else, it gave Southerners, many for the first time, a sense of corporate identity," noted an observer of the process.[3] Even the citizens of Tennessee, who had previously disavowed the idea of secession, overwhelmingly voted in favor of separation from the Union once Lincoln called for troops to suppress the rebellion. Hundreds of suggestions poured in from all levels and classes of Southern society when a committee of the Confederate Congress asked for designs for a new national flag. Nine out of ten of these were from women. A Southern woman's diary noted in April 1861: "Upon returning to my boarding-house . . . I found the ladies making secession flags. Indeed, the ladies everywhere seem imbued with the spirit of patriotism, and never fail to exert their influence in behalf of Southern independence."[4] Women wore secession flags as part of their daily costume in the streets. Southern ladies formed gunboat societies that sponsored dances, bake sales, rummage sales, and auctions to raise money for the building of ironclads for the infant Confederate navy to use in defending the harbors and waterways. Southern women were intensely aware of the need to maintain a Southern tradition and culture that "had roots several decades deep," and their diaries and letters are replete with nationalistic themes.[5]

The strongest feature of Southern nationalism was to be found on the battlefield. The South was ripe for war. The Baltimore *American and Commercial Advertiser* reported on April 22, 1861, that hundreds of impetuous young Marylanders had left the city in wagons, carriages, and buggies or on horseback to wage war against the invaders from the North. Although volunteers dedicated themselves to the defense of their individual states, the Southern army quickly showed a new unity and esprit de corps. For the first time in their lives many young men traveled away from their homes and interacted with people who were not also neighbors or relations. They accepted strangers as brethren, bonded to them by a larger identity. An analysis of the surviving letters and diaries of Confederate soldiers suggests that many expressed a patriotic allegiance to the Confederacy as a "country." Soldiers typically referred to sacrificing themselves on the "altar" of their country; yet they were equally expressive in their desire to defend their state, their home and hearth, and their families. The conflict between the love of those things familiar, personal, or close and dedication to the more abstract and intangible new nation troubled many Confederates; but the paradox brought forth by this dichotomy of motivation was not insoluble. The urge to defend one's state and family, which brought many volunteers to the battlefield in 1861, took on greater scope when the Federals launched a massive invasion of the South in 1862. Those from Tennessee and Louisiana who had fought initially to liberate their homes from the "varlet's threat" quickly extended their commitment to the Southern nation as a whole, particularly when their principal cities fell to federal forces. Many Confederates came to realize that the defense of their home and hearth was best prosecuted by winning the war, even if that meant fighting on fields foreign to their domestic concerns. A Southern soldier wrote of both his nationalism and his identity as a Southerner: "My *country* shall be freed from the fiendish vandals who thirst for the extermination of a *people* who are actuated by motives . . . far above those that influence and characterize the enemy."[6] Individuals may have continued to do things as Texans or Floridians, but on the whole they identified themselves as Confederates united in the defense of an independent Southern nation.

The nationalist movement with which the South most closely identified was the American Revolution, and references were consistently made to it throughout the prewar period and through the Civil War years. Southerners viewed their struggle as a continuation of that of 1776. They felt that the original Revolutionary dream had not been completely fulfilled and that the original Constitution had been corrupted by Yankee degeneracy and immorality. It is important to note that many of the expressions of Revolutionary ideals credited to Southern apologists in the nineteenth century were also found with surprising regularity in diaries, journals, and letters from the front to loved ones at home. As these contemporary documents were not written for publication or for use as propaganda, it is hopeless to hold the position that their regular appearance in private letters is anything but a heartfelt outpouring of genuine sentiment.

Reestablishing the American Revolution

It was commonly held that the fires of revolution, first kindled in Massachusetts, would have gone out had it not been for the sympathy, aid, and manpower provided by Virginia and South Carolina. There was a factual legitimacy to this claim. The views of Henry "Light Horse Harry" Lee, a Revolutionary War hero, devoted friend of Washington, and the father of Robert E. Lee, were typical of those of many Southerners. He wrote that the American victories in New Jersey, New York, and Pennsylvania were inconsequential in the ultimate attainment of independence. Indeed, although he participated actively in these campaigns, Lee felt that much of the martial effort in the North resulted in a string of abject failures, wherein even the victories proved indecisive in securing independence. The signal victories of the war over the British forces, and the ultimate victory at Yorktown, were perceived to have been Southern victories, and the outcome of the Revolution had been decided south of the Mason-Dixon line. Many Southerners were of the opinion that they were, thereby, the natural guardians of Revolutionary ideals.

Southern political and military leaders of the American Revolution were held in awe. Thomas Jefferson, Patrick Henry, and Richard Henry Lee were viewed as the political giants who had fathered independence. The figure of George Washington was consistently recalled in this regard both in public documents and in private papers. Besides Washington, a litany of Southern battlefield heroes was commonly called forth to support the myth. The military legacy of a successful militia uprising against the overwhelming force of the regular British army, whether martial mythology or historical reality, was to have far-reaching effects in the organization of the infant Confederate army.

Southerners argued that it was illogical for the North to enshrine radical revolutionaries such as Sam Adams and Patrick Henry as Founding Fathers, but consider Edmund Ruffin a demented old man and William Yancey a traitor when they championed the same political ideals that led to revolution in 1775. The political concepts that fired a just revolution in the eighteenth century were no less valid in the nineteenth century.

The new Confederate Constitution was closer to the U.S. Constitution than it was to a revolutionary document. With the exception of a few omissions and changes in phraseology, the two documents are almost identical. As the purpose of disunion was to establish a government that would preserve Southern culture and society as it *was*, this is not surprising. The act of secession was a conservative political uprising, and the Confederate Constitution has been described as "a theoretical time capsule that embodies the distinctive principles of republican government."[7] These principles tended to focus on the Anti-Federalist view of the government which had been obscured by the development and implementation of Federalist political theory since 1789. Jefferson Davis wrote, "We have changed our constituent parts, but not the system of our government."[8] This statement exemplifies the true nature of the Confederacy as the Southerners saw it. The new government was to be a continuation of those ideals fostered in the first American Revolution which had been altered by a fanatical and immoral North.

However, as champions of a new revolution and defenders of the Southern nation, the Confederates gave up much of what they held dear. The South embraced a centralized government fully as determined to control the reins of government as that in Washington. The concept of states' rights was sacrificed—not without the determined resistance of some state governments—for the defense of the country as a whole. Southern cities swelled in size, urbanization increased, factories and manufacturing took on a new importance, and men and women went to work much like the wage earners of the North. Ultimately even slavery changed as the Confederate Congress provided for the enlistment of black soldiers and dallied with bartering black emancipation for foreign recognition in the name of independence.

The planter aristocracy was sorely tested, and in many cases their social and financial prominence did not meet the test. Although wealth and social position maintained their hold on the structure of Southern society, the military created new avenues to prominence. Many aristocratic families lost scions to the fates of battle, while many of the masters of plantations proved unfortunate choices as military leaders.

The infant national government brought prominence and power to many of those who had been outside the upper classes of society before the war. Alexander Stephens, who was from a poor Georgia family, nonetheless became the vice-president of the new country. Judah Benjamin, outside the pale of acceptability in the North because of his Jewish ancestry, rose to be one of the most capable members of the Confederate cabinet and a respected and loyal friend of President Jefferson Davis. The greatest hero in the South during the war was an orphan and an impoverished college professor who raised himself to the rank of lieutenant general—Thomas J. "Stonewall" Jackson.

Before secession, the majority of manufactured goods needed in the South came from the Northern states. Those not made in the North were imported from Europe and entered the country through Northern ports to be shipped south by means of railroads, river steamers, and coasting vessels. The prospect of war with the North ended any hope of continuing this trade. At the same time imports from Europe, which had been negligible before the war, were now becoming vital to the life of the new Southern nation. Since the Confederacy had no large-scale shipbuilding industry, lacking both facilities and shipwrights—and since the small facilities that did exist were totally dedicated to the building of gunboats and ironclads—the effort to develop a substantial trade with Europe focused on foreign vessels as carriers and made the new nation as dependent on foreign powers as it had been on the North.

Below the mouth of the Chesapeake Bay, the Southern coast was largely a ridge of sand occasionally broken by the mouths of rivers which discharged sediment into the bays and inlets that could afford ships a

A *Leslie's* illustration by William Waud of the undiminished nationalism of the people of New Orleans even in the face of the loss of the city. Note the prominence of the Confederate national flag and its similarity to the U.S. flag of the Revolution.

safe haven. This silt was incorporated into a natural series of banks, shoals, and sandbars inimical to deepwater shipping. As a consequence there were few harbors in the South that were not subject to continually shifting navigational obstructions, and few large ports capable of receiving oceangoing vessels had developed.

Two of the best ports available to the South—Norfolk, Virginia, and New Orleans, Louisiana—were quickly taken by federal forces. Norfolk gave access to Richmond by way of the James River, and New Orleans ranked first as a Southern port in terms of wealth, volume of trade, and the number of alternate entrances to its harbor for oceangoing vessels. The federal government further hampered the Southern effort to import necessities by blockading the few good remaining ports along the coast. Of these, Wilmington, North Carolina; Charleston, South Carolina; Savannah, Georgia; Mobile, Alabama; and Galveston, Texas, were the most important. Each of these, with the exception of Galveston, was connected by rail to the rest of the South. After June 1863, Wilmington proved the most important element in the Confederate supply system both because of its rail connections and because of its geographical location near the focus of the war in the east.

A unifying feature of the Southern nation in its struggle with the North was the continued existence of the blockade runners. Often called the "lifeline of the Confederacy," the blockade runners were largely foreign-owned vessels that attempted to evade the federal blockade and bring military and other goods into Southern ports. The inability of the federal navy to stop these vessels served as a rallying point for Southern nationalism. The Confederacy imported a remarkable amount of military supplies through the blockade. More than 400,000 rifles, 3 million pounds of lead, and 2 million pounds of saltpeter for gunpowder production, as well as food, clothing, shoes, accouterments, medicines, and paper, were brought through the blockade. To pay for these supplies more than 500,000 bales of cotton were shipped out of the South during the war and bonds worth millions of Confederate dollars were issued to creditors.

Blockade Runners

The price of consumer goods was most directly affected by the blockade. From 1860 to 1863 the monthly cost of feeding a small family was reported to have gone from $6.55 to $68.25.[9] The following prices were recorded in the months indicated by a concerned observer: In May 1862: meat—50 cents per pound; butter—75 cents per pound; coffee—$1.50; tea—$10; boots—$30; men's shoes—$18; ladies' shoes—$15; shirts—$6; room and board for one—$30 to $40 per month; and house rent per year—$1,000.[10] In September 1862: firewood—$16 per cord; coal—$9 per load; blankets—$25; sheets—$15; and bleached cotton shirting—$1 per yard.[11] In March 1863: cornmeal—$8 per bushel; chickens—$5 each; turkeys—$20 each; turnip greens—$8 per bushel; bacon—$1.50 per pound; bread—20 cents per loaf; and flour—$39 per hundredweight barrel.[12]

With a scarce supply of gold and the value of the Confederate dollar down to $18.50 per federal greenback by November 1863, the Southern government began impressing items of all kinds—"horses, wagons, hogs, cattle, grain, potatoes—leaving the farmers only enough for their own subsistence."[13] In March 1863 the Confederate War Department issued a schedule of standardized prices for impressed goods that reflected only half of their market value. Some counties were so alarmed by this development that they threatened to take steps to prohibit the export of foodstuffs from within their boundaries to the rest of the country.

The eventual success or failure of the Confederacy was largely dependent on the will of the people to support the war by enduring privation and tolerating wartime prices. Unfortunately, profits and patriotism were often in conflict when it came to blockade running. Of course, without profits there would have been no blockade runners at all. Yet the huge profits brought by private rather than military goods continued to hamper the ability of the Confederacy to use the blockade runners to their best advantage. Nonmilitary goods vied for scarce cargo space on the runners and sold for incredibly high prices in the market-place, thereby fueling inflation. For a short time the Richmond government tried to enforce regulations reserving a large fraction of the cargo space in each blockade runner for military goods. This plan was aided by the dedication of Wilmington as a port of entry for military imports, while Charleston was left in the hands of private shippers.

The average lifetime of a blockade runner was two round trips. Besides a small number of sailing vessels, just under 300 individual steam-powered vessels tested the blockade, and two-thirds of these were either captured or destroyed. Nonetheless, of 1,300 attempted runs, over 1,000 were successful, and the supply line was maintained until the very last months of the war. Regardless of the inefficiencies of the blockade running system, no battle or campaign of the war was lost by the Confederacy for lack of arms or ammunition, due almost solely to the success of the runners.[14]

The Bread Riots
A severe food shortage seems to have developed in urban areas of the South in the latter part of March 1863. Initially a group of women in Salisbury, North Carolina, demanded that store owners charge them no more than the fixed price the government would ordinarily pay for foodstuffs and goods. Some of the merchants obliged the ladies by lowering their prices. There were several such episodes in the South at the same time. The most significant took place in the capital city of Richmond, where Mary Jackson promoted a concerted action by the women of that city to influence the price of goods and foodstuffs.

Beginning at the Belvidere Hill Baptist Church, the women, armed with persuaders such as pistols, knives, and hatchets, and led by Mary Jackson, marched on Capital Square in protest. Here the governor of Virginia, John Letcher, spoke to the crowd and expressed his sympathy, but he offered no concrete solution to their problem. As the crowd disgorged from the square, the gathering of women clearly became a mob and began to loot the stores and take the goods of the merchants. Seemingly no attempt was made to buy articles at any price, including prices fixed by the government. A number of merchants simply tried to close their doors, and at least one, a Mr. Knott, tried to appease the women by handing out packages of sewing needles—considered a luxury item at the time.

This episode was widely reported in the antigovernment papers and the Northern press as a "bread riot." Although there is no indication that any bread was taken or asked for, some foodstuffs, including bread, meat, and rice, were distributed to the needy by the Young Men's Christian Association. "Boots are not bread, brooms are not bread, men's hats are not bread, and I have never heard of anybody's eating them," retorted a government clerk to the reports.

The riot was not a particularly large affair, and from its beginning at the Belvidere Church to its end in the downtown merchant quarter, it lasted little more than two hours. Nonetheless, President Davis had gone so far as to threaten to have the mob fired upon by the Public Guard which had mobilized in the streets. The Richmond *Examiner* suggested that future rioters be shot on the spot. The City Council initiated a formal investigation of the affair and found the riot to be totally unjustified. Several of the instigators of the protest were arrested. Of these, twelve women were convicted of misdemeanors, and four men and one woman, Mary Jackson, were convicted of felonies.[15]

Southern nationalism, and the traditional "Old South," died as surely in the city streets and farmyards as it did on the battlefields. The Southern landscape was littered with debris—skeletons of horses and mules left unburied, human remains washed from their shallow graves, broken muskets, and wagon wheels decorated the sides of rutted ditches that once were pleasant lanes through the countryside. Homes had been shelled or dismantled to build fortifications, roads, and bridges. Parts of the South were said to actually stink with the odor of death.

The immediate cause of defeat was a lack of sufficient manpower for the Confederate armies, but the inability of the civilian population to withstand any more war after four years of mourning their loved ones ensured that the war would not long endure. For four brief years Southerners, charged with a spirit of revolution and nationalism, took charge of their own destiny. In the aftermath of the war the unique Confederate identity would never be the same again. Yet the new South, rising from the ashes of the old, would reassert many of its traditional ideologies from the postwar years to the present.[16]

NOTES

1. Drew Gilpin Faust, *The Creation of Confederate Nationalism: Ideology and Identity in the Civil War South* (Baton Rouge: Louisiana State University Press, 1988), 3–4.

2. Ibid., 15, 36.

3. Thomas, 114.

4. Faust, *Nationalism*, 8; Miers, 3.

5. James M. McPherson, *For Cause and Comrades: Why Men Fought in the Civil War* (New York: Oxford University Press, 1997), 95. See Croushore, 30.

6. James West Smith, "A Confederate Soldier's Diary: Vicksburg in 1863," *Southwest Review* 28 (1943): 304, 312.

7. Marshall L. DeRosa, *The Confederate Constitution of 1861* (Columbia: University of Missouri Press, 1991), 17.

8. Thomas, 40.

9. Douglas O. Tice, "Bread or Blood: The Richmond Bread Riot," *Civil War Times Illustrated*, February 1974, 12.

10. Miers, 79.

11. Ibid., 99.

12. Ibid., 178.

13. Ibid., 310–312.

14. For a detailed discussion of blockade running and its effect on the South, see Stephen R. Wise, *Lifeline of the Confederacy: Blockade Running During the Civil War* (Columbia: University of South Carolina Press, 1988).

15. Tice, 14–16.

16. Thomas, 127.

5

The Peculiar Institution: Slavery

"I feel that it is degrading the human race to have white men for servants."

—A Congressman from Maryland, 1831

History inexplicably continues to blame the English for creating a system of "American" plantation slavery when the system is documented to have existed before the New World was discovered and more than a century before the English set foot in any colony of their own. The African slave trade was begun by Arab and Muslim traders in the fifteenth century, and the Portuguese adapted slavery to their immensely profitable sugar plantations in the islands of the eastern Atlantic before the discovery of the New World. Three-quarters of all the Africans brought to the New World were imported by Spain and Portugal.

The Slave Trade

Unfortunately, the early history of slavery in North America is poorly documented and inconclusive. It seems certain that none of the founders of the first English colonies anticipated a dependence on black slaves. While the first Negroes brought to the English colonies were formerly thought to have been exclusively slaves, recent research suggests that many of them were actually indentured servants or free craftsmen. It is equally clear, however, that there were distinctions made between black and white laborers and servants in even the earliest English colonies; but in a society where whites were often degraded and treated as brutally

The slave patrol at work. All blacks, free or slave, were required to have a pass when off the plantation and not accompanied by a white. Failure to obey the slave patrol could end in detention or even death. Sketch by F. B. Schell.

as slaves, social distinctions often proved more important than racial ones.[1]

The distinction between free blacks, black indentured servants, and black slaves quickly blurred. Free blacks seem to have preferred to live in an urban setting and were twice as likely to live in cities as slaves, who were primarily agricultural workers. In cosmopolitan areas free blacks and slave craftsmen found opportunities for employment, exposure to black culture and religion, and the company of other freemen. However, the majority of free blacks lived on the margins of poverty and were subject to detention and questioning by the authorities without cause. They were continually encouraged to sell themselves back into slavery.[2]

By the beginning of the eighteenth century, race-based slavery firmly established itself in English North America in place of indentured service. Historians have been hard pressed to explain the sudden shift from white indentured labor to black slavery, as indentured servants were less expensive to maintain and generally more tractable workers. One theory suggests that whites became unwilling to undergo the physical hardships required of work on another man's plantation, opting instead to hack out a living for themselves on the frontier. The absurd theory that the black race was better suited to the hot climate of the South than the white was put to rest by John Quincy Adams: "Europeans cultivate the land in Greece and in Sicily; why should they not do so in Virginia or the Carolinas? It is not hotter there."[3]

During the eighteenth century slave labor proved profitable only on large-scale plantations that produced a cash crop. At the time only tobacco and sugar seemed to satisfy this requirement. Growing tobacco had saved the Virginia and Carolina colonies from extinction once the quest for gold and precious metals had been quelled by failure. Tobacco was used as cash, in lieu of cash payments, and as collateral for loans. Tobacco bonds, which encumbered the profits of future crops, were even accepted in lieu of taxes. But intensive tobacco farming was hard on the soil, stripping it of valuable nutrients that could not easily be replaced in an era before synthetic fertilizers. The production of sugar was particularly lucrative, but sugar cultivation was hard on the slaves, who suffered ghastly levels of mortality in the pest-infested humidity of the cane fields. If a large planter of tobacco or sugar were fortunate enough to have three good agricultural years in a row, he could become fabulously wealthy.[4]

Fortunes made in growing sugar and tobacco altered the entire state of colonial society. Whites living in the Southern colonies developed a class structure based on "all the ideals, all the passions, all the prejudices of an aristocracy." Many built manor houses that rivaled the great homes of Europe. So common were these residences that a substantial immigrant population made up of Italian stonemasons, bricklayers, and plasterers came to reside in the South and was supported almost solely by this form of construction.

Rich Southerners maintained their "planter aristocracy" through the Revolution and into the nineteenth century. Certainly there were upper and working classes among the whites, but nowhere was the equality between white men so complete as in their ability to force Negroes to work without working themselves; and the laws of the new republic lent authority to the white man by divesting the black of two-fifths of his very humanity.[5]

Of the 10,000 plantations that came to rely on slave labor in the antebellum period, fewer than 10 percent had more than one hundred slaves. The institution of slavery had been in decline for some time before the war, particularly, among the small tobacco planters who had worn out their soil. A South Carolina planter in 1831 reported: "It is an extraordinary thing how far public opinion is becoming enlightened about slavery. The idea that it is a great evil and that one could do without it is gaining ground more and more. . . . We have seen it abolished in the State of New York, then in Pennsylvania; it holds on to a precarious existence in Maryland; there is talk against it in the Legislature of Virginia."[6]

The importation of slaves into the United States was outlawed in 1808, but the ownership and selling of slaves within the confines of the country continued. Not until 1848 was slavery abolished in most of New England. This was accomplished by gradual emancipation and not without considerable turmoil over the incorporation of free blacks into New England society. It is an amazing facet of the war that the New England states should so strongly oppose slavery in 1860 when they had tolerated or supported it a mere twelve years earlier.

Cotton saved the plantation system and breathed new life into slavery. By mid-century cotton accounted for two-thirds of the exports of the country and created an unprecedented demand for agricultural laborers. The widespread adoption of the cotton gin, which economically removed the seeds from desirable long staple varieties of cotton, resurrected the plantations of the Deep South in the antebellum period. A slave, who could process 100 pounds of cotton per day without the cotton gin, could produce 1,000 pounds of fiber in the same time with it. Estimates show that by 1860 there were more than 3.6 million black slaves in the states that were to form the Confederacy. Profits from cotton in the Carolinas and from sugar in Louisiana provided a financial bulwark for slavery in the Deep South. The archaic plantation system would have faded into obscurity were it not for the ability of slavery to provide the labor needed to produce these crops.

Virginia, noted for its production of tobacco rather than as a cotton producer, became a major supplier of slaves to other areas of the South. In 1860 the estimated value of all the slave property in the Old Dominion alone was more than $300 million dollars.[7] Virginians found that they could make more profit selling slaves than using them as laborers. In the three decades before the war, more than a quarter million slaves were "sold south" from Virginia alone. In 1860 young black men aged nineteen to twenty-four could bring between $1,300 and $1,700 in the slave market; and young women between sixteen and twenty, from $1,200 to $1,500. Slaves with skills brought higher prices. Blacksmiths, wheelwrights, and furniture makers sold at a premium, as did particularly comely young women. Children, the aged, and the unskilled brought less. A healthy child four months old was considered worth $100 in North Carolina. The average price for a slave, taking all ages and sexes into account, has been estimated to have been $1,500. The largest number of slaves purchased were young men. Few women, children, or older slaves saw regular trading. This difference helps to explain the high average of $1,500. It should be noted, to place these values in perspective, that a white overseer on a moderate sized plantation could expect to receive a salary of only $200 to $500 for an entire year's work.[8]

Outside the Deep South economic and moral attitudes toward the "peculiar institution" had begun to change before the turn of the century. In the border states the importance of slavery as an institution continued to erode. Kentucky and Tennessee had few slaves, as they were too mountainous to grow cotton economically. One county in western Virginia was so removed from slavery that there was not a single black person, slave or free, within its bounds in 1860. Nonetheless, as an institution race-based slavery had a long lifeline. In Maryland and Delaware slaves were found mostly in the cities, serving as tradesmen, artisans, and household help. "I feel that it is degrading the human race to have white men for servants," said a border state congressman. "When one comes to change my plate, I am always tempted to offer him my place at table."[9]

Historians are greatly divided on the extent of the various physical mistreatments to which slaves were exposed, and the psychological effects of being held in bondage can only be surmised. A Northern visitor to the South testified, "It is almost impossible to believe that human nature can endure such hardships and sufferings as the slaves have to go through."[10] Though slavery was certainly a great evil and was oppressive everywhere, the burden imposed on the individual slave varied greatly depending on the master and the region of the country in which the slave resided. Profession and practice with regard to slavery were so complex that they were frequently radically different things, and generalizations in this area must be carefully drawn. Unquestionably, the practices that served to underpin the institution of slavery in the South were becoming more harsh as the century progressed. This was especially true with respect to questions of black education, manumission, provision of physical care, and the status of blacks, both free and slave.

Plantation Slavery

There seems to have been a striking difference between the treatment of slaves in the small towns and cities of the South and that of blacks held on large plantations. Both the material mistreatment of the "whip-driven" slave on the plantation and the freedom enjoyed by urban slaves, as well as black freemen, were exaggerated by anti-slavery advocates at the time and subsequently by some serious historical scholars. Notwithstanding such exaggeration, there was almost certainly a relative disadvantage to being a plantation slave.

The systemic abuse of black freemen was generally limited to the rural areas of the South and was much less common before the war than after.[11] Southern blacks lived hard lives, yet many displayed fortitude, courage, and a sense of dignity throughout. Nonetheless, on the eve of the Civil War there were blacks in the South, themselves free, who owned slaves, used slave labor in their businesses, and condoned slavery. Black slave masters, especially shippers, tradesmen, and artisans, owned many of their fellow Negro workers, an arrangement often entered into in lieu of an apprenticeship agreement. Incredibly, many of the free Negro tradesmen and artisans invested heavily in these slaves.

This was especially true of free Negroes who owned shipping concerns where slaves served as shipwrights, sailmakers, and stevedores. It has been documented that in 1830 more than 2,000 black slaves were owned by free Negro masters in New Orleans alone.[12]

The campaign to emancipate these slaves raised interesting questions about the sympathies of free Negroes who owned slaves. Black masters, who sometimes also owned the members of their families, had their rights recognized in law in most states. They could therefore stabilize their workforce and provide a modicum of legal protection for their loved ones. These men were highly educated, cultured, and sophisticated in their outlook, and they were decidedly against any form of gradual emancipation without indemnification. At the beginning of the war many of them were openly Confederate in their outlook.[13]

The available evidence about the conditions surrounding slavery comes to us from a variety of sources, some of which hardly inspire confidence as to their reliability. Slave biographies and narratives based on oral interviews are one major source of information. Many of these were taken down in the 1920s and 1930s by historians desperate to document the details of slave life before its participants faded away. These narratives were given by people who were, on the average, over eighty years old and had been children when the Civil War began. Additional sources are found in the letters, diaries, and contemporary writings of the slaveholders, and in the collections of plantation records, Freedmen's Bureau documents, and other written material dealing with the slave trade and plantation management that survived the war. Each of these must be subjected to the same type of evaluation by which all sources of historical information are judged.[14]

Slave autobiographies, in particular, have been used by historians extensively, and perhaps too uncritically, because they are few in number. Under close scrutiny they often turn out to be carefully crafted propaganda pieces, rooted in truth but designed by the abolitionists to appeal to all the dissimilar reform groups of the North. In the 1860s there was an explosion of handwritten testimony from slaves recently freed by federal troops. New Orleans fell to federal troops early in the war, and there was an active attempt to document the system of slavery in the area around that city. While historians know more about slaves in New Orleans during the war than in any other Southern city, it was hardly an archetype of Southern slavery. New Orleans boasted the largest black community of any city in the country at the time, composed of numerous free black businessmen and artisans, urbanized former slaves, and recent refugees from the plantations.

Nonetheless, the data that were compiled are useful, particularly since the slaves could not be expected to leave much in the way of other written documentation. Much of the material collected took the form of anecdotal statements by former slaves assembled by well meaning, but not unbiased, investigators.[15] It is not enough to say that all sources are biased. Some sources suffer from other limiting characteristics beyond their obvious intent, such as the author's selective memory or his desire to make himself seem heroic. It is almost impossible to correct the data that we have for the prejudice of "untrained, negligent, or incompetent" nineteenth-century researchers. Such data have been used by scholars, authors, playwrights, and screenwriters to distort the picture of slavery beyond our ability to know the truth.[16]

The accounts of slave society written by slaveowners are used sparingly and with great caution by historians even though they are plentiful and vastly superior sources of detailed information. These sources of information about slavery reside largely in the daily reports of plantation activities and the internal records of slave trading establishments. Considering them along with published tracts on the "Management of Negroes," private letters and papers of slaveholders, and advertisements for fugitives, we can at least surmise an accurate picture of what slaves looked like and did, even if we cannot get a reliable view of how they felt or what they thought. These sources provide firsthand accounts, rather than hearsay evidence, of slavery. They are contemporary with the events and are considered by most open-minded historians to have been written "with the substantial integrity needed for accuracy in business accounts."[17]

If we properly discount the reliability of the self-serving firsthand documents produced by slaveowners and their apologists, must we not take into account the subjective influences brought to bear on the autobiographies and narratives of slaves published and recorded by abolitionists? One outstanding slave autobiography, favorable to slavery, is almost totally ignored by historians as "obviously unreliable," yet there is no evidence that the feelings expressed therein are bogus or recorded under duress. The pamphlet, *Slavery and Abolitionism, as Viewed by a Georgia Slave*, by Harrison Berry, a shoemaker and slave, warned against the promises of the abolitionists and pointed to the potential poverty that blacks would experience if let free in an anti-black society. In urging his fellow blacks to be submissive to their owners, Berry was perhaps the only person to address the nation directly on the subject of bondage while still a slave, and he seemingly never disavowed these sentiments.[18]

The "Narrative" of Frederick Douglass is a commonly referenced work in this regard. Douglass was a slave in Baltimore for more than twenty years, and his book, published by the American Anti-slavery Society, was replete with descriptions of the physical abuses of slavery, including whippings, rape, unwarranted punishments, and cold-blooded murder. The work appealed to a wider audience of reformers than just those who favored emancipation. Proponents of women's rights, temperance, public education, and immigration reform all found something to stir them in Douglass' work.

Southern readers pointed with incredulity to many of Douglass' child-hood memories of the whipping and murder of his fellow slaves. As he carefully omitted corroborating details from the incidents, many whites were convinced that the stories were patently false. His accounts of two slaves being murdered in unrelated incidents by individual masters on adjoining plantations within hours of one another rang false to all but the most dedicated of abolitionist ears. Nevertheless, between 1845 and 1850 the book sold more than 30,000 copies and was regarded by many in the North as a true picture of slavery in Maryland. The *New York Tribune* reviewer, himself an abolitionist, praised the book upon its pub-lication for its simplicity, truth, coherence, and warmth.

Slave Clothing   It would be an error to generalize about the standards of slave attire before the war based on Civil War documents. The physical appearance of slaves in the war-torn South was widely documented by the illustrated newspapers of the day and, to a lesser extent, by the science of photography; but little of their condition prior to the war had been so documented. Drawings are val-uable, but often reflect the bias of the artists, who tended to portray blacks as the North expected to see them. The photographers of the pe-riod, notorious for staging their shots, took very few pictures of common slaves. An exception to this is the series of photos taken immediately after the war that documents the scarred condition of an elderly man's back.

Slaves were a valuable form of property, and, as such, their owners had a financial incentive to keep them in good health. Plantation slaves were often clothed in coarse but durable trousers, shirts, and skirts made from "Negro-cloth," usually a form of coarse linen. Shoes were pur-chased for the plantation workers by the barrel, and most former slaves complained of rarely having had shoes that fit well. In 1839 a visitor from the North testified as follows: "The allowance of clothing on [one] plantation, to each slave, was given out at Christmas for the year, and consisted of one pair of coarse shoes, and enough coarse cloth to make a jacket and trousers. . . . The slaves on this plantation, being near Wil-mington, procured themselves extra clothing by working Sundays and moonlighting nights." The women received the same allowance of cloth as the men. It is certain that slaves were provided with better clothing before the war than after the federal blockade took effect.[19]

Slave Work Week   Slavery called for long hours of work and trying condi-tions by modern standards. Most slaves worked from sunup to sundown in the fields, or until the work was fin-ished when working indoors. During harvest or corn husk-ing slaves could be found working into the early hours of the morning.

A *Leslie's* illustration by Edwin Forbes of "contrabands"—slaves who have fled to the federal lines. Federal officials were hard pressed to decide the status of these unfortunates.

Slaughtering, in late fall, was a bloody and offensive task that allowed no interruption for rest. Nonetheless, the testimony of former slaves suggests that there was time to do extra work "on the side." The work week ran from Monday to Saturday noon and respected the Sabbath. Attendance at church services in clean clothes was required. Most blacks were restricted to the plantation and lived in the village of shanty huts provided for them. Any slave found off the plantation without a pass ran the danger of being "whipped on the spot" by the slave patrol, and if he resisted capture he could be shot. Slave housing was poor; heat in winter and ventilation in summer were generally haphazard, if not altogether absent. The plantations were therefore a strange combination of labor camp, racial community, and Christian mission.[20]

The food provided for slaves was of poor quality by modern standards, and the diet was periodically unbalanced. **Slave Food** Yet even the slave narratives suggest that foodstuffs were often abundant. Much of the food given to slaves was thought to be offensive or unwholesome. Whites normally did not eat chicken necks, gizzards, or pig's feet; and the small intestines of hogs, made up into chitlins, and kush, a mixture of bacon fat and cornmeal, were considered less than appealing to the delicate palates of white slaveowners. Wheat flour, white bread, and beef were almost unknown to slaves. Nonetheless, ham and gravy, fried chicken, ashcake, and hoecake—all standards in modest white households—were also found in slave kitchens. To supplement their diet, slaves were allowed to grow their own vegetables and to catch fish, squirrels, raccoons, opossums, and rabbits.[21]

Slaves were periodically issued molasses, salt pork, okra, peas, collard greens, turnips, and black-eyed peas. These foods supplemented a steady diet of cornmeal, fresh or parched corn, and potatoes or yams. Salted codfish was a staple of the slave diet in many localities. Purchased from the New England fisheries, it was identical to a familiar staple item in many European communities, especially those along the Atlantic and Mediterranean coasts of Spain and Italy. Surprisingly, slaves seem to have received sufficient calories and nutrients from this diet to allow for the heavy labor to which they were put.

Slave Entertainment
Slaves had no form of entertainment outside of that which they provided for themselves. As their work was tiring to the point of exhaustion, the very idea of leisure activities was displaced by a need for rest, if not sleep. Nonetheless, slaves found personal tasks to perform in their nonlaboring hours. Mending clothing, tending gardens, fishing and hunting, and caring for children and relatives took up much of their time. There were opportunities for enjoying music, dancing, storytelling, and simple sports such as footraces. Amusements included pitching horseshoes, gambling, cockfighting, and playing at marbles, checkers, or games of African origin. A good deal of time was spent in community activities such as church services, visits to the sick and elderly, and other comparable family activities.

Legal Rights for Slaves and Discipline
Unlike white employees, slaves were not free to change their condition should it become too burdensome. They could be physically chastised by their masters for many forms of disobedience, for insolence involving a white person, and for petty crimes. Incredibly, masters did not have unlimited legal power over their slaves. A slave accused of a felony could not be purposely mutilated, maimed, or killed as a punishment without the intervention of a court. The jurisdiction of these courts varied from place to place, but generally their procedures were set down in the Black Codes.

Of course, a slave defendant was not entitled to a jury trial. However, a hearing officer was required to determine the merits of the case and to act as a finder of fact. The county would then mete out punishment to slaves found to be guilty of serious crimes. As the hearing officers came from the community of free white slaveholders, questions of guilt or innocence were often moot. Nonetheless, the slave was allowed to make a defense. In such a case, the defendant needed to rely upon his own testimony or the testimony of other slaves. Slaves could not subpoena whites to testify. Both the Black Codes and custom gave great leeway to the officers of the court in determining the nature of any punishment.

As slaves were valuable property, masters looked down on any form of physical punishment that permanently devalued their slaves. Some masters intervened in behalf of their slaves even when their guilt had been firmly established. Hamstringing, various forms of dismemberment, and death, while not complete figments of the abolitionists' imaginations, were uncommon punishments for mere disobedience or petty crime. If only for economic reasons, the master wanted to maintain a chastised but physically capable slave in his employ, not a handicapped cripple. Punishments most often took the form of an informal laying on of the ever-present lash, while a hitching up to the whipping post for a formal flogging was reserved for major offenses. Masters also had the option of selling the unrepentant slave to the far South, into the interior, or to the disease-infested sugar plantations in lieu of punishment. The slaves themselves attest to such goings-on, and in very few narratives are such events absent.

Slaveowners rarely punished their bondsmen personally. This was left to the overseer. Much of the physical abuse distributed to slaves came from these often coarse and uncultivated men. Overseers came and went on individual plantations, and "some were too severe on the Negroes . . . brutified by their employment, [and] little better than the Negroes they managed."[22] These white men were aided by slave drivers, who, although black slaves themselves, could apply the lash with pitiless regularity and were used to chase down fugitives. Some blacks, like the slave drivers, were characterized as "white folks' servants," devoted to the master and his family and alienated from the general slave community. They were viewed by other slaves with disgust, as it was feared that they might curry favor with the master at the expense of other slaves by betraying them.

Ostensibly, flogging was the most widespread form of cruelty practiced by these persons; yet Americans believed even the most outrageous tales of immense abuse. Corporal punishment in many forms was highly evident throughout white society even in the North. Schoolmasters caned their disobedient or lazy students; fathers accompanied their progeny on repeated trips to the woodshed with razor strop or belt in hand; prisoners were ruthlessly beaten with sticks and whips by their jailers; and soldiers and sailors were frequently punished by flogging, sometimes to the point of death. Notwithstanding these facts, slaves were certainly exposed to excessive and unwarranted cruelty through no fault of their own.

While on an intellectual level Southerners claimed racial superiority for the white race, they nonetheless depended on the Negro to tend their animals, repair their vehicles, cook their food, and care for their children.

White slaveowners were intimately involved with blacks almost all of their lives. In the isolation of the great plantations, it was possible that most of a white person's dealings, in human terms, were either with family members or blacks. Some slaves were able to accompany their owners on trips to the town or city, and, once there, they were sent off on their own, with a pass, to do their master's business. It is strange to consider that white slaveowners, who so underestimated the value of human beings as to enslave them, were also able to entrust their bondsmen with the well-being and protection of their property and families. This fact seems to say much more about the humanity and responsibility exhibited by the slaves themselves than about their masters.

Race-based slavery promoted a type of equality among all white Southerners regardless of their social status. The lowliest white man could find comfort in the knowledge that he was the legal superior of even the wealthiest black freeman. Yet many slaveowners found it undesirable to have lower-class whites living on the fringes of plantations, where the slaves could be "impaired by contact with white labor."[23] Although it is uncertain with how much respect these whites viewed the Negro freeman, it would be common for them to have to deal with free blacks as laborers, tradesmen, and artisans. The working white population in much of the South exhibited far less abhorrence of blacks than did many in the upper and middle classes in the North.[24]

Draft Riots   European immigrants showed a particularly strong prejudice against the Negro. This was most obviously manifest during the 1863 New York City draft riots. Beyond a few recruiters and government officials who happened to be in the wrong place at the time, the targets of the mostly Irish rioters were generally Negroes.[25] *Harper's* reported that "no class of our foreign population is more jealous of its own liberties than the Irish, and there is also none which more strongly resents every liberty accorded to the Negro race." One black was "seized by the mob, and, after his life had been nearly beaten out, his body was suspended from a tree, a fire kindled under him, and, in the midst of excruciating torments, he expired." There may have been upwards of seventy black victims among the servants and workers of the hotels and restaurants in New York. An observer noted, "These things were done deliberately, and not in the heat of passion . . . and were moved by a political prejudice."[26]

By comparison Southerners were generally ambivalent in their attitude toward Negroes, requiring considerable formality from them, but treating them with disdain or paying them no mind at all. In some circumstances slaves were able to earn a small amount of cash by doing extra work, turning their talents to a particularly artful or craftsmanlike project, or receiving the equivalent of tips. One slave, "a money making and saving boy," was said to have accumulated more than $500 in this manner, only to have it stolen by a foraging party of black federal soldiers. Very elderly slaves, unable to work in their old age, were often "pensioned off," being provided with a small sum of cash or being given a shack and a regular issue of food on the plantation. Some states had laws requiring slaveowners to make such provisions so that elderly slaves, and those freed under manumission provisions, did not become a burden on society.[27]

Even in the absence of physical abuse or brutality, the institution of slavery did great harm to the bondsman. Southern blacks countered by drawing great strength from a number of traditional and cultural sources. In the years before the **Black Churches** abolition of the slave trade new arrivals from Africa exhibited a heavy dependence on their own tribal religions. In Louisiana and the West Indies many African religious practices came to be fused into a widespread religion known as Voodoo, "which penetrated into every level of Black society." Slaves bought charms and amulets in order to control their masters, obtain money, ensure love or good health, or bring harm and even death to enemies and nonbelievers. The New Orleans *Delta* reported in 1854 that the participants "strip themselves naked and then commence a strange, wild sort of Indian dance." Wild orgies, the drinking of blood, necromancy, and human sacrifice were all attributed to Voodoo by white observers.[28]

White society deemed such activities pagan, innately evil, and inconsistent with its own dedication to Christianity. Many African religious practices were rooted in a communication with the natural world and the joyful expression of an overt sexuality that shocked the more prudish Protestants. By extension, whites came to be intolerant of all forms of African culture that they did not understand. Slaveowners, even benevolent ones, effectively stripped the black of his tribal religious culture. Slaves were expected to exhibit moral behavior reflecting the mores of the God-fearing Christians whom they served. The responsibility for Christianizing the slaves, baptizing their infants, and nurturing in them a fear of the Lord was seriously regarded by whites. Many slaves were therefore forced to attend conventional religious instruction for the good of their souls.

White Southerners used their religion to validate the concept of race-based slavery, but their religion made the masters neither more humane to their slaves nor more likely to emancipate them.[29] Some of the most brutal masters were avid churchgoers. A Southern woman wrote in her journal with regard to slaveowning, "The purest and holiest men have owned them, and I see nothing in the scriptures which forbids it."[30] White ministers often preached to the blacks in a manner calculated to make the slave satisfied with his lot as an expression of the will of God. It was not unusual for the white clergy to own one or two slaves as servants. Sometimes slaves were provided by the congregation as part of the living given to the minister. Some churches, especially the Methodists and Baptists of the South, thought the social issues surrounding slavery scarcely worth consideration when contrasted to the saving of the heathen soul. Since many of the white man's churches upheld slavery, many blacks became suspicious of organized religions with white origins.[31]

There were churches established exclusively for slaves by their owners, but the presiding white ministers, who were in the forefront of defending slavery from the pulpit as the natural and correct place for the black race, were generally disliked. Most free Negroes in New Orleans attended the Catholic Church, where they enjoyed an almost equal standing with the white congregation. Separate black congregations grew in number among many sects because the white congregations of their denomination did not welcome black freemen. A growing army of black ministers was thereby able to found parishes among the freemen and slaves of the South. The African Methodist Episcopal (A.M.E.) Churches had the most prominent black ministers of the period. In New Orleans there was a congregation supported by more than 600 slaves of the Methodist Church; and the black Baptist Church had 500 members. White authorities feared any large meeting of blacks and broke up these religious services on a regular basis for the most trivial of reasons.

There were two very different types of religious services common to black churches. In the upper-class churches, populated by large numbers of freemen, there was a great dedication to religious form and ceremony. The services were less passionate and affected a greater intellectual appeal and attention to social problems than in the lower-class churches. The communicants of the lower-class churches were primarily composed of slaves and poor Negroes who held a strong belief in the power of God in their everyday lives. They emphasized revelations, visions, dreams, and outward expressions of redemption. Worship was often accompanied by shouts, cries, dancing, and other forms of joyful noise. Nonetheless, in each form, some of the African music, folk heritage, and dance survived. With time blacks were able to blend many of their African beliefs with the biblical teachings of Christianity. Both types of worship, although generally dividing the black community along class lines, served to uphold the structure of black life in a nation that cared little for Negroes except as chattels and laborers. The church proved to be one of the more durable black institutions.

The Slave Family   Another important social institution among blacks was the family. That the slave family was an incredibly unstable institution was only partially due to the influence of whites. A former slave noted, "There were on this plantation about seventy slaves, male and female: some were married, and others lived together as man and wife, without even a mock ceremony. . . . The slaves, however, think much of being married by a clergyman." Since marriage was considered a legal medium by which property was handed down, and the slave had no property, the law saw no reason to recognize the union of slaves as binding. Some morally scrupulous planters encouraged slave marriage as opposed to the immorality of open promiscuity.[32]

Investigators in New Orleans during the federal occupation recorded more than 500 marriages that had taken place while the couples involved had been slaves. Of these, fewer than 100 had remained unbroken. While some unions lasted from 20 to 40 years, the average length of a slave marriage was a mere 5.6 years. Records indicate that 70 percent of these marriages ended due to death or personal choice, and only 30 percent of the slave unions were broken up by the planters. Many planters professed an aversion to breaking up slave families because the practice increased unrest among the blacks; but the extravagant lifestyle of the planters, coupled with the regularity of foreclosures on mortgages and demands for the repayment of loans, caused most slaves to see the auction block at least once in their lives. Slaves could be bought or sold, rented out, gambled away, or left in a will as an inheritance to almost anyone; and the law did not provide for the continuity of the slave family as a unit.

Slave children did not belong to their parents but generally were considered the property of the mother's master. The father and the father's master, should he be a different person, were denied any standing in regard to the offspring of slave unions. "Women were generally shown some indulgence for three or four weeks previous to childbirth . . . [and] they are generally allowed four weeks after the birth of a child, before they are compelled to go into the field, they then take the child with them."[33] The offspring of a free man with a slave woman was thereby a slave; yet the offspring of a slave with a free woman was considered to be freeborn even if the woman were black. Even the children of a white master by a slave mother were born slaves. In the case of a dispute in this regard, with very few exceptions, whenever a slave's human rights came into conflict with a master's property rights, the courts invariably decided in favor of the master. The first activity of many refugee slaves during the war was to begin a search for their missing mates or children.

One of the unique features of slavery in this period was the pervasiveness of miscegenation,[34] or interracial **Miscegenation** sexual activity. The desire of white men to have sexual contact with black females was seemingly so common in the South that no social stigma was attached to it; whereas illicit liaisons between whites, extending even to white couples who were engaged to be married, were roundly condemned. White men involved in sexual relationships with black women, slave or free, seem to have received a special dispensation from Southern society. Indeed, a man who openly kept a white mistress would be turned out of society; yet, if he chose a "colored" one, and produced a whole family of mixed-race children from the relationship, he was seemingly absolved from any shame and highly regarded by his fellows.

Mixed-race sexual relations were not unknown in the North, and black-white marriages were legally void in several Northern states. Nonetheless, Northerners viewed miscegenation as a form of moral degeneracy, singularly "Southern," and rooted in the immorality of slavery. A European traveler to America found that blacks treated those of mixed race with disdain and hate. "They think them much closer to the Whites than to the Blacks."[35] An antebellum abolitionist author confidently reported that half the slave population of the South was mixed with white blood, and his assertion was accepted as gospel by willing readers. Statistical analysis suggests, however, that fewer than 10 percent of the slaves in the South were of mixed ancestry; and a portion of these had native American blood. Only a small percentage of the children born to slaves in a given year were fathered by white men. A high incidence of illegitimacy among poor populations, as well as a lack of careful records, makes the question of establishing absolute paternity difficult to answer.

Over time there developed an absurd theory that a single drop of black blood polluted the human being. Yet some Southerners suggested the equally preposterous notion that miscegenation improved the black population by breeding "whiteness" into it and would gradually eliminate the black race from America by dilution. Abolitionists spread the probably specious story of a slaveowner who offered a white man "twenty dollars for every one of his female slaves, whom he would get in the family way."[36] The extent of miscegenation is somewhat obscured by the methods used by nineteenth-century investigators to quantify the mixed-race population of the South as mulattos, quadroons, and octoroons by the criteria of the outward appearance of the skin and the absence or presence of certain defining racial features. A large population of mixed-race persons "passing for white" may also have obscured any meaningful estimates at the time.

Some white men, abjuring any justification for the satisfaction of their lustful desires, simply considered every slave cabin a bordello. In 1851 a Louisiana court recognized the virtual helplessness of the female slave in this situation, finding that she was "particularly exposed to the seductions of an unprincipled master."[37] A free black of New Orleans ascribed a loss of all feelings of morality and chastity among female slaves to this helplessness. "The practice of indiscriminate sexual intercourse ... was so universal that a chaste colored girl at the age of seventeen was almost unknown."[38]

The anti-slavery audiences of the North were horrified by descriptions of a planter who proposed intercourse with his female slave. If she would not comply, he could send for the overseer and have her flogged. "Seeing that her case was hopeless, her back smarting with the scourging she had received, and dreading a repetition, [she] gave herself up to be the victim of his brutal lusts."[39]

Notwithstanding such anecdotal evidence to the contrary, slave women rarely needed to be beaten into submission in such a manner. Consent was never more than a minor factor in any relationship between master and slave, and rape would seem a more straightforward and timely answer to the bestial needs of this particularly unethical master. No court would have heard a case of rape brought by a black slave against a white man.

Evidence suggests that female slaves were more often bribed, cajoled, or simply seduced by their masters or their master's sons. When the harsh realities of servitude were the only available alternative, any romantic notions involving the practices of miscegenation should best be avoided as sentiment rather than as an unbiased assessment of the situation in which these young women were placed.[40] Notwithstanding this reservation, there is documentary evidence, as well as anecdotal accounts, that some white Southerners demonstrated a long commitment to their black mistresses, recognized their mixed-race offspring, and attempted to provide for their upkeep and well-being. Often this took the form of a public admission after death, and many interracial alliances were recognized in a planter's will. The white children of such masters often went to great lengths to undo those parts of their father's will favorable to their biracial siblings.

The openness of many of these liaisons scandalized the social and religious elite everywhere. Nonetheless, some men of wealth seemingly relied on the common practice of supplying themselves with a quadroon mistress for short-term affairs. "They [the mistresses] are furnished with a Chamber and a sitting room and servants, and the comforts and elegancies of life. It generally costs from $1500 to $2000 a year to keep a quadroon."[41] The slave market records show that mixed-race, "light-skinned girls" brought far higher prices at auction than did prime field hands. In a documented case $8,000 was paid for a "particularly beautiful Negro woman." Moreover, to those who lacked the price of a slave or the wherewithal to maintain a mistress, the services of black prostitutes were sold at a premium, and comely slave girls brought exaggerated prices on the block from whoremongers who then hired them out as concubines.[42]

Southern ladies universally frowned upon any husband who was too open in his lustfulness; and while it seems that they could do little to enforce their displeasure on the male population at large, they could become quite angry and vengeful when the husband was theirs. More than one planter, taken with the beauty of a comely black slave, was forced to sell her or otherwise remove her from the reach of his wife. Evidence suggests that many of the petty lashings and beatings visited on the slaves were brought on by the vengeance of a jealous plantation wife taken out on the concubines and mixed-race children of her husband.

The question of how common sexual affairs between slaves and masters actually were, as opposed to how often they appear as titillating tidbits of gossip in journals and letters, is undecided. It is certain that the abolitionists exaggerated the universality of the documented cases. Southern slaveowners went to great lengths to structure laws and cultural norms that would prohibit such interaction. Many slaveholding states passed anti-miscegenation measures providing severe social penalties for white men who openly bedded black women and massive physical retaliation upon any black men who had sexual relations with white women. Although these measures ostensibly prohibited all interracial unions, for the white male they only made the offspring of his intercourse illegitimate.

The concept of white women sleeping with black men, a possible consequence of the moral hypocrisy surrounding such practices, was a proposition too explosive for the delicate egos of white males. White women were expected to respond to blacks as they would to any animate property, such as pets. The diaries and letters of young women and girls are full of references to the indelicacy of naked blacks, even adult males. Young women were expected to steel themselves into viewing the naked slave as a dehumanized object, no more indelicate than livestock in the barnyard.[43] Documented cases of the daughters of wealthy plantation owners bearing mixed-race children are rare, and, when found, are accompanied by tales of social rebuff and revulsion. Only after the war did liaisons involving white women and black men become more common and open to public knowledge; nonetheless, such women were universally labeled "sluts."[44]

NOTES

1. David Brion Davis, *Slavery in the Colonial Chesapeake* (Williamsburg: Colonial Williamsburg Foundation, 1994), 5.

2. A freeman could sell himself as an indentured servant for life, contract his conditions of employment, choose his master, and retain the cash under the laws of Virginia and other colonies.

3. Mayer, 61.

4. Davis, 4, 6, 22.

5. Mayer, 61.

6. Ibid., 116. Comments are attributed to an American diplomat, Joel R. Poinsett (1779–1851).

7. Jordan, 5–11, 21.

8. The view that slaves were bred for sale is not universally accepted by historians. In a 1980 work Kenneth M. Stampp of the University of California, Berkeley, wrote, "No conventional historian of the past generation claimed that slaves were bred in the Old South in the manner here described." Stampp, *The Imperiled Union* (New York: Oxford University Press, 1980), 92. The authors have deferred in this regard to the more recent work of Ervin L. Jordan.

9. Mayer, 61.

10. Horatio T. Strother, *The Underground Railroad in Connecticut* (Middletown: Wesleyan University Press, 1962), 201. From the narrative of Nehemiah Caulkins, a Northern visitor to North Carolina, published by Theodore Weld in 1839.

11. Sewell, 15; Jordan, 9, 22.

12. John W. Blassingame, *Black New Orleans* (Chicago: Chicago University Press, 1973), 33.

13. Ibid.

14. The Smithsonian Institution has audiovisual tape and film of former slaves whose ages are close to 100 years.

15. Alice Dana Adams, *The Neglected Period of Anti-slavery in America* (Boston: Corner House, 1973), 75, 77; Jordan, 14.

16. Stampp, *Imperiled Union*, 81.

17. Ibid., 43–45.

18. Harrison Berry, *Slavery and Abolitionism, as Viewed by a Georgia Slave* (Atlanta: M. Lynch, 1861).

19. Strother, 197.

20. Ibid., 203.

21. Recent archeology on slave quarters in Virginia has found evidence that some slaves may have been allowed the use of firearms.

22. Walter Sullivan, *The War the Women Lived: Female Voices from the Confederate South* (Nashville: J. S. Sanders, 1995), 5.

23. Kenneth M. Stampp, *The Peculiar Institution* (New York: Vintage, 1956), 150–151.

24. Jordan, 22.

25. Blassingame, *Black New Orleans*, 20–21. This is a phenomenon still present in American society, with new immigrant groups vying for the last practical social level that will sustain survival.

26. Alfred H. Guernsey and Henry M. Alden, ed., *Harper's History of the Great Rebellion* (New York: Gramercy Books, 1866), 652.

27. Dolly Sumner Lunt, *A Woman's Wartime Journal* (Atlanta: Cherokee, 1994), 26.

28. Blassingame, *Black New Orleans* 5–6.

29. Frederick Douglass, *Narrative of the Life of an American Slave, Written by Himself* (1845; New York: Penguin, 1968), 67.

30. Lunt, 38.

31. In a research study of New England towns done in 1987 under a grant from the Connecticut Council for the Humanities, it was found that many min-

isters and preachers had households which were comprised of both slaves and free blacks under the same roof.

32. See Theodore Weld, *American Slavery as It Is* (New York: N.p., 1839).

33. Strother, 195.

34. Although mixed-race sexual relations have an ancient history, *Webster's* dictionary claims that the word "miscegenation" did not appear in print until 1864.

35. Mayer, 116.

36. Strother, 207.

37. Quoted in Blassingame, *Black New Orleans*, 83.

38. Quoted in ibid.

39. Strother, 206.

40. There is considerable disagreement over the level of true affection found between such couples. Noted Civil War historian Eugene D. Genovese claims that many slaves fell in love with their masters and vice versa. In *The Plantation Mistress: Woman's World in the Old South* (New York: Pantheon Books, 1982), Catherine Clinton finds such a conclusion lacking in sensitivity with regard to the dynamics of sexual exploitation. The authors have decided to defer to Clinton's view.

41. Herbert A. Kellar, ed., "The Diary of James D. Davidson," *Journal of Southern History* 1 (1935): 348. Davidson was a visitor to Louisiana in 1836.

42. *New Orleans as It Is* (New Orleans: N.p., 1850), 35–45. See Blassingame, *Black New Orleans*, chap. 1.

43. Clinton, 111, 208–209, 221.

44. See ibid. 199–222.

6

Abolition

"I want to see those hot-headed abolitionists put in the front rank
and shot first."

—A federal soldier in 1861

Attacks on slavery in the early years of the republic had
been based on the ideals set forth in the Declaration of   **The**
Independence and the incompatibility of slavery with the   **Anti-slavery**
concept that "all men are created equal." Many Americans   **Movement**
freed their slaves during and immediately after the Revolution—a circumstance not confined to the North. Following the Revolution a large number of Southerners spoke about the abolition of slavery
in abstract terms, and others were sufficiently dedicated to its ultimate
eradication to provide for private manumission of their slave property.
Yet early opposition to emancipation, including that of Thomas Jefferson,
was based largely on the racist concept that the inherent inequality in
the races would prevent their living in peace and prosperity together.
Allegiance to slavery as an institution was rarely expressed. That was to
come later in the turmoil over states' rights.

Proponents of emancipation looked to gradualism and colonization,
rather than immediate emancipation and inclusion, to relieve the supposed incongruities of the races living peacefully together. Gradual
emancipation provided that children born as slaves could be freed on
attaining maturity, having been given a skill or education in the interim

so that they might provide for themselves. Similarly formed legislation had quietly obliterated slavery throughout the New England states by mid-century. Private parties among anti-slavery proponents favored the removal of free blacks to colonies established far from the Americas. The African city of Monrovia was founded as a "freemen's colony" in 1821 in this manner. Less dramatic suggestions were also made to remove freed blacks to the Indian Territories, Florida, the Caribbean Islands, and Central America.

While many Northerners were against slavery, they were also remarkably prejudiced against blacks. They were averse to having them live in their communities and inclined to leave the issue of universal emancipation alone. Radical abolitionists—always a minority among anti-slavery advocates—were loath to accept the slow pace of gradual emancipation and were becoming increasingly militant in their frustration. This militancy was not universally shared even among anti-slavery proponents. Abolitionist speakers were threatened with tar and feathers in New England towns as late as 1850, and an anti-slavery speaker, Elijah P. Lovejoy, was murdered by a mob in the free state of Illinois in 1837. It was widely held that free blacks would come North to compete for scarce jobs in the cities, and an economic downturn in 1857 did not help to relieve this fear.[1]

The treatment of blacks in Northern states was often brutish, and they were despised and treated with contempt. In the decades after independence, towns and cities had been flooded by thousands of freed blacks, some of whom had fought in the Revolutionary army; and any plan for a general abolition of slavery had to deal with the touchy problem of free blacks living in a white-dominated, racist society. This led many sympathetic whites to fear for the ultimate welfare and safety of a black population suddenly foisted on an unfriendly America should the radicals attain their goal of universal emancipation.[2]

Even among those who volunteered to fight for the preservation of the Union, there was little sympathy for the abolitionists. Wrote one federal soldier at the beginning of the war, "I don't blame the South an atom. They have been driven to desperation by such lunatics as Garrison and Phillips, and these men ought to be hung for it." Another federal recruit said, "I want to see those hot-headed abolitionists put in the front rank and shot first."[3]

There was a growing recognition, however, that slavery was a great moral and social evil that must be ended soon. But it was also true that slavery had become uneconomical for the smaller planters. As early as 1816, several Southern states, Virginia, Georgia, Maryland, and Tennessee included, had asked that a site for colonization by freed blacks be procured, and they had jointly petitioned the federal government for financial aid to offset the monetary loss involved in emancipating their

Federal authorities initially put escaped slaves to work digging entrenchments and fixing railroads. Some Northern artists had an unfortunate habit of showing blacks in a stereotypical manner that mirrored the expectations of the Northern public. Sketch by W. T. Crane of *Leslie's*.

slaves. The British government had successfully indemnified its slave-owners for their loss when the slave trade was ended in 1808, but a similar arrangement was not possible in antebellum America, either financially or politically.

In 1817 the American Colonization Society was formed to encourage free blacks to return to Africa. The organizational meeting was held in no less a prestigious place than the chambers of the House of Representatives. Among its founders were Henry Clay, Andrew Jackson, and Francis Scott Key. The society drew its initial support from all sections of the country and from both slavery and anti-slavery advocates. Colonization societies outnumbered abolition societies in America right up to the opening of the war. Within two decades of its founding, more than 140 branches of the American Colonization Society were formed in the Southern states, with the majority of chapters in Virginia, Kentucky, and Tennessee. In the North approximately 100 societies were formed—radical abolition seemingly stealing some of the colonialists' thunder—the majority established in the states of Ohio, New York, and Pennsylvania. Only in Massachusetts did immediate abolition have a greater following than colonization. Of all the states, only Rhode Island and South Carolina had no colonization societies—both had been major import markets in the days of the Atlantic slave trade. Unquestionably, the intervention of

Northern moralists into the evolution of anti-slavery at this point provided a "fateful check" to any hope of abolition without considerable turmoil.[4]

A minority of free blacks espoused great interest in their African homeland, yet a larger number were interested not in Africa, but in other areas outside the United States. Canada, Central America, and Haiti were all mentioned as possible sites for black emigration. Several prominent free blacks, such as poet James M. Whitfield, the Rev. Henry H. Garnet, and Dr. Martin R. Delancy, called for an emphasis on black nationalism and militant black unity. It was feared that in the United States blacks could always expect to be crawling in the dust at the feet of their former oppressors.[5]

Colonization was very popular politically. At the time, it was estimated by the proponents of colonization that slavery could be abolished by 1890. During the debates with Stephen Douglas in 1858, Lincoln had expressed both support for colonization and a belief in an inherent inequality among the races. He disclaimed any hopes for "social and political equality of the White and Black races," and disavowed any plan to make "voters or jurors of Negroes, nor of qualifying them to hold office, nor to intermarry with white people." Most important, he pledged his support for colonization of freed slaves, saying, "There is a physical difference between the White and Black races which I believe will forever forbid the two races living together on terms of social and political equality." True to his word, in 1862, one year before the Emancipation Proclamation, the president signed a congressional appropriation of $100,000 for the purpose of encouraging black colonization.[6]

But the abolitionists demanded immediate, unreimbursed emancipation and integration of freed blacks into white society, not gradualism and separation. No price, including war and disunion, was too great to pay in the cause of ending slavery and racial prejudice. The rhetoric of Wendell Phillips, a leading abolitionist in Massachusetts, provided an example to the South, and all of America, of just how far the radicals were willing to go when he suggested "trampling the laws and Constitution of the country" to gain their ends. Such rhetoric was seen as a call for civil disorder, even violence, on a massive level.[7]

The radical abolitionists berated the gradualists and colonialists as being less than completely dedicated to the cause of emancipation. In *Thoughts on African Colonization* (1832), William Lloyd Garrison went so far as to suggest that the gradualists and colonialists were actually covert supporters of slavery, allowing Northern slaveowners to "sell their slaves south," thereby recouping their considerable investment in slave property. Garrison argued that colonization would make Americans "abominably hypocritical" by allowing free blacks to remain among them only "as inferior beings, deprived of all the valuable privileges of freemen, separated by the brand of indelible ignominy, and debased to a level with the beasts."[8]

Garrison may have been the most vehement of the radical abolitionists. Although he did not, in any real sense, lead the American anti-slavery movement, he was possibly the most conspicuous of the radicals. In 1845 he wrote in the highly idealized style typical of the movement: "Be faithful, be vigilant, be untiring in your efforts to break every yoke, and let the oppressed go free. Come what may—*cost what it may*—inscribe on the banner which you unfurl to the breeze, as your religious and political motto—'No Compromise with Slavery! No Union with Slaveholders!' "[9]

Although calls to violence were not characteristic of the abolition movement, the rhetoric of the outspoken radicals was couched in inflammatory and unambiguous terms aimed at ending slavery—"Law or No law, constitution or no constitution."[10] Abolitionists vowed to work with "invincible determination" regardless of the consequences. The radicals publicly disavowed the unsettling concept of slaves shedding the blood of their oppressors, but they recognized that there was "no neutral ground in this matter, and the time is near when they will be compelled to take sides."[11]

In the call for a slave rebellion, the goal of which was "to attack the slave power in its most vulnerable point," the South perceived a very real physical threat. There had been three important black insurrections in the South: the Gabriel revolt in 1800, the Denmark Vesey revolt in 1822, and the Nat Turner revolt in 1831. Only the Turner revolt had led to any deaths among whites, but these had numbered mostly women and children among the sixty or so killed. Coupled with the knowledge of major slave revolts and mass murders in the West Indies, such doings were taken seriously by slaveowners. Abolitionists endorsed John Brown's attempt to foment an armed slave rebellion in Virginia by attacking Harper's Ferry in 1858. Against this background the writings and speeches of the radicals proved truly heavy rhetoric.[12]

Young Kate Stone's diary reflected her fears in an encounter with slaves recently freed by federal forces in April 1863: "Looking out the window, we saw three fiendish looking, black Negroes standing around George Richards, two with their guns leveled and almost touching his breast. He was deathly pale but did not move. We thought he would be killed instantly. But after a few words from George . . . they lowered their guns and rushed into the house . . . to rob and terrorize us."[13]

Those who identified themselves as abolitionists gen-   **Abolitionists** erally eschewed allegiance to a particular religious group, but a good number were intimately involved in their religions, particularly the newly formed sect of Unitarianism. However, those belonging to the Congregational, Presbyterian, and Quaker denominations predominated in the movement. The Methodists and Baptists

were quite split over the issue, and very few Catholics rose to prominence in the largely Protestant anti-slavery circles. The Quaker sect was
probably the most unified in its position against slavery. Yet the crusade
for the immediate social and political equality of blacks was championed
with a religious fervor by many men and women.

Lewis Tappan, a New York merchant, abandoned his Calvinist roots
to become the treasurer of the American Unitarian Association. He was
a supporter of the American Board of Commissioners for Foreign
Missions and the American Bible Society. In 1833 he established the
American Anti-Slavery Society in New York, but split with the
Massachusetts-based abolitionists over ancillary issues raised by Garrison. Thereafter, he worked increasingly for the Negro through the
American Missionary Association and through support of the Underground Railroad.

Theodore Tilton joined the *New York Observer*, a Presbyterian weekly,
in 1853. However, he found the paper's editorial attitude toward abolition lukewarm and moved on to become the editor of the *Independent*, a
Congregational journal with more radical views on emancipation. Tilton
turned the *Independent* into a first-class journal. He attracted writers such
as E. B. Browning, Whittier, Lowell, Garrison, and Seward, and he regularly printed the sermons of Henry Ward Beecher, the prominent pastor
of the Plymouth Church in Brooklyn, New York. Tilton and Beecher
joined forces in 1861 and used the paper to fight aggressively for emancipation and a more vigorous prosecution of the war. Tilton's promising
career was ruined in a failed lawsuit against the preacher in which an
affair between his wife and Beecher was made public.

Sidney H. Gay was the editor of the *New York Tribune* from 1857 to
1865. As a young man Gay had become convinced that slavery in any
form was absolutely and morally wrong. He became a member of Garrison's group of abolitionists and edited the *American Anti-Slavery Standard* in New York from 1843 to 1857.

Stirred by the death of the abolitionist Elijah P. Lovejoy at the hands
of a mob in Illinois in 1837, Edmund Quincy shocked his family, who
were quite moderate on the issue, by becoming a Garrisonian abolitionist
and vice-president of the American Anti-Slavery Society. He was a prominent member of the Nonresistance Society, which agitated for the secession of New England from the Union over the issue of slavery. Quincy
was well known in literary circles, and his writings on the subject furnish
an interesting history of the abolition movement in America.

Like many of the female radicals of the period, Abby K. Foster was an
abolitionist as well as a women's rights activist. Originally from a Quaker
background, she began to lecture for abolition in 1837. She conducted
her campaign with Angelina Grimké, reportedly becoming the first

woman in the United States to address a mixed audience in public. For this she was denounced by the clergy, who considered her a menace to public morals, and her speeches were periodically broken up by mob violence. Her presence as a delegate to the World Anti-Slavery Conference in London in 1840 caused serious disturbances, as women delegates were refused recognition. As a pioneer feminist and a leader of the radical abolitionists, she was a well-known figure in the North and a target for hatred in the South.

Angelina and Sarah Grimké were sisters born to a slaveowning family in South Carolina. Upon their father's death, the young sisters were able to persuade their mother to apportion the family slaves to them as a share of their family estate, upon which they freed them at once. Originally members of the Episcopal Church, they were attracted to the Quaker sect by friends who lived in Philadelphia, but found that they lacked the self-restraint to curb their unequivocal hatred of slaveowners. In 1836 Angelina wrote an *Appeal to the Christian Women of the South*, which urged Southern women to speak and act out against slavery. In South Carolina the sixty-six-page pamphlet was confiscated and burned by postmasters, and the author was threatened with imprisonment if she returned to the state. Angelina followed this work in 1837 with an *Appeal to the Women of the Nominally Free States*, in which she strongly insisted that the women residing in free states were equally guilty for the national shame of continued slavery.

Sarah and Angelina began their careers by addressing small groups of women on both feminist and anti-slavery topics, and ultimately entered the lecture circuit. So great was the opposition to women speaking in public that the sisters found that they were spending as much time defending their feminism as preaching their anti-slavery ideals. John Greenleaf Whittier came to their defense, referring to them as "Carolina's high souled daughters" in his writings; but, at the same time, he privately suggested that they limit their efforts to the cause of emancipation.

The efforts of the sisters were important in the development of both the feminist and abolitionist causes, and it is difficult to determine to which cause they were most dedicated. Angelina confirmed her position in the anti-slavery community when she married abolition activist and author Theodore D. Weld in 1838. As a youth, Sarah Grimké found that it was impossible for her to study law because she was a woman. From this situation flowed her natural devotion to the cause of women's rights. Sarah wrote *Letters on the Equality of the Sexes and the Condition of Women* in the year of her sister's marriage. Her correspondence with her brother-in-law is a source of information about the cause of abolition in this period. As Southern advocates of radical abolition and feminism, the Grimké sisters were particularly detested by traditionally minded

Southern women, who took pains to target them in their journals and letters.

Activists were not the only targets of Southern ire. An outspoken Southern woman listed a number of pro-abolitionists among the day's popular writers and politicians in the following diatribe: "On one side Mrs. Stowe, Greeley, Thoreau, Emerson, Sumner, in nice New England Homes—clean, clear, sweet-smelling—shut up in libraries, writing books which ease their hearts of their bitterness to us, or editing newspapers— all of which pays better than anything else in the world." The same woman called anti-slavery "the cheapest philanthropy trade in the world" and castigated the abolitionists for "setting John Brown to come down here and cut our throats in Christ's name."[14]

Contrary to the common Southern perceptions of abolitionists— preaching and teaching "hate as a gospel and the sacred duty of murder and insurrection"—the use of violence to attain emancipation never had a great appeal to the mass of people in the North, and the more pro- vocative tactics and strategies of the radicals rarely had any effect outside of New England. Anti-slavery, as a movement, was far too decentralized and subject to too many local variations to march in lockstep behind the radicals.[15]

Garrison, in particular, was prone to involving himself in factional disputes within the movement. His refusal to endorse a political solution to slavery based on compromise, his attacks on the religious institutions of the nation as supporters of slavery in the 1840s, and his continued characterization of the South as an aggressive enemy of all American institutions left him outside the mainstream of anti-slavery sentiment. He attacked the Constitution as a "guilty and bloodstained instrument," called for the secession of the New England states from the Union, dis- rupted religious services at "pro-slavery" churches, and castigated the clergy and the anti-slavery moderates as conspiring with Southern slave power. These positions caused a split in the movement in 1840. None- theless, Garrison remains a central figure in the controversy that led to the Civil War simply because the South took him seriously and believed that he had a much greater following than reality justified.[16]

Black Anti-slavery Activists One of the many themes of the abolitionists was that the slave was "capable of high attainments as an intellectual and moral being—needing nothing but a comparatively small amount of cultivation to make him an ornament of society and a blessing to his race." Emancipation advocates declared that only the great weight of slavery had deteriorated the nat- ural goodness and intelligence the Negro had brought from Africa. "It has a natural, an inevitable tendency to brutalize every noble faculty of man." Frederick Douglass served as a favorite symbol of the ideally regenerated freeman, and was portrayed as a victim of slavery with a "godlike nature" and a "richly endowed" intellect. Douglass was showcased as a naturally eloquent "prodigy—in soul manifestly created but a little lower than the angels."[17]

From 1841 to 1860, Douglass was the most prominent black abolitionist, "filled by his escape to freedom with noble thoughts and thrilling reflections." Yet, among black activists there were several equally eminent success stories. These included Charles Lenox Remond, one of the first black anti-slavery activists; Williams Wells Brown, the first black playwright; Frances E.W. Harper, a prominent poet; Henry Bibb, a former slave and editor of a Canadian newspaper; John Mercer Langston, a free lawyer from Ohio; Martin R. Delancy, a Harvard-trained physician; and Rev. Henry Highland Garnet, the first black man to speak in the U.S. House of Representatives.

Several black newspapers were printed in the antebellum period that vied for prominence in anti-slavery circles with Garrison's *Liberator*. The *Impartial Citizen* was printed in Syracuse, New York, beginning in 1848; the *Colored Man's Journal* was popular in the 1850s in New York City; San Francisco had the *Mirror of the Times* in the 1850s; and the *Alienated American* was published briefly in Cleveland, Ohio. One of the earliest papers was *Freedom's Journal*, established in 1827 by John B. Russwurm, the first Negro to receive a degree from an American college.

One of the most popular black papers of the 1850s was *Frederick Douglass' Paper*, later called *Douglass' Monthly Magazine*. Unlike the other black papers, which were locally popular and short-lived, Douglass' work was circulated through eighteen states and two foreign countries. It had more than 4,000 subscribers and survived for more than thirteen years. Not only did these papers showcase the ability of blacks to write and edit, but they also hinted at the large number of blacks among their subscribers who could read.

While Southern slaveholders may have been willing to forego slavery as an institution if their financial invest- **Slaveowners** ment in slaves were indemnified, the mass of Southern society was totally unwilling to be chastised by self-righteous Northern idealists or to tolerate the integration of blacks into white society as equals. It has been estimated that the large slaveowners comprised as little as 3 percent of Southern whites, and fewer than 6 percent owned any slaves at all. The majority of these small slaveholders had fewer than five slaves and labored in the fields beside them. Nonetheless, in 1850 slaveholders represented a majority of the delegates in the legislatures of all but two Southern states. Only in South Carolina were they dominant. In Louisiana and Texas nearly two-thirds of the legislators owned no slaves at all. It is estimated that only 40 percent of all county offices

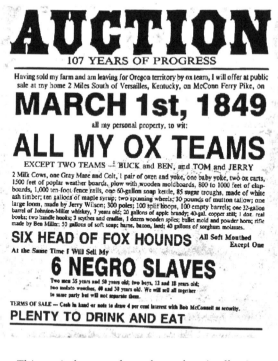

AUCTION

107 YEARS OF PROGRESS

Having sold my farm and am leaving for Oregon territory by ox team, I will offer at public
sale at my home 2 Miles South of Versailles, Kentucky, on McConn Ferry Pike, on

MARCH 1st, 1849

all my personal property, to wit:

ALL MY OX TEAMS

EXCEPT TWO TEAMS — BUCK and BEN, and TOM and JERRY

2 Milk Cows, one Gray Mare and Colt, 1 pair of oxen and yoke, one baby yoke, two ox carts,
1500 feet of poplar weather boards, plow with wooden moldboards, 800 to 1000 feet of clap-
boards, 1,000 ten-foot fence rails, one 60-gallon soap kettle, 85 sugar troughs, made of white
ash timber; ten gallons of maple syrup; two spinning wheels; 30 pounds of mutton tallow; one
large loom, made by Jerry Wilson; 300 poles; 100 split hoops, 100 empty barrels; one 32-gallon
barrel of Johnson-Miller whiskey, 7 years old; 20 gallons of apple brandy; 40-gal. copper still; 1 doz. real
books; two handle hooks; 3 scythes and cradles, 1 dozen wooden spiles; bullet mold and powder horn; rifle
made by Ben Miller; 50 gallons of soft soap; hams, bacon, lard; 40 gallons of sorghum molasses.

SIX HEAD OF FOX HOUNDS   All Soft Mouthed Except One

At the Same Time I Will Sell My

6 NEGRO SLAVES

Two men 35 years and 50 years old; two boys, 12 and 18 years old;
two mulatto wenches, 40 and 30 years old. We will sell all together
to same party but will not separate them.

TERMS OF SALE — Cash in hand or note to draw 4 per cent interest with Bob McConnell as security.

PLENTY TO DRINK AND EAT

This period poster from the authors' collection
chillingly illustrates the status of Negro slaves as
they are listed for sale amid ox teams, foxhounds,
and sundry farm goods.

in the Deep South were held by nonslaveholders, giving slaveowners
control far out of proportion to their numbers.[18]

The impracticality of blacks being integrated into the fabric of American society in the antebellum period can best be measured by the resistance to racial integration seen in the South after a costly and painful
war had forced emancipation upon it. With no solution to the perceived
problems of free black participation in white society, and faced with
economic ruin if forced to forfeit their considerable investment in black
labor, Southerners were forced to turn any moderate attitudes they may
have possessed toward gradual emancipation into a total defense of
Southern society against any disruption from without. Impelled by a
growing body of public opinion in the North that slavery must be abolished *at all costs*, the South launched an equally militant defense of the
institution, portraying it as a positive good—a civilizing and caring medium for blacks who would otherwise revert to the brutality of their
African origins. A Southern woman wrote of her slaveowning relations,
"They strive to ameliorate the condition of these Africans in every par-

ticular ... [and] live their own lives in peace [as] if they were African missionaries."[19]

A number of important legal cases involving slaves and the efforts of abolitionists preceded the outbreak of war. Three of the more interesting are the *Amistad* case, the Lemmon case, and the Dred Scott case. That not all of these **Slavery and the Courts** cases were decided in the same direction suggests some ambiguity within the courts, but it should be noted that some of these decisions were handed down by state courts, while others were decided by federal judges. The depth of the discrepancies found in these decisions was symptomatic of the preoccupation with these matters as an outgrowth of the ongoing disputes tearing at the country.

The *Amistad* was a slave ship belonging to Spanish owners that sailed from Havana in June 1839 for another Cuban port. The master of the ship had on board over **Mutiny on the** *Amistad* fifty blacks, including four children. All of them were so recently imported from Africa that most spoke neither English nor any other European language. On the journey the blacks, under the leadership of a warrior named Cinque, overcame the crew and took control of the ship. In the process, they killed the captain and the ship's cook. With the coerced help of the surviving crew, they proceeded to sail north along the Atlantic coast of the United States.

Some months later, the vessel was found at anchor off the shore of Long Island, New York. A boarding party from the USS *Washington* commanded by Lt. Cmdr. T.R. Gedney, USN, took the *Amistad* into the port of New London, Connecticut, along with the blacks. Gedney brought a case in the U.S. district court in New Haven for the salvage rights to the ship, which included the fair market value of the "slaves" on board.

John H. Hyde, an abolition sympathizer and the editor of the New London *Gazette*, wrote a story about the incident, making the blacks instant celebrities. The Anti-Slavery Society in Connecticut contacted Roger S. Baldwin, a New York attorney, to defend the rights of the Africans found aboard the *Amistad*. With financing arranged by Louis Tappan, the Committee of Friends of the Amistad Africans was formed. The abolitionists brought suit in the Connecticut state courts before Judge Andrew T. Judson, claiming the freedom of the Africans under existing U.S. law, as the United States had joined with Britain to prohibit slave trading in 1808. Under several treaties between 1817 and 1830, the Spanish had also made the slave trade illegal.

The abolitionists' lawyers argued that the blacks had the status of free men on the grounds that they were free-born Africans, not subjects of Spain or any other country. They were in fact of the Mendi tribe and had been kidnapped as free men from their homeland in Sierra Leone, and illegally transported to a Spanish possession, and were therefore free under Spanish law as well. Since the treaties between the United States and Spain did not require that the Africans be returned to Spanish territory, the court ruled that they were at liberty to return to Africa if they wished.

Abolitionist forces were initially elated but quickly became alarmed when it was learned that the Van Buren administration in Washington was determined to overturn this decision so as not to offend the sensibilities of the South in the election of 1840. The case was appealed to the Supreme Court, and Justice Joseph Story delivered its opinion in 1841. The Court awarded Lt. Cmdr. Gedney the salvage rights to the ship and its cargo, but freed the Africans on the grounds that they had always been free men and had never become slaves under Spanish law. This was deft footwork if there ever was any. By declaring that the Africans were free by the law of Spain, the Court was able to sidestep any accusations of freeing slaves or setting precedents for the emancipation of American-born blacks under U.S. law.[20]

It had taken almost three years for the Africans on board the *Amistad* to regain their freedom. In the interim, they were housed in Westville, Connecticut, about two miles outside New Haven. Under the care of the abolitionists, many of the Africans learned to speak and write English, studied the Bible, and became "civilized Christian Men." One was later to serve as an English interpreter in an African mission in Sierra Leone, and one of the female children became a teacher. On November 27, 1841, with money raised for the purpose among interested British abolitionists, thirty-five of the surviving Africans returned to their homeland along with five white missionaries and teachers. A Christian mission to Africa was established there and remained prosperous for many decades. It is interesting to note that little money was raised among American abolitionists for the return trip to Africa even though it seemed supportive of the growing colonization movement.[21]

In 1852 Jonathan and Juliet Lemmon decided to move **The Lemmon** from Virginia to Texas and take the eight slaves that be-**Case** longed to Mrs. Lemmon with them. Although the details of the trip are confused and unimportant, it was decided to take a side trip by steamer to New York City and then book a luxury passage from there to New Orleans. The slaves were thereby brought into New York Harbor while New York was a free state. Jonathan Lemmon, conscious of a possible problem, made plans to transfer the slaves to a southbound steamer without actually landing them in New York for fear that the abolitionists would make an effort to rescue them. But his plans failed, and the owners and the slaves were arrested as soon as they touched land and were brought before the New York State courts.

The state argued that Lemmon was a slave trader and that these blacks were confined and held against their will. The attorneys for the Lemmons argued that they had the right under federal law to transport their "property" anywhere in the country. Moreover, it was argued that the slaves had never touched free soil except for the purpose of passage and transit. Justice Elijah Paine granted the state's writ, citing the anti-slavery statutes of New York as his authority. He ordered the eight slaves freed. Paine's decision was greeted with approbation by the New York press, free blacks, and abolitionists everywhere. Nevertheless, a group of New York businessmen raised funds to compensate the Lemmons for their loss. The Lemmons received $5,200 in indemnification and returned to Virginia, while the former slaves were secretly whisked off to Canada to ensure their future safety.[22]

In 1857, in a much more celebrated case, the Supreme Court decided that the Missouri Compromise was uncon- **The** stitutional, and that a black slave, Dred Scott, taken from **Dred Scott** slave territory in Missouri to free soil in Illinois, "had never **Decision** ceased to be a slave" and so could not claim his freedom in a federal court because he lacked standing as a citizen with the right to sue. The decision effectively denied the right of Congress to prohibit slaveowning "anywhere within the United States."[23]

An outburst of protest greeted the Dred Scott decision in the North, and the Republicans made it a cornerstone of their 1860 presidential election campaign. Meanwhile, in March 1860, the New York State court of appeals chose to rehear the Lemmon case, and ruled again in favor of the slaves. Southern slaveowners were horrified by the decision and threatened to take it to the Supreme Court. However, the outbreak of the war prevented the case from ever again being heard.

NOTES

1. *Dictionary of American Biography*, ed. Dumas Malone (New York: Scribner's Sons, 1943). The information on prominent abolitionists that follows is taken largely from this source.

2. Adams, 66–81. The infant U.S. government promised to free black slaves that fought the British at the end of the Revolutionary War. They kept their word and provided pensions for the veterans. The British governor of Virginia, Lord Dunmore, made similar promises, but chose to send black volunteers who supported the British as slaves to the West Indies at the close of the conflict. See David O. White, *Connecticut's Black Soldiers of the Revolution* (Chester: Pequot Press, 1973).

3. John D. Billings, *Hardtack and Coffee* (Boston: G.M. Smith, 1887), 20.

4. Adams, 105, 107. Data taken from the table on p. 106.

5. John W. Blassingame, *The Clarion Voice* (Washington: National Parks Service, 1976), 18.

6. See ibid., 18–20.

7. Douglass, xvii.

8. William Lloyd Garrison, *Thoughts on African Colonization* (Boston: N.p., 1832), 134.

9. Douglass, xiv. Emphasis added.

10. Garrison, *The Liberator*, (Boston), December 15, 1837.

11. Ibid.

12. Ibid., May 31, 1844.

13. Sullivan, 91–92.

14. C. Vann Woodward, *Mary Chesnut's Civil War* (New Haven: Yale University Press, 1981), 245.

15. Clifford Dowdey, *The Great Plantation* (Charles City, VA: Berkeley Plantation Press, 1957), 300.

16. Garrison, *The Liberator*, March 31, 1832.

17. Douglass, vi, 24 .

18. Ibid., vii.

19. Dowdey, 300; C. V. Woodward, 245.

20. Fred J. Cook, "The Slave Ship Rebellion," *American Heritage*, February 1957, 60–64, 104–115.

21. Howard Jones, *Mutiny on the "Amistad"* (New York: Oxford University Press, 1987), 3–21.

22. Jordan, 13–14.

23. Bowman, 38.

Part II

Soldiers' Lives

7

Billy Yank and Johnny Reb

"Dearest and most intimate friends and companions."
—Thomas A. Ashby

The men who opposed one another on the battlefields of the Civil War were more alike than different. Generally, the soldiers on both sides came from similar backgrounds, spoke the same language (although sometimes with widely divergent regional accents), had the same political history, cherished the same Constitution, and suffered the same hardships and dangers offered by soldiering. But the differences between Billy Yank and Johnny Reb were nonetheless meaningful enough to sustain four years of bloody conflict and may help to explain the relationship between these enemies.[1]

Common Soldiers

The great difference between Billy Yank and Johnny Reb seems to have been in their style of fighting—a characteristic noted by many observers. "Three points I noted with regard to our opponents," observed federal captain John W. De Forest. "They aimed better than our men; they covered themselves (in case of need) more carefully and effectively; they could move in a swarm, without much care for alignment and touching elbows. In short, they fought more like [Indians], or like hunters, than we. The result was that they lost fewer men, though they were far inferior in numbers."[2]

Applying statistical analysis to the Civil War is difficult at best and foolhardy at worst, yet the war generated a noble body of data that begs

Civil war reenactors: Mark Gilbert, 7th Virginia
Cavalry, and Keith Curtis and Jim Volo, 1st
Connecticut Cavalry. Dorothy Volo photo.

to be interpreted. Still, hard and fast conclusions based solely on these
data should be avoided. Facts and figures on the men who faced one
another in 1861–62 are largely unreliable when grouped together with
those of 1863–64. The volunteers of the earlier period tended to differ
significantly from the troops of the later war, which included draftees,
substitutes, and bounty claimers. Moreover, it is difficult to ascertain
reliable statistics for Southern troops, as they are simply not available
for all theaters or periods of the conflict. Similar inherent inaccuracies in
the data notwithstanding, some simple facts stand out about the men
who fought in the Civil War.[3]

Of all the soldiers that served in the war, it has been estimated that
between 30 percent and 40 percent were Confederates, yet a reliable figure for their absolute number can not be obtained because records for
the western armies are lacking. Between 1 and 1.5 million men may have
served in the Rebel army. In contrast, the records of the United States
Government, which are much more complete and reliable, show that
federal forces numbered precisely 2.2 million men. Approximately three-
quarters of each opposing force was composed of infantry, with cavalry
making up 15 percent and artillery about 7 percent. The remaining portion was composed of engineers, medical personnel, teamsters, and other
ancillary personnel. About 10 percent of each army served as officers.
Only 3 percent of all federal personnel served in the navy, and less than
1 percent served in the minuscule Confederate navy.

The average age of the men at enlistment in the federal army was just under twenty-six. The Confederates averaged just over twenty-six years, a remarkable agreement with the federal figure when the traditional view of the Rebels is of an army composed of old men and young boys. The height and weight of federal recruits is well documented; they averaged 5 feet, 8 inches and 145 pounds. As nineteenth-century men were about this size on average, it can be presumed that Confederates were of a similar height and weight. Of the federal soldiers, 29 percent were married when they enlisted, while more than 36 percent of their Southern counterparts seem to have been married men. This may reflect a greater mobilization of the available population in the manpower-hungry South.

While many men wrote regularly to their families and expressed pitiable longing and loneliness for them, a federal officer testified about receiving a letter from a destitute wife, anxious for news of her husband's health. The wife had received no word of him in months and only nine dollars since he had enlisted. She and her children had therefore been evicted from their home. "Here are four pages of pathos that make me want . . . to kick him for not deserving them," wrote the officer. "Apparently a fairly educated and quite worthy girl has married a good-looking youth of inferior nature and breeding who has not the energy to toil effectively for her, nor the affection to endure privations for her sake."[4]

While only 5 percent of all federal soldiers were killed or mortally wounded in combat, almost 12 percent of the Confederates suffered a similar fate. The death rate from all causes, including accidents and sickness, was much higher. Six hundred thirty thousand Americans died in the conflict. As many as 25 percent of all Southern soldiers may have died. The North actually suffered more war deaths, almost three men for every two lost by the South. The Battle at Gettysburg had the highest number of casualties in the war, but it was one of the largest battles in terms of the number of men engaged. In terms of the number of wounded and killed as a portion of the forces engaged, the bloodiest battle of the war was Shiloh; the bloodiest single day took place at Antietam; and the greatest losses suffered in the shortest time were at Cold Harbor, where up to 7,000 men fell in just twenty minutes. The single worst one-month period for casualties was May 1864. Almost 100,000 Americans lost their lives or were wounded in battle in this period, and Grant was called a butcher for continuing his campaign. The willingness of Civil War soldiers to face death in a conflict that offered no chance of personal gain remains one of the most remarkable characteristics of the war.

Billy Yank was generally better educated than Johnny Reb, owing, in part, to the greater number of prestigious colleges and universities located in the North and the greater emphasis placed on basic public education at the lower academic levels. While the South had a number of impressive universities, their number was small in proportion to the total in the country; and Southerners were wary of public education. The rate of illiteracy among Civil War soldiers should not be overemphasized, however. Most of the troops could write their names and read from the Bible. However, the spelling and grammar found in letters, diaries, and journals frequently fell well below schoolroom standards. A typical white regiment on either side of the contest probably had few illiterates, and many units had none at all. The highest rate of illiteracy was found among black units. This is to be expected, as many of these soldiers had been denied an education. Nonetheless, there were many well-educated black freemen in the ranks. Even the totally unlettered soldier could easily impose himself on a literate comrade to read a newspaper out loud or to write a letter home for him.

The vast majority of the men who served were neither professional soldiers nor draftees. The largest percentage were farmers before the war. The Southern soldier was more likely to be an agricultural worker of some type than the immigrant recruit from the more highly industrialized North. The available data make no distinction between the plantation owner, the small farm owner or his children, and the paid agricultural worker. The data also ignore all those who were too young to have an occupation when they enlisted, such as teenagers and students. Many of these were listed as unskilled workers.

Skilled laborers made up the second largest group of men to serve in either army. These skilled laborers included carpenters and furniture makers, masons, machinists, wheelwrights and cartwrights, barrel makers and coopers, shoemakers and leather workers, smiths of many kinds, and other skilled tradesmen. The particular trade by which an artisan made his living rarely prepared him for military service. Exceptions to this may have been made for artisans like butchers, blacksmiths, and farriers, who were organized within the service to practice their trades for the army.

Professional and white-collar occupations made up the largest portion of those who served as officers. Professional men included lawyers, physicians, clergymen, engineers, professors, and army and navy officers. The "white-collar" category is somewhat obscured, as it is distinguished from the professional class more by degree than by any other characteristic, and many men often crossed the line between the two. These included bankers, merchants, manufacturers, journalists, clerks, bookkeepers, and schoolteachers.

Notwithstanding their civilian occupations, each man came with a set of values that mirrored the home and community he left behind. The majority of the recruits in the first year of the war were volunteers, and they pledged themselves to serve for three months, expecting that the

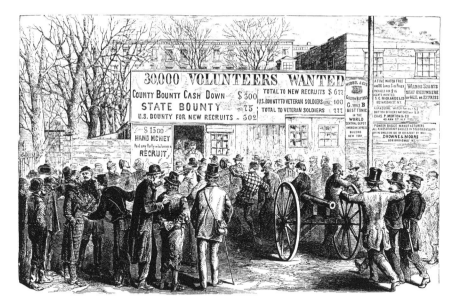

An 1864 *Leslie's* illustration of the New York City Hall Park Recruiting Office.
Although bounties were offered to new recruits, it should be remembered that
all those who served in the first two years of the war were volunteers.

first major battle would decide the issue of secession. Nonetheless, their
commitment to serve, their personal and economic sacrifice, and the distress experienced by their families and loved ones should not be minimized because of this limited initial commitment. The motivation of most
volunteers seems to have been rooted in the compelling and deeply personal forces of duty and honor. In 1861 both of these were closely linked
with concepts of masculinity, morality, conscience, and romance.[5]

It is strange that federal volunteers most often associated their service
with duty, while honor seems to have motivated Confederate volunteers.
Although the two are not mutually exclusive, there is some truth in viewing the South as a society with a profound sense of honor, whereas the
North was driven by a communal conscience analogous to a compact
made with God. Americans of the early nineteenth century were strongly
influenced by such sentiments. The consciousness of duty resonated particularly well with the parallel development of social reform in the
North. To shirk duty was to violate the collective conscience and to offend morality by omission. Duty was viewed as a personal responsibility
rather than a collective obligation. "We all of us have a duty to perform
in this life," wrote one volunteer. It was not enough to support the war
from a distance when duty required that a man place his life on the line.
Many Confederates also cited obligations to duty, but they were much
more likely to speak of honor.[6]

Honor was primarily a masculine concept that dealt with one's public image and reputation. There is ample evidence of a link among the romantic themes of adventure, glory, and honor that appeared in the popular literature of the period and the letters and diaries of the Southern volunteers. Nonetheless, Southerners also viewed honor in a contemporary light, and the continued popularity of dueling attests to the vitality of the sentiment in the Southern psyche. Confederate soldiers often wrote of being dishonored in the eyes of their "revolutionary ancestors" should they fail to defend the cause. Nonetheless, the appeals to duty and honor were most often found among the letters and journals of the more literate upper classes.[7]

Among less popular motivations such as adventure, excitement, patriotism, and ideology, Civil War soldiers were also affected by a need to prove their masculinity. Southerners tended to be more boastful in this regard than the Yankees. "They were amiable, gentle, and unselfish in disposition, yet were fearless and daring in spirit, and devoted . . . to those bodily exercises that make the strong and vigorous man," noted one observer.[8] Northerners tended to be more circumspect, worrying whether they would pass the test of manhood posed by battle. The psychological importance of passing this test should not be minimized. Particularly among the young volunteers, the experience of battle, "seeing the elephant" in nineteenth-century terms, was seen as a rite of passage.

A young woman wrote, "It seems very patriotic and grand . . . for one's country to die. . . . A lot of us girls went down to the train and took flowers to the soldiers as they were passing through and they cut buttons from their coats and gave [them] to us as souvenirs." Young men quickly repudiated the romance, adventure, and glory of war once they had "seen the elephant," but a young man's performance on the battlefield quite literally separated the men from the boys.[9]

Perhaps the many references to sentiment were a reaction to the pressures brought upon the men by the communities and social groups to which they belonged. As volunteers generally served in companies and regiments raised from the eligible men in a local neighborhood, it may have been socially impossible for them to do otherwise. A contemporary commentator noted, "The associations of . . . boyhood and early manhood were with these people . . . [their] dearest and most intimate friends and companions. . . . These men found gratification in a military organization composed of those of their own class."[10]

If the recruits' own motivations for volunteering, as set down in their personal letters and diaries, are not accepted at face value, it is difficult to rationalize how so many individuals could have been willing to die for a cause or how such massive volunteer armies could have been raised. Nonetheless, it remains an extraordinary fact that during the first year of the war all those who enlisted and fought on one side or the other chose to do so.

While the vast majority of soldiers, both North and South, were native-born Americans, a large number of foreigners were to be found in both armies. It has been estimated that between 20 percent and 25 percent of the Union army was foreign born. Millions of Europeans had migrated to North America in the decades before the war, and the majority had settled in the North. Most of these had established themselves in the great urban areas. Close to 4 million aliens were living in the North when the war began. They tended to identify with that section of the country, and joined the federal forces. As little as 4 or 5 percent of the Confederate army was composed of foreigners. There were fewer than 1 million foreign-born residents in the Confederacy, and therefore they made up a smaller proportion of the Southern forces. The crews of the minuscule Confederate navy were almost entirely recruited from abroad. As a proportion of the available population, however, foreigners seemed to have supported both the North and South equally.

Almost 8 percent of the federal generals and 2 percent of the Confederate generals were foreign born. The government at Washington gave serious consideration to offering the command of its armies to the Italian patriot Giuseppe Garibaldi, who had lived in Staten Island, New York, briefly in the 1850s, but the freedom fighter demurred. Federal general Philip H. Sheridan, who in later years alternately claimed Albany, Boston, and Somerset, Ohio, as his birthplace, was certainly of Irish extraction, and probably was born in Ireland—a difference unimportant until postwar supporters wished him to run for the presidency. The four Solomon brothers from Prussia had fought on the losing side of a revolt in their homeland in 1848. All fought for the federal cause in 1861. One of them was the wartime governor of Wisconsin, while two others served as colonels and the last as a brigadier.[11]

The largest group of foreigners to serve in federal ranks, about 200,000, were of German origin. The Irish were next, numbering about 150,000, followed by the Canadians and the English, each totaling about 50,000 men. Scandinavians, Frenchmen, Italians, and other nationalities also served in small numbers. Although the largest foreign group to serve the Confederacy seems to have been the Irish, other nationalities were also present in the Rebel ranks, including Englishmen, Canadians, Frenchmen, Italians, and Mexicans.

The motivation for foreign-born soldiers to participate in an internecine conflict in the absence of obvious personal advantages is difficult to pin down. Some, like British officer Sir Percy Wyndham, who had once served with Garibaldi in Italy, were simply soldiers of fortune. Men from the socially unacceptable and impoverished immigrant populations may have served in an attempt to win a place for themselves and their families in postwar American society. In this they were at least partially successful—as with the Irish, who came to dominate early twentieth-century urban politics. Whatever their motivation, the foreign-born soldiers generally gave a good account of themselves. The Irish troops, in particular, provided some of the most momentous and courageous combat of the war. The fighting reputations of the federal Irish Brigade and the Louisiana Tigers, both composed of working-class Irish immigrants, stand up well beside the reputations of any native-born American unit on either side of the contest. Many units, like these, were solidly foreign or ethnically related in their composition; but others, like the 5th Confederate Regiment, a "foreign legion" serving under General Hood in Tennessee, were composed of men from many nationalities.

Blacks, Jews, and Native Americans were also represented in the service. Throughout the war, blacks were generally made to serve in non-combatant roles at the front in order to free white soldiers for the battle line. A federal officer in occupied New Orleans, where some of the first black regiments, with black and white officers, were raised, expressed the following thought: "The colored troops will probably be kept near here and used to garrison unhealthy positions; they will be called on for fatigue duty such as making roads, building bridges and draining marshes; they will seldom be put into battle." Allotted to white regiments, blacks dug ditches, built fortifications, and served as laborers, wagoners, carpenters, farriers, orderlies, stevedores, track layers, and porters.[12]

Ultimately, the Union had almost 180,000 black soldiers under arms. The acceptance of the "Sable Arm" of the federal army was not immediate, however. Although free blacks were enlisted, they were placed in segregated units largely under the command of white officers who felt that such an assignment would "afford small chance for distinction." Based upon prejudicial notions that they could not equal white soldiers in a fight, these units were often given noncombatant duties far from the front. However, it should be noted that the Union army expected menial services from all its troops regardless of race—a policy that raised some objections among the insecure Irish, who were asked to labor beside the blacks. Ultimately, under severe pressure from Northern abolitionists, black troops were placed in combat roles, where their performance proved laudable, and at times heroic. The best known black unit was the 54th Massachusetts Colored Infantry, but other black units were raised throughout the occupied South as well as in almost every Northern state. Although the use of black combat troops was not necessary "to win the war," blacks came to represent 9 percent of all Union forces—a higher proportion of free blacks in service than were represented by their percentage in Northern society.

Initially, white federal troops were opposed to this policy. Black men wearing the same uniforms as whites had disturbing implications of equality for men whose own status in a recently restructured Northern society was suspect. Many white soldiers, willing to die in order to free a black man from slavery, were unwilling to fight beside him. Federal soldiers from the border states strongly expressed a reluctance to serve in the same army with men who had been considered menials, servants, and chattels. However, basic logic, which dictated that blacks could stop Confederate bullets just as easily as whites, overcame such bias. This thread of reasoning quickly made many a Northern segregationist into a closet abolitionist.[13]

The immediate reaction of the Southern government to the arming of blacks by federal forces was to declare that any black found in arms against the South, and any white federal officer found leading such men, would be executed upon capture. Few individual Confederate soldiers acknowledged killing blacks in their letters and diaries. Nor did they express much racist sentiment. The cases of massive race-based retaliation were reserved for the battles at Fort Pillow, Tennessee; Poison Springs, Arkansas; Plymouth, North Carolina; and the "Crater" at Petersburg, Virginia. In each of these instances it is quite certain that blacks were purposely killed after they had surrendered to Confederate troops.

Southern forces used blacks almost exclusively as laborers and servants. A Southern woman noted, "We have never made the cowardly Negro fight, and it is strange, passing strange, that the all-powerful Yankee nation with the whole world to back them ... should at last take the poor Negro to help them out against this little Confederacy." Nonetheless, a vocal minority in the South had called for the arming of blacks from the beginning of the war, and even General Lee called for their enlistment. At the end of March 1865, the Confederate Congress, sorely pressed for manpower, approved the enrollment of armed blacks in the Southern forces, offering freedom as a reward. This promise lured many blacks, even in the face of the Emancipation Proclamation, and a number actually came to serve under arms in the Confederate army. The question of what effect black Confederate soldiers would have had on the white Southerners fighting beside them was made moot by the collapse of the war effort almost immediately thereafter.[14]

With the exception of their indefensible attitude toward blacks, and prejudicial statements by individuals, the Southern government was remarkably open to adherents to their cause from many ethnic and religious groups. It is a paradox of the war that the South was more accepting of ethnic and religious differences than the North. This paradoxical openness dates from the beginning of the conflict and may have been forced upon the South by its own geographic and demographic character. Mexican-Americans and those of mixed ethnic parentage, particularly those of French and Spanish background from the Gulf Coast, were common in the service of the South. Religious diversity found greater acceptance in the South than in many Northern cities. Two members of the Richmond cabinet and a number of soldiers and officers of the Confederate army were Jewish. Moreover, the Confederate forces boasted several brigades of Native Americans composed of Cherokees, Choctaws, and Seminoles, and several generals were of mixed or nonwhite heritage: General Pierre G. T. Beauregard (Creole-French), General William B. Taliaferro (Italian-English), General Patrick Cleburne (Irish-English), General Stand Wati (Native American). If the Confederate forces exhibited any bias, it was that of favoring Virginians for high-ranking positions. In 1863 ten of the fifteen highest-ranking Confederate officers were from Virginia—a situation that was found intolerable by many outspoken officers from the other states.[15]

The North, by contrast, was replete with anti-Catholic and anti-Semitic feeling; and few whites in the North, even those who espoused the abolition of slavery, believed that they shared any equality with the black race. Northerners were generally intolerant of immigrants, especially the Irish. Moreover, the federal government had a history of poor relationships with Indian groups, and Washington raised only a single Native American brigade, most of whom were Creeks. Other tribal groups generally remained aloof from the war. The Santee Sioux of Minnesota took advantage of the weakened federal presence on the plains to rise up and attack the local white settlers in 1862.

The most conspicuous case of overt anti-Semitism to take place in the war was the promulgation of General Order No. 11 by General U. S. Grant in December 1862. Grant ordered all Jews "as a class" expelled from the Department of Tennessee (a war zone dissected for the purpose of command and supply). This order—misdirected at Jewish merchants dealing with the army commissary, and certainly inappropriate on the part of Grant—caused severe hardship for the local Jewish community and raised a wail of protest in the North. Nonetheless, the highest-ranking Jewish officer in the Army of the Tennessee, Colonel Marcus M. Spiegel, took no note of the order in his letters and continued to express a growing admiration for Grant. Under direction from the Lincoln administration, Grant rescinded the order in less than a fortnight.[16]

Boys in War   The enlistment of minors in the nineteenth century was based on tradition, and boys had served in armies and aboard vessels for centuries. Minors under sixteen were allowed to enlist in the armies and navies of both forces. More than 40,000 minors may have served in the war, and the majority managed to survive. Many boys considerably younger than fourteen served. While figures for the Confederacy are unavailable or incomplete, in the federal army alone there were 300 boys aged thirteen or under and two dozen who were ten or under.

Parental consent was needed in both the federal and Confederate forces for minors to enlist. On this subject Lincoln wrote to the secretary of the navy, "The United States don't need the services of boys who disobey their parents." It is hard to imagine under what circumstances parents would send such young children to war. Yet it was not until March 1864 that the federal Congress prohibited the enlistment of persons under sixteen under any circumstances.[17]

Underage youths managed to scheme their way into the ranks of both armies. Hard-pressed enlistment officers often turned a blind eye to the evident youth of willing recruits in order to fill their recruitment quotas. Many boys entered the Confederate state militias as railroad and bridge guards or served in the mounted guerrilla units. They often performed necessary but routine duties that freed older soldiers to fight. They functioned as water carriers, barbers, orderlies, kitchen help, mounted couriers, or hospital attendants. Youngsters served at sea as cabin boys, as galley helpers, and as powder-monkeys, bringing shot and powder to the gundecks in battle.

However, most boys served as musicians, drummers, or buglers. These helped to organize the daily routine of the camp by signaling reveille, assembly, officers' call, sick call, and taps; and their music provided a form of entertainment for the troops and a festive flare on formal occasions such as regimental reviews. Yet, the primary purpose of music on the battlefield was to communicate orders over the din of warfare. Precisely blown bugle calls and accurately played drumbeats could carry commands more clearly than the human voice at great distances and more quickly than the fleetest runner or mounted courier. Drummers were generally assigned to infantry regiments behind which they marched into battle. Buglers were allocated to the cavalry or horse artillery, as the bugle is more convenient to carry and play while mounted and riding across the field than the drum.

However, very young or small boys faced some unique obstacles in these positions. Some cavalry buglers were too short to mount a horse and had to be hoisted into the saddle, and young drummers often had great difficulty in maintaining the regulation twenty-eight-inch pace while marching beside the troops carrying a regulation size drum. Moreover, small uniforms needed to be secured and replaced periodically. This was usually done at the expense of the officers, who sometimes provided elaborate and impractical outfits. Properly enlisted boys were paid and drew supplies like the soldier, but frequently needed items such as child-sized shoes, socks, and shirts were often difficult to resupply.

John Lincoln Clem (1852–1937) was nine years old in June 1861 when he stowed away in a regimental baggage car and attached himself to the 22nd Michigan, whose officers appointed him the drummer for Company C. At the Battle of Shiloh a shell had shattered his drum, earning him the sobriquet "Johnny Shiloh." At the age of thirteen, he was discharged, only to return to the army as an officer in 1871. He retired as a major general at age sixty-five, and in 1916 was the last man then active in the service who had served in the Civil War.[18]

Partisan Warfare   In the spring of 1861 enthusiasm for secession spurred Southerners to join the Confederate army. The expectation of an eyeball-to-eyeball standoff across the Potomac or an early Southern victory convinced the South that few men would actually be needed. Enlistments of from six months to one year were common in these early days. Volunteers swelled the recruiting offices, and the Confederate War Department had to turn away more than 200,000 men because they could not adequately provide supplies for them.

The most devoted to the cause enlisted at once, and early volunteers usually joined a local company raised by some prominent citizen in the neighborhood. Following the traditions of the militia, or citizen soldiers, of the Revolutionary Era, most of the men furnished their own weapons; in a few cases, weapons were furnished by the person forming the company. The Southern press glorified these small local commands, and Northern newspapers defamed them, often associating their operations with depredations and irregularities. The scores of small companies, raised in the Revolutionary tradition and operating independently, drained the manpower pool of the main army.

Conscription   Ultimately, the South was forced to resort to conscription to preserve its forces in the field. The Confederate Conscription Act was the first general draft of soldiers in America. Neither the Confederate Congress nor Jefferson Davis wanted it, but conscription was seen as an absolute necessity. Its purpose was twofold. The twelve-month enlistments entered into in the spring of 1861 were about to run out. It was feared that these men, now veterans of war and free from many of the romantic notions they had brought to their first muster, would fail to reenlist. The Conscription Act ensured that the Confederacy would retain the men it had in the army, and, since the war had already lasted longer than anyone had predicted, it provided for the additional men that would be needed.

The Confederate Congress passed the Conscription Act of 1862 by more than a two to one vote. The act made all white males from the ages of eighteen to thirty-five eligible for three years of service. Men who had already served one year were made responsible for two more. The U.S. Congress followed with its own Conscription Act in August of the same year, but Lincoln refused to sign it into law until March 1863. The draft, almost identical in its characteristics both North and South, was universally unpopular, but it was accepted with a certain equanimity, rather than reservation, in the South. In the North, the first drawing of names in July 1863 set off a violent four-day riot, with a mob of over 50,000 working men swarming through New York. Federal troops, just back from the grim scene at Gettysburg, were called upon to quell the riots, which left more than 1,000 rioters dead. Small disturbances also broke out in Boston, Troy, New York, and other towns in the East and in Ohio.

Failure to comply with the draft could end in arrest and imprisonment. Conscripts were generally brought to training camps, given cursory medical exams, vaccinated, and given some basic military instruction. Their time in camp and the extent of their training were dependent in large part on the immediate needs of the army. Now considered soldiers, they were shipped off to join regiments from their own states in the field. It has been estimated that over 300,000 men, from 25 to 30 percent of the army, were conscripts during the course of the war.

There were a number of ways by which a man could avoid the draft. If he was found to have a physical disability he would be exempt. Disqualifying disabilities included genuine health problems like blindness, missing limbs, lung disease, venereal disease, or an unsound heart. Other genuine problems were less evident. Urine samples were taken; a man's balance and coordination were tested; and even if he could see, his eyesight needed to be normal or at least correctable with the use of glasses. Those who were epileptic or insane were exempt. Chronic conditions such as coughing, shortness of breath, and back pain were more difficult to prove and harder for the authorities to evaluate. Two very simple physical characteristics also freed a man from conscription. First, he could not be less than 5 feet 6 inches tall, which suggests that people were not really shorter in the nineteenth century than they are today. Second, as a purely practical matter, he needed at least two opposed teeth because the bullet cartridge needed to be torn open with the teeth in firing the musket.

A man could have an exemption from the draft based on a war-related occupation considered more critical to the cause than his service at the front. Among those exempt from the draft were iron founders, machinists, miners, and railroad workers; ferrymen, pilots, and steamboat workers; government officials, clerks, and telegraphers; ministers, professors, teachers of the handicapped, and private teachers with more than twenty pupils. There were protests over the exemptions; but the only outcome of a public outcry was an extension of the exemption to physicians, leather workers, blacksmiths, millers, munitions workers, shipyard workers, salt makers, charcoal burners, some stockmen, some printers,

Town of Paris, Me.

At a Town Meeting held on the 12th day of November, A. D. 1863,

VOTED, That the town pay Three Hundred Dollars to each person who will volunteer to fill the quota of the town under the last call of the President for three hundred thousand men: to be paid when they are mustered into the service of the United States.

VOTED, That the Selectmen be authorized to pay those who may volunteer either in money or Town Scrip, at their discretion.

ATTEST: _____ *Town Clerk.*

A true copy of Record,

ATTEST: _____ *Town Clerk.*

An enlistment bounty of $300 was to be paid in cash or town scrip by the town of Paris, Maine, in order to help fill the local recruitment quota. From the authors' collection.

and one editor for each paper. Conscientious objectors who belonged to recognized nonviolent sects did not have to serve if they provided a substitute or paid $500 to the government.

One of the more flagrant exemptions was that one slaveowner, or a slave overseer who had more than twenty slaves under his care, would be exempt from each plantation. White overseers were exempt because of a practical consideration—the ever-present fear of slave uprisings. Many felt that this exemption led to "a rich man's war and a poor man's fight." Although this attitude was strongly held in many circles, many slaveowners and their sons voluntarily served in the war, very often as well-placed officers and leaders of local partisan groups. As an example, Wade Hampton, a leading slaveowner—considered to be the richest man in the South before the war—served with great distinction throughout and was wounded several times. Both his brother and his son lost their lives in battle.

Finally, a man could buy his way out of the draft by finding a substitute. As much as $400 in gold was offered in 1863 for a draft substitute. There was a tremendous amount of fraud perpetrated in the hiring of substitutes, and this may have been the greatest weakness of the draft system. Physically unsound men were found to replace sound substitutes before they reached the training camps; underaged boys and overaged men were used in the same manner; and many paid substitutes simply deserted, often repeating the process over and over again under different names.

The Conscription Acts and the exemptions were modified as the war progressed, and more and more men became eligible for the draft. The federal act made all men twenty to forty-five eligible. The manpower-starved Confederates accepted boys of seventeen years of age and men between forty-six and fifty as local defense forces or as railroad guards. These men who were too young or too old to fight on the front lines were able to free thousands of soldiers to do so. The draft had the positive effect of retaining veteran soldiers in the ranks. Without these the Southern armies would soon have collapsed. The conscription system was nonetheless amazingly inefficient and filled with abuses; moreover, it provided a rallying point for antiwar sentiment.

At the beginning of the war prisoners were released upon their parole, or promise, not to fight again until legitimately **Prisoners** exchanged for a prisoner from the other side. Parolees were **of War** generally sent home or placed on restricted duty until the exchange could be effected. Some federal soldiers, wishing to avoid serving in the field for an extended period of time in subfreezing temperatures, contrived their own capture in order to obtain a parole. An investigation was called when the number of parolees suddenly increased as the first winter of the war wore on. It was found in one case that local residents of Northern Virginia kept a supply of blank paroles on hand, all authentically signed by proper Confederate officers, attesting that the bearer had been captured and released. These were traded to federal soldiers for such rare items as coffee and sugar. In this way the civilians had founded a lucrative business with a willing clientele. The practice was ended when the Washington government refused to exchange prisoners with the manpower-hungry South. Thereafter, federal and Confederate prisoners were denied parole and held in prison camps for the duration. The unsavory reputations of Libby Prison and Andersonville, in which thousands died of neglect, quickly dissuaded many federal soldiers from voluntarily being made a prisoner.

For some concerned officials the disbandment of the armies at the end of the war was not an encouraging pros- **Disbanding** pect. The federal army alone had just over 1 million men **the Armies** under arms at the war's end. Besides the sudden influx into the peacetime economy of almost 2 million soldiers, the close of hostilities also meant the end of a large number of war-related industries in the North. Thousands of men would be thrown out of work. Although there were many fewer Southerners under arms at the end of the war—men had been abandoning the Confederate cause for some months—the South, with its economy all but destroyed, faced massive unemployment. Even agricultural workers had to face the destruction of their farm buildings and livestock. Wells and fields had been fouled, and almost every fence rail in the South had been torn down or burned. The cost of replacing the fences on Southern farms alone proved a substantial economic burden estimated to be in the millions.[19]

In the North "all the anticipations of evil proved groundless." Freed of the sectional controversies of the antebellum period, massive economic growth seemed to take hold after the war. The war destroyed the hold that the anti-industrial South had on federal policy and paved the way for industrial development by placing factions sympathetic to business in undisputed control of the country. The federal soldiers who left the army in late 1865 and early 1866 "reentered civilian life with apparent contentment and even with certain advantages." Speaker of the House James G. Blaine noted that veterans "were found to be models of industry and intelligence." The experience of war had "proved an admirable school" and given the soldiers "habits of promptness and punctuality, order and neatness, which added largely to their efficiency in what ever field they were called to labor."[20]

NOTES

1. The origins of the terms "Billy Yank" and "Johnny Reb" in reference to Civil War soldiers are not quite apparent. It is evident, however, that the soldiers referred to themselves and their enemies using these terms.

2. Croushore, 190. De Forest uses the unfortunate term "redskins" at this point.

3. McPherson, preface.

4. Croushore, 46.

5. See John Keegan, *The Mask of Command* (New York: Vintage, 1987), 191; McPherson, *For Cause*, 94. John Keegan may have exaggerated this characteristic of Civil War armies in his study, but there is general truth in the statement.

6. McPherson, *For Cause*, 24.

7. Ibid.

8. Thomas A. Ashby, *The Life of Turner Ashby* (New York: Neal Publishing, 1914), 29–30.

9. Richards, 131.

10. Ashby, 34, 40.

11. Lewis, 36.

12. Croushore, 50–51.

13. McPherson, *For Cause*, 126.

14. Lunt, 37.

15. Gen. Wade Hampton was particularly outspoken against Gen. J.E.B. Stuart's attitude toward officers who were not from Virginia. In fairness, Lee's second in command was a non-Virginian, James Longstreet. See John S. Mosby, *Stuart's Cavalry in the Gettysburg Campaign* (New York: Moffat, Yard & Co., 1908), 90–119, 191–200.

16. Byrne and Soman, 191–193.

17. David Mallinson, "Armed with Only Their Drums," *America's Civil War*, November 1992, 8.

18. Ibid., 70–73.

19. V. C. Jones, 45.

20. James G. Blaine, "The Disbanding of the Northern Army, 1865," in Francis W. Halsey, ed., Great Epochs in American History (New York: Funk & Wagnalls, 1884), 201–204. Blaine was Speaker in 1861–62 and again beginning in 1869.

8

Hardtack and Coffee

"It seemed at first that we would starve."
—Federal Private Rice C. Bull

The federal soldier had the most abundant food allowance of any fighting man in the world at the time, and shortages were commonly short-lived. Most of the food ration was grown in the North and shipped to the theater of operations by using a diverse network of railways and roads, and by taking advantage of an almost unchallenged ability to ship supplies by water. The soldiers commonly referred to food as "grub."[1]

Supplying the Army with Grub

Southern soldiers, serving in the midst of a largely agricultural area, began the war with sufficient foodstuffs. However, living off the land and relying on seasonal harvests led alternately to a superabundance of food or almost none. The Confederacy was hampered in its effort to ship foodstuffs by a lack of adequate railway facilities, by an inability to maintain control of the major water arteries within its own territory, and by the increasingly successful interdiction efforts of federal forces. "Sometimes there was an abundant issue of bread, and no meat; then meat in any quantity, and no flour or meal; sugar in abundance, and no coffee to be had for love or money."[2]

"A soldier in the Army of Northern Virginia was fortunate when he had his flour, meat, sugar, and coffee all at the same time and in proper quantity."[3] Although blessed with widespread fields tended by an army of slaves, most plantations produced cash crops of tobacco or cotton, not food. Foodstuffs were provided predominantly by small farms with few or no slaves. With the increased demand for manpower on the battlefield, white Southern farmers were increasingly becoming fighters, leaving the farm work to less productive old men, boys, and women. The farms of the Shenandoah Valley in Virginia and of middle Tennessee served as breadbaskets for the Rebel army for almost four years. Most farm families in these areas managed to raise a garden crop or fatten a hog specifically for the troops, and they gladly shared their food surplus with them when they had it. Many citizens gave handouts to soldiers from their own tables; and city dwellers reduced the number of their daily meals in an effort to support the cause.

Army Food Standard rations were issued in bulk by the company. The company cooks were generally appointed, and arrangements were made for company cooking with company cooking utensils. In his basic kit each Civil War soldier had a tin cup and plate as well as a spoon, knife, and fork which he kept in his haversack. One federal private recalled his first company meal: "The rice was badly burned and unedible; the hardtack, the first we had ever seen, was of good quality but we had not yet learned to appreciate its value. The pork was very salty, and the coffee had not been made by an expert. . . . It seemed at first that we would starve."[4]

Southern men initially formed messes, each consisting of about ten men, many employing a Negro man as a cook. These cooks quickly disappeared from the line of march, and rarely were any soldiers other than officers so served. A Virginia foot soldier provided an insight into early Rebel eating etiquette once the Negro cook for his mess was gone. "We made a fire under the shade of a tree, made up our bread of meal, sliced our fat meat, and commenced to cook. In about two minutes both meat and bread were burned on one side. . . . We were disgusted; but the next day we had better success, and in a few days we got along all right."[5]

Cookware Initially the government in Richmond ignored the need for the wide-scale provision of camp equipment, and little beyond firearms, bayonets, and canteens was issued. On the other hand, the federal authorities encumbered their troops with several standard items of camp equipment, including kettles, mess pans, and coffeepots. A set of metal crutches with a sturdy crossbar served to hang the pots over the fire. The kettles were made of tinned sheet iron in sizes that allowed them to be nested within each other for ease of transportation. Large iron mess pans were used to serve the food. The company mess kettles were provided to make coffee, soups, and stews, but in typical soldierly fashion, they proved excellent for washing clothes. The mess pans were made to fry pork and bacon, yet they also served as washbasins. Such double duty was less than polite society would have tolerated, but for the soldiers any other course was considered impractical.

Each company was initially issued a mule upon which the company cookware was to be carried on the march. Camp cooking equipment was cumbersome and took up much of the limited space assigned to each company in the regimental baggage train. As the mules required careful attention, they quickly disappeared from the line of march; and the company cooking gear, whether through design or by accident, frequently deteriorated or was purposely abandoned. The concept of company cooking quickly disappeared under all but the most favorable of circumstances.

In this manner both Johnny Reb and Billy Yank found themselves in surprisingly similar situations. Each soldier was obliged to use only the limited array of cookware that he could carry. A coffee boiler of some sort was considered a necessity, and any utensil that could serve as a frying pan became indispensable. Small groups of men would pool their money to purchase a coffee boiler or a real frying pan from the sutler, and each would take turns carrying it on the march. The person so designated often was entitled to the utensil's first use when camp was made. If one of the owners was wounded, killed, or otherwise removed from the companionship of his fellow investors, his share could be sold to an outsider.

A particularly common cookware solution was to unsolder the seam between the two halves of an extra canteen acquired from the battlefield. Each half served as a tolerable lightweight frying pan or plate and could be carried strapped over the canteen. Tin cans with wire handles served as tolerable coffee boilers. As with the soldiers of most wars, Civil War soldiers quickly adopted any serviceable device that proved light to carry and easy to replace.

Hundreds of officers and men were engaged in the day-to-day duty of providing food for the troops. The **The Commissary** overall responsibility fell to the Subsistence Department in Washington, headed by a commissary general who contracted for the various types of rations with private manufacturers or packers. The foodstuffs were then apportioned to the respective army commissaries, and by them, in turn, to the corps, brigade, and regimental commissaries. They were then distributed to the troops. Washington continued, from the beginning of the war until its end, to let contracts to private suppliers for all of its rations in this manner.

The Richmond government tried to institute a Confederate Subsistence Department, but found that the independent spirit of the state governments hampered such unified efforts. Although the problem existed in different degrees from state to state, supplies were greedily guarded for

The massive logistical support available to federal troops is made clear in this illustration of a New York City wharf in 1861.

consumption by only the troops of the state that provided them. Individual states exacerbated the supply problem by competing for the same scarce resources. As Confederate currency became inflated and prices soared, the Subsistence Department found it necessary to purchase food-stuffs with cotton bonds. The secretary of war made no secret of the fact that it was not possible to provision the troops as Richmond wished, yet the soldiers seem to have taken the shortages in stride.

Foodstuffs
The government rations distributed to the troops varied slightly with the season and the availability of local supply. Nonetheless, a complete list of all the possibilities is short. These included hardtack, coffee, sugar, soft bread, flour, rice, cornmeal, dried peas, dried beans, desiccated vegetables or dried fruits, fresh or dried potatoes (called chips), salt pork, bacon or ham, pickled beef (called salt horse), fresh meat, and occasionally onions, molasses, salt, pepper, and vinegar.

With only a rudimentary understanding of balanced nutrition, it is a wonder that any soldier survived the war on such a diet. However, the standard ration provided a daily average of over 3,000 calories, heavy in carbohydrates and fats, but providing few vitamins or complete proteins.

The vitamin deficiencies and the lack of protein could have been devastating. An unrelieved diet of cornmeal and salt pork, while sufficient in calories, would ultimately produce such diseases as scurvy and pellagra. Fresh meats will provide protein but cannot afford sufficient protein to make up the deficit alone. Both beans and cornmeal are high protein sources but are individually incomplete in amino acids; yet, in combination they are complementary and provide all the essentials needed to sustain health. Rice and peas are another complementary pair with similar characteristics. In offering these pairs among a small variety of foodstuffs, the government unwittingly supplied a nearly complete diet to its soldiers, yet the unresolved question of a lack of essential vitamins had serious health consequences that cost many lives.

The lack of variety in the soldiers' diet resulted from the need to keep the rations from spoiling while they were being shipped and stored for use. In the absence of refrigeration, meats, if not freshly slaughtered, had to be salted or pickled; and breads, vegetables, and fruits, if not for immediate consumption, had to be dried. Salting and drying retarded the growth of bacteria, as did pickling, smoking, and sugar curing. With the exception of meals aboard naval vessels, there is an amazing absence from the records of cheese being issued as a regular part of the ration.

Canned Foods. Some canned foods were utilized by the army. The technology of preserving foods in tinned iron cans had been developed by the French in the first decade of the century and was first patented in America by Ezra Daggett in 1825. The heat used in preparing the contents destroyed the bacteria, and the sealed container prevented new contamination. Although the process was decades old, some enlisted men saw their very first canned foods during the war.

The officers' mess and hospitals seemed to have had a significant variety of canned items, but they were seldom available to the troops unless they were purchased from the sutlers. By 1861 the list of common canned items had expanded to include several types of meat, peas, sardines, peaches, and other fruits; but the most common canned item encountered in the field was condensed milk, much of which was purchased by contract from Gail Borden.

Camp Rations. There were two standard rations in the federal army. One was the camp ration, and the other was the campaign or marching ration. The camp ration tended to be more diverse, and for one soldier in the federal army consisted of meat (1 1/4 lbs. of salted or fresh beef, or 3/4 lb. of pork or bacon); and bread (1 lb., 6 oz. of soft bread or flour, or 1 lb. of hardtack, or 1 1/4 lbs. of cornmeal). He also received approximately 1 1/2 ounces of dried vegetables, rice, dried potatoes, peas, or beans. Fresh potatoes were to be had, but fresh vegetables were rare and allotted in only very small quantities. Salt and pepper were allowed in minuscule quantities. About 1/2 ounce of vinegar was provided for each man daily to help prevent scurvy. About the same amount of molasses was allowed when available.

Marching Rations. The marching ration consisted of 1 lb., or 8 crackers, of hard bread; 3/4 lb. of salt pork, or 1 1/4 lbs. of fresh meat; sugar, coffee, and salt. The beans, rice, and so on, were not issued to the soldier when on the march, as he could not carry them. The other parts of the camp ration "were forfeited, and reverted to the government." The revenue from the uncollected rations was supposed to revert to the regiment and be distributed to the rank and file as cash, but few soldiers saw a cent of the money. This was seen by some observers as "an injustice to the rank and file."[6]

The soldier added both quantity and variety to his diet in many ways. Gifts of food from home were always welcome. These included hams, smoked meats and cheeses, pickles, onions, potatoes, chocolate, condensed milk, sugar, salt butter, coffee, tea, cakes, cookies, applesauce, and preserves. Due to delays in delivery, many times the baked goods proved to be stale, the butter rancid, and the preserves, put up in glass jars, too fragile to ship to the front lines without breaking. Intoxicating liquors were frowned upon by the army hierarchy, but were often smuggled through hidden in other packages.

Sutlers. Sutlers were businessmen and storekeepers who set up their enterprises within the army camps, and sometimes traveled with the army on campaign. With and without the sanction of the government, sutlers provided a variety of items to the federal forces in the form of pies, cakes, cookies, fudge, raisins, eggs, fresh fruits, salted or smoked fish, and soda pop. Clinton Parkhurst, 16th Iowa Volunteers, described a camp sutlery in 1862. "There was a sutler shop, with its gaudily adorned cans of fruits and jelly and the breath of rumor hinted that the peach cans ... contained brandy. ... Cheese, butter, crackers, nuts, candy, sardines, oysters, euchre decks, boot blacking, paper collars, and a myriad other luxuries of civilization reposed within our grasp." The sutlers often took advantage of the men by charging premium prices, but in general, the sutlery provided a worthwhile, if expensive, service to the troops. The sutlers' tents and wagons quickly became a favorite haunt of off-duty soldiers with a few dollars in their pockets.[7]

Confederates were almost always on the edge of starvation once the first days of the war were past. A federal soldier noted that his opponents were "very seldom well supplied, [but] they often bravely fought when even weak with hunger."[8] They were known to have depended on cowpeas, or field peas, to round out their sparse rations. General Lee considered these field legumes one of the Confederacy's best friends. The men also grubbed for wild onions, scallions, dandelions, and ground-nuts. Swamp cabbage could be made palatable by having the unpleasant flavor boiled out of it. The closest thing to a sutler's wagon seen by most Confederate troops was a cider cart or fruit wagon pushed by a slave or a roadside display of pies and cakes set up by a civilian.

The sutler's shop was a favorite place for soldiers to spend their pay and find "luxury" items.

Officers' Mess. Officers, of course, fared better than the enlisted men. Negro cooks, some slaves and others freemen, were a common feature of the officers' mess of both armies. Southern gentlemen tended to support their own needs, including that of food, from private resources, although they received a pay based on their rank. Federal officers were given a monthly cash allowance for the purchase of food from the brigade commissary. In addition, each field officer was given an allowance for staff, servants, tents, wagons, horses, and forage in proportion to his rank. General officers required significantly more elaborate quarters than their juniors and were paid accordingly. These gentlemen could afford to have imported items, canned delicacies, cheeses, brandied fruits, wines, and liquor on their tables. The Union officers' mess at Manassas in 1862 contained lobster salad, canned peaches, pickled and smoked oysters, and a stock of Rhine wine. The federal authorities furnished no rations to company officers without payment and would not honor their credit. If the officers were too prodigal, or if the paymaster's cash was withheld by unforeseen circumstances, they "went hungry for lack of money."[9]

Foraging. Both sides resorted to foraging for foodstuffs, and sent out groups of men, usually cavalry, to strip the countryside of provisions—a standard practice of armies since ancient times. Many farms were visited repeatedly and stripped bare by friend and foe alike. The farms in middle Tennessee and the Shenandoah Valley became the prime focus of foragers time and again. The area around Winchester, Virginia, changing hands more than a dozen times, was left sorely pressed and economically destitute by constant foraging. "It was a woeful sight for civilized eyes," wrote a federal soldier.[10]

Although both sides initially tried to moderate the activities of their foragers to keep from alienating the local residents, a good deal of unofficial foraging was practiced by individual soldiers. A federal soldier wrote in his diary, "I succeeded in getting a meal from a lusty colored woman who lived in a small cabin; gave her fifty cents and had a fine meal of fresh pork, sweet potatoes, and pones."[11]

In the final year of the war federal troops systematically and vigorously searched even the poverty-stricken homes of Southern sympathizers to remove any provisions that could be of use to the Rebel army. In a conscious attempt to disable the Army of Northern Virginia the effort was carried out with ruthless efficiency. The incredibly large herds of army horses, requiring unending amounts of fodder, stripped the valleys of hay and grass. Provisions that could not be carried off were destroyed; livestock were slaughtered; freshwater wells were fouled; 2,000 barns were destroyed; and fields were burned. "As a warlike measure it was very effective."[12]

Gathering provisions from the countryside had both advantages and disadvantages. Fresh meat and vegetables were joyfully received by men who had nothing but salted and dried foods to eat. But foraging could slow the advance of an army. The soldiers found that it was difficult duty, and detachments were commonly gone for an entire day, leaving before dawn and returning after midnight. Seeking supplies over a wide area put a strain on the army's horses and wagons and weakened the strength of the army in the interim. Foragers needed to advance cautiously, avoiding enemy patrols, as they would inevitably be outnumbered and overwhelmed by even a small force.[13]

Foragers brought in foodstuffs common to the civilian farm diet. This usually included ham, bacon, cornmeal, roasting ears of corn, and sweet potatoes. Livestock, in the form of cattle, pigs, hogs, sheep, chickens, geese, and turkeys, was sometimes driven into camp to be slaughtered. The meat was often thin and tough, especially if taken from a Southern farm late in the war; but the soldiers usually found it possible to prepare it for consumption without extensive processing. Roasting ears were a particular favorite as they could be thrown into the fire ash with the shucks on, cooked, and retrieved with little ceremony; but recruits

The return of the foraging party. The entire camp rejoiced when foragers returned with fresh meat and vegetables stripped from the farms of the unfortunate local population (*Leslie's*).

quickly found that green ears of corn, consumed without proper preparation, brought on stomach and lower bowel ailments that could have been avoided by a judicious roasting.

The troops often resorted to the unauthorized stealing and killing of livestock. "Bear hunting" seems to have been a popular pastime for foragers in both armies. Pigs, which generally were allowed to roam the scrub and woodlots of most farms, seem to have been a favorite target of the "bear" hunters. One forager, caught with a roasting pig on the spit by the enraged farmer who owned it, excused his acquisition of the meat by explaining that the pig had violated the grain allotted to the horses of his artillery battery. The horses, swore the soldier, had sensed the pig's intrusion, kicked out, and killed the pig instantly. To mollify him, the farmer was invited to partake of the meat, but he came to suspect the soldier's sincerity "after his teeth had come down hard on a pistol bullet, and continued to doubt, though assured that it was the head of a horse-shoe nail."[14]

By sending a hind-quarter to the company officers, and by similarly placating the sergeants, the soldiers "alloyed any murmurs over violated discipline."[15] Nor were the officers beyond doing a little offhand foraging. "We officers have been obliged to . . . come down to the same rations that the privates live on. . . . I have a man out when on the march foraging for fresh meat, chickens, garden sauce, etc. So I think I shall make out to live."[16]

Federal foragers could wipe a Southern farmstead clean in a few minutes without the least pity. "To my smoke-house, my dairy, pantry, kitchen, and cellar, like famished wolves they came," claimed a Southern housewife in 1864, "breaking locks and whatever is in their way. . . . in a twinkling my flour, my meat, my lard, butter, eggs, pickles of various kinds. . . . wine, jars, and jugs are all gone. My eighteen fat turkeys, my hens, chickens, and fowls, my young pigs, are shot down in my yard and hunted as if they were rebels themselves." The woman's four horses and a mule were also taken. After pleading with the NCO in charge of the foragers to spare her something, she was told, "I cannot help you, Madam; it is orders."[17]

Soldiers were death on Southern gardens. "A five acre field of potatoes went in short order," and the fence rails "vanish[ed] as if by magic, for cooks must have firing wood, and everybody must have tent pins. Lucky is the man who has been able to steal a hatchet; he is much courted and truckled to by his comrades."[18] A federal officer noted, "It is woeful to see how this lately prosperous region is being laid waste. Negroes and runaway soldiers roam everywhere, foraging for provisions, breaking into and plundering the deserted houses, and destroying furniture, books and pictures in mere wantonness."[19]

Southern foragers understood the "terrible necessity" of depriving friendly families of most of their stock of food in order to feed the army, and some voluntarily cut cord wood, helped with the harvest, repaired farm machinery, and toiled at any other farm work in repayment for the willing donation of food. A favorite ploy of Southern foragers was to linger about the house of an unsuspecting farm family until they were at supper, "and then modestly approach and knock at the door." This procedure almost always resulted in an invitation to dinner as "honored guests."[20]

Fresh Meat. In the summer of 1861 the Washington government decided to organize a separate and independent department within the Army of the Potomac for supplying fresh beef to the troops. The man responsible for supplying live cattle for slaughter to the army for the rest of the war was Captain John H. Woodward.

Keeping the army in fresh beef was no easy task. Woodward determined to furnish the whole army with a fresh ration of beef two days in each week, requiring that eighty to ninety animals would be killed daily. He erected a small building called the Headquarters of the Fresh Beef Department at the present site of the Washington Monument, which was incomplete at the time. "Immediately in the rear of the Headquarters there was a supply of beef cattle sufficient to subsist [an] army for a week, capable of transporting itself as fast as the army could march."[21]

As the Army of the Potomac began the failed Peninsular campaign in the spring of 1862, Woodward moved his operation to White House, Virginia. Ultimately, General McClellan ordered a withdrawal that was accompanied by an appalling destruction of supplies; but Woodward contrived to save 2,700 head of cattle in the retreat, his herders driving them across the peninsula to a new base.[22]

The cattle herds used to feed the federal armies were generally composed of essentially wild steers just off the western ranges, and a herd of 2,500 to 3,000 beef cattle could cause considerable damage to farms, fences, and growing crops. Nonetheless, Woodward was so successful in moving his cattle that by 1864 his superiors expected him to work miracles. In crossing the James River near Petersburg the beef had to cross a portion of water more than three-fourths of a mile wide. In the past Woodward's herders had forded many small streams and rivers with large herds by having the cattle swim across, but an allowance had to be made in this case for the width and depth of the river. A pontoon bridge across the river was available, but with a width of only twelve feet and no side rails, it was considered impossible for a herd of cattle to be driven across in a body. Woodward resorted to one of the strangest solutions of the war. He put two soldiers on the bridge followed by two cattle; then two more men followed by two more cattle; and so on. The plan worked perfectly. The cattle followed the men without bunching or falling from the planking into the water. Woodward thought it "an inspiring sight, to see more than 3000 head of wild cattle moving in close order over a bridge nearly a mile long and twelve feet wide, without a rail on either side, supported by boats . . . steadily and easily and without confusion."[23]

Of all the war escapades initiated by the Confederate cavalry, General Wade Hampton's "Beef Steak Raid" most captures the imagination. Confederate food supply had become critical by the fall of 1864. Hampton developed a well-timed and well-executed plan to capture a herd of cattle at the federal supply depot beyond General Lee's lines. Striking at 3 A.M., Hampton's men managed to rustle more than 2,400 head of cattle and reenter Lee's lines. No more welcome raiding party ever returned to camp. The Beef Steak Raid was as brilliant an operation as any completed in the war. Hampton had brought in more than 2 million pounds of beef, or enough to feed 50,000 men for forty days.[24]

Preserved Meats. When fresh meat was not available the enlisted men were provided with a basic preserved meat ration of pork—boiled ham, salt pork, or bacon being most common. The South quickly realized that it would experience a meat shortage, and Richmond established an extensive government pork-packing program in close proximity to the rail and river transportation of Tennessee. These plants and their associated salt works were constantly in danger of capture or destruction by federal forces.

Federal forces also relied heavily on preserved pork. Pork's prominence as a foodstuff, when compared to preserved beef, did not lie in any intrinsic nutritional value, although the high fat content provided an excellent source of caloric intake. It was simply easier to preserve than beef and tasted better than pickled beef, which was so poor and unpalatable that the soldiers called it "salt horse." No effort was made to comply with dietary restrictions due to individual medical or religious preferences.[25]

In camp boiled ham was often pulled from a barrel into which it had been packed for some months in a thick covering of grease that came from the boiling. The meat came out in long, "unappetizing strips," and "when brought to the surface the sound of the suction was like the noise made when one pulled his feet out of Virginia mud." The grease was scraped off and saved by many soldiers to be used as an ingredient in other recipes. The meat could be fried, roasted, or eaten sliced between two pieces of soft bread or with hardtack.[26]

Salt pork was easy to make and had been used since colonial times as a mainstay of the diet for soldiers and sailors. Salt pork was a favorite among veteran soldiers, who sometimes declined fresh beef for a good piece of salt pork, but recruits had to learn to ignore its overwhelmingly salty flavor and to appreciate its nutritional qualities. The amount of salt used in its processing was staggering, but salt pork could last, unspoiled, for a long time in a sealed barrel. However, once a barrel was opened, the meat had to be used quickly or it would spoil. One reason for the spoiling of salted meats in transit was the lack of good barrels, which sometimes opened between the staves. Southern armies suffered severely from increasing numbers of poorly made barrels as experienced coopers, white and black, were drafted to fill the ranks on the firing lines or streamed north to freedom. So great was the domestic war demand that there developed a worldwide shortage of quality American barrel staves.

Bacon was a common foodstuff reminiscent of home cooking which proved highly acceptable to the tastes of most soldiers. Bacon was made from the sides or flanks of the hog, kept in a slab, soaked in brine, and smoked. This operation cured the meat and so retarded the growth of bacteria that bacon could be kept for long periods of time. Thick slices could be cut from a single slab for several days with no noticeable deterioration of the remainder, and several rations of bacon could be carried in a haversack, wrapped in an oilcloth, without spoiling for some time.

Fresh Bread. Fresh bread was almost unheard of on campaign in the field. However, several soldiers attest to its presence in established camps. The federal government provided a few portable regimental ovens and built bakeries where they were practical. "Our regiment built a large, double log cabin for a bakery, with brick ovens, and a professional baker from the ranks took charge. We drew flour, and every day had an abundance of as fine fresh bread as was ever laid on a millionaire's table.''[27] One soldier wrote home of how he could not live by bread alone: "Of late we have drawn flour and soft bread. The flour we make biscuits and pancakes of. I think I can beat the natives making wheat pancakes. I get them as light and nice as you please and we think they make pretty good eating. But the hardest of it is we have to pay 60 cents per pound for all the butter we get. This makes it pretty high living for a soldier.''[28]

Hardtack. The staple ration of the federal army was a square cracker, 3 1/8 by 2 7/8 inches, with small holes in its top, known as hardtack. Referred to as both army bread and biscuit, it was a very dry, incredibly hard product without leavening, and bore little resemblance to either. The army was not being purposely cruel to its soldiers by giving them hardtack to eat. Hardtack was not a new product. It was used as ship's bread for centuries. The dryness and hardness were functional characteristics. It was dry when packaged to keep the cracker from spoiling, and hard so it could be carried in the soldier's haversack without crumbling.

Hardtack provided a good-quality ration when combined with other foods, but it took some time for the soldiers to learn to appreciate its value. Nine to ten crackers comprised a daily ration weighing only about one pound. It was therefore easy for soldiers to carry several days' rations with them in their haversacks. Hardtack was made edible by soaking it in water or coffee, or cracking it—a process that sometimes required a rock and a gun butt. Water-softened crackers were sometimes compared to gutta-percha, a sticky natural material that becomes just soft enough when boiled to be molded into shape. Crumbled hardtack was sometimes mixed with pork grease to form a hot meal called "skillygalee.''[29] Soldiers with strong teeth were known to nibble at the edges of the dry cracker in camp or on the march. One soldier found this process like "biting into a wooden shingle" with the flavor of "wallpaper paste," but the taste could be improved by adding sugar or salt saved from other parts of the daily ration.[30]

A soldier wrote home to his girlfriend—with some sarcasm—about the unrelenting presence of hardtack in his diet, "Nett, I have become a model cook since entering the Army, and I think you will agree with me when I tell you how many kinds of dishes I can make out of hardtack, 1st make pancakes out of them, 2nd hoecake, 3rd flour gravy, 4th sauce, 5th coffee, 6th, fry them.''[31] An officer wrote home sarcastically, "We are living very high nowadays, have pork, hardtack and coffee for breakfast and of course for dinner coffee, hardtack, and pork for a change. Then for supper we have a little coffee, pork, and fried hardtack. . . . I am in danger of getting the gout on account of so high living.''[32]

Federal hardtack was made by machine in a factory. Plain white flour was mixed with water and a little salt into a very stiff dough. The dough was rolled thin, about one half inch, and cut into squares by machines, sometimes with the baking company's name pressed into the top, as in "U.S. Marvin's Hardtack" and "Holmes & Coutts, Army Bread, New York."[33] The finished crackers were carefully stacked into wooden boxes in lots weighing fifty pounds.[34] Although most hardtack was made in Baltimore, contractors were located across the North, and hardtack was often months old before it was issued to the troops. When the crackers were poor, they were either too hard, or moldy and wet, or infested with maggots and weevils. It was not unusual for a man to find the surface of his pot of coffee swimming with weevils after breaking up hardtack in it. But the pests were easily skimmed off and left no distinctive flavor behind. If a soldier cared to do so, he could expel the weevils by toasting the bread at the fire. These conditions were mostly due to exposure to the weather, as thousands of boxes marked "Army Bread" piled up at some railway station inadequately sheltered from the weather. Such wanton disregard by federal authorities rankled many Southern sympathizers conscious of their starving forces in the field.[35]

Empty hardtack boxes were common enough in the camps. Although the boxes were sometimes used whole as stools and tables, the wood panels more often became raw material for the building of shelters. They were worked into field fortifications to hold sand and dirt in place, or laid on the ground to provide better footing in the all too common mud. The planks were also used as grave markers. Few of the original boxes survived the war, as they provided a good source of firewood.

Cornbread. The supply-starved Confederates appreciated captured federal hardtack in place of the cornbread that was the staple of their daily diet. At times the entire Southern army seemed to run on nothing but cornbread and captured hardtack. The cornbread was usually coarse, dry, and rather tasteless. Baked loaves of cornbread were sometimes available to the troops, but most often dry, ground meal was issued from which the Confederate soldier needed to make his own bread. Without an oven he needed to resort to his ingenuity. A thick corn disk, called hoecake or ashcake, could be made by mixing cornmeal with water and salt into a thick paste in an oilcloth and baking the product in a frying pan or on a hot, flat stone. Such cakes could withstand moderate abuse in a haversack and, like hardtack, were a sight common at mealtime and during breaks along the line of march.

Cornmeal could be mixed with hot water to form a mush, and was sometimes eaten with honey, molasses, or milk if they were available. Some soldiers improvised a full dinner stew called Confederate cush, or kush, of cornmeal mush, cooked meat, garlic, and bacon grease, ironically similar to a common preparation of plantation slaves. Cornmeal was also added to soups as a thickener.

Coffee. The importance of coffee to the Civil War soldier cannot be underestimated. Their diaries and letters are full of reverent references to the hot brown liquid. Coffee was included in the official federal ration, as was sugar to sweeten it. Condensed milk of two brands, Lewis' and Borden's, and a dry powder called the "Essence of Coffee" were available through the sutlers.[36]

Federal soldiers rarely had trouble getting their regular daily ration of 1 1/2 ounces of coffee beans. Confederate soldiers showed an equally intense liking for coffee, but due to the effectiveness of the blockade, they often had to do without coffee or find a coffee bean substitute. Several substitute materials were commonly used either to make coffee or to stretch a limited supply. Acorn coffee was made from the parched meat of the shelled nut roasted in a little bacon fat. Kernel corn, dried apples, wheat, seeds, and dried yams were tried, but wild chicory root seems to have served best. The quality of this substitute coffee was questionable, and Confederates would take great risks to trade scarce Southern tobacco for good Union coffee by trading with the enemy pickets across the lines.

The Army of the Potomac used eighty tons of coffee and sugar every week. Nonetheless, federal soldiers were very concerned lest they somehow be deprived of even the smallest part of this coffee and sugar allowance, and steps were taken to ensure that favoritism in apportioning the ration was thwarted. The appropriate amount having been issued on a company level, the orderly sergeant would place a gum blanket on the ground and make as many piles of coffee beans and sugar as there were men to receive the ration. Great care was taken to ensure that the piles were uniform. To prevent any charge of unfairness, the sergeant would turn his back, and an assistant would point to a pile randomly. The sergeant would call out the company roll by name, and the named man would retrieve his allowance. The veteran soon learned to place both the sugar and the coffee together in a cloth bag and scoop out the two together without ceremony, but some men preferred to keep them separate and use each in proportion to their taste.

Coffee was furnished to the soldier as green beans from the sack. Roasting was done in a camp kettle, which often meant the beans were burned rather than roasted. To "grind" the beans the soldier seized his musket by the barrel and used the butt as a tamper. The ground coffee more properly should have been called "cracked coffee," as many of the grains were halved, more quartered, and the rest of a very coarse texture. Yet an army surgeon believed that army coffee had "no equal as a preparation for a hard day's march, nor any rival as a restorative after one."[37]

The army recognized this value, and each soldier was issued a tin dipper in which to boil his coffee. This was a large metal cup holding between a pint and a quart of liquid. The ground coffee was placed directly into the water without a filter of any sort. With little enthusiasm, Pvt. John D. Billings recalled making coffee with the tin dipper, which proved "an unfortunate dish for that purpose, forever tipping over and spilling the coffee into the fire." Such utensils soon disappeared, to be replaced by a tin can with an improvised wire handle. Astonished recruits were amazed to see veteran soldiers holding this improvisation on the end of a stick, boiling their coffee at the campfire in happy security.[38] For those who recoiled at resorting to cast-off tin cans, sutlers offered an improved device for boiling coffee with a hinged lid and a stout wire handle by which it might be hung over the fire. The price of such an article could strain the financial resources of a single soldier, but several men might pool their money to purchase one and take turns carrying it.

The Civil War soldier would not be denied his coffee. If an early morning march was intended, and fires were permitted, the march was preceded by a pot of coffee. If a halt was ordered in mid-afternoon, coffee was made. Coffee making equipment was generally carried strapped to the outside of the kit where it was easily accessible. The movement of an army could be heard from far off by the resulting unmuffled rattling of countless coffee boilers and tin cups. So significant was this noise that special orders were frequently issued prior to stealthy movements of the army to place these items inside the haversack. At the end of each day's march, as soon as the army began to bivouac, small groups of men would invariably make the preparation of coffee their first task. A supper of hardtack and coffee followed, and then each man would roll up in his blankets for the night.

In camp, company cooks were issued large coffeepots holding several gallons. John Billings recalled, "It was coffee at meals and between meals; and men going on guard and coming off guard drank it at all hours of the night."[39] The U.S. Christian Commission made the rounds of the camps with "coffee wagons" made from old artillery limbers nicknamed by the troops "the Christian Light Artillery."[40] The coffee wagon was provided with compartments for ingredients and three large coffee boilers that could produce ninety gallons of coffee every hour. Whatever grumbling there may have been about the quality of the other rations, "there was but one opinion of the coffee which was served out, and that was of unqualified approval."[41]

Salt and Life. Salt was as indispensable to an army as gunpowder. Besides its use in preserving foods, heavy doses of salt were needed to maintain the health of horses and in tanning leather for shoes, saddles, belts, and cartridge boxes. Common salt could be mined or retrieved by evaporating seawater. The Federals east of the Appalachian Mountains relied extensively on the saltworks at Onondaga Lake near Syracuse, New York, for this important substance. Here the brine, which welled up naturally from the floor of the lake, had provided an extensive source of salt for decades. More than 9 million barrels of salt, worth in excess of $30 million, were produced in New York in 1862 alone. The captured saltworks of the Kanawha River Valley in Virginia were also important to federal forces. On the eve of the war a new source west of the mountains at the Saginaw River site in Michigan was found. The rapid wartime development of this resource yielded more than 500,000 barrels of salt annually. So successful were the Federals at processing domestic sources that Washington did not need to import foreign salt.[42]

Southern saltworks were a priority target for the invading Federals. Only five months into the war the Southern papers began to fret over a shortage of salt. Besides hundreds of coastal evaporating operations, there were only five principal sources of salt, in Louisiana, Alabama, Virginia, and Kentucky. The major production center in the Kanawha Valley was lost to the South with the defection of western Virginia. The Louisiana saltworks were lost to occupying federal troops about halfway through the war. Saltville, Kentucky, was the largest salt supplier in the upper Confederacy, making 3,000 bushels of salt a day, and it could have supplied the needs of the entire Confederacy alone if enough workers and rail connections had been available. Saltville was continually threatened by no less than two federal armies, yet it was the only Southern provider to remain in operation throughout the conflict.

Although the troops of both armies were at times very hungry, no battle or campaign of the war was lost solely due to a lack of food, and even the Southern forces, who were often at the point of starvation, were provided with at least minimal levels of nutrition to support four years of conflict. Veteran soldiers believed that they had "reached the soldierly perfection" when two or three pieces of hardtack and some coffee could be made to satisfy their hunger for an entire day.[43]

NOTES

1. Croushore, 162.
2. McCarthy, 55.
3. Ibid., 57.
4. K. Jack Bauer, ed., *Soldiering: The Civil War Diary of Rice C. Bull* (Novato: Presidio, 1977), 11–12.
5. James I. Robertson, Jr., ed., *One of Jackson's Foot Cavalry* (Wilmington, NC: Broadfoot Reprints, 1987), 4–5.
6. Billings, 112.
7. Clinton Parkhurst. "Corinth: Tenting on the Old Camp Ground," *Civil War Times Illustrated*, January 1987, 30–35.
8. Ibid., 33.
9. Billings, 112–113; Croushore, 161.

10. Croushore, 197.

11. Bauer, 168. One of the objectives of the Gettysburg campaign was General Lee's wish to forage in the untouched countryside of Maryland and Pennsylvania, thereby relieving the pressure on the Shenandoah Valley, which would be free to harvest its crops. Lee carefully timed his march to coincide with the ripening of the July harvest.

12. Croushore, 197.

13. Stuart's cavalry was out of touch with Lee's army for several days during the Gettysburg campaign on such a mission. Although he brought in more than 100 wagonloads of provisions, the absence of his men may have contributed to the Confederate defeat.

14. McCarthy, 66–67.

15. Parkhurst, 35.

16. William Walton, ed., *A Civil War Courtship: The Letters of Edwin Weller from Antietam to Atlanta* (New York: Doubleday, 1980), 84.

17. Lunt, 35.

18. V. C. Jones, 45; Croushore, 79.

19. Croushore, 73.

20. McCarthy, 60–61.

21. John H. Woodward, "Herding Beef for the Union Army," *Civil War Times Illustrated* December 1970, 28–39.

22. Ibid., 31.

23. Ibid., 36.

24. The Hollywood film *Alvarez Kelly* starring William Holden and Richard Widmark is based on this real-life exploit.

25. Byrne and Soman, 6.

26. Bauer, 91.

27. Parkhurst, 33.

28. Walton, 28.

29. Billings,114–116.

30. Bauer, 11.

31. Walton, 28.

32. Ibid., 90.

33. Francis A. Lord. *Civil War Collector's Encyclopedia*, 5 vols. (Edison: Blue & Gray Press, 1995), 2: 58–59.

34. J. J. Scroggs, "A Tour of a Hardtack Factory: Diary of J. J. Scroggs 5th US Colored Infantry," *Civil War Times Illustrated*, October 1972, 34.

35. Billings, 114–116.

36. Lord, *Encyclopedia*, 2: 58–59.

37. A. C. Swartwelder, "This Invaluable Beverage: The Recollections of Dr. A. C. Swartwelder," *Civil War Times Illustrated*, October, 1975, 10–11.

38. Billings, 114–116.

39. Ibid.

40. Lord, *Encyclopedia*, 58–59.

41. Billings, 116.

42. Emerson David Fite, *Social and Industrial Conditions in the North During the Civil War* (Williamstown: Corner House, 1976), 26.

43. Bauer, 11–12.

9

Tenting Tonight:
The Soldier's Life

"We soon became used to the little tents and were thankful to have them."

—A federal private

Civil War soldiers found shelter from the elements in many ways. Which of these was used depended largely on the season **Shelter** of the year and the accident of location. Permanent and semi-permanent shelters, barracks or huts, made largely of wooden planks or logs, were considered to be winter or permanent quarters. When on campaign the army was constantly on the move, and permanent structures were obviously impractical. Shelter was then provided almost exclusively by canvas tents. As the campaigning season truly began in late spring or early summer and ran on into early winter, the soldiers were under some sort of canvas shelter for most of the year, under a wide variety of weather conditions ranging from dry heat to wet, snowy cold.

The science of encamping an army is called *castramentation*, derived from *castra*, the Latin word for "camp." The armies of ancient Rome were highly regarded for the regularity of their Legionary camps, which served as a model of proper Civil War castramentation. A castramentation officer was usually appointed from among the subalterns to arrange the regimental quarters. A standard plan was followed as well as the vagaries of the campground allowed; yet in an establishment as big as an army, so many regiments needed to be accommodated that even on the best of sites some regiments were allotted poor ground. This led to some unfortunate consequences for the newly raised units and inexperienced officers of the volunteer regiments when the precincts of the camp reached into uneven, wet, or swampy ground.

The regimental site would be broken down by the castramentation officer according to battalions and companies. An effort was made to keep the company organization together, and a single company usually occupied a whole lane called a company street. These streets often ended on a main road through the encampment. One of the more difficult tasks of the castramentation officer was to locate the latrines, which were usually no more than simple slit trenches. These needed to be within a convenient distance of the company but placed far enough away from both his regiment and all others to mask the odors that would unfortunately be present.

The textbook scheme dictated exactly the relative position of each billet, whether that of an officer, an NCO, or an enlisted man, in a double row along the company street. NCOs and officers were expected to maintain a certain level of social distinction and separate themselves from the private soldiers. Regimental areas such as headquarters, the hospital, and the commissary were also carefully dictated so that those new to a particular encampment, who were nonetheless familiar with the system, could comfortably make their way around without the least perplexity. Civilian commissions, Bible societies, missions, and sutlers usually occupied an area separate from the soldiers. Nonetheless, an "astonished" federal officer found one brigade encamped "with no boundary lines between the different regiments, all being tumbled together higgledy-piddledy, officers mixed up anyhow with the men, and the brigade commander in the middle."[1]

Winter quarters for sixteen men were to be made of wooden planks or logs with a one-room layout, sixteen by twenty feet. A single entrance was made at the narrow end along a company street and was opposed at the rear by a fireplace with a chimney of crossed, notched sticks coated with mud. A cord or more of firewood would be stacked outside each hut. The roof was made with riven boards split from short logs or the sides of hardtack boxes used as shingles. Inside, the hut was designed to have wooden bunk beds paralleling the long walls, and was supposed to accommodate sixteen men. The bunks were "simply broad shelves one above the other, wide enough to accommodate two men spoon fashion." Straw-filled canvas sacks, called ticking, served as mattresses. No provision was made for any flooring other than the packed earth.[2]

The soldiers were expected to build their own winter shelters with the tools given to them. No provision was made for furnishings beyond the creativity of the occupants. "We built bunks clear of the ground, to sleep on; made rustic arbors about our streets . . . every rude improvement was encouraged by the company officers." The hut could be furnished with tables and chairs in the form of discarded barrels and hardtack crates; a shelf was usually made for the all-important fresh water bucket of tinned iron. Canvas flies and shelter halves were sometimes stretched over the rafters to improve the roofs. The ingenuity of the occupants usually provided for a small section of wall or a part of a log to be removed to provide light and ventilation if a window could not be "found" for the purpose. The soldiers sometimes crowned the chimney with a nail keg or flour barrel to improve the draw of the fireplace; but, as these caught fire with frustrating regularity, only constant attention kept the entire structure from burning.[3]

A sergeant described the NCO hut that he built in a letter to his friend: "We have been at work for about a week past building log huts to make us comfortable. We have about half of them finished. I have succeeded in getting one built for myself and a very comfortable one too. It is about as large as Moily Walker's front room, with a good fireplace in it. Two nice bunks and a stationary table built up on one side, and stools around it, these with other little conveniences make it quite comfortable."[4]

Officers' huts were constructed by details of soldiers in a similar fashion and were of the same dimensions, with the exception that the layout called for two rooms with separate doors. Company captains and adjutants rated separate rooms, while junior officers were normally expected to double up. A federal officer wrote in 1864, "I am not as nicely furnished as regards furniture as I was at Atlanta, but I still have enough to be quite comfortably situated. My furniture consists of a bedstead, bedding, etc. three chairs, one camp stool, one table and my office desk and table, also a wash bowl and pitcher. My room has a good fireplace in it." Not infrequently officers absented themselves from the army during the winter to sleep in private residences. "Since I wrote you last our regiment and brigade have moved camp about a mile and a half. . . . My office is [now] located in a dwelling house and I again have a parlor of the house for my office room and a room just across the hall for storing my things in."[5]

During most of the year, and in the South even during the winter, the troops found shelter under canvas. Tents came in various standard patterns, but the ingenuity of the individual soldier provided infinite variations. An officer noted the vagaries of living under canvas for long periods. "Rain streams at will through numerous rents and holes in the moldy, rotten canvas. Nearly every night half the men are wet through while asleep unless they wake up, stack their clothing in the darkness, and sit on it with their rubber blankets over their heads."[6]

The Sibley tent was invented by Henry Sibley in 1857 while he was an active duty officer with the U.S. Army. When the war arrived Sibley joined the South, ultimately attaining the rank of Brigadier. Nonetheless, the Sibley, or Bell Tent, went to war on the side of the Federals. The pattern resembled a Native American tepee with a large canvas cone eighteen feet in diameter and twelve high with a single entrance and a smoke hole at the top one foot in diameter. This served the dual purposes of providing ventilation and emitting smoke in cold weather. A canvas cap was provided to close the hole in foul weather. Unlike the tepee with its numerous long poles, the Sibley tent sported a unique design innovation that provided for a single nine-foot center pole resting on an iron tripod. The tripod could be adjusted to tighten or relieve the tension in the canvas. The area under the tripod provided a place for a conical sheetiron stove. With its several short lengths of stovepipe protruding through the opening at the top, the Sibley stove provided a good deal of smoke-free heat.

Sibley tents were comfortable and capacious for a dozen men under moderate weather conditions, but they quickly disappeared from the line of march principally because their large canvas sheathing proved cumbersome to transport. Even in moderate weather, the tents could become foul and unwholesome if closed up for long periods. In some cases only the tripods were retained to be used over the company fireplace. Though the federal government withdrew the tent from active campaigning, it continued to be popular with the state militias camped outside the war zone.

The "A" or wedge tent was quite common during the Civil War. The one-piece canvas tent was stretched over a horizontal bar six to seven feet long supported at each end by an upright pole of about the same length. One end of the wedge was split up the center into flaps, which could be opened and fixed back to provide ventilation or tied closed in foul weather. The rectangular floor was about seven feet square. The shape permitted standing only in the very center, but six men could comfortably occupy the floor space with their equipment by "spooning" together to fit. The tent was widely used during the war, but took up too much room on the march, and was most often seen in camps of instruction and used by troops permanently located near important military centers.

Wall tents were often used by officers for their quarters or as headquarters tents. An extra piece of canvas fly, of the same size as the roof of the tent, could be stretched over it to provide extra protection from the sun and rain. The air space between the fly and the actual roof of the tent also served tolerably well as insulation. The fly was sometimes placed in front of the entrance, creating a porch-like area, or set alone as an airy canopy or sunscreen. The wall tent used poles much like those of the wedge tent, but it required more than two dozen tent stakes and a dozen supporting ropes to erect properly. The all-around canvas wall served well, "as one could stand erect and move about in them with

"Tenting Tonight," a favorite camp song of the
period, may have envisioned neat company streets
such as these, with dog tents (above) and wedge tents
(below), set up by modern Civil War enthusiasts in
Pennsylvania. James Volo photo.

tolerable freedom." In long-term camps wall tents were often provided
with platform floors made of wooden planking.[7]

The dog tent, or shelter tent, was used almost exclusively by the Federals, and its squat shape became symbolic of the rank and file federal
soldier on campaign. Open at both ends, the dog tent was composed of
two shelter halves joined by an overlapping seam fastened with a series
of brass buttons and buttonholes provided for the purpose. Each half
was approximately 5 1/2 × 4 1/2 feet fitted with loops for tent stakes
on the long side. In an open field two muskets with bayonets fixed could
be stuck into the ground and a stout guy rope tied between the trigger
guards to support the ridge of the tent. "As you make by leaning two
cards against each other," the buttoned pair of shelter halves was quickly
draped over the rope and fixed to the ground by stakes. This was not
the use the military had visualized for muskets and bayonets, but it was
more practical than carrying tent poles or having thousands of men trying to find new ones each night. In wooded areas the guy rope might

be tied between two trees, and artillerymen commonly draped the shelter halves over the wagon tongue of their limber. The dog tent provided a space about six feet square on the ground and nearly four feet high at the apex and could be erected in a matter of minutes by veteran troops.[8]

If time and material permitted, the soldiers used tree limbs and green boughs to build canopies over their little structures to keep off the sun, or they raised the entire enterprise off the ground several feet and built a platform on which to rest away from the ground. It was not uncommon to see the bottom of dog tents raised several feet on a stockade of logs or planks, which made them very spacious and comfortable for winter quarters. "In stockading a tent the posts were split in halves, and the cleft sides all turned inward so as to make a clean and comely inside." By far the most common way of "logging up a tent" was by notching the logs together at the corners like a cabin. This took much less time and material than splitting out planks.[9]

A favorite alternative was to place a large bed of straw, hay, or leaves a foot or more thick between two large logs. Over this snug nest the tent could be pitched. Covered with a rubber blanket in case of rain, such "straw pens" could provide a comfortable shelter for a season. In cold, dry weather some men burrowed into the ground, digging a trench under the shelter. This "lowering the floor instead of raising the ceiling" concept had several drawbacks, as digging was hard work and rain quickly filled the trenches with water in all but the best locations. Since the army might move at any moment, most men chose not to invest the physical effort needed to make these modifications until they had gone into winter quarters.

Although the dog tent was designed for two men, ice in the washbasin, numb fingers, and frosty breath often brought three men to bunk together. This allowed a third shelter half to be draped over the open end of the tent or over the seam at the top, or placed on the ground with the gum blanket as an additional barrier against dampness. Three blankets were now available. One was spread beneath and the other two on top of the men, who spooned together to conserve body heat. Shelter tents were otherwise free of all creature comforts. As one soldier noted: "These tents were to be used chiefly for sleeping, as one could barely sit erect at the highest place in the center. They were far from comfortable living quarters. Yet they were the only kind of shelter we would have in the field during our term of service . . . and we soon became used to the little tents and were thankful to have them."[10]

The success of the shelter tent lay in the ease with which it could be erected and carried. Recruits rolled it with the blanket on top of the knapsack. Besides the convenience of always having the tent in their possession, soldiers understood that the elimination of baggage allowed more wagons to be used to bring food to the front. Veterans, having dispensed with their knapsacks as useless impedimenta, commonly rolled their blanket, shelter half, and rubber blanket lengthwise and wore them as a tube over their left shoulder in bandolier fashion with the ends tied at the right hip. Some men of macabre disposition abandoned their shelter halves on the morning of battle in the knowledge that they could resupply themselves at day's end from the unclaimed baggage of those killed in the engagement.[11]

In the early days of the war several Confederate units provided themselves with tents, but these quickly disappeared. Shelters of any kind were rarely seen in the field. Rather, two men generally slept together, each having a blanket and an oilcloth. The oilcloth served as an inferior alternative to the gum rubber blankets carried by the Federals. One oilcloth went on the ground. The two bunkmates covered themselves with one or both blankets, with the second oilcloth on top to protect them from the elements. Their haversacks served as pillows. Confederate encampments came to be characterized by numerous small "mounds" of sleeping men rather than neatly arranged tent lines.[12] One Southerner noted in a letter, "Bivouacked for the night in an open field. The night was very cold and the only way we could keep warm was to build up a good fire and sit or wrap ourselves up in our blankets and lay down beside it."[13]

While Confederates were characteristically destitute of equipment, federal recruits came to the war zone over- **Equipment** loaded with useless articles of convenience. However, the equipment retained and valued by veteran soldiers of both armies was remarkably similar. Woolen uniforms—jackets and trousers—were almost universal, as wool retains its insulating qualities even when wet. Armies on the march in warm weather "could be smelled before they were seen." Soldiers were issued unbleached cotton or linen shirts, but wore a variety of civilian colors and patterns. The most characteristic hat of the period was the cloth kepi, which was a cap fashioned after a style made popular in European armies. Slouch hats, with a wide brim all around, were issued to some regiments and were particularly popular with troops in the western theater.[14]

Uniforms came in a variety of colors, and the lack of a standard color scheme quickly proved the cause of serious confusion. In the Battle of Bull Run, Southern troops were fired upon by their own side after being identified as Federals because of their blue jackets, and vice versa. As the war continued the Confederates generally limited their colors to gray and butternut. The Federals commonly resorted to dark blue jackets, but in some cases, as with Zouaves and Berdan's Sharpshooters, vivid red or forest green might predominate. Federal trousers, of heavy kersey wool held up by tape suspenders, were sky blue in color. Confederate trousers were black, blue, gray, or butternut. As the war progressed, the

The men of the Stone family, from the cartes de
viste album of Margie Stone, exhibit a number of
uniform types worn by federal officers. The man at
the lower right appears to be wearing a naval
uniform. From the authors' collection.

South relied increasingly on captured federal clothing supplies or un-
dyed cloth. By 1863 many Southerners were wearing sky blue trousers
or trousers made of linen canvas, cottonade, or tent cloth.

Shoes were issued to the infantry and were made of leather—uppers,
soles, and heels. Leather laces were worked through as few as two sets
of unreinforced eyelets. The most common shoe was the brogan, or
workman's shoe of European design. The brogan covered the entire foot,
coming up to the anklebone. The brogan was often fitted with metal
plates on the heels to protect against wear. Leather or cloth leggings were
often buckled on over brogans to protect the lower leg. Federal shoes
were dyed black, as were Confederate ones at first. Later in the war,

when black dye became unavailable, Southern leather goods were done in russet brown. A severe leather shortage caused some Rebel shoes to be made with wooden soles.

Both shoes and boots were issued to the cavalry, the horse artillery, and mounted officers to protect the leg from the chafing of the stirrup leathers. Very stylish boots, hearkening back to the days of the English cavaliers, were very popular among the gallants of the Confederate and federal cavalry, but by the end of the war many riders found that shoes were more comfortable and serviceable. Federal riders were issued pants with a double layer of fabric on the inseam to be worn with shoes when astride.

The prescribed uniform allowance for a one-year enlistment in 1861 was identical in both armies and included the following items: hat (1); kepi or cap (2); havelock, or cap cover (1); coat (2); trousers (3); shirt (3); blouse (1); drawers (3); shoes, pair (2); stockings, pair (2); stock, or tie (1); greatcoat (1); wool blanket (1); ground sheet, gum rubber blanket or oilcloth (1). Theoretically the year's allotment was divided into two batches, one for issue in the spring and one in the fall. The Confederacy quickly found that it was unable to provide many of these items, and Southern troops often equipped themselves with captured federal equipment.

With the exception of the cavalry, who were provided with a wide assortment of firearms including pistols and rapid-fire repeaters, both armies issued muzzle-loading rifled muskets with percussion cap ignition to the infantry. Most commonly they were American made .58 caliber Springfields or British .577 caliber Enfields. The soldiers found Enfields more accurate than Springfields. "At long range we are rather afraid of them," admitted a federal officer in 1864. Troops would "trade" their weapon for an Enfield on the battlefield if the opportunity presented itself, and whole companies were sometimes rearmed in such a manner after a major engagement.[15]

The similarity in musket calibers proved a great advantage in distributing supplies and was a godsend to the Confederacy, which could use captured federal ammunition. The ammunition for Springfields and Enfields was interchangeable for all practical purposes, but cavalry ammunition was generally made in a smaller caliber, .52 caliber being a popular size, to relieve some of the recoil experienced with lighter weapons. The most common pistol calibers were .36, .44, and .45, but almost any size bullet might be fired in anger from the hundreds of private weapons carried to the battlefield by recruits. Thousands of pistols, sometimes advertised as "lifesavers," were returned to families in the North by Federals who found them useless encumbrances once they had become veterans.

With the minié ball, a conical bullet with a hollowed base, the rifled musket was capable of hitting a man-sized target at 800 yards and had plain sights that were adjustable to that range. Effectively, a target the size of a man could barely be seen at 800 yards. However, used in a volley—hundreds of muskets firing simultaneously—the musket could be deadly over open ground. The need to ram down the charge before firing slowed the sustained rate of fire of most troops to about three aimed shots per minute.

Sharpshooting, the use of carefully aimed shots by individuals designated to pick off officers, artillerymen, or other conspicuous persons, was a peculiar characteristic of the Civil War battlefield that hearkened back to the activities of the fringe-shirted riflemen of the Revolution. Generally, no special weapon was used for this purpose, though many sharpshooters were equipped with telescopic sights.

Breechloaders like the Sharps or Smith carbines could fire nine rounds a minute, and the fully self-contained brass cartridge of the Spencer repeating rifle allowed for twenty. There was a genuine concern among military experts, lasting through World War I and diminishing only after World War II, that the soldiers would quickly expend all of their available ammunition with repeating weapons. Nonetheless, breechloading designs and revolvers were widely issued to the cavalry and other specialty troops.[16]

The majority of muskets were fitted with a socket bayonet about eighteen inches long. Some regiments were issued short swords, instead of bayonets, that could be fitted to the barrel of the musket. Although great reliance was placed by military tacticians on the ability of "cold steel" to drive the enemy from the field, in practice very few combatants came to such close quarters before the psychological effect of the bayonet caused one side or the other to flee. Captain J. W. De Forest noted that "bayonet fighting occurs mainly in newspaper and other works of fiction." Bayonets, however, proved to be excellent digging tools, skewers for roasting meat and potatoes, and good candle holders.[17]

The deadly accuracy of the rifled musket at a distance, combined with the use of entrenchments and fortified positions, caused bayonet wounds to account for a very small percentage of injuries. As the war progressed and troops settled into trenches and fortifications for prolonged sieges, head wounds "between the brim of the hat and the top of the head" predominated, and most of these occurred in the first day after entrenching as the enemy sharpshooters probed for defensive weaknesses and the occupants had not yet identified the "dangerous locations." The soldiers learned to cut "loopholes" in the works or erect "head logs" to defend against these wounds. Placed on the top of the parapet with widely separated supports, the head log provided a small space beneath which the men could fire without exposing the top of their heads.[18]

Woolen blankets were issued in warm weather, and lined woolen

This *Leslie's* illustration by A. Berghaus clearly shows the euphoria with which the 6th Massachusetts Regiment was greeted when mounting the "cars" in Jersey City. Note the greatcoats with their elbow-length capes.

greatcoats, weighing several pounds, were provided for winter. The greatcoats were particularly effective in retaining body heat, but having both blanket and greatcoat simultaneously was thought to be too cumbersome. While most men cherished their blankets, some threw them away on a hot march and regretted their actions when the weather changed. Green troops marched poorly, "straggling about the roads . . . and the fields." Their columns, flanked by discarded equipment, were described as "a spectacle of disorder."[19]

All federal troops were issued a thin canvas ground sheet coated with gum rubber, called a "rubber blanket" by most men. Some soldiers carried two, as they could be rolled very tightly. There is some disagreement among historians as to whether rubber blankets were designed to be worn as ponchos in case of rain or if the soldiers altered them to be used in this manner. About 6 1/2 feet long and 3 1/2 feet wide, rubber blankets were provided with eyelets in the sides and ends which allowed them to be used in the same manner as the shelter half. Confederates were issued oilcloths to ward off rain and damp, but they highly prized gum rubber blankets.

Soldiers were expected to carry their field equipment, extra clothing, and personal items in a knapsack. Blankets and dog tents were rolled and fastened to the top of the knapsack. Numerous knapsack designs were patented during the war, but most proved uncomfortable on long marches. On going into battle it was common for the troops to pile their marching gear and knapsacks in a remote spot to which they would return if they were victorious. Should the encounter go against them, the baggage would almost certainly pass into the hands of the enemy.

Private Jay Butler recalled his headlong retreat at the Battle of Stones River: "When we got back as far as my knapsack, I picked it up and attempted to carry it and did so for a quarter of a mile when I found that I was getting behind and that the bullets came nearer and thicker, so I dropped it, took out my rubber blanket and went on my way feeling very down hearted at leaving so many good and useful articles to the enemy."[20]

The string of Confederate victories in the first two years of the war helped supply the Rebel army with captured equipment and conveniences otherwise unavailable to Southern soldiers. Breechloading weapons, shoes, blankets, and gum rubber blankets were particularly valued prizes. Captured brass-cartridge weapons proved less valuable to Confederates than one would suppose, as the South was incapable of producing replacement ammunition.

Uniforms   Confederate soldiers acquired so much federal equipment that it was difficult to discriminate between friend and foe simply by uniform. "A Rebel Captain and some of his men were clothed in our uniform," wrote a frustrated federal officer, "a growing practice, so reprehensible that it should be met with condign [well-deserved] punishment, as the deception engendered is always apt to cost lives and disasters." In winter, large contingents of Southern troops were seen sporting sky blue federal trousers and greatcoats. Federal commanders insisted that Southern troops captured wearing federal equipment be treated as spies. The South countered that such items were legitimate objects of capture under the rules of war, to be used at the pleasure of the captors, leaving a dispute that was never resolved.[21]

A resident of Winchester, Virginia, Cornelia McDonald, described the uniform of a fallen Southern gallant with the rank of major in 1862. "He was dressed in a beautiful new uniform, gray and buff; a splendid red silk scarf was around his waist." As the officer was dead, "his sword was lying by his side . . . not a drop of blood stained his clothing." He was a young man with "fine soft hair" and a "long jet black beard" through which he had received a death wound, shot in the chin.[22] However, young Sarah Morgan, in describing the uniform of two Southern officers serving in Louisiana, may have come closer to a picture of reality: "Yesterday two Colonels . . . dined here. Their personal appearance was by no means calculated to fill one with awe, or even to give one an idea of their rank; for their dress consisted of merely cottonade pants, flannel shirts, and extremely short jackets, which, however, is rapidly becoming the uniform of the Confederate States."[23]

Morgan recorded the following description of the enlisted men in the fall of 1862. "What a sad site[*sic*]. . . . Men that had fought at Shiloh and Baton R., were barefooted. Rags was their only uniform, for very few possessed a complete suit, and those wore all varieties of colors and cuts. Hats could be seen of every style and shape."[24] A Federal writer described the clothing of a fallen foe in 1864: "His feet, wrapped in rags, had coarse shoes upon them, so worn and full of holes that they were only held together by many pieces of thick twine. Ragged trousers, a jacket, and a shirt of . . . 'tow cloth,' a straw hat, which had lost a large portion of both crown and brim."[25]

By way of comparison, federal general Philip Sheridan was said to be neatly and properly uniformed even in the hottest weather in "a double-breasted frock coat; pantaloons outside his boots, strapped down, and chafing against small brass spurs." He frequently eschewed his kepi for a slouch hat.[26] Nonetheless, a federal officer wrote from the field in August 1864, "We are the seediest and most disreputable gang to look at that you can imagine. I have but one shirt and one pair of socks, and my coat and trousers are as ragged as a tramp's, and my shoes are innocent of blacking."[27]

Each soldier was furnished with a canteen, cartridge box, and haversack, which were worn on his body over the shoulder along with the musket. Most veteran troops quickly discarded all other encumbrances and reveled in campaigning with as little equipment as possible. "Everyone is stripped for the march, carrying his own blanket, shelter tent, haversack and canteen, whether he be captain or private." Such discrimination in the choice of equipment quickly distinguished veteran units from new recruits in the federal armies, while a lack of equipment became characteristic of the largely destitute Confederate forces.[28]

Most soldiers kept their most personal items in their haversacks or in their pockets, along with two or three days' rations, a "housewife" or sewing kit, a tin cup, and any extra ammunition. A Confederate haversack found on the field in 1864 contained "a jack-knife, a plug twist of tobacco, a tin cup, and about two quarts of coarsely cracked corn, with perhaps an ounce of salt tied in a rag."[29]

The single complaint most often expressed by Civil War soldiers was that of being bored. Camp life was "one everlasting monotone, yesterday, today, and to- **Camp Life and Recreation** morrow." Pickets, or sentries, went on duty at the front for two days in every six. A federal officer noted that guard duty was the very last duty that soldiers learned to perform "accurately and thoroughly," as they were required to shoot any man, including comrades, found running the guard. Burial and fatigue details took up much of a soldier's remaining time not devoted to drill. If there was anything that the troops needed to excel in, it was tactical evolution. An officer noted

The advertising section of many Northern newspapers offered an amazing variety of goods for the soldier volunteer.

with remarkable pride, "We had been drilled in battalion and drilled in brigade till we went like a machine." Yet the soldiers repudiated such regimental pride and complained, "The first thing in the morning is drill, then drill again. Between drills . . . we sometimes stop . . . and have a roll call." If things went wrong during drill, especially if an officer blundered, the general quickly moved to "the scene of confusion with a face of anguish." By the time the camp was established, firewood gathered, cooking finished, and weapons cleaned, the soldier had little free daylight time for entertainment.[30]

A federal officer observed, "I had no amusement beyond occasional old newspapers and rare walks to the position of some neighboring battery or regiment."[31] Nonetheless, individuals and groups did find some time for entertaining activities. Letter and journal writing, reading, whittling, drawing, and painting were common entertainments. Games such as checkers, chess, dice, and dominoes were popular with small groups, as were card games such as poker, cribbage, euchre, and "old sledge." Game boards were often drawn on the inside of the ever-present gum blanket, and stones, bones, and corncobs served as game pieces. Gambling was strictly forbidden by military law, but the prohibition was almost impossible to enforce. Soldiers were reluctant to have dice and cards found among any personal effects that might be sent home upon their death, and often disposed of them before going into battle. A popular, but probably specious, story that made the rounds of the camps was that of an inveterate card player who received a ball to his chest which passed through all the cards of a deck he was carrying save one, the ace of spades, which saved his life.[32]

Large group activities included snowball fights, chasing greased pigs or climbing poles, and playing football and baseball. Singing was a very popular activity. Generally speaking, the soldiers were interested in sentimental rather than patriotic tunes. Ballads such as "Just Before the Battle, Mother" and "Somebody's Darling" were very popular. The men sang about their sweethearts in "Aura Lea," "Lorena," and "The Yellow Rose of Texas." A Rebel favorite was "All Quiet Along the Potomac," and "Tenting Tonight on the Old Camp Ground" was a Northern favorite. "Dixie," "John Brown's Body," "The Bonnie Blue Flag," and "The Battle Cry of Freedom" were sung less often by the toil-weary troops than by the patriotic populace.[33]

In sharp contrast with the romantic image of groups of soldiers huddled in comradeship around the campfire, many men separated themselves from the group each night and settled at small solitary fires at the edge of the camp. After a full day of marching between twenty and thirty miles, the men's feet were often blistered nearly all over so that they could hardly take a step further. Edwin Weller, 107th New York Volunteers, found that "on taking some salt and water and bathing my feet thoroughly and then applying liquor I managed to get myself in tolerably good marching order for the next day."[34] Other men simply fell to the ground to rest, too tired to invest the further effort of pitching a tent, and happy to go to their blankets to sleep supperless and unsheltered. "The march done, the fevered feet bare to the evening breeze, the aching limbs outstretched, the head laid on the blanket roll which had been such a burden through the day, the pipe in the mouth, nature revived a little and found that life retained some of its sweetness." One Federal noted of day-to-day soldiering, "It is a healthy, monotonous, stupid life, and makes one long to go somewhere, even at the risk of being shot."[35]

NOTES

1. Croushore, 165.
2. McCarthy, 84.

3. Parkhurst, 30–35.

4. Walton, 17.

5. Ibid., 141–142.

6. Croushore, 44.

7. Billings, 50.

8. Croushore, 164.

9. Billings, 49.

10. Bauer, 10.

11. Gregory A. Coco, *The Civil War Infantryman: In Camp, on the March, and in Battle* (Gettysburg: Thomas, 1996), 54.

12. McCarthy, 25.

13. Walton, 18.

14. Lewis, 6.

15. Croushore, 196.

16. Dismounted federal cavalry using such weapons proved significant in retarding the Southern advance on the first day of the Battle of Gettysburg.

17. Croushore, 117–118.

18. Ibid., 66.

19. Ibid., 56.

20. Peter Cozzens, *No Better Place to Die: The Battle of Stones River* (Urbana: University of Illinois Press, 1990), 99. Quoting a private letter made public in 1930.

21. V. C. Jones, chap. 13, note 4, 388.

22. Minrose C. Gwin, ed., *Cornelia Peake McDonald: A Woman's Civil War. A Diary with Reminiscences of the War from March 1862* (Madison: University of Wisconsin, 1992), 53.

23. Charles East, ed., *Sarah Morgan: The Civil War Diary of a Southern Woman* (New York: Simon & Schuster, 1991), 218.

24. Ibid., 274.

25. Millard K. Bushrod, *Old Jube: A Biography of General Jubal A. Early* (Shippensburg, PA: Beidel, 1955), 247. Bushrod quotes E. Merton Coulter.

26. Lewis, 33.

27. Croushore, 167.

28. Ibid., 165.

29. Bushrod, 247.

30. Croushore, 54, 79; Bruce Catton, *The Picture History of the Civil War* (New York: American Heritage, 1960), 369, 375.

31. Croushore, 144.

32. V. C. Jones, 102.

33. Catton, 379.

34. Walton, 18, 23–24.

35. Croushore, 7, 96.

10

Tactics and Strategy

"I used to think . . . that I knew what muddy roads was."
—Private Edwin Weller

There was little strategic direction given to federal forces beyond a roughly drawn plan by Lt. Gen. Winfield Scott to ex-   **Strategy**
haust the resources of the Confederacy by blockading its ports
and controlling the flow of goods on the Mississippi River. Known as
the Anaconda Plan, this general outline was supplemented by the direct
guidance provided by Lincoln from the White House. The strategy was
essentially geographic and offensive. The South considered it an invasion, and the plan most certainly had all of the required defining characteristics. Although Scott was quickly replaced as the army commander,
the three-pronged drive into the South he envisioned was essentially the
strategic plan that won the war for the North.

The Confederacy would effectively be cut into thirds. One prong was
to operate along the Mississippi—simultaneously driving north through
New Orleans and south from Kentucky. The objective, unrealistically
optimistic in light of future events, was to control the river with a considerable economy of force. While not conquering extensive areas on
either side of the river, the joint military and inland naval operations
would effectively isolate the considerable agricultural resources of the
western third of the Confederacy from the rest and make importation of

foreign provisions from Europe through Mexico and Texas very difficult for the supply-starved Southerners.

The second prong visualized an attack from Kentucky into middle and eastern Tennessee. This would remove the agricultural breadbasket of Tennessee from Confederate control, cut the railways between west and east, and support the pro-Union sympathizers who inhabited much of Kentucky and eastern Tennessee. The hard core of the South's nominal industrial base was found in a corridor from central Virginia south to Alabama with its few factories, powder mills, and blast furnaces. With a foothold in Tennessee firmly established, a great advance through this region would sweep into Georgia, through Atlanta, and into the Carolinas. Upon completion of this phase, the main Rebel army in Virginia would be isolated and placed between the pincer of federal armies driving from the north and the southwest.

Finally there was to be an advance down the eastern seaboard with Richmond as its objective. The South would be denied its capital as well as munitions plants, iron foundries, and a major railroad hub. It was hoped that with Richmond gone, Virginia, and possibly the entire South, might be driven from the war quickly. This eastern offensive particularly caught the popular sentiment of the North, and "On to Richmond" became a common rallying cry. However, it seemed to some observers that the drive to Richmond might be the least advisable strategy. The terrain of Northern Virginia was well suited to defense, obstructed by rivers, areas of dense undergrowth, mountains to the west, and the great bay of the Chesapeake to the east. Moreover, a major defeat of federal forces might expose Washington to counterattack and capture.

The inability of the Federals to prosecute a more vigorous offensive in Northern Virginia was symptomatic of a defensive attitude among the political and military leaders in the capital, particularly Army Chief of Staff Henry W. Halleck, Secretary of War Edwin Stanton, and Abraham Lincoln. The federal army commanders were required to protect the capital, the lines of supply wagons, and an avenue of retreat, and at the same time counteract any initiatives of the enemy. The forces entombed in the Washington defenses under these policies, over 100,000 men, more than matched the size of all of Lee's forces, and the main federal field army was almost twice this number. Moreover, federal commanders were required to maintain armies of occupation in quickly conquered areas such as western Virginia and New Orleans.[1]

The Confederate strategy was essentially defensive. To maintain their quest for independence, the Southern states needed only to resist the invading forces of the North until their infant government was recognized by the world community. For this reason they wished to be viewed as the victims of aggression. It was obvious to the Confederate leaders, if not the general public, that the Confederate government could function equally well anywhere within the Southern states and need not occupy any territory that they did not already hold. While no point was vital to the existence of the government, any successful attack on the life blood of the Confederacy's economic and physical infrastructure could easily disrupt the new nation.

Unfortunately, Southern strategy continued to emphasize a total defense of its territory throughout the war. Southern leaders were particularly worried about losing control of areas where Unionists might free the slaves and thereby instigate widespread slave insurrections. They also feared the vast economic cost represented by seized cotton, destroyed manors, and burned fields. This defensive outlook caused the Confederates to disperse their forces widely. The country was organized into an array of impracticably large departments and districts based on state lines and geographical imperatives that were not always adapted to the prosecution of the war.[2]

The state of Virginia immediately took on a leading role in the war because it faced the federal capital at Washington   **Geography** directly across the Potomac River. Four pivotal military campaigns were fought on Virginia soil, making the region known as northern Virginia the main theater of the Civil War in the east. These campaigns were the First Manassas (Bull Run) campaign of 1861; the 1862 Peninsular campaign between the York and James Rivers; the Second Manassas, Fredericksburg, and Chancellorsville engagements of 1862; and the series of battles from the Wilderness to Petersburg in 1864–65. The major incursions of Southern forces into Maryland (1862) and Pennsylvania (1863), which ended in the battles of Antietam and Gettysburg, respectively, were initiated from bases in Virginia. Moreover, the Confederate capital at Richmond was guarded primarily by General Lee and the Army of Northern Virginia.

As a primary theater of the war, Virginia's geography posed one of the most important variables to Civil War operations. What remained of the commonwealth after the mountainous northwestern region became the new pro-Union state of West Virginia[3] was divided into eastern and western regions by the Blue Ridge Mountains, which rise at Harper's Ferry and proceed southwesterly, dividing the Shenandoah Valley from the rest of the state. With the exception of the line of hills pretentiously called the Bull Run Mountains, the area was relatively flat. In the southeastern portion of the state was the Great Dismal Swamp, a 700-acre bog that historically provided a refuge for runaway slaves and made major military operations difficult.

To the east of the Blue Ridge were two discernible areas, the tidewater and the piedmont. The tidewater was on the coastal plain that bordered the Chesapeake Bay; and it was from here to the south along the coast that most of the large-scale cotton and tobacco plantations were located

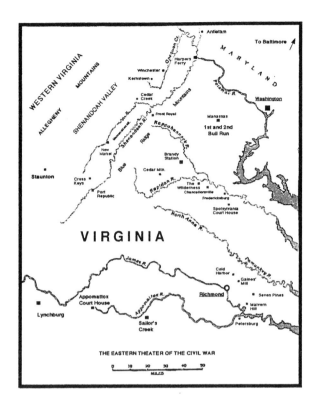

THE EASTERN THEATER OF THE CIVIL WAR

along with their population of free blacks and slaves. The state was cut by numerous rivers which flowed generally from the mountains of the west to the Atlantic coast, each posing a natural obstacle to an invading army from the North. The major rivers that flowed through the piedmont to the tidewater had their origins in the Blue Ridge and included the Potomac, the Rappahannock and the Rapidan, the York, and the James. The piedmont, although fairly open, was dissected by streams, creeks, and runs, and had a large area of dense woods and scrub known as the Wilderness.

The rivers and their tributaries had worn gaps in the mountain ranges and hills that served as connections to the great valley of the Shenandoah River in the west. This river flowed northeast into the upper reaches of the Potomac at Harper's Ferry. The Shenandoah Valley pointed like a dagger at the city of Washington, yet it angled away to the southwest of Richmond to connect with the heart of the Confederate rail system. The valley boasted a good road, a branch of the Manassas Gap Railroad, and two waterways: the North and South Branches of the Shenandoah River. Although impractical for navigation, these branches joined at

Front Royal after coming around the major topographical feature of the valley, Massanutten Mountain. This large ridge split the valley from Front Royal in the lower valley to Cross Keys in the upper valley, leaving a width of barely four miles. A federal line officer noted, "Its eastern flank and a long stretch of its front are covered by the winding gorge of the North Fork of the Shenandoah River. The only feasible road of attack is from the west over successive ranges of wooded hills which are themselves easily defensible." The geography of the valley was used with great effect by General Jackson to bewilder and evade the superior federal forces sent against him in 1862.[4]

Of secondary importance to Virginia as a field of battle was the western theater, which centered on Tennessee. While the people of Tennessee voted overwhelmingly for secession, the eastern half of the state was decidedly pro-Union. This split in sentiment and the effort to bring Kentucky into the Confederate fold brought forth much of the guerrilla warfare that came to characterize the western theater of operations. Tennessee provided more troops to the war effort than any other Southern state—a total of 145,000 men, of whom 30,000 served with the Federals. More than 450 large engagements and thousands of skirmishes were fought in Tennessee and the surrounding border areas of Kentucky, Mississippi, Georgia, and Alabama. While many were minor affairs in the ultimate scheme of things, several pivotal battles were fought there. These included the Battles of Forts Henry and Donelson, Shiloh, Chickamauga, Stones River, Chattanooga, Franklin, and Nashville.[5]

Geographically, Tennessee is divided into three regions: east, middle, and west Tennessee. Stretching across the state from Alabama to Kentucky is the Cumberland plateau of middle Tennessee, which includes the capital at Nashville and the Stones River Valley. This valley, along with its adjacent area, was a rich agricultural region in the 1860s and served as an important source of food supply for the Confederate forces.

The state was cut by both the Tennessee River and the Cumberland, which flowed into the Ohio River in its northwest corner. The Cumberland River allowed access across the heartland of the state. Unlike the waterways of Virginia, which could be used as defensive lines and might serve to hamper federal movements toward the south, the Mississippi and the western Tennessee Rivers were a "double barrel shotgun pointed at the heart of the South" because they had the potential of allowing deep penetrations by Union forces.[6]

The ability of the U.S. Navy ironclads and gunboats to exploit these waterways characterized many of the engagements in the western theater of the war. The South attempted to confound the federal advantage in gunboats by building forts along the riverbanks. The battles at Fort Henry on the Tennessee, Fort Donelson on the Cumberland, Island Number 10, Vicksburg, and Port Hudson on the Mississippi were fought to provide free navigation by Union forces. The battle of Shiloh (Pittsburgh Landing) was fought on the banks of the Tennessee River, and federal gunboats were able to bring fire to bear on the Confederates from the banks of the river at a pivotal point in the battle.

Raiders   Several of the most successful Confederate commanders were to take on the mantle of legend by prosecuting guerrilla warfare. Among these were Turner Ashby of the 7th Virginia Cavalry, who, "leaping over stone fences" and "crying out to his men to charge the enemy," was so impetuous that his recklessness sometimes caused him to be separated from his men. Ashby's early death in June 1862 left his unit and the entire South "heartbroken." The general's remains were "wrapped in a Confederate flag and tended by a guard of honor" to be buried at the University of Virginia.[7]

Another audacious small unit commander was John Singleton Mosby, the Gray Ghost. Mosby's name was feared by federal privates because of his lightning attacks on their outposts and pickets across Northern Virginia. Lee recognized the partisan leader's boldness and tactical genius but berated him for centering his attention on supply wagons instead of the enemy's communications. Mosby's operations so frustrated General George A. Custer that he ordered six of Mosby's men executed after they were captured. One of these was a teenage boy. Mosby proposed hanging an equal number of Custer's men in retaliation. Lee sanctioned the executions of the Federals, who were chosen by lot from a group of prisoners. Mosby survived the war and wrote one of the more controversial histories of the conflict.[8]

Widely regarded as one of the most brilliant generals on either side, Nathan Bedford Forrest recruited and equipped a cavalry battalion at his own expense that destroyed railroads, captured stores, and generally disrupted federal plans in the western theater. Federal soldiers feared this man, who killed in single combat more men than any other general officer of the war. He was said to have had twenty-nine horses shot out from under him. Nonetheless, Forrest's reputation was tainted by his association with the massacre of black soldiers at Fort Pillow and his founding of the Ku Klux Klan.[9]

John Hunt Morgan raised a brigade of pro-Southern Kentucky horsemen and first achieved fame in 1862 by making a 1,000-mile raid through Kentucky and middle Tennessee. In 1863, just as the Confederacy was reeling from its loss at Gettysburg, Morgan crossed the Ohio River into the North and raided through Southern Indiana and Ohio. He was finally captured, but in November of the same year he made a daring escape back into the South.[10]

These raiders illustrated the South's advantage in fighting on the defensive in its own territory. With 2,500 men Morgan and Forrest immobilized an invading army of 40,000. By successfully destroying lines

Southern raiders, or guerrillas, were tremendously successful in acquiring supplies destined for federal troops. The continued success of these raiders proved an embarrassment to federal commanders in areas of the South that had been occupied by Northern troops.

of communication and worrying the flanks of federal columns, "partisan rangers" became heroes in the eyes of the Southern public but came to be frowned upon by the Richmond government. Partisans were accused, with some justification, of acting the role of highwaymen and plunderers, especially in the border states.

Never before in history had civilian resources been so hard pressed by fellow Americans. "The South, with its chivalric traditions and romantic self image, had been avidly solicitous of noncombatants." This view of warfare might be considered quaint by today's standards, yet the men who fought the Civil War felt that the unwritten rules of civilized combat should be honored. At Lee's insistence orders were issued to combine all local partisan groups into the regular organization of the Confederate army.[11]

The abominable condition of Southern roads during the rainy season and in the winter added to the importance of **Railroads** its railways. Although the South controlled only one-third the railway mileage of the North, the Southern railways were strategically located within the theater of operations and were used with great tactical skill by Confederate commanders. Virginia was crossed by several important railways that could be used with great effect to move supplies and manpower throughout the eastern theater. At First Bull Run Con-

A *Leslie's* illustration of a group of five new locomotive engines produced by
the U.S. Military Rail Road in 1864. Sketch by F. B. Schell.

federate reinforcements were brought to the field by rail in time to turn
the tide of battle and rout the Federals.

Much of the northern rail mileage was used for the distribution of
manufactures in the Northeast. The most prominent railways—the Pennsylvania, the Erie, and the New York Central—were outside the war
zone. Those in New England were almost entirely shut off from army
transport. However, the north-south lines—the Illinois Central and the
Cleveland, Columbus, and Cincinnati—prospered on army business.

The Baltimore and Ohio, with a right of way in the war zone, was
strategically important as a line of communications between Washington
and Ohio. In May 1861 General Jackson was able to "steal" 300 railroad
cars and 56 locomotives from the B. & O. in a single operation. Much of
this rolling stock was horse-drawn down the Shenandoah Valley Pike
from Winchester to Strasburg to be used on the Southern railways. At a
later date, when loss of the line to federal forces seemed imminent, Jackson was given the task of destroying the 400-mile railway. He burned
the bridges, derailed the freight cars, and burned more than forty engines. The Federals learned to repair the damage quickly, but raids along
the B. & O. were a constant source of trouble to federal commanders.

The railways of the western theater, which had been built in the 1850s,
far in advance of any immediate need, proved very important. The line
between Louisville, Kentucky, and Nashville, Tennessee, provided a vital

link for the invading Federals. Yet no strategic railways were built, and no thought was given to the development of the principles of military operations and maintenance of railways. "In no direction could cars run long distances without changes and delays." Freight, as well as passengers and their luggage, often had to detrain and cross town from one line to another either by wagon or on foot. The construction of five short connections between competing lines, for a total of 140 miles, would have provided the Federals with an uninterrupted railway from Washington to the entire North.[12]

An obstacle to rail transport in all parts of the country was the different gauges, or track widths, used on different lines. In New York and New England a gauge of 4 feet 8 1/2 inches was used. In Ohio, and to the west and south of Philadelphia, the gauge was 4 feet 10 inches. Some rails were placed as much as 6 feet apart in special cases. Many ingenious expedients were used to overcome this problem. These included third rails, wide wheels that would accommodate both narrow and wide track, and adjustable train axles. The longest single gauge track of the war belonged to the Atlantic and Great Western line, which connected New York with St. Louis more than 1,000 miles away.[13]

There was an attempt by Richmond to adopt a standard gauge of 5 feet throughout the nation,[14] but a national dedication to the ideal of states' rights generally got in the way of any standardization. The length of Southern railway mileage, the tonnage of rolling stock and engines, and the number of interconnecting systems were severely limited throughout the war. Nonetheless, there were more than 1,000 miles of strategically important track in Tennessee alone with connections passing to the southeast. The heart of this rail network lay in Corinth, Mississippi. The line connecting Cairo, Illinois, with Corinth drove directly south and continued on to New Orleans, creating a network that pumped vital supplies from the Gulf north to Tennessee and east to Virginia. The Confederates were therefore theoretically able to use their railways to bring troops from the Deep South into Virginia or the western theater. In 1862 more than 2,500 men and their equipment were brought to Nashville from Louisiana in just two weeks—a remarkable feat given the dilapidated state of the railways and the fact that the troops had to wait for available cars or march between unconnected lines.

A major limitation on the use of Southern railways for military purposes remained a lack of maintenance. In April 1863 Lee wrote to the War Office that "unless the railroads be repaired, so as to admit of speedier transportation of supplies," he could not maintain his position.[15] Damaged cars and worn-out engines became the victims of the South's limited industrial technology. A damaged locomotive boiler might take more than a thousand man-hours to repair if the boiler plate were found to do the job. Tracks and especially wooden ties were simply unable to

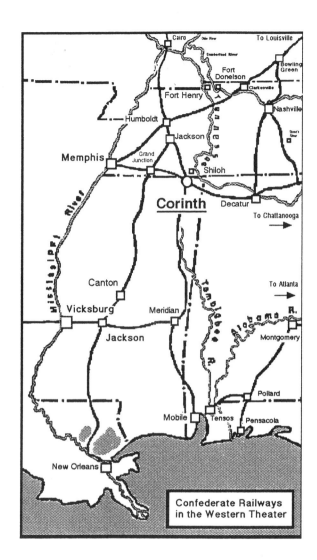

Confederate Railways
in the Western Theater

withstand the wear and tear of wartime demand. "There were no means at hand for their repair. The wooden ties rotted, the machinery was almost exhausted, the rails were worn out, and thus the speed and capacity of the trains were greatly reduced." An engine could be required to lug a supply train weighing up to 120 tons.[16]

Roads   If railroads were the arteries of the nation, then the roads were its veins.[17] A long march on dirt roads was almost inevitable for the soldiers of both armies. The very poor condition of Southern roads and turnpikes was one of the few circumstances for which the federal army did not provide in its initial offensive planning. The Confederates understood the defensive qualities of many of the roads in northern Virginia, which were "very narrow—mere ditches," surrounded by dense forests of second growth pine or virgin oak that would snarl the movement of an invading army with its wagons and artillery.[18] "We were not able to march but three miles . . . as we are never allowed to march any faster than the artillery and baggage train can move." With high humidity and abundant vegetation, the rain-soaked road surfaces of Virginia remained wet and were churned into a sticky morass that was barely passable. "Yesterday we had another very hard rain storm which makes the roads much worse than before," wrote a soldier in March 1863. "I used to think when at the North that I knew what muddy roads was, but they do not compare at all with the roads here."[19]

Northern commanders greatly anticipated the improvement of the roads when the mud froze as it did in the North during November and December, providing a supportive surface on which to march troops, haul supplies, or move artillery. However, increased daytime temperatures prevented the freezing of the roadways until much later in the season than Northerners expected. Federal operations in the early winter of 1863 therefore encountered an unforeseen obstacle. "We have experienced a severe snow storm," wrote a soldier in a letter home, "but the last two days have been so warm that it has all nearly disappeared making the mud much deeper than it was before. It will now be impossible for the Army of the Potomac to make a forward movement short of five or six weeks."[20]

The armies spent considerable time and effort building "corduroy" roads by laying bundles of saplings and small tree trunks across the muddiest parts of the road surface. Although uneven and bumpy, they allowed the wheeled vehicles to pass without sinking into the mud. Corduroy was very hard on the foot soldier and almost impossible for the cavalry, who often opted to ride across the open fields. Plank roads, as the name suggests, were municipal roads built with several layers of wooden planking covered with dirt. The Orange Plank Road and the Orange Turnpike, connecting Fredericksburg and Chancellorsville with the valley of western Virginia, were two of the good roads that proved critical to the strategy of the opposing forces.

The Columbia Pike south out of Nashville was a well-maintained road of macadam—a type of compressed broken stone. The Valley Pike, the main road that ran down the center of the Shenandoah Valley, was also of macadam and proved a veritable highway for the South. Flanked by the North Branch of the Shenandoah River and the western part of the Manassas Gap Railroad, the advantages of such a surface to the movement of military forces were obvious. The Valley Pike played a prominent role in Jackson's Valley campaign of 1862; and in subsequent years it figured prominently in the operations of Confederate general Jubal Early no less than it did in the operations of federal generals Franz Sigel, David Hunter, and Philip Sheridan. The battles at Cross Keys, Port Republic, New Market, Front Royal, Cedar Creek, and Kernstown were overshadowed only by the more than a dozen seesaw occupations of the city of Winchester, which straddled the pike.[21]

Military Organization The organization of the Federal and Confederate armies was based upon the division of the available number of infantry soldiers into manageable tactical units. A clerk in the Confederate War Office wrote in April 1861: "A great many separate companies are accepted [for enlistment] . . . provided they have arms. . . . What a deal of annoyance and labor it will be to organize these into battalions, regiments, brigades, and divisions. And then comes the appointment of staff and field officers."[22]

In the first major battle of the war, First Manassas or Bull Run, 60,000 men were divided into numerous divisions and brigades. Both sides had about 30,000 men available to fight—the largest forces seen on the North American continent up to that time. None of the senior field officers or generals, even those with combat experience, had ever directed one-tenth this number. The Federals were organized under General Irvin McDowell into five divisions, representing ten brigades. The South fielded two armies, under P.G.T. Beauregard and Joseph E. Johnston, divided into six and four brigades, respectively. There were also numerous legions, companies of volunteers, and militias that defy placement in an ordinary structural organization. In a blend of confusion, incompetence, and providence only 60 percent of these men saw action in the first major battle of the war, yet almost 10 percent of these became casualties. This result taught many lessons to both sides about organization. By 1863 army organization had become somewhat standardized, and enlistments for three years, or the duration of the war, were common.

To the individual soldier the eight or ten men who were his messmates were the most important part of the army organization. Several messes formed a battalion, or half a company, under the command of a junior officer and various company NCOs. In the federal army there were twenty battalions, or ten companies, per regiment with an approximate strength of 1,200 men. The Confederates, forsaking the battalion as a formal unit, simply had ten companies per regiment. Two companies were designated to act as skirmishers each day and formed the advance and rear guard for each regiment. On paper Southern regiments were larger than their federal counterparts, with strengths up to 1,550 men— an advantage that disappeared as the war progressed and the South suffered from a lack of manpower.

It was not unusual for a regiment to lose 30 percent of its men while awaiting deployment to the front. A federal officer observed, "There is a constant drain on the troops in the field, much heavier than a civilian would suppose. Something like one fifth of the men who enlist are not tough enough nor brave enough to be soldiers." The men "disappeared" in various ways, including death by hardship and disease, or through desertion. Others were tolled off on special duties as "bakers, hospital nurses, wagoners, [or] quartermaster's drudges," and a fair number were working out the sentences of court-martial. Regiments were usually commanded by colonels, with captains directing individual companies.[23]

Generally, a regiment stayed together for the duration of the war and fought without replacements until its numbers were so exhausted by death, disease, or disability that it was no longer practical for it to continue to exist. It was thought that the relative stability of the same men eating and living together for the duration of their enlistments fostered cooperation, raised morale, and sustained each soldier's courage under fire. While this system produced units composed of battle-hardened veterans, a lengthy conflict sometimes resulted in widespread mourning among the families of a single town as its young men were continually exposed to the carnage of battle. Newly raised regiments with muster rolls filled with recruits lacked the hard-won experience of veteran units and were more likely to break and run when hard pressed. Veterans quickly learned to hold their ground on defense, but they were more likely to "go to ground" or take advantage of available cover during a charge. A federal officer bemoaned the policy. "It is a pity that our new levies cannot be clapped into the old organizations.... They would be something like veterans in a fortnight; whereas it will take six months to bring them to the same point under their own raw officers and sergeants."[24]

Regiments from the same geographical area were often brigaded together to achieve a greater feeling of unity and to maintain the fiction of state control. The brigade, commanded by a brigadier general, was the smallest practical tactical unit. Brigades were assigned to divisions, divisions to corps, and corps to armies. The brigade's several regiments tended to serve together through many campaigns, although their number varied somewhat depending on their individual strength. As few veteran regiments were ever brought up to strength, it is difficult to determine the numbers of soldiers in a brigade by simply counting the regiments on each side.

Many hundreds of men "belong to an army but never fight," observed one officer. These included "the cooks, the officers' servants, the hospital gangs, the quartermaster's people, the 'present sick,' and the habitual skulkers." The last were particularly disliked by their fellows because, while they failed to have the "courage" to desert, they also lacked the courage to take their place on the front lines. After some months of active campaigning a brigade might look like a pitiable force. Even though composed of at least a dozen regiments, some brigades numbered not more than 800 men, "all jaded and dispirited."[25]

Confederates tended to identify their place in the army establishment by referring to the names of their commanders, while federal soldiers utilized the numbers and letters assigned to their units. So common was this difference that when Lt. Gen. James Longstreet, lost after a nighttime arrival on a battlefield, and calling out to some soldiers asking their unit, received their prompt numerical designations. He was quickly convinced that he had blundered into the federal lines and made a discreet retreat in the opposite direction.[26]

A Confederate soldier therefore might have his mail sent to Pvt. Jonathan Reb, Army of Northern Virginia, 43rd North Carolina Regiment, Captain Hatcher's Company, Daniel's Brigade of Rode's Division. A Northern soldier might describe his place in the federal army as Pvt. William Yank, 2nd Battalion, Company A, 124th New York Volunteers, serving in the 1st Brigade of the 2nd Division, III Corps of the Army of the Potomac.

Armies   To prosecute an effective war strategy it was necessary to wage war in more than one theater at a time. Due to the enormity of the boundary between the North and the South and the need to garrison the border states, both the Federals and the Confederates divided their military strength into large groups called armies. Armies were commanded by a full general or lieutenant general.

Federal armies were designated by the names of the rivers along which they pursued their campaigns, as in the Army of the Potomac, Cumberland, James, Ohio, or Tennessee. Briefly, there was an Army of West Virginia. Not all of these existed simultaneously. The Confederates generally named their armies for the territory they were defending, as in the Army of Northern Virginia, Mississippi, or Tennessee. Overall control of federal armies resided in the Army Chief of Staff, General Henry W. Halleck, and in the President. The Confederates had no overall commander other than Jefferson Davis—each area commander reporting directly to him. Lee therefore had authority over only the Army of Northern Virginia; but a restrained Davis was less willing to interfere in strategy and day-to-day operations than the more willing Lincoln.

Confederate armies were almost always smaller than federal armies, but the advantage of numbers could not always be brought to bear. In 1862 the Army of the Potomac under General Ambrose Burnside numbered up to 250,000 men. The principal Confederate force of General Robert E. Lee's Army of Northern Virginia was 70,000 men strong during most of the war, but Lee was often able to convince the Federals that he had two to three times this number.

Federal and Confederate armies were surprisingly similar in their structure. The army headquarters was made up of the staff officers and some troops assigned to protect the establishment and the commander from attack. A troop of cavalry was usually detached to serve as couriers. A signal unit and an engineering unit were almost always present. Headquarters personnel alone could number up to 3,000 individuals.

Staff duties were primarily organizational rather than directly related to combat. The adjutant general kept track of all the operations of the different branches and did most of the paperwork for the commander. The inspector general was responsible for training, discipline, and fighting efficiency. The provost, or military police, and the judge advocate's office, or courts-martial, were operated under the inspector general. The quartermaster general assumed all those duties that related to providing for the troops and controlled service units such as supply-train troops, hospital personnel, and payroll clerks.

An army was really too large a unit for tactical purposes. While European armies had always been subdivided in some manner, Civil War armies generally followed the structural pattern established by Napoleon in 1804 and were subdivided into corps. The corps was a major conceptual breakthrough in military science and came to be composed of "separate, self-contained, and interchangeable parts," having its own balance of infantry, artillery, and mounted components. Napoleon mastered the armies of Europe with this organization, and his methods and strategy had been emphasized at the military schools and academies in which most Civil War general officers had learned their trade.[27]

Corps and Divisions

While both sides in the Civil War established a separate cavalry corps enhanced by horse artillery designed for raiding and scouting, individual cavalry regiments were often attached to corps to provide mounted scouts, flankers, or videttes. An observer of Southern cavalry organization noted: "These are the troops for quick marches, surprises, and captures. And our people, even down to little boys, are expert riders. . . . We should want all our men [to] fight in the saddle who could not or would not march in the infantry. And mounted men are content to use the double-barreled shotgun—one barrel for ball, the other for buck-shot and close quarters."[28]

While the federal armies consisted of several corps, the Confederates initially resisted their adoption, relying instead on a larger and less independent unit called the division. After 1862, however, the Confederacy incorporated their divisions into corps to provide for better articulation of forces and to allow a larger number of senior field officers to be in direct control of the troops in battle. The new corps commanders, particularly Jackson and Longstreet, whose talents may have initiated the change in organization, were made more independent of the army com-

The cavalry arm of the federal army (above) began
the war with a decided disadvantage when
compared to the South's mounted force. The
Confederate cavalry literally rode circles around the
federal army on at least three occasions during the
war. Not until the Battle of Brandy Station, Virginia,
did the federal cavalry show any ability to cope
with Southern horsemen. James and Dorothy Volo
photo.

mander than previously. They were given additional rank to comple-
ment their new status and responsibility. Some of the best soldiers of the
war rose to fame as corps commanders.

Civil War forces exhibited an amazing articulation and speed of maneuver for armies that moved on foot. Military theorists believed that
corps, separated by no more than a day's march, could move more rapidly than an army marching in column together. An army column might
move with its rear more than a day's march from the advanced elements.
A force of equal size, advancing in parallel columns as corps, extended
over a larger front and a much shorter length, as the corps individually
had more roads over which to travel. Such a formation could cover a
wider territory when foraging, had a greater possibility of finding the
enemy, and could concentrate quickly.

In the Gettysburg campaign the Federals fielded seven infantry corps, which concentrated on the sleepy town along the many roads that intersected there. In anticipation of the invasion of Pennsylvania, Lee had reorganized his army into three large corps with a total of nine divisions. The Southern corps were almost twice the size of their federal counterparts so that the South had an initial numerical advantage as the head of the column approached on the first day. The advantages of marching in corps notwithstanding, the rear of Lee's army and much of his cavalry did not arrive until the second day of the battle, a fateful circumstance for Pickett's division, chosen to make the third day's charge because it had remained unengaged. By then the Federals (93,000 men) had a small advantage in numbers over the Confederates (78,000 men).

Civil War commanders relied on linear tactics and the weight of the bayonet charge to fight and win their battles. The ability **Tactics** of long lines of troops to face each other across open rolling fields and woodlots, banging away with a deadly hail of musket fire within sight of one another, was extraordinary. Once engaged, the roar of musketry became almost continuous. Units maneuvered under the weight of this fire in great phalanxes trying to bring flanking fire on the enemy position. Either through the weight of fire or through the terror of the bayonet charge, the ultimate goal was to cause the enemy line to break, become disordered, and flee the field.

Military opponents commonly tried to avoid battle until each saw some advantage to the possible outcome. A general seeking battle commonly tried to trap the enemy against an obstacle such as a river, swamp, or mountain range or to turn his flank with the potential of forcing a battle on the enemy in a less than advantageous position. The "strategic turning maneuver" and the advantage of operating on "interior lines" gave the field commander the ability to entangle a stronger enemy in battle by concentrating his forces at a predetermined point in space or at a specified point in time. If positioned on interior lines, his forces had the inherent advantages of shorter distances to travel than the surrounding enemy. By concentrating a higher proportion of his forces than the enemy could engage at a single point, a general could defeat the enemy in detail and reconcentrate to fight at another point. Both Confederate and federal commanders utilized these principles, and this somewhat offset the advantages inherent in such tactics.

Communications were particularly important to the management of a battle when separate parts of the army were **Ancillary** spread across miles of war zone. The use of flag bearers and **Units** drummers was essential for the maintenance of alignment and the transmission of orders on the company and regimental level; but across greater distances a more effective method of managing the army was needed. During the 1850s the U.S. Army had adopted a "wig wag"

Besides adding color to the display of battle, flag
bearers and drummers served a practical purpose on
the battlefield. It was a great honor to be chosen as
a flag bearer, and only a very brave man was
willing to accept the appointment. James Volo
photo.

flag system for field communications. This flag system remained the
principal means of passing orders and intelligence for both the federal
and Confederate armies throughout the war.

At the outbreak of hostilities both armies lacked a military telegraph
system. While the Confederacy continued to rely almost solely on flags
and civilian telegraph lines, the Federals established a military telegraph
to supplement the older system. The Signal Corps advocated the use of
"flying" telegraphic teams organized around light telegraphic wagons
which would move with the army, erect telegraph lines, and gain tactical
control on the battlefield with the use of dial-type message encoding
equipment. The rival U.S. Military Telegraph Service obtained its equipment and personnel from the existing civilian companies and relied on
the more common Morse type telegraphic equipment. The Washington
office of the U.S. Military Telegraph Service quickly became a sanctuary

for President Lincoln where "he could escape other cares of his office and obtain a little quiet, except for the clatter of the telegraph keys."[29]

The medical services of the armed forces were almost nonexistent. The federal army began the war with fewer than 120 surgeons and assistant surgeons, and some of these were dismissed for suspected disloyalty and served with the Confederate forces. Medical officers and their assistants were commonly assigned to individual regiments, and musicians served as stretcher bearers.[30]

Prior to the Civil War the U.S. Army had not provided ambulances for the wounded and sick. In 1859 experimental carts were tested on the western plains and a less than satisfactory two-wheel version was adopted. Not until 1863 did the federal army organize and outfit a formal ambulance corps for the Army of the Potomac. Under General Order No. 85 only four-wheel, two-horse carts would be used as ambulances. Each ambulance had five men assigned as stretcher bearers and drivers. Three ambulances were permanently allocated to each infantry regiment, two to each cavalry regiment, and one to each artillery battery. Moreover, two army wagons were designated to carry only medical supplies for each corps, and two more were placed at the division level. "Obviously, this organization was sorely needed, but it fell far short of the real need," as three ambulances were "hardly adequate" to support a regiment of 1,000 men.[31]

Once off the battlefield the plight of the wounded was complicated by limited medical knowledge, malnutrition, and disease. While American military hospitals were better than those in Europe, they were nonetheless inadequate. Civilian corpsmen, hired by the army at $20.50 per month to staff army hospitals, often proved unreliable. A nursing service, directed by Dorothea Dix and staffed by women, had been established to care for the wounded and sick in the numerous soldiers' rests and regimental hospitals; but the recruitment of nurses was hobbled by the strict "moral" requirements Dix placed on potential candidates. Women were required to be of high moral character, no less than thirty years of age, plain looking, and unadorned. There was no requirement that they be efficient or capable.

In March 1863 Secretary of War Edwin M. Stanton established a Corps of Invalids from among the "walking wounded" and "convalescent soldiers" of the army to serve as nurses and medical aides. More than 60,000 men ultimately served in the invalid corps "scattered randomly" among the regiments of the army. Although only 42 members of the corps were killed in action, more than 1,600 died of the diseases to which they were exposed in the sick wards. The invalid corps concept received little support from the army hierarchy, and General Grant opposed all plans for retaining it as a part of the postwar army.[32]

Thousands of Catholic nuns served as nurses in the federal military hospitals of Boston, New York, Philadelphia, Baltimore, Washington, and other cities. Sisters of Charity, Sisters of Mercy, and Sisters of Saint Vincent de Paul were all conspicuous in their unique religious habits. The nuns volunteered to serve without pay even though they were often abused by anti-Catholic hospital personnel and patients. Their patience, skill, and persistence won over a good number of bigots. "My mind was filled with prejudice," wrote one soldier. "I did not believe that anything good could come from the Sisters. But now I see my mistake all too clearly."[33]

Catholic sisters were "conspicuously neutral" in their attitude toward the war. Confederate hospitals in Richmond, Charleston, Nashville, and New Orleans were also staffed with at least some Catholic nuns. The sisters consistently failed to leave their work when the vagaries of war changed the nature of the occupying force from South to North, and in Vicksburg they suffered the siege and ensuing bombardment with the beleaguered of the city. The sisters proved to be expert medical and surgical nurses, as they had experienced service in asylums and civilian hospitals during their long novitiates. A Southern woman noted that the work of the sisters made "all the difference in the world" in the Confederate hospitals of Richmond.[34]

A number of civilian organizations helped to fill the need for additional medical care. The Women's American Association for Relief was closely associated with a number of eminent doctors in New York and furnished medical supplies to the army. Beyond this the U.S. Sanitary Commission made provisions for the relief of the sick, provided ambulances, and cared for the wounded and the dead. Commission representatives, operating in the east and in the west, oversaw the diet and personal cleanliness of the soldiers in camp, provided housing for white refugee families, and raised money to expand their work. A single Sanitary Commission fundraiser in New York City raised over $1 million. A woman wrote, "The amount realized will no doubt do much toward relieving the poor wounded and suffering soldiers than all the surgeons do. No one can know how much good is done by the Sanitary Commission who is not in the Army."[35]

The South mounted a less formal assault on the medical chaos that plagued the Confederate forces. Less than thirty surgeons and surgeon's assistants from the old army chose to serve with the Confederacy, and wounded or sick men were often left to the tender care of their mates or the local populace. The military hospitals of the South were overwhelmed by the task before them, and wounded men were often shipped home to recuperate under the care of their families. Those who were capable, but still considered invalids, were formed into local militias and railroad guards, rather than hospital orderlies, by the manpower-hungry state governments.

Ambulances were provided by subscription. A newly painted Confederate ambulance, apparently donated by a well-meaning supporter from Fairfax, was among the early acquisitions of federal pickets in Northern Virginia. "This capture was an object of much curiosity around the Federal camp near Alexandria. Soldiers stood off and stared at it in awe . . . an omen of what might lie in store for them, this wagon designed for toting the wounded or the dead."[36]

Sincere religious reflection characterized both armies as the war wore on. The Christian Commission and its western affiliate were late in forming, and there is some dispute over the role they played in the war. Both sprang from an **Moral Awakening** association of the YMCA, the American Bible Society, and the American Tract Society, and they were somewhat more evangelical in their agenda than the Sanitary Commission. Most historians agree that the Christian Commissions provided quality reading materials for the troops and established a moral standard for the soldiers of the federal army. However, their agenda was essentially religious in nature. Although there was some friction between the various organizing groups, no less than $500 million was raised by the Christian Commissions for religious and philanthropic purposes.[37]

Most regiments had resident chaplains. One Confederate general, Leonidas Polk, was a consecrated bishop of the Episcopal Church. Religious tracts and Bibles were circulated throughout the army camps. Nonetheless, federal captain J. W. De Forest observed that "the men are not as *good* as they were once; they drink harder and swear more and gamble deeper." The same officer noted, however, that "the swearing mania was irrepressible. In the excitement of the charge it seemed as if every extremity of language was excusable, providing it would help toward victory." Bible societies, moral reform organizations, and social uplift associations of all kinds sent missionaries and representatives into the field in an attempt to improve the physical and moral environment of the troops.[38]

Public demonstrations of piety and religious worship, organized by ministers, priests, lay preachers, and the men themselves, were common events in camp and were well attended by the troops. General Jackson's fanatical Presbyterian evangelical devotion came to be almost stereotypical of Confederate religious sentiment. Nonetheless, when two dozen general officers of the Confederate army were seen at the same church service in 1864, it was suggested that "less piety and more drilling of commands would suit the times better."[39]

Women   Women were active in all of the efforts to improve the mo-
at War   rality of the troops, and for the first time the female presence
               with the army was not solely represented by the traditional
camp followers. While it has been proven that a substantial number of
women were able to pass themselves off as men and serve in the armed
forces, their number was too small to effect any advantage or disadvantage to the troops. Most women chose to act in less startling ways to
support the war effort. A number of war-related jobs were filled by
women. Females served as clerks in the clothing branch of the Quartermaster's Department and filled the ammunition cartridges and artillery
shells with powder at the armories, laboring at this dangerous and exacting task for low wages. Both sides utilized women in these capaci-
ties.[40]

A number of wives and female relatives traveled with the army to
sew, nurse, and wash clothes. Federal captain John W. De Forest was
constantly plagued by his wife's requests to join him on the field, and
many of his responses to her were phrased in such a way as to discourage her gently. Confederate general John B. Gordon had his beautiful
young wife with him at all times on campaign. Fanny Gordon "turned
her two children, aged four and six, over to Gordon's mother, climbed
into a buggy, and with one of the family slaves driving she followed her
man." Generals John C. Breckinridge and Thomas Rosser brought their
wives along as well when things were quiet—much to the chagrin of
their superior, General Jubal Early, who was driven to "distraction" by
women on campaign. But Mrs. Gordon was there *all the time*, and Early
was overheard to say, "I wish the Yankees would capture Mrs. Gordon
and hold her till this war is over."[41]

Major General Benjamin Butler, in charge of the occupied city of New
Orleans, may have made the most insulting gesture of the entire war
with regard to women. He declared that since federal officers had been
"subjected to repeated insults from the women" of that city, any lady
would, upon repetition of the offense, "be regarded and held liable to
be treated as a woman of the town plying her vocation." The order was
severely protested in the South and in Europe.[42] Nonetheless, prostitutes
and women of loose morals were much in evidence in the Army of the
Potomac under General Joseph Hooker. Historians disagree on the ety-
mology of the term "hooker," which may or may not proceed from this
circumstance as a synonym for prostitute. Nonetheless, a righteous general officer from among the federal forces noted, "The condition of morals among officers who [find] congenial companionship in the society of
such women is apparent and needs no coloring from pen or pencil."[43]

NOTES

1. Lewis, 51.

2. Archer Jones, *Confederate Strategy from Shiloh to Vicksburg* (Baton Rouge: Louisiana State University Press, 1991), 8–27.

3. West Virginia was to propose a constitution in which gradual emancipation would take place after July 4, 1863. It prohibited slavery but required freed blacks to remove themselves from the state. Jordan, 20.

4. Croushore, 192.

5. General Joe Wheeler fought twenty-six rearguard actions in just two weeks in 1862.

6. Shelby Foote, *The Civil War: A Narrative, Fort Sumter to Perryville* (New York: Vintage, 1986), 173.

7. Richard Armstrong, *Seventh Virginia Cavalry* (Lynchburg: H. E. Howard, 1992), 32–37; Ashby, 216–220, 269–275.

8. Mosby. Mosby was almost the only defender of Stuart's actions before and after the battle. Today Stuart's leading apologist is Mark Nesbit, *Saber and Scapegoat: J.E.B. Stuart and the Gettysburg Controversy* (Mechanicsburg: Stackpole, 1994). Nesbit dispels many "lost cause" myths surrounding Stuart's actions and attempts to justify the cavalry leader's decisions at the time of the campaign.

9. Brian Steel Wills, *A Battle from the Start: The Life of Nathan Bedford Forrest* (New York: HarperCollins, 1992), 1–3.

10. James M. McPherson, *Battle Cry of Freedom* (New York: Oxford University Press, 1988), 514–515, 763.

11. V.C. Jones, 107; Lewis, 59.

12. Francis A. Lord, "The United States Military Railroad Service: Vehicle to Victory," *Civil War Times Illustrated*, October 1962, 6–11, 46–50.

13. Fite, 56.

14. Ibid., 57n.

15. Miers, 187.

16. Cozzens, 32; David B. Sabine, "Resources Compared: North Versus South," *Civil War Times Illustrated*, February 1968, 5–15; Guernsey and Alden, 792.

17. Sabine, 12.

18. V. C. Jones, 26. Quoting the report of Gen. Philip St. George Cocke on the defenses of northern Virginia.

19. Walton, 29.

20. Ibid., 24.

21. See George E. Woodward, *Woodward's Architecture and Rural Art*, 2 vols. (New York: Privately printed, 1867–1868), 1:32–37. John L. McAdam was a Scottish engineer who had developed a road which came to be called macadam—a covering of broken stone, in three layers consolidated by the passage of surface traffic.

22. Miers, 22, 29.

23. Croushore, 34–36.

24. Ibid., 77–78.

25. Ibid., 141, 173.

26. J. B. Mitchell, 165.

27. Archer Jones, *The Art of War in the Western World* (New York: Oxford University Press, 1987), 314.

28. Miers, 31.

29. Wilbur S. Nye, "The U.S. Military Telegraph Services," *Civil War Times Illustrated*, November 1968, 28–34; Raymond W. Smith, "Don't Cut! Signal Telegraph," *Civil War Times Illustrated*, May 1976, 18–28.

30. Robert E. Denny, *Civil War Medicine: Care and Comfort for the Wounded* (New York: Sterling, 1995), 10.

31. Ibid., 226–227.

32. Byron Stinson, "The Invalid Corps," *Civil War Times Illustrated*, May 1971, 20–27.

33. Michael F. Fitzpatrick, "The Mercy Brigade," *Civil War Times Illustrated*, October 1997, 34–40.

34. Ibid., 36.

35. Walton, 72.

36. V. C. Jones, 34. Referring to the *Official Records of the Rebellion*, II, 299.

37. Guernsey and Alden, 792.

38. Croushore, 65, 80.

39. C. V. Woodward, 585.

40. McPherson, *Battle Cry*, 35. Edward D.C. Campbell, Jr., and Kym S. Rice, eds., *A Woman's War: Southern Women, Civil War and the Confederate Legacy* (Charlottesville: University Press of Virginia, 1996), 102. "Camp followers" were not necessarily prostitutes.

41. See Croushore, 148–152, "Don't come on here unless I write for you. You could sleep in a tent, you say. Not in mine; I have none," 162–163; and Lewis, 114–116.

42. Campbell and Rice, frontispiece. From a broadside of General Order No. 28, May 15, 1862.

43. V. C. Jones, 149. Quoting General Lafayette Baker.

11

Seeing the Elephant: The Realities of Life in Battle

"The battle . . . the dreadful splendor . . . all my description must fall vastly short."

—Col. Wm. B. Hazen, Army of the Cumberland

Civil War battlefields were much more extensive than most people would suppose. Even in small engagements, hundreds if not thousands of men might be involved. In large battles a mounted officer, who could freely gallop from place to place, could scarcely travel over the entire field during the course of a day. Dense woods choked with heavy undergrowth or crossed with streams and marshes added to the difficulty of moving large bodies of troops. Commanders were forced to rely almost entirely on the reports of aides or couriers in formulating the military situation on different parts of the field.

With upwards of 100,000 men involved in battle, the individual soldiers saw only what occurred in their own regiment or company, and they were limited to a very narrow view of what was going on. Soldiers commonly heard more than they saw and relied on the reports of those coming from the front, which were sometimes incomplete or based on rumor. Nonetheless, this information formed part of the experience of battle for most soldiers. Although we have no way of knowing the experience of those who were killed outright, the survivors and those wounded who lived long enough to record their feelings have left us a storehouse of journals, diaries, and letters containing the expression of what a Civil War battle was like.

Civil War battles had several distinct parts. The armies roused themselves in the morning and marched out with little foreknowledge that a fateful engagement was about to take place. The opponents sent out scouts to probe in the direction of the enemy, and, ultimately, the armies came into contact and began to skirmish. In each regiment of ten companies, two were detailed each day to act as skirmishers. These men fanned out before their regiments and engaged the enemy's skirmishers or outposts. Skirmishing between outposts was a constant activity in the war zone, but skirmishers were trained to avoid precipitating an unwanted engagement by pressing too closely. "Skirmishing is not dangerous," observed an imperturbable federal captain. "Two men mortally and two severely wounded constituted my whole loss in something like three hours fighting out of a company of forty-one muskets." This loss of 10 percent of his force seemed small in contrast to the large losses of a major battle.[1]

Rarely, the opposing commanders decided to make a major fight of a small meeting, or they had a general engagement thrust upon them. A major engagement had many requirements beyond intelligence of the enemy's strength and position. Tactics and strategy were chosen to fit the particular situation, orders dictated, and units informed of their part in the cataclysm. It took time for forces to be marshaled. The column, sometimes miles long, had to be brought up to the battlefield, organized, and sent to strategic positions along the battlefront. Artillery positions and fields of fire had to be found and exploited. The cavalry might be sent to feel out the flanks of the enemy and to determine the possible success of a turning movement. A reserve was organized, and hospitals, signal stations, and supply units were set up. Beginning slowly, the battle began to rage furiously as more and more troops became engaged.

Soldiers often reported a lull in battle, sometimes immediately following a remarkable effort by both sides. Very often a series of small climaxes taken together made it obvious that one side was dominating the field. The opposing sides might now call a truce to care for their wounded and dead, and the losing commander would prepare a rearguard action to cover his retreat. The ability to effectively disengage from the victorious enemy without exposing one's forces to renewed attacks was the true test of a battlefield commander.

A soldier's experiences in battle are both common and unique. More than 10,000 individual engagements made up the Civil War, and no two were exactly the same. Most diaries, letters, and journals of the men who fought describe their experiences in battle. As noted by Col. William. B. Hazen, "The battle . . . the dreadful splendor . . . all my description must fall vastly short."[2] The authors have therefore chosen to simply let the soldiers speak. In what follows no attempt has been made to describe any particular battle. The flow of the narrative imitates the characteristic development of a major engagement. Some sentence restructuring and editing of proper names and units have been done for the sake of continuity. The name of the individual, his rank, and his affiliation are provided with each report. It is hoped that the result will remain true to the spirit of what each man contributed to the written record of the Civil War battle experience.

MARCHING TO WAR

We have received orders to cook all our rations, strike our tents very quietly, and be ready to move at any time, which we all think means that we are going to move against the enemy[3] across the river. They, also, have been exhibiting signs of uneasiness for some days past. . . . I am writing to you now for fear I may not have the opportunity again shortly. I fear not the result, am confident that we, through God, will be victorious.[4]
            —*Sgt. Alexander T. Barclay, 4th VA Infantry*

We have been on the march since yesterday, a week. . . . I would take any amount that this trip has the most beautiful scenery I ever beheld since I have been in the army, which is some time.[5]
            —*Lt. William B. Taylor, 11th NC Infantry*

We found several patriotic ladies with small feet and big umbrellas waiting to receive us. . . . One of the ladies had an enormous wreath which she was anxious to place on the neck of the General's charger. The horse objected to it seriously.[6]
            —*Lt. F. W. Dawson, Staff Officer, ANV*

No one who has not had the experience knows what a soldier undergoes on a march. We start off on a march some beautiful morning in spring. At midday slight clouds are seen floating about; these thicken . . . the rain commences and soon pours down. Poor fellow! He pulls down his hat, buttons up his jacket, pulls up his collar, and tries to protect his gun. In a short while he feels the water running down his arms and legs. . . . We went through equal trials in very dusty marches.[7]
            —*Pvt. J. H. Worsham, 21st VA Infantry*

We were about proceeding on our march. . . . [when] the men were allowed to light fires and dry the clothes in which they had shiv-

Civil war enthusiasts, many of whom are experts on
the period, recreate the lifestyle of federal troops
and the spectacle of battle at public reenactments.
James Volo photo.

ered all night. At 3 PM we received orders to recross the river, and
all the drying of clothes had to be done again in the evening.[8]
                                              —*Col. David W. Aiken, 7th SC Infantry*

We soon came to Dumfries Creek which has swollen very much
during the night taking away the bridge over the stream. . . . We
marched between twenty and thirty miles and when night came
my feet were blistered nearly all over so that fifteen minutes after
we halted I could hardly walk a step but on taking some salt and
water and bathing my feet thoroughly and then applying liquor I
managed to get myself in tolerably good marching order for the
next day.[9]
                                              —*Pvt. Edwin Weller, 107th NY Volunteers*

Angry was the glare of the sun during those fearful days. . . . Chok-
ing, blinding were the clouds of dust that rose from beneath the
army's steady tread; parching was that unquenchable thirst which

dried the tongue to its very roots. The men fell by tens, twenties, nay by hundreds along the dusty roads. Such days as these prove the true soldier.[10]

—*Capt. John E. Dooley, 1st VA Infantry*

MAKING CONTACT

The column, hitherto moving forward with the steadiness of a mighty river, hesitates, halts, steps back, then forward, hesitates again, halts. The colonels talk to the brigadier, the brigadiers talk to the major-general, some officers hurry forward and others hurry to the rear. The infantry stands to one side of the road while the cavalry trots by to the front. . . . Most of the men know . . . they are on the edge of battle. . . . The skirmishers step into the woods and carefully go forward. They load, fire, and reload rapidly while standing six to twelve feet apart, calling to each other, laughing, shouting and cheering. . . . They have at last driven the enemy skirmishers in upon the line of battle, and are waiting. A score of men have fallen here, some killed outright, some slightly, some sorely and some mortally wounded.[11]

—*Pvt. Carlton McCarthy, 2nd Richmond Howitzers*

At first when the boys brought news of the engagement to the company, we were loath to believe them and had it not been for the serious faces of those who gave us the information we would have been tempted to treat it as an attempt at a scare. Quite a number of the members of the company . . . returned with a report confirming the tidings already received. Soon afterwards a number of prisoners, about 300, were marched past where we were resting. As soon as we saw them we crowded up close to the road to get a good look at them. They all seemed to be in the best of spirits, evidently glad to escape the pending battle.[12]

—*Pvt. Joseph A. Lumbard, 147th PA Infantry*

The orders were to be ready at a moment's notice. The lines were forming. Batteries were being placed into position. Dark columns stood motionless. . . . Hospitals were established in the rear, and the musicians and other non-combatants were detailed to bear the stretchers and attend the ambulances. Medical stores were unpacked and countless rolls of bandages placed at hand for use.[13]

—*Ebenezer Hannaford, 6th OH Volunteers*

Hundreds of Civil War enthusiasts recreate a
column of march (above) while others defend an
artillery battery (below) during a Civil War battle
reenactment. James Volo photo.

I now formed my division in the woods. . . . I told the General that
the column seemed to be heavily engaged. I thought I had better
go in. He replied: "I do not wish to bring on a general engagement
today; the rest of the army is not up." . . . Very soon [however] an
aide came to me with orders to attack.[14]

—Mjr. Gen. Henry Heth, Division Cmdr. CSA

A DAY OF BATTLE

In general, the terror of battle is not an abiding impression, but
comes and goes like throbs of pain; and this is especially the case
with veterans who have learned to know when there is a pressing
danger and when not; the moment a peril has passed they are as
tranquil as if it had never come near.[15]

—Capt. John W. De Forest, 12th CT

We soon came to the top of a hill in full view of the field and valley and upon the hill we had the fight. Here men jumped over a fence to the left and formed in battle line. In a short time a line of the enemy came out of the woods in front of us about a mile off; soon another; and yet another. They kept steadily advancing until we could see their officers stepping in front swinging their swords. Suddenly a cloud of smoke arose from their line and almost instantly the balls began to whistle about us and the men next to my right fell. The order rang along the line . . . to load and fire at will, as they call it. I think we fired about five rounds. . . . As soon as the report of our muskets were [sic] heard we knew that a very small part of our line was there. The enemy did not return our fire but came rushing down the hill yelling.[16]

—*Sgt. Edwin A. Gearhart, 142nd PA Infantry*

At every step some poor fellow would fall, and as his pitiful cry would come to my ear I almost imagined it the wail of some loved one he had left at home."[17]

—*Capt. John T. James, 11th VA Infantry*

The Colonel was all impatience. "Where the hell is my flag?" He shouted [to the flagbearer], "If I can't get you killed in ten minutes, by God, I'll post you right up among the batteries!"[18]

—*Capt. Abner Small, 16th ME Infantry*

One of our own batteries stationed on a hill in the rear of our line fired two shots which fell short and killed two of our company. I was sent back to inform the Colonel of the fact. . . . I mounted an orderly's horse, a great lumbering beast. As I reached a hill I was obliged to follow the ridge for several hundred yards. The enemy sharpshooters opened fire upon me. . . : I lost my hat, and as it was a new one and cost me seven and a half dollars, I drew my saber and ran the point through the hat and recovered it. I next lost my Navy Colt revolver, but if it had been made of gold, studded with diamonds I would not have stopped for it.[19]

—*Col. Elisha Hunt Rhodes, 2nd RI Volunteers*

There was the thunder of guns, a shrieking, whistling, moaning of shells, before they burst, sometimes like rockets in the air. . . . No results of this conflict could be noted; no shifting of scenes or movement of actors in the great struggle could be observed. It was simply noise, flash, and roar. I had the sensation of a lifetime."[20]

—*William H. Bayly, 13-year-old resident of Gettysburg*

The appearance of the landscape northward from this point was singular and doleful. Hundreds of noncombatants, and many who should have been in the ranks, with many whose bloody clothing showed that their fighting for that day had ended, were drifting rearward confusedly, yet with curious deliberation. Over the space of a mile square the fields, long since stripped of their rail fences, were dotted with wagons, ambulances, pack mules, army followers and stray soldiers, none of them running. . . .

Defeated and retreating soldiers do not fly at full speed for any considerable distance. After a run of a hundred yards, or less, even though the bullets are still whizzing around them, they drop into a walk. . . .Thence forward they tramp steadily rearward, not in the least wild with fright, but discreetly.[21]

—*Capt. John W. De Forest, 12th CT*

It was a moment of contending emotions of pride, hope and sadness as our gallant boys stood face to face with those heights, ready to charge upon them. At double-quick and in splendid style they crossed the plain. Our line was perfect. The men could not have made a better appearance had they been on drill.

Just in the rear of the division three batteries of Parrott guns were playing into the works of the enemy, while from the heights above, all the opposing batteries poured a terrible and destructive fire upon the advancing lines. Having gained the rifle pits at the base of the hills, they pushed forward to capture the heights. . . .

There were the hills, enough to fatigue any man to climb them without a load and with no one to oppose. But the boys pushed nobly, steadily on, the enemy steadily retreating . . . our men were falling in every direction . . . but with shouts and cheers . . . with bayonettes fixed, mounted the heights, the enemy retreating in confusion.[22]

—*George T. Stevens, Surgeon, 77th NY Volunteers*

The works commenced were only piles of rails and logs not capable of resisting shells, so we got tools and commenced ditching. By 10 AM we had pretty good works. . . . Soon after two lines of battle burst out of the woods in front of us, and started up, on the charge. . . . They came up within 50 paces of the works, before being repulsed. . . .

We have been kept close by sharpshooters, having nothing to protect us but our works. The enemy is on the edge of the woods, three or four hundred yards off while we are in an open field. We could not get out after water until dark. . . . The fire was kept up some time wounding several others, but killing no more. We have

been enfiladed all day and have lost many killed and wounded—
at night strengthened our works—worked all night.[23]

—*Pvt. John S. Jackman, 1st KY Infantry*

WOUNDED IN BATTLE

Some of the wounded from the battlefield began to arrive where I
was staying. They reported hard fighting, many wounded and
killed, and were afraid our troops would be defeated and perhaps
routed. The first wounded soldier whom I met had his thumbs tied
up. This I thought dreadful, and told him so. . . . Soon two officers
carrying their arms in slings made their appearance, and I more
fully began to realize that something terrible had taken place. Now
the wounded began to come in greater numbers. Some limping,
some with their heads and arms in bandages, some crawling, others
carried on stretchers or brought in ambulances. Suffering, cast
down and dejected, it was truly a pitiable gathering.[24]

—*Tillie Pierce, 15-year-old resident of Gettysburg*

At a distance of about one hundred and fifty yards the enemy were
lying down, and rose up in masses and fired one volley. I and one
other member of the Brigade fell wounded . . . the bullet cut across
my bowels and made a long and ugly wound . . . I was feeling no
pain, but felt somewhat dazed. . . .

The grape shot and shell were pouring thick and fast in our rear,
a great number falling short of their intended mark, and it made
me hopeful that it would soon put an end to my existence. I turned
my head to the enemy, thinking that I might be so fortunate as to
get shot dead. . . . [25]

As there was no sign of discharge [from the wound] . . . I thought
[after a time] that possibly I was not mortally wounded. Then fear
was uppermost and I crawled about 50 feet to a well rotted stump,
thinking it would protect me from shot. I was not much more than
settled behind it when the idea struck me that a grape [from artillery canister] could go through, so I dragged myself to a good sized
tree about 100 feet off and stayed there some time in a reclining
position, with head and shoulder resting against the tree. All the
while the battle was roaring across the creek.[26]

—*Pvt. William A. Fletcher, 5th TX Infantry*

[A] man lay near me, dying from a terrible wound through the
abdomen, his fair face growing whiter with every laboring breath
and his light blue eyes fixed vacantly on the glaring sky . . . I

glanced at him pitifully from time to time as he patiently and silently drew towards his end. Such individual cases of suffering are far more moving than a broad spectacle of slaughter.[27]

—*Captain John W. De Forest, 12th CT*

A terrific explosion occurred . . . I found myself lying off from my former position and gasping for breath. Around me were brains, blood, and skull bones. The two men who lay to my left had been blown off just above the ears, and that shell had exploded almost directly over me. It had broken several ribs and bruised my left lung cutting my jacket into shreds. My Colonel asked me if I was badly hurt to which I replied I thought I was and called for that which a wounded soldier first wants, a drink of water.[28]

—*Sgt. David E. Johnston, 7th VA Infantry*

We were in this wheat field and the grain stood almost breast high. The enemy had their slight protection, but we were in the open, without a thing better than a wheat straw to catch a Minnie bullet that weighed an ounce. Of course our men began to tumble. They lay where they fell, or, if able started for the rear. Near to me I saw a man go down, shot through the neck. I made a movement to get his gun, but at that moment I was struck in the shoulder. It did not hurt and the blow simply caused me to step back. I found that I could not work my arm, but . . . it was not serious enough to justify my leaving the fighting line. So I remained, and some time after felt a blow on my left leg, and it gave way, so that I knew the leg was broken. . . . While lying here entirely helpless, and hearing those vicious bullets singing over my head, I suffered from fear.[29]

—*Lt. Charles A. Fuller, 61st NY Infantry*

The road where we lay was covered with our dead and wounded. A battery of the enemy came thundering along it, and when the officer commanding it saw our dead and wounded on the road, he halted his battery to avoid running over them and his men carefully lifted the dead to one side and carried the wounded to the cellar of a house, supplied them with water, and said they would return and care for them when they had caught the rest of us.[30]

—*Sgt. Edward R. Bowen, 114th PA Infantry*

I do not know how long it was before I became conscious but the battle was raging furiously; two dead men who were not there when I fell were lying close to me, one across my feet. . . . Two stretcher-bearers came and carried me back about fifty yards to a small stream that ran parallel to our battle line. Here was a de-

Chew's battery of horse artillery fires a blank round
(above) and watches as the infantry line fires a
volley (below). Civil War photographs were unable
to catch such action shots, as the photographic
plates were too slow in reacting to available light.
James Volo photo.

pression in the ground some three or four feet below the general
level where the wounded would be protected from the musket
fire. . . .

When I reached the stream the banks were already lined with
many dead and wounded. Some had been carried there, others had
dragged themselves to the place to die. Many were needlessly
bleeding to death. Many died who would have lived if only the
simplest treatment had been in the hands of the men themselves.[31]

My mind was clear . . . I knew I could not get to the rear without
help, so made no further attempt. Fortunately my canteen had been
filled; my thirst had become great and I had some water to wash
the blood from my face.

During this time the battle on our front continued with unles-
sening fury. . . . Looking back I saw a scattered line of the enemy
coming toward us on the double quick. . . . They had to cross

around or over the wounded and were cautioned by their officers to be careful not to disturb them more than was necessary. They passed over us carefully, without any unkind actions or words.[32]
—*Pvt. Rice C. Bull, 123rd NY Volunteers*

I felt a burning, stinging sensation in my thigh, and as if all the blood in my body was rushing to one spot. Finding I was falling on my face, I gave myself a sudden twist which brought me into a sitting position facing the enemy, with my broken leg doubled up over the other. Taking it up tenderly, I put it in its natural position; then tied my handkerchief above the wound, took the bayonet off my gun and made a tourniquet with it. I then took my knapsack off and put it under my head for a pillow. Having made myself comfortable . . . every moment I expected would be my last.[33]
—*Pvt. David R. Howard, 1st MD Battalion*

CLIMAX

At sunrise our Division advanced against the enemy's works. . . . We lay about forty yards apart. . . . To expose one's person was sure death. . . . Both armies were like hornets. We dug holes with our bayonets to protect ourselves and more than one poor fellow was shot before his little dugout would protect him. We lay there expecting every minute to be gobbled up. The shells passed over us both ways. Some of them fell short of going where they were started for and burst over our heads. We made ourselves in as small bulk as possible. This was a very dangerous position, but we took our chances and trusted to providence. . . . Time goes slowly.

At 7 PM everything became as quiet as the grave, we felt it was the calm before the storm. We fixed ourselves as well as possible to be ready for what was coming, and at 8 PM it came. The enemy charged our works. . . . These were long fierce charges—they came right up to the works but they could not effect a lodgement . . . We could hear their officers shouting, "Forward, forward!" On they came to be mowed down by the thousand, but we never thought of getting driven out.

At daylight all was quiet. The enemy advanced a white flag, asking permission to bury their dead, which was granted. We had an armistice of two hours. The quietness was really oppressive. It positively made us lonesome for the continual racket which we had endured for so long, both day and night. We sat on the works and

This period lithograph shows a much more sanitary view of a medical field station than was the case. The nineteenth-century public was ill prepared for the grim reality of the war.

let our legs dangle over the front and watched the enemy carry off their dead comrades in silence. . . . When the two hours was up we got back into our holes, and they did the same.[34]

       —Pvt. Daniel Chisholm, 116th PA Infantry

THE AFTERMATH

With us for a time all was quiet. There was nothing to disturb us but the occasional cries and groans of the wounded; not a word of complaint was heard. . . . Nearly all knew we were not only wounded but were now prisoners. . . .

  The enemy's surgeons went among our wounded looking for those that required amputation. . . . The arms and legs were thrown on the ground, only a few feet from the wounded who lay nearby. As each amputation was completed the wounded man was carried to an old house and laid on the floor. They said they could do nothing at that time for those others less critically wounded. . . . The condition of most of these was deplorable.[35]

—*Pvt. Rice C. Bull, 123rd NY Volunteers*

Our men had 60 rounds of cartridges each when they went into an action and had used it nearly all when the enemy ran. Our regiment went into the fight with about 650 men and, as we lost about 100 in killed and wounded, you may know that we had pretty hot work. . . . I don't know the total loss in our brigade but should think about 450 killed and wounded. The enemy loss is pretty heavy but I don't believe they lost more than us as they were well protected by their breast works.[36]

—*Lt. George Washington Whitman, 13th NY Militia*

Some of them lay dead within twenty feet of our works—the dead look horrible all swelled up and black in the face. . . . After there was nothing left but stains of blood, broken and twisted guns, old hats, canteens, every one of them reminders of the death and carnage that reigned a few short hours before.[37]

—*Pvt. Daniel Chisholm, 116th PA Infantry*

The ground here is very hard, full of rocks and stones, the digging very laborious work, and the dead are many. As the time is short, they got but very shallow graves. In fact, most of them were buried in trenches dug not over 18 inches deep, and as near where they fell as was possible so as not to have to carry them far. I saw 60 buried in one trench and not one was carried more than 25 feet.[38]

—*Sgt. George A. Bowen, 12th NJ Infantry*

The Pickets on both sides have agreed not to fire on each other, and are getting very friendly. They trade Tobacco for Coffee, and also exchange newspapers, etc. . . .

This is a beautiful Sabbath day. Quiet. The regiment has marching orders and we lay around in the sun wondering where to go next. At dusk we quietly packed up and fell back without noise or confusion and struck out through the darkness leaving the battlefield behind. This has been a hot place for us as our thinned ranks show.[39]

—*Pvt. Daniel Chisholm, 116th PA Infantry*

[A]n enemy officer came and took a list of all prisoners, having each one sign a parole not to enter active service again until properly exchanged. . . . On returning home, after the battle, I found that my family was notified that I had been badly wounded, it was thought mortally, and was left on the battlefield. Great was their joy when two weeks later, after they had abandoned hope of my being alive, they received a letter from me sent from the hospital.[40]

—*Pvt. Rice C. Bull, 123rd NY Volunteers*

Tell my father I died with my face to the enemy.[41]

—*Col. Isaac E. Avery, 6th NC Infantry*

My Dear Papa,

When our great victory was just over the exultation was so great that one didn't think of our fearful losses, but now I can't help feeling a great weight at my heart.[42]

—*Capt. Henry L. Abbott, 20th ME Infantry*

NOTES

1. Croushore, 114. Casualties in excess of 50 percent were not uncommon.

2. Cozzens, 165.

3. The term "enemy" has been used to replace Yankees, Federals, Rebs, Johnnies, etc. General Robert E. Lee eschewed the use of the term "enemy." Rather, he habitually referred to the Federals as "those people."

4. Editors of Time-Life, *Voices of the Civil War* (New York: Time-Life, 1995): [1863 Maryland campaign], Sgt. Alexander T. Barclay, 4th VA Inf., 16. Hereafter cited as *Voices*, with campaign, person, unit, and page where appropriate. The excerpts from letters, diaries, and journals found in this publication were originally printed in the lifetime of their authors and can be found separately in their entirety.

5. Ibid.: [1863 Maryland campaign], Lt. William B. Taylor, 11th NC Inf., 21.

6. Ibid.: [1863 Maryland campaign], Lt. Francis W. Dawson, Staff Officer, Longstreet's Command, 33. The abbreviation "ANV" stands for Army of Northern Virginia.

7. Robertson: Pvt. John H. Worsham, 21st VA Inf., 96–97.

8. *Voices*: [Gettysburg], Col. David W. Aiken, 7th SC Inf., 22.

9. Walton: [On the March], Pvt. Edwin Weller, 107th NY Volunteers, 18, 23–24.

10. *Voices*: [Gettysburg], Capt. John E. Dooley, 1st VA Inf., 35.

11. McCarthy: Pvt. Carlton McCarthy, 2nd Co., Richmond Howitzers, 94.

12. *Voices*: [Gettysburg], Pvt. Joseph A. Lumbard, 147th PA Inf., 41.

13. Ebenezer Hannaford, *The Story of a Regiment: A History of the Campaigns, and Associations in the Field of the Sixth Regiment Ohio Volunteer Infantry* (Cincinnati: Privately printed, 1868): Ebenezer Hannaford, 6th Ohio Volunteers, 811–812.

14. *Voices*: [Gettysburg], Mjr. Gen. Henry Heth, Division Commander, CSA, 40.

15. Croushore, 59.

16. *Voices*: [Gettysburg], Sgt. Edwin A. Gearhart, 142nd PA Inf., 49.

17. Ibid.: [Gettysburg], Capt. John T. James, 11th VA Inf., 121.

18. Ibid.: [Gettysburg], Capt. Abner Small, 16th ME Inf., 116.

19. Robert Hunt Rhodes, ed., *All for the Union*, by Col. Elisha Hunt Rhodes (1985; reprint, New York: Random House, 1995): Col. Elisha Hunt Rhodes, 2nd RI Volunteers, 143–144.

20. *Voices*: [Gettysburg], William H. Bayly, thirteen-year-old resident of Gettysburg, 105.

21. Croushore, 213–214, 220.

22. George T. Stevens, *Three Years in the Sixth Corps* (Albany: S. R. Gray, 1866), 196–197. Surgeon Stevens was a witness to the second battle before Fredericksburg. The first storming of Marye's Heights had ended in a bloody repulse.

23. William C. Davis, ed., *Diary of a Confederate Soldier*, by John S. Jackman (Columbia: University of South Carolina Press, 1990): Pvt. John S. Jackman of the Orphan Brigade, 123–124.

24. *Voices*: [Gettysburg], Tillie Pierce, fifteen years old, 62. Tillie Pierce's memoirs of the Gettysburg battle were featured on an episode of *Civil War Journal*, a series produced by the Arts and Entertainment Network in 1997.

25. Stomach wounds were thought to end only in a long, agonizing death.

26. Fletcher: [Second Manassas], Pvt. William A. Fletcher, Co. F, 5th TX, 50–56.

27. Croushore, 138.

28. *Voices*: [Gettysburg], Sgt. David E. Johnston, 7th VA Inf., 117.

29. Ibid.: [Gettysburg], Lt. Charles Fuller, 61st NY Inf., 86.

30. Ibid.: Sgt. Edward R. Bowen, 114th PA Inf., 92.

31. No first aid appliances were supplied to the soldiers, although many items such as tourniquets and other "lifesavers" were available from sutlers.

32. Bauer: [Chancellorsville], Pvt. Rice C. Bull, 123rd NY, 58–63.

33. *Voices*: [Gettysburg], Pvt. David R. Howard, 1st Maryland Battalion, 110.

34. W. Springer Menge and J. August Shimrak, eds., *The Civil War Notebook of Daniel Chisholm* (New York: Ballantine, 1989): [Cold Harbor], Pvt. Daniel Chisholm, Co. K, 116th PA, Irish Brigade, 19–22.

35. Bauer: [Chancellorsville], Pvt. Rice C. Bull, 123rd NY, 58–63.

36. Jerome M. Loving, ed., *Civil War Letters of George Washington Whitman* (Durham: Duke University Press, 1975): [Battle of New Bern, NC], 13th Regiment of NY State Militia, 46–47.

37. Menge and Shimrak: [Cold Harbor], Pvt. Daniel Chisholm, Co. K, 116th PA, Irish Brigade, 19–22.

38. *Voices*: [Gettysburg], Sgt. George A. Bowen, 12th NJ Infantry, 147.

39. Menge and Shimrak: [Cold Harbor], Pvt. Daniel Chisholm, Co. K, 116th PA, Irish Brigade, 19–22.

40. Bauer: [Chancellorsville], Pvt. Rice C. Bull, 123rd NY, 58–63.

41. *Voices*: [Gettysburg], Col. Isaac E. Avery, 6th NC, 102. Written in a scribbled hand as he was dying.

42. Ibid.: [Gettysburg], Capt. Henry L. Abbott, 20th ME Inf., 159.

Part III

Civilians' Lives

The visions of a nation wrenched apart by civil war and of soldiers battling on many fronts are often used to capture the emotion and turmoil of the period. But while the physical debris of war was obvious, the full extent of the tragedy was somewhat obscured. The broken implements of battle, the uneven lines of shallow graves, the torn earth upturned by shot and shell rather than by the plow were all visible evidence of the tragedy that had been visited upon the nation. Yet the same imagery proved equally valid when applied to families and civilians during those troubled times.

The war placed the institution of the family under a siege equally as violent as any that occurred on the field of battle. Loved ones were wrenched apart as men and boys marched off to fight, many never to return—sometimes not even in death. Economic shortages, strained agricultural productivity, and social upheaval beset civilians in various forms. Like brave soldiers themselves, many civilians managed to stand apart from the war and cope with its vagaries while trying to preserve some semblance of their social order, standard of living, and values. Thus, even though the war might rage at their very doorsteps, the civilians lived through it and in spite of it.

12

Be It Ever So Humble

What have husbands to do with housekeeping? If they furnish the
funds to supply the family, is that not sufficient?
—*The Housekeeper's Encyclopedia*

Home ownership served as an ideal during the Civil War era, but many
families, especially in cities, had to settle for apartments, boarding
houses, and tenements. Even among individual homeowners, the diversity of the residences included mansions, villas, multistory houses, cot-
tages, cabins, and soddies. The Irish immigrants were noted by observers
at the time for building shanties—structures that were virtual shacks.

Architectural pattern books abounded, containing a wide variety of
house plans of different sizes and prices. Even periodicals carried house
plans. The typical middle-class home had three types of rooms. There
were public rooms such as the hall, parlor, dining room, and library.
Bedchambers were considered private rooms and were almost exclusively located on the second floor. The mere placement of a bedroom on
the first floor of a two-story home other than in the event of sickness
was considered risqué in many circles. The final category included work-
rooms such as the kitchen, pantry, laundry, scullery, and cellar.

In addition to the practical purposes of providing a barrier
against the cold or containing the mud and dirt from outside, **The Front**
the front hall of a Victorian home had a very important social **Hall**
function. Business dealings in these times were much more

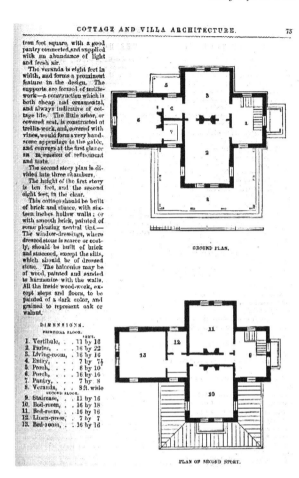

A floor plan from *Arthur's Home Magazine* (1855).

likely to be done face to face, and the front hall provided a reception area where these dealings could take place without exposing the family's private quarters. In the absence of a servants' entrance, shopping purchases were often delivered here, and in urban areas, mail might be delivered several times a day.

It was important that the front hall be decorated in a fashion appropriate to the social standing of the family. The hall was likely to be furnished with a pair of chairs for visitors, a mirror for checking one's appearance, and a table to receive calling cards. Upscale homes often had massive pieces of furniture that combined several of these features. Floors could be tiled for the practical purpose of accommodating the dirt of a high-traffic area. Nonetheless, Elizabeth Blair Lee wrote in 1863, "I have enquired about carpets & oil cloth—the latter is much the cheapest for the Hall—the best quality costs $1.25 to $1.50 for square yard—a poor carpet costs that & dust makes the oil cloth best in other respects."[1]

Calling was a required social function governed by convention. On the topic of calls, *Martine's Hand-Book of Etiquette* stated, "Such visits are necessary, in order to maintain good feeling between the members of society; they are required by the custom of the age in which we live, and must be carefully attended to."[2] Martine counseled that ceremonial calls be kept brief. "Half an hour amply suffices for a visit of ceremony. If the visitor be a lady, she may remove her victorine, but on no account either the shawl or bonnet, even if politely requested to do so by the mistress of the house. Some trouble is necessarily required in replacing them, and this ought to be avoided."[3] Upon exiting, the caller would leave a card, which would be placed in a cardholder in the front hall. Elaborate cardholders were made from silver or china. Ladies' magazines contained patterns for crafted ones. "In leaving cards you must thus distribute them: one for the lady of the house and her daughters . . . one for the master of the house, and if there be a grown up son or a near male relation staying in the house, one for him."[4]

Socially conscious women kept a list of family members and business acquaintances who formed a basic calling circle. It would be expected that persons on this list would be visited at least twice a year. Failure to reciprocate would be considered a grievous slight. Naturally, close friends and family would see each other more frequently. Martine warned, "Keep a strict account of your ceremonial visits. This is needful, because time passes rapidly; and take note of how soon your calls are returned. You will thus be able, in most cases, to form an opinion whether or not your frequent visits are desired."[5] Brides were kept particularly busy making rounds as they introduced themselves in their new social position. Women were reminded that "it is the custom for a wife to take her husband's cards with her, and to leave one or two with her own."[6]

The parlor was the most public room in the Victorian house. Parlors were common to both the North and the **The Parlor** South and across the middle class. Some more affluent homes had a front parlor solely dedicated to formal visitations and a back parlor for family use, but a single parlor was most common. The parlor was the place where visitors would be received, and therefore where the first impressions of a family were formed. Decorating decisions were made in a very calculated manner so as to project the image a family wished to convey. The parlor contained a family's "best" in every way. It would have the highest ceilings, the largest fireplace, and the most elaborate furnishings. The central feature of most parlors was a large circular table with a kerosene or oil lamp. Here the family would

A back-to-back advertisement for parlor accessories
from *Arthur's Home Magazine* of 1855.

gather to write, read, converse, play games, or engage in needlework.
The need to gather around the central light, which may have been the
only one in the room, helped to foster a communal attitude. The parlor
table allowed family members to be together, yet various members of
the family could be engaged in a variety of pastimes. They were able to
function as individuals yet remain a part of the family community as a
whole.

The second focal point of the parlor was the fireplace. The mantel was
often heavily decorated with pictures, collected natural objects, or me-
mentos. What could not fit on the mantel would be placed on shelves or
etageres around the room. An intense appreciation of nature prevailed
during this time, leading to the collection of seashells, fossils, minerals,
pinecones, and dried flowers, which were all displayed in the parlor. It
was felt that natural objects reflected the harmony of nature and civilization. Homes decorated with objects of nature were thought to demonstrate nature's beauty in family life. Additionally, using natural objects

as decorative accents showed a wife's sense of economy, an attribute much extolled.

Other furnishings might include an upholstered sofa, armchairs, and a pair of easy chairs all done in matching fabric. Rocking chairs were very much in fashion during the 1860s, and parlors were just one room in which they might be found. Common upholstery materials included brocades, silk damask, and tapestry, which were adorned with tassels, cords, and fringe. It was not unusual for sofa ensembles to contain a large gentleman's armchair and a smaller chair with half arms for the lady, which accommodated her wide skirts and kept her posture properly erect. The placement of chairs around the room allowed social groupings to change as activities varied. A person might move from the solitary activity of reading quietly to join a game with other family members at the table. Sofas were designed with slight curves to encourage conversation.

Ownership of a piano or parlor organ heralded solid middle-class status. In 1855 a German-born American piano maker named Henry Steinway began to manufacture a piano with a cast-iron frame that gave its sound much greater brilliance and power than earlier forms. There have been no fundamental changes in the design and construction of pianos since 1855. This improvement prompted widespread interest in pianos and musical compositions for it. More than 20,000 pianos a year were being produced in the United States by the time of the war. Retailers offered terms even for their least expensive models, which sold for as little as $300, and advertisements for pianos and organs filled period newspapers.[7]

Families enjoyed singing and listening to pieces played on the piano. The piano was generally considered to be a feminine instrument, and women actively cultivated their musical skills. The pursuit of musical excellence may not always have been motivated by a love of harmonious tones. The piano provided a reason for courting couples to be in relatively close quarters during a time when proper behavior generally forbade such intimacy. By the piano, however, the couple could exchange glances as the young woman played. The young man could bend close, as he courteously turned pages for the seated player. "Young ladies are the principal interpreters of domestic music," stated *Macmillan's Magazine* in 1860.[8] This feminine interpretation led to the selection of many feminine accessories to adorn the piano top.

The sheet music industry was already well established and flourishing. The war created an even greater demand as people sought patriotic and war-related music. Three days after the firing upon Fort Sumter, George F. Root's "The First Gun Is Fired! May God Protect the Right!" was for sale. Two of the most popular songs, "Dixie's Land" and "The Battle Hymn of the Republic," remain favorites even today. Other popular

Advertisements like these for pianofortes and
sewing machines continued to appear throughout
the war in Northern magazines. This is from
Arthur's Home Magazine (1855).

themes for parlor music included soldier life and battlefield deaths. The
sheet music itself was often beautifully lithographed, providing the additional bonus of an inexpensive piece of artwork for the parlor. With
the outbreak of war, these images often contained patriotic and battlefield scenes that brought the war into the parlor. So much piano sheet
music was acquired by some that separate pieces of furniture were required to hold it. Possession of such a piece of furniture was an addi-

Cartes de visite are displayed on a period album
from the authors' collection.

tional status symbol. Parlor organs tended to be an outgrowth of
domestic religious worship which celebrated hymns and church music.
These were particularly important to homes that actively fostered the
Christian development of family.

Assorted small tables around the parlor contained additional bric-a-
brac or perhaps a photograph album used to collect "cartes de visite,"
which were photographs a little larger than modern business cards
mounted on thick cardboard stock. Filling albums with cartes de visite
was quite a family hobby. Edwin Weller wrote to his fiancée, "I should
be pleased to aid you in filling up your Album with nice Pictures, and
will do so if I have an opportunity for I think they [other soldiers] could
not place their Photographs in better hands than yours."[9] Some albums
were elaborate and decorated with silver or brass clasps and covered
with velvet, wood, or mother of pearl. Inside, the album contained
twenty or more pages of precut frames ready to receive the cartes. While
the cartes became relatively inexpensive, at least one photographer advertised on the back of his work, "CARTES DE VISITE, 6 for $1.00."
Filling an album was an accomplishment likely to be achieved only by
a middle- or upper-class family.[10]

People generally stood for photographs at landmark times in their life
such as just after marriage or betrothal, following the birth of a child, or
before leaving for war. Cartes could also be purchased. Collectors acquired pictures of famous people or cartes that expressed a religious
sentiment. Soldiers of both armies exchanged cartes with comrades. Weller later wrote, "I have had some new photographs sent me. . . . I had
these last ones taken for the officers of our Regt. who have wanted my

photograph ever since I returned but I thought I would let some of my friends have the best of exchanging and giving some of the officers those I had taken first." Soldiers also purchased cartes depicting the generals of their army and prominent officers, creating a pictorial documentation of their battle experience.[11]

The walls of a home were often wallpapered. Patterns showing large bouquets tied with ribbons or of oversized fruit became popular a decade before the war and stayed in style into the 1860s. Walls were usually further ornamented with paintings and, for the less affluent, prints. Attractive prints of good quality and color became readily available during the 1860s, and many families took advantage of this new technology. Subjects included farmyard scenarios, riverscapes, European scenes, hunting vignettes, still lifes, and biblical tableaus. The popularity of farmyard pictures in homes decorated in brocade and tassels can be attributed to the passion for harmony with nature and an underlying yearning for simpler times.

European subjects might be reminders of the travels family members might have made, a fact the family would have been desirous to publicize. Another popular subject was famous people, both historical and contemporary. The prominent people came from musical, literary, political, and military venues. Representations of these people might take the form of a painting, print, engraving, or bust. Which public figures a family chose to decorate their home made a powerful statement about the owners.

Not only did the selection of these works of art show good taste and education, they served as silent but concrete reminders of revered values. George Washington, for example, was admired as a selfless leader who put the public interest above his private preferences. The presence of his picture in the parlor showed that these attributes were valued by the family. These pictures served as constant reminders to children of what was expected of them in adulthood. Many of the women depicted in this form were wives of famous men, such as Mary Todd Lincoln, or entertainers like the singer Jenny Lind. The message for young girls was one of the expectation that they would be quiet movers gently working behind the scenes. Many women of the Civil War era understood this and participated in benevolent activities such as serving in hospitals, sewing for troops, and assisting orphans and needy families.

Floors were carpeted. However, carpets were sold by the linear yard and were a little more than two feet wide. They had to be pieced and sewn together much like wallpaper. Patterns tended to be floral or other naturals. Susan Evans wrote to her sister, Emma Sargent Barbour, about the installation of new carpet in July 1861. About a dozen women came to assist her in the installation. "I had to help cut the breadth, but we were not very experienced hands and consequently the carpet was cut wrong, or rather one breadth fell short. We measured it before hand, but could not seem to make the figures match any other way."[12] Carpets would additionally be covered by mats in high-traffic areas or where fireplace sparks were likely. Elizabeth Blair Lee compared prices of two merchants in Washington and Philadelphia and stated that they ranged from $150 to $262 for a carpet in October 1863.

Victorians revered intellectual pursuits. Books were therefore a must in the parlor. By 1860 more than 90 percent of white men and women could read. Diary entries refer to reading more than to any other pastime. Large, heavy Bibles were most often displayed on the central table as a symbol of family religious life. Other books were frequently displayed on tables or built-in bookshelves. Books brought learning and the world outside into the home. A parlor containing books showed that the owners valued knowledge and wished to better themselves. The information contained therein provided greater understanding of the natural world and the Lord's works. Literary allusions were not limited to pictures of famous authors or samples of their works. Statues and ceramics depicting scenes from literary works were used to decorate the parlor. Harriet Beecher Stowe's Uncle Tom and Little Eva were popular images in Northern homes.

Windows were almost buried beneath a shroud of fabrics. Closest to the window would be a thin curtain most likely of lace. This would be covered with a second layer made of heavy fabric which could be closely drawn to block out the light entirely. The ensemble would be topped off with a valance fashionably trimmed with cords, tassels, and braid. Overall, the Victorian parlor was a place of abundant accumulation. It also gives insight into the spirit and the structure of the society of which it was a part.

The Library

Although it was common to see period house plans showing libraries—and trade catalogs displayed library furniture—only the rich and the upper middle class could afford libraries. The library was truly a man's domain. It was a place to which he could retreat and engage in the kind of activities not traditionally associated with home life. Here a man could smoke, drink, and discuss money, politics, and war without exposing the rest of the family to such vulgarities. Libraries were usually on the ground floor but off to one side. Decorations were more subdued than in the parlor. Walls were paneled or done in dark-colored paper. Heavy bookshelves were often featured. Other furniture would include a desk or writing table, large gentlemen's chairs, and various tables. If a man had hobbies or interests, it would be here that he would pursue them. Specimen cases containing fossils or insects would be displayed among accompanying magnifying glasses and other optical aids.

The Dining   The luxury of a room dedicated solely to the purpose of
Room   dining was another badge of middle-class status. Families
                  of lesser means ate in the kitchen or in an area adjacent to
the parlor set aside for dining. Dining room furniture tended to be massive, often of mahogany or other dark wood. Elizabeth Blair Lee wrote
to her naval officer husband in October 1863, "I have look [*sic*] at some
furniture & find that dining room furniture alone will cost four hundred
dollars of oil walnut which is as cheap as oak."[13] The standard number
of chairs was eight. A sideboard was common, providing an excellent
place to display oversized serving pieces and candelabras. Walls tended
to be dark to show up well under candlelight, the standard lighting for
this room. Even during luncheons it would not be unusual to draw the
draperies and eat by candlelight. The formal dining experience was one
of tremendous ritual and ostentation. Books of etiquette contained pages
upon pages of rules guiding proper behavior while dining. Certain foods
required highly specialized serving or eating utensils, and form was extremely important. Ten of the thirty pages Martine dedicates to dining
in his etiquette book pertain solely to carving. Beginning in the mid-
nineteenth century the upper class developed a passion for complicating
the dining process by introducing needless table items such as spoon
warmers in an attempt to ritualize the process and to distinguish those
"in the know."

                  The one utilitarian room in the mid-nineteenth-century
The Kitchen   house was the kitchen. It was here that the most mundane,
                  labor-intensive household duties took place. The kitchen
was always located on the ground floor and had a door to the outside
to facilitate deliveries. It was not necessary for the kitchen to be adjacent
to the dining room, and in certain circles distance was considered an
asset, keeping odors contained. Kitchen furnishings were functional and
simple. There was usually a large central work table and a cupboard for
storing dishes.

Miss Beecher's Domestic Receipt Book advises, "The kitchen floor should
be covered with an oil cloth. . . . Nothing is cleansed so easily as an oil
cloth, and it is much better than a painted floor, because it can be moved
to be painted."[14] In many homes the kitchen was also the scullery and the
laundry. If that were the case, there would also be a deep sink with a drying rack for washing vegetables and pots. Indoor sinks generally had hand
pumps but no drains, so that dirty water had to be bailed out and emptied
outside. Dishes were washed in a large wooden bowl as a measure to keep
down breakage. Pots were stored by hanging them from racks.

In many homes the dominant feature in the kitchen would have been
the wood-burning stove. Stoves had become fairly standard in Northern
middle-class homes by the 1860s. In rural areas, particularly among the
lower classes, cooking was still done on the hearth. There were those

who felt that the hearth was the traditional heart of the home and resisted the kitchen stove.

Other furnishings included the ice chest and meat safe. The meat safe was a kind of screened cupboard that protected the meat from insects, pests, and vermin but did nothing to regulate temperature. Dry goods such as flour, sugar, and cornmeal were stored in crockery or wooden containers. Rural kitchens and those of families of lesser means were also likely to be more family oriented. They may well have been used for activities such as sewing or helping children with studies and would probably contain additional furnishings to suit their multiuse needs.

The bedroom of the 1860s was very different from that of the previous century. It was no longer a semi-public **The Bedrooms** place in which one received close acquaintances. It was now a very private place that would not even be referred to in polite conversation. Bed curtains had disappeared.

After her husband sent her some linen samples for bed linens, Elizabeth Blair Lee wrote, "The linen is wonderfully cheap—Cotton that width costs in the city $1, 25 cts & not of the best quality—that linen here would sell for $1, 50 to 60 cts . . . you could not do better to buy than buy two pairs— they will take about 11 yards—I have 12 prs of double linen sheets & two prs single . . . & two pairs of Blankets—for we cannot get any blankets here for less than six dollars. I would like one pair."[15]

Cribs and cradles were frequently found close to the parents' bed to facilitate breastfeeding and as a precaution should the child take ill during the night. Older children in lower economic situations might also sleep in the same room. Children of wealthy families would sleep in the nursery with their nanny.

Families who could afford it had a nursery for the children. As the 1860s progressed, children came to be **The Nursery** thought of as innocent beings in need of protection and sheltered from exposure to the world outside. The nursery provided this environment. It could limit the amount and kind of stimulation a child received and might possibly protect him or her from accidents and disease. Accidents and common childhood diseases claimed nearly half of all children before the age of five. Modest households had a single nursery room, often found on the third floor. Affluent households could afford both day and night nurseries. These rooms were designed to withstand the abuse children can inflict on furnishings. Walls were often whitewashed. Curtains were simple. There would be a table with several chairs, perhaps simple pine furniture bought for that purpose or cast-off furniture from other rooms. There were shelves and cupboards for books and toys and perhaps an armchair or two. Nurseries often doubled as schoolrooms and would also contain globes, maps, and perhaps a blackboard for instruction.

The Necessary   While wealthy families might have had inside plumbing and the accompanying bathroom facilities, most people had to make do with ceramic washbasins and pitchers on a washstand. Full baths were labor-intensive events that involved bringing up heated water from the kitchen to the bedchamber so that a compact metal tub could be filled. This relegated total-immersion baths to special occasions. Sponge baths were the more common occurrence. Outhouses were not convenient at night, so most bedrooms contained a covered chamberpot. Some chamberpots were hidden in various pieces of furniture (mostly chairs and stools), but some were merely stored beneath the bed until they were emptied into the slop jar in the morning.

Clothing was stored in chests of drawers and wardrobes. Built-in closets were just beginning to come into vogue in the 1860s. Beside the bed might be found a small table upon which to rest the chamber stick used to guide one to the bedroom upon retiring. Oil lamps were usually not found in bedrooms, as carrying an oil lamp with its liquid fuel from room to room was a dangerous endeavor. People did not sit in bed and read before sleeping, nor did they lounge about in their lingerie. Bedrooms were likely to be drafty places most of the year.

NOTES

1. Virginia Jeans Laas, ed., *Wartime Washington: Letters of Elizabeth Blair Lee* (Chicago: University of Illinois Press, 1991), 313.

2. Arthur Martine, *Martine's Hand-Book of Etiquette, and Guide to True Politeness* (New York: Dick & Fitzgerald, 1866), 113.

3. Ibid., 112–113.

4. Ibid., 116.

5. Ibid.

6. Ibid.

7. Richard Crawford, *The Civil War Songbook* (New York: Dover, 1977), v.

8. Patricia Anderson, "Romantic Strains of the Parlor Piano," *Victorian* 3, no. 3 (1997): 22.

9. Walton, 25.

10. Carte de visite in the authors' collection from Isaac S. Lachman, 984 North Second Street, Philadelphia.

11. Walton, 65.

12. Shirley Blotnick Moskow, *Emma's World: An Intimate Look at Lives Touched by the Civil War Era* (Far Hills, NJ: New Horizons Press, 1990), 68.

13. Laas, 212.

14. Catherine E. Beecher, *Miss Beecher's Domestic Receipt Book* (New York: Harper & Brothers, 1850), 253.

15. Laas, 313.

13

Leisure Time

One book, wisely selected and properly studied, can do more to improve the mind, and enrich the understanding, than skimming over the surface of an entire library.
—Reverend Doctor Joel Hawes, 1835

Literacy was quite high in Civil War America. In the South at least 70 percent of the white male population could read, **Literature** and in the North the ability to read may have run as high as 90 percent.[1] Prior to 1820, English texts, less expensive and more fashionable, had almost closed the literary market to American authors. The emergence of a new popularity of reading and writing among the middle class underpinned a new national interest in publishing and professional authorship. This circumstance was further fostered by the need to while away long hours of boredom created by the lack of normal social activities brought on by the war. Four types of reading material have been identified as popular with Civil War era readers: religious reading, purposeful (or instructive) reading, newspaper and magazine reading, and reading for escape. These categories, while somewhat arbitrary, can serve to describe the majority of the printed materials sought by nineteenth-century readers.[2]

Beginning in the second decade of the nineteenth century, the novel, the most popular form of escapism, was found to have a growing acceptance and appeal among the general reading public. Middle- and

News, information, and entertainment. The
importance of the printed word in nineteenth-
century America cannot be overestimated.

upper-class women have long been recognized as the chief consumers
of this literary form. So great was the popularity of the novel that it
drew criticism. As late as 1856 the *Code of Public Instruction* for the State
of New York recognized the "necessity" of excluding from all libraries
"novels, romances and other fictitious creations of the imagination, including a large proportion of the lighter literature of the day. The propriety of a peremptory and uncompromising exclusion of those
catch-penny, but revolting publications which cultivate the taste for the
marvelous, the tragic, the horrible and the supernatural . . . [is without]
the slightest argument." The code also expressed an "obvious" disgust
for works dealing with "pirates, banditti and desperadoes of every description."[3] A guide to propriety for mothers written by Lydia Child
decried "the profligate and strongly exciting works" found in the public
libraries. "The necessity of fierce excitement in reading is a sort of intel-

lectual intemperance" producing, in the estimation of the guide's author, "weakness and delirium" in women and young girls. The Pelham novels and the works of Byron, Edward Maturin, Matthew G. Lewis, and Ann Radcliffe were all identified as having "an unhealthy influence upon the soul" that should be avoided.[4]

Of these, the only meaningful name is that of Lord Byron, who, with Shakespeare and Charles Dickens, was among the most famous of British authors known to those outside of Britain. Mrs. Child does not identify her reason for including him in this list, but his collected works along with his letters and journals were available to most American readers in a multivolume edition. Byron typified the romantic movement in literature, and politically he was a "genuine and burning liberal." His advanced political views may have made him suspect.[5]

The "Pelham novels" referred to by Mrs. Child may be the works of Camden Pelham, who wrote *The Chronicles of Crime*, a series of memoirs and anecdotes about British criminals "from the earliest period to 1841." They were illustrated by H. K. Browne, the famous illustrator of Dickens' works who went by the pseudonym "Phiz." The historical novels of Irish American author Edward Maturin were particularly steeped in the romantic. They included *Montezuma, the Last of the Aztecs*, a brilliant, if overly impassioned, history; *Benjamin, the Jew of Granada*, set in fifteenth-century Moslem Spain; and *Eva, or the Isles of Life and Death*, a romance of twelfth-century England. One of his more fiery books was *Bianca*, a story of a passionate love between a woman from Italy and a man from Ireland.[6]

Ann Radcliffe's novels, many written in the late 1790s, were primarily "time-fillers for literarily inclined young women who had no children and did not care for society." Although she died in 1823, Mrs. Radcliffe was the main source of "horror stories with a twist" for nineteenth-century readers. The significance of her "horror-mongering" on later romantic literature can not be overestimated. Terror connoisseurs found her heroines melancholy, quick to weep, and endearingly practical. In *The Italian* she created a romantic villain who brought the physical aspects of terror to perfection. This villain, repelled by the enormity of his crime, but fascinated by the looming tragedy of his fate, was the basis for similar characters used by Maturin, Byron, Lewis, and Scott. Her last novel, released in 1826, was *Gaston de Blondeville*. Actually written in 1802, this work preceded Scott's first historical novels and attempted for the first time to paint an authentic historical picture.[7]

Almost totally forgotten today, Matthew G. Lewis was a follower of Mrs. Radcliffe whose writings "ran heavily to the florid romantic." His first novel, *Ambrosio, the Monk*, was universally read and widely condemned in Britain and America. Lewis was charged with being immoral and irreligious when it was discovered that he was recommending that certain passages from the Bible be kept from the young. His work was considered "vicious" and "terrible." Often referred to as the "immoral monk Lewis," he was a man of genuine philanthropy and humane instincts. After inheriting a plantation in Jamaica along with 500 black slaves, Lewis instituted a series of reforms that were "regarded as mad" by his contemporaries. He attested to their effectiveness in *The Journal of a West India Proprietor*, which was published just before his death from yellow fever. Besides several dramas, Lewis produced two romantic novels—*The Bravo of Venice* and *Feudal Tyrants*—as well as *Tales of Terror* and *Romantic Tales*, which were based on German and Spanish legends; and in collaboration with Scott, a collection of ballads, *Tales of Wonder*. His work is generally neglected today, but he had tremendous influence on the romantic writers of his day.[8]

Like Mrs. Child, the Reverend Doctor Joel Hawes similarly warned young men that in the choice of books there was a "great need of caution." He believed that a person's character could be "ruined by reading a single volume." Yet he confessed that one book, "wisely selected and properly studied," could "do more to improve the mind, and enrich the understanding, than skimming over the surface of an entire library."[9]

Notwithstanding such warnings, novels remained popular, and the potency of this literature to govern the mind of readers proved to have not been underestimated by the good reverend. Fictional characters possessed a remarkable ability to influence nineteenth-century readers. Uncle Tom, Topsy, Ivanhoe, Hawkeye, Hester Prynne, and Ebenezer Scrooge were deeply familiar characters to a society that read as much as nineteenth-century Americans did. These characters often seemed to become nearly as real and as influential to the reader as actual friends and relations.[10]

The works of the English novelist and social commentator Charles Dickens were widely read in America. In Dickens' very popular works both sections of the country found some character, situation, or condition that seemed to bolster the very different views of modern society Americans held. Many social reformers, like Dickens himself, championed the cause of the poor. Nonetheless, Dickens was generally unconcerned with the economic aspects of social reform, choosing rather to deal with an increased appreciation of the value of the human being. Ignorance, for him, was the great cause of human misery. In 1843 he gave a speech in the city of Manchester in which he pleaded for a heightened sense of humanitarianism and an improvement in the system of public education in Britain. In contrast to the "ragged schools" that had been set up by well-meaning but untrained volunteer teachers to give England's poor children the rudiments of an education, Dickens proposed that the surest improvement in the nation's future was tied to a public investment in education sponsored by the government.

Dickens' stories emphasized the need to change traditional ways of thinking. But many in the South misread Dickens' message and saw the misfortune, destitution, and disease that fills his works as characteristic of all urban life. Modern urban life was the great evil haunting the romantic domains of the Southern imagination. Dickens' novels mirrored the inevitable bleak future of America if Northern concepts of social progress continued to be implemented as English ones had for decades without noticeably improving society.

Although thoroughly English in its setting and personalities, *A Christmas Carol*, first published in 1843, seemed to embody the very limitations of modern society in mid-century in the interactions of Scrooge with the other characters. The story portrays a secular rather than a traditionally religious attitude toward the holidays. The spirits and ghosts of Christmas are remarkably worldly in their appearance and temporal in their outlook. The awakening of a social conscience in Scrooge is their chief endeavor. Ultimately it is the specter of an unlamented death, a topic of great concern in the nineteenth century, that brings Scrooge around. Yet even a morally awakened Scrooge refuses to devote his life to social work. Instead, he acts out his reformation on a very personal level.[11]

Southerners despised such ambiguous social remedies as the poorhouses and the workhouses that filled Dickens' pages. The debtors' prison of *Little Dorrit* and the orphanage of *Oliver Twist* were obviously not sufficient to solve the social ills of an urban society. Southerners were left with a portrait of cities, like those of the North, veritably teeming with the exploited masses from which they chose to be separated.[12]

Apologists for the Southern way of life proclaimed that Scrooge's treatment of Bob Cratchit emphasized the abuses possible in an age governed by the "work for wage" system that so lacked a sense of personal involvement and family dedication. The personal responsibility many Southerners felt toward their neighbors, their workers, and even their slaves seemed noble in contrast to the socially anonymous caretaking for the unfortunates found in Dickens' works.

Southern intellectuals of the prewar period were also widely read in the literature of European romanticism, and they used romantic allusions freely in their writing. Confederate General John B. Gordon, who rose to popular prominence when badly wounded at the Battle of Antietam, was described as being "pure as Galahad, knightly as King Arthur . . . [and] as brave as Lancelot . . . a Chevalier Bayard."[13] Southern papers spoke of heroics and crusades. The Richmond *Southern Illustrated News* reported the final minutes of General George Pickett's charge at Gettysburg as "noble and gallant."[14]

The most popular book of the war period was *Les Miserables*. This was closely followed by Tennyson's 1864 narrative poem *Enoch Arden*, in which a shipwrecked sailor returns home to find that his wife, thinking him dead, has remarried. Sir Walter Scott's Waverley novels were immensely popular. Their theme of the Scottish struggle to throw off the dominance and oppression of the English served as an analogy for the position in which the South saw itself with respect to the North. Scott's use of romantic characters, lords and ladies, knights in armor, and grand estates was particularly resonant with the Southern image of itself. So familiar was Scott's work to Southerners that in later years Mark Twain only half-jokingly blamed Scott for causing the Civil War.

Second only to Scott's in popularity were the American adventure novels of James Fenimore Cooper. Although his first novel was poorly accepted by American readers, largely because it imitated the British form, Cooper's second work, *The Spy*, published in 1822, was an outstanding success. Cooper's subsequent novels emphasized American manners and scenes as interesting and important. Still, many Americans considered novels to be "trivial, feminine, and vaguely dishonorable" because they appealed to the emotions and aroused the imagination. Nonetheless, Cooper found that there was a great demand for adventure tales derived from the Revolution, and his writing was sufficiently manly and moral to find acceptance by a wide audience.[15]

Like Scott, Cooper promoted a social vision of a stable and genteel society governed by its natural aristocracy, "perpetuating property, order, and liberty" as represented by a reunited American gentry. That this view resonated with the Southern image of itself would have upset Cooper, with his very Northern attitudes. *The Pioneers*, Cooper's third book, was dedicated to the proposition that the American republic, poised on the verge of "demagoguery, deceit, hypocrisy, and turmoil," could be transformed into a stable, prosperous, and just society. Although the theme of "reconciliation . . . on conservative terms" was almost three decades old, Cooper's novels were very popular with the soldiers, mainly because of their masculine adventure themes, and were often found among their most prized possessions. Dog-eared copies circulated through the camps and were often read aloud around the campfire to eager audiences.

A federal officer, Captain John W. De Forest, found himself "a tolerably instructed man, having read *The Book of the Indians*, all of Cooper's novels, and some of the works of Captain Mayne Reid." Reid was a close friend of Edgar Allan Poe, and his novels were mainly adventure stories. Beginning in 1850, he published *The Rifle Rangers: Adventures of an Officer in Southern Mexico*, which was based on his own service in the 1846 war; *The Scalp Hunters; The War Trail*; and *Forest Exiles*. In 1853 he wrote a novel inspired by his fifteen-year-old spouse, appropriately titled *The Child Wife*, and in 1856 he wrote a play called *The Quadroon*. De Forest reported that he inexplicably found his thoughts "ranging from the expectation of a [musket] ball through the spine to a recollection of Coo-

THE

WILD MAN OF THE WEST.

A Tale of the Rocky Mountains.

BY

R. M. BALLANTYNE,

AUTHOR OF "THE RED ERIC," ETC.

BOSTON:
CROSBY AND NICHOLS.
NEW YORK: OLIVER S. FELT, 36 WALKER STREET.
1864.

THE NARROW ESCAPE.

The title page of a popular adventure novel from 1864. Similar works drew
criticism from more conservative quarters of society.

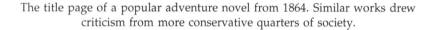

per's most celebrated Indians" while under fire during the siege of Port
Hudson.[16]

Nathaniel Hawthorne, convinced that most American literature ran too
close to the British style, devoted himself to a uniquely symbolic and
allegorical form. *The Scarlet Letter*, published in 1850, was certainly familiar to American readers, and its author was considered a literary giant. But Hawthorne's persistent dark emphasis on guilt and sorrow ran
counter to the popular tastes and religious sentiment of Americans at
mid-century. In 1851 and 1852, respectively, he published *The House of
the Seven Gables* and *The Blithedale Romance*. This last was a study of failed
utopian efforts to improve society. He served as the U.S. Consul at Liv-
erpool, England, for four years, and was photographed by Mathew
Brady before his death in 1864.

When Harriet Beecher Stowe published *Uncle Tom's Cabin* in 1852, the
book sold 300,000 copies in America and Britain in one year. Mrs.
Stowe's work was one of total fiction; it stressed the evils of slavery and
presented a picture of total brutality. Mrs. Stowe had no personal knowledge of slavery. The factual basis for the story was Theodore D. Weld's
radical abolitionist tract entitled *Slavery as It Is: The Testimony of a Thousand Witnesses*, which was published in 1839. *Uncle Tom's Cabin* was im-

mensely more effective in preaching the anti-slavery message in the form of a novel than the earlier tract had ever dreamed of being.

The South considered Mrs. Stowe's work a slander and regarded it as abolitionist propaganda. A Southern woman, familiar with slavery and slaves, wrote that she could not read a book so filled with distortions as it was "too sickening" to think that any man would send "his little son to beat a human being tied to a tree." The same woman goes on to suggest, using other literary references, that Mrs. Stowe's work portrays as much fiction as Squeers beating Smike in Dickens' *Nicholas Nickleby* or the gouging of Gloucester's eyes in Shakespeare's *King Lear*. "How delightfully pharisaic a feeling it must be, to rise up superior and fancy [to] we [who] are so degraded as to defend and like to live with such degraded creatures around us . . . as Legree."[17]

Nonetheless, amicably disposed Northerners found the passages describing the murderous brutality of Simon Legree indicative of the typical behavior of Southern slaveowners. The significance of the story, as of many of the attacks on the institution of slavery, lay in its ability to dramatize and emotionalize the issue. Writing and speech making on the subject of slavery in particular—and of the Southern culture in general—were becoming increasingly stereotypical, and the stereotypes, even when presented in novels, were taking on a reality in the minds of the people.

Although soldiers were quick to write home about finishing *Nicholas Nickelby*, *The Pickwick Papers*, *The Deerslayer*, *Ivanhoe*, or other works of obvious quality, they also read a great deal of low-quality material. Many of these works have been identified. They include such masculine titles as *Con Cregan*, *Gold Friend*, *The Quadroon of Louisiana*, *Son of the Wilderness*, *Scar Chief the Wild Halfbreed*, *Wild West Scenes*, and *Our Own Heroes*, but also more popular works such as *Lady Audley's Secret*, *The Mystery*, *Macaria*, and *Louisa Elton*.[18]

Soldiers, "burdened by huge blocks of time during which they have nothing to do but wait," were suddenly possessed of an abundant amount of time to read which "had previously been in short supply to American men." Of the five most common leisure-time camp activities—individual foraging, gambling, sleeping, talking, and reading—only reading was seen to be "a positive force" for the improvement of the troops.[19]

American books were in large supply for the first time during the war. In 1834 fewer than 500 titles were published in the United States. By 1862 this number had grown to almost 4,000.[20] By coincidence the first "dime novels" were published in June 1860. These were inexpensive paperbound adventure stories. The first title, *Malaeska, the Indian Wife of the White Hunter*, by Ann Stephens, makes it abundantly clear that this was escapist literature of the lowest class. Publisher Irwin P. Beadle's dime novels and their many imitators initiated a whole era of cheap publishing just eight months prior to the war.[21]

At the time there were a number of distinguished American authors of an age to serve in the field and provide a firsthand professional description of the face of war. Theodore Winthrop had written a number of successful books prior to the war, and he volunteered to serve. Unfortunately, Winthrop was killed in one of the first engagements of the war at Great Bethel in June 1861.

Another young author distinguished before the outbreak of hostilities was John W. De Forest. From 1851 through 1859 De Forest wrote several books, including the *History of the Indians of Connecticut* and the novels *Witching Times, Oriental Acquaintance, European Acquaintance*, and *Seacliff*. De Forest went to war as a captain with the 12th Connecticut Volunteers. Many of his battlefield reports were printed by *Harper's Monthly*, and in 1864 he wrote *Miss Ravenel's Conversion from Secession to Loyalty*. In these De Forest shared the simple truth of life in the army and on the battlefield.[22]

The enormous hunger for reading material in the camps was supplied to some extent by social and religious agencies which recognized the need. In part the soldiers and their comrades found their own supply of reading material, but both armies were largely at the mercy of outside sources for their books and newspapers. Much of the work involved in providing books to the troops was done by the U.S. Christian Commission, which supplied both religious and secular reading material. Almost 1 million Bibles were distributed to the troops, and more than 30,000 other volumes were circulated through a system of almost 300 portable libraries. Each contained from 70 to 125 volumes which were transported and stored in wooden, shelved boxes about three feet square. Many of the books were printed in smaller than standard size and included classical titles as well as history, poetry, science, philosophy, and religion. The Confederate Bible Society and the South Carolina Tract Society provided religious works for the Southern troops, but the South had no system of portable libraries.[23]

There were millions of newspaper subscribers in the country on the eve of the war, and the papers were par- **Newspapers** ticularly adept at bringing the war to the homefront.[24] People wanted to know what was happening to their friends and relations on faraway battlefields, and they looked to newspapers such as *Leslie's* or *Harper's* to make sense of the confusion of war reports. New York publisher Frank Leslie produced amazingly moving woodcut illustrations for his *Illustrated Newspaper* from 1861 through 1865. His use of graphics and terse prose to interpret ongoing news events was a new concept in the American newspaper business that was quickly adopted by other news agencies. In a day when a partisan press was the rule,

There was no lack of illustrated newspapers in Civil
War America, but the quality of their artwork was
not consistent.

Leslie's stood apart. Except for tolerating anti-Irish sentiment and portraying Negroes in a stereotypical and condescending manner, *Leslie's*
condoned little that was political.

Frank Leslie, whose true name was Henry Carter, had emigrated from
Britain in 1848. There he had worked as an engraver for the *Illustrated
London News*, which was the first newspaper to employ graphics. In London Leslie learned the processes for turning pencil sketches into woodcut
engravings that could be transferred to newsprint. In 1852 P. T. Barnum,
the famed American showman, developed a process by which the sketch
was divided into several pieces to be engraved on as many blocks by
individual engravers, then carefully assembled into a single printing surface.[25] Leslie was hired by Barnum as a supervising engraver for the
short-lived *Illustrated News*. Leaving Barnum, by 1854 he had set up his
own organization and published the first issue of *Frank Leslie's Ladies'
Gazette of Paris, London, and New York*, one of the first illustrated fashion
magazines in America. This was quickly followed by the *Illustrated Newspaper* in 1855. Leslie employed more than 130 engraving and print artists
as well as a substantial number of roving sketch artists.

Frank Leslie introduced a number of papers to Civil War readers: the *Illustrated Zeitung*, a German-language edition aimed at the German immigrant population of the North; the *Budget of Fun*, a whimsical publication featuring cheap fiction; the *Ten Cent Monthly*; the *Lady's Illustrated Almanac*; and the *Lady's Magazine and Gazette of Fashion*. All of these bore his name: *Frank Leslie's*.

Within four years two independent graphic news weeklies were launched in competition with Leslie's newspaper empire: *Harper's Weekly* and the *New York Illustrated News*. Fletcher Harper, the well-financed publisher from Harper and Brothers, actively tried to recruit Leslie's artists and engravers, and aggressively tried to exceed Leslie's circulation. Leslie provided poor and erratic pay for his artists, many of whom he lost to competitors. By the opening of the war the two newspapers were within 10,000 copies of one another, with the *New York Illustrated News* a distant third.

Two of the best sketch artists of the period were the brothers William and Alfred Waud. William worked for *Leslie's* and Alfred for *Harper's*. William proved particularly adept at ingratiating himself with the social elite of South Carolina during the secession crisis. Because of the paper's uncommitted stance, wherever Waud traveled he found individuals to be cooperative and helpful. Leslie instructed him to use the utmost care in making his sketches and to avoid giving any indication of political sympathies toward one side or the other. Nonetheless, Waud left *Leslie's* in 1863 to work at *Harper's* with brother Alfred and another fine artist, Theodore Davis.

William Waud's genius and discretion were matched by an army of artists who continued to be employed by *Leslie's*, including Eugene Benson, a young artist who eagerly went to the front to record the visual images of battle; Arthur Lumley, who was hired to follow the Army of the Potomac full-time; Henry Lovie, who found his fame in sketching George B. McClellan; C. S. Hall and F. H Schell, who recorded the war in northern Virginia; F. B. Schell, who covered the Vicksburg campaign; and Edwin Forbes, who stayed with the Army of the Potomac until 1864 and became Leslie's most prolific artist. This twenty-two-year-old artist followed the federal army from 1862. Forbes was not interested in the great generals and battles of the war, but rather in the day-to-day activities and lifestyle of the soldiers. So well drawn were Forbes' sketches that "readers . . . scanned the drawings in *Leslie's* for familiar faces."[26]

Reporting from the battlefield was exacting and dangerous work. Many artists fell ill with the same maladies that afflicted the troops. Two of Leslie's artists were captured and released by Lee, and one part-time artist, James O'Niell, was killed in combat. C.E.F. Hillen was badly wounded in the Atlanta campaign. They often found it difficult to get their sketches from the battlefield to the engravers. *Leslie's* failed to have a correspondent with Sherman on his campaign to the sea, while *Harper's* artists accompanied the general. Consequently, by 1864 *Harper's* and other Northern journals had surged ahead of *Leslie's* in circulation.[27]

The quality of the sketches by battlefield artists was not always reproduced faithfully by the engravers, and in viewing these graphic scenes great care must be taken. What the artist drew was not so much reproduced as copied. Though the artists accompanied the army and witnessed battles, they were often in a hurry to get their work back to the engravers. Unfinished sketches of prominent figures in the scene with backgrounds and lines of soldiers "roughed in" and labeled as "trees here" or "artillery battery here" were often sent off to the engravers to be filled by hands whose eyes had never seen battle. In many cases this made the scene more one created by imagination than reality. The results were sometimes unfortunate. As a consequence the contemporary accounts of the war were far from accurately illustrated.[28]

The South had been generally dependent on Northern publishers to print its books and newspapers. In the entire South there was only one type factory, no facilities for printing maps, and an entire inability to make inexpensive wood-pulp paper. In 1860 a well-illustrated magazine such as *Harper's* or *Leslie's* could not be published in the South. The *Southern Illustrated News* and other papers were often limited to a single sheet of newsprint. These publications made an attempt to mimic *Harper's* and *Leslie's* with crude engravings but were obviously not comparable to the Northern news outlets.[29]

Moreover, the Confederate mails were two to three times more expensive than those in the North, severely limiting circulation. Even soldiers at the front had to pay to have newspapers and mail brought to them, and by 1864 the Confederate postal system had so completely broken down that thousands of personal letters remained undelivered. The inability of the Confederacy to establish and maintain an information system based on the printed word rather than hearsay and word of mouth had no little effect on the deterioration of Southern morale. Nonetheless, patriotic Southerners bombarded their newspapers with so much unsolicited poetry on national themes that some publications began charging to print it. Newspapers like the *Montgomery Daily Advertiser* were particularly successful in creating a wide public identification with the stirring events of the winter and spring of 1861.[30]

Availability of Reading Material   The upper classes were particularly well positioned to enjoy the pleasures of books and writing and had greater access to the printed word than the rest of the Southern population. Consequently, the aristocratic plantation owners came to share a sense of cultural commonality through their newspapers and popular literature, while the rest of the population received its information chiefly from conversation, verbal discussion, and religious exhortation.[31]

What people read during the war was dependent on what was available. In the Northern urban centers there was an almost unlimited amount and variety of reading material, so what was read in the South becomes more interesting. Southern civilians had their literary choices disrupted not only by the vagaries of the war, but also by the blockade. Newspapers printed what was available. Confederate battlefield heroes and other men of prominence were given front-page treatment. The boredom of battle reports, advertisements, and political tracts was broken, for example, when the personal letters of federal general Custer to a young woman were captured. The Richmond papers printed them and provided "some spicy reading" for the ladies.[32]

Books were read, reread, and loaned among friends and acquaintances. Many women and men turned to instructive reading, spending time with books on history, geography, painting, foreign languages, surveying, and needlework. A number of books were available on etiquette, manners, propriety, the rearing of children, husbandry, and oratory. There was a renewed interest in the Bible and religious tracts, the plays of Shakespeare, and the novels of Dickens, Scott, and Cooper.

A Virginia judge, Nathaniel B. Tucker, had turned secessionist and dedicated a novel to the cause of Virginian secession in 1830. Entitled *The Partisan Leader*, the novel portrayed a unionized but unhappy Virginia in the evil grasp of Northern masters while a newly seceded and independent Southern confederacy enjoyed freedom and prosperity. While the author did not survive to see disunion, his novel became the subject of a popular Southern literary revival.

New works were scarce in the South. Nonetheless, several popular works were printed. In 1863 the Richmond *Southern Illustrated News* offered $1,000 cash to the author of the "best illustrated romance to be submitted to them between the present date and October 1 next." Many novels first appeared as serials in weekly newspapers, to be published in book form only after their popularity had been established. This had been true of the works of Dickens in England and of Stowe in America.[33]

Although authorship by women was generally frowned upon before 1850, several novels were written by Southern **Women Writers** women in the period. Women who practiced the profession of letters seem to have been viewed with less disapprobation than those who became teachers, nurses, or lawyers. Several women were acclaimed in the Southern press for their published work. The great sensation of the Southern literary world seems to have been a novel by Augusta Jane Evans, published in 1864 and entitled *Macaria, or Altars of Sacrifice*. The author dedicated this novel, about a pair of heroines sacrificing their romantic love for dedication to the cause, to the Confederate forces.[34]

Photography The photographers who documented the Crimean War from 1854 to 1856 would be very upset to hear that the Civil War was the first to be photographed. It was not. Nor was it the first to use observation balloons, telegraphy, rifled muskets, repeating weapons, or railroads. All of these "firsts" are reserved for European wars. Yet the Civil War was the first American war to use these advances so extensively.

Hundreds of wartime photographs of the Civil War are available, and periodically new ones are found. Photographs of wartime battlefields and personalities were shown in galleries in the major cities of the North. The photographic galleries in New York and Washington in particular were very popular, and admission was expensive. The pictures, including some of the first to show war dead on the battlefield, were poignant, and may have helped to create antiwar feeling in the North. The wet plate process used in taking them was very slow and precluded any action shots. Unfortunately, some of the pictures of battlefield dead were staged by photographers who arrived days after the conflict when most of the bodies were buried. Northern photographers arriving at Gettysburg found the Confederate dead to be more available for their work, as the Federals had buried their own dead first. As a consequence, members of the burial detail were asked to pose as Federal war dead, which they did, sprawling in grotesque positions on the rocks of Little Round Top and the Devil's Den.

Mathew Brady is possibly the best known photographer of the period. People flocked to his studios to have photographic portraits taken in their best clothes. Cartes de visite were possibly the most popular form of civilian photograph. Thousands of such wartime photos exist. Several "cabinet photos" of Abraham Lincoln (on the order of 5" X 8") were taken by Brady. However, very few "Brady" battlefield photographs were actually taken by him. Brady was practically blind and wore dark blue glasses to protect his eyes from the light. His assistants, sent out in photographic wagons with their wet glass plates, took most of the extraordinary pictures that were credited to his studio.

One of these assistants, Alexander Gardner, left Brady's employ and struck out on his own. Gardner is said to have taken almost 75 percent of the extant photographs of the Army of the Potomac. Gardner served the army by photographically reproducing maps and other documents. By the war's end, Gardner had displaced Brady as the leading American photographer, and it was he who photographed the Lincoln funeral procession and the trial of the assassination conspirators.

Another Brady assistant was George N. Bernard, whose first war photographs were taken of the Manassas battlefield in 1862. Breaking with

The carte de visite was a popular form of
photography. The wedding photo on the left is
particularly unusual, as the bride has a white
wedding dress. This reflects a relatively new fashion
at that time yet to be embraced by a majority of
women.

Brady in 1863, he moved to the western theater of war to document
Sherman's march from Tennessee through Georgia and to the sea. He
was the official photographer of the Military Department of the Mississippi.[35]

Captain Andrew J. Russell, noted for his Union Pacific photographs
after the war, was also an official army photographer during the war.
As such he is the only such soldier-photographer of the period. Russell's
duties included photographing the work of the Army Engineers and the
reconstruction of damaged railways in order to create a visual record for
the use of similar units in the future.[36]

The South also had its photographers. George S. Cook, J. D. Edwards,
and A. D. Lytle were able photographers committed to the Southern
cause, but their work was much more circumspect than that of their
fellows from the North, being generally limited to portraiture. The
South's limited technical facilities forced the public to be content with
rough woodcuts and engravings. Lytle pulled off one of the great espionage feats of the war. Concealing himself, he was able to get two photos
of General Benjamin Grierson's 1,700-man Northern cavalry encamping
on their raid from Vicksburg to Baton Rouge.[37]

Almost no technology existed for reproducing photographs for the print media. The usual way of reproducing a photograph for a newspaper or magazine was to have an artist redraw it and make a woodcut or engraving, as was done with battlefield sketches. This process neutralized most of the advantages of photography for the newspapers. Only original prints were available to the public, and since enlargement equipment was as yet in a formative stage of development, prints were almost always made by placing the glass plate negative in contact with the photosensitive paper and exposing them to the sun. This results in a "contact print" the same size as the glass plate negative.

Optical Novelties
Americans seem to have enjoyed a variety of optical phenomena in their drawing rooms and parlors. Some photographs were stereotypes, two simultaneously recorded images set side by side, giving a three-dimensional view when seen through a viewer designed for the purpose, known as a stereoscope or stereopticon. Such devices go back to 1838, and stereotypes of period places, buildings, monuments, and naval vessels predominate. Very few stereotypes of battle dead survive, and no stereotypes of the poor or of the squalid condition of the nation's slums are known. Photographers understood that to sell their pictures they would have to appeal to well-heeled customers who did not wish to be reminded of the nation's failures.[38]

Propelled by a fascination with photography, optical novelties were very much in vogue. The magic lantern had been around for over 200 years, used by showmen and hucksters to beguile audiences with mystical images. It consisted of a metal box into which an oil lamp was placed; a polished metal reflector which focused the light on a painted slide; and a hole with a lens through which the light was projected. These lanterns were notably improved as a result of photographic discoveries, and their use became widespread. Lanterns were used by lecturers to enhance their presentations, and they became very popular as a parlor toy to show comic pictures. A number of hand-colored glass slides of the war have recently been restored.

Another optical curiosity was the zoetrope. This consisted of a revolving drum with equally spaced slits around the sides. The interior of the drum contained a series of sequential pictures. The pictures were taken by a series of still cameras activated by trip wires. Walking men and running horses were prominent subjects of the zoetrope. When the drum was rotated, the pictures gave the impression that they were moving. Because it could be viewed by many people at one time, the zoetrope enjoyed popularity as a parlor amusement.

A similar device was the phantascope. This simple contrivance was comprised of a cardboard disc with a series of slits equally spaced around the center and a handle that acted as a pivot around which the phantascope was rotated. The reverse side contained a series of pictures set between the slits. When the operator held the device in front of a mirror and rotated the disc, the pictures appeared to be moving.

The decade beginning in 1860 spawned an abundance of cultural institutions in the North and West. War involve- **Cultural** ment and subsequent poverty retarded a similar movement **Institutions** in the South for almost twenty years. The interest in art, music, literature, and nature that permeated the parlor surged forth, creating museums, symphonies, libraries, and parks. These, in turn, engendered a plethora of ancillary institutions such as literary societies, study groups, and reading clubs.

These organizations were gender specific. Male organizations attracted businessmen and professionals. In addition to the obvious activities such organizations would conduct, they created a venue which was ripe for the founding of additional social projects. The distaff version of these clubs provided activities for middle- and upper-class women beyond domestic and church endeavors. The clubs furnished an arena for women to pursue their intellectual development. Study clubs met twice monthly for ten months a year to discuss such topics as literature, history, and art. Meetings commonly were held in members' homes and consisted of conversation, presentation of papers, and subsequent discussions.

Many civilians, particularly the women who were doomed to sit out the war while their husbands and lovers fought, **Reading** found reading one of the few sources of entertainment avail- **Clubs** able to them. Like their loved ones in the army camps, many women read in groups and met regularly to do so. Books were frequently read aloud, making it possible to share the books and newspapers that were "all too scarce in the print-starved Confederacy." Even in the North, where books were widely available, oral presentation by an articulate reader often enhanced the literature and allowed the majority of the women to do other chores such as sewing and embroidery. Reading aloud became an activity with many of the characteristics of theater. Books provided women with an almost pure escape from the realities of war, suffering, and death. More important, oral presentation discouraged continual war gossip among the women, and the camaraderie of the group helped to alleviate depression and gloom among those who were without loved ones, displaced from their homes, and anxious about their own futures.[39]

To some extent, literary society or study club meetings took the place of the public lectures that had enjoyed tremendous **Lectures** popularity from about 1840 forward. The war had interrupted many lecture series, which were curtailed, and in some cases suspended. Lectures had been particularly popular among ambitious young men, many of whom joined their cause on the battleline. Northerners demanded that the remaining lecturers make their concern matters related to the conflict. Topics sought by lecture audiences included denunciations of the South, glorification of Union causes, and narrations detailing the reforms that would follow the Northern victory. Popular speakers included Senator Charles Sumner, Major General Cassius Clay, Theodore Tilton, and Wendell Phillips.

Games

Games have always been popular in America. One popular game was solitaire, played on a circular board containing thirty-three holes. Marbles or pegs were placed in all but the center hole. A peg was moved forward, backward, or sideways, but not diagonally, over an adjacent peg, which was then removed from the board. The game ended when the remaining pegs could not make a move. The object of the game was to have only a single peg remaining, preferably in the center hole.

Board games were just coming into their own in America. Most board game publishers were located in the Northeast, particularly in Boston and New York. "The Mansion of Happiness, an Instructive Moral and Entertaining Amusement" is generally acknowledged as the first board game published in the United States. This 1843 game closely resembles the formerly imported "The Game of Goose," but had a distinctly moral message. Players landing on squares marked "gratitude" or "honesty" advanced more rapidly toward their goal. "The Game of Goose" was a board game distinguished by an elaborate spiral containing sixty-three squares. Players rolled the dice and advanced along the board, incurring a variety of changes in fortune involving penalties and bonuses. The game dated from the eighteenth century and served as inspiration for a host of imitators.

American board makers copied other games as well. "The Game of Pope and Pagan, or the Siege of the Stronghold of Satan by the Christian Army" and "Mohamet and Saladin, or the Battle for Palestine" were both based on the centuries-old game fox and geese. Other published games took the form of card games and included, "Dr. Busby," "Yankee Trader," "Uncle Tom's Cabin," "Heroes," "Master Redbury and His Pupils," and "Trades." The last of these consisted of lithographed cards; some depicted such tradesmen as shoemakers, farriers, and taxgatherers, and others showed the symbols of each trade. The object of the game was to collect tricks which matched the tradesman and the symbol. It is thought that this game served as the inspiration for the very popular English game "Happy Families."

Other popular games included cribbage, checkers, tangrams, and lotto—a forerunner of bingo—which was played with cards of three horizontal and nine vertical rows. Five numbers from one to ninety appeared on the cards, with the remaining spaces blank. Children's versions of the game were developed to teach spelling, multiplication, botany, and history.

Craft projects appeared regularly in many ladies'
magazines. This pair is from an issue of *Peterson's
Magazine.*

Women engaged in a variety of needlework crafts including
tatting, knitting, crocheting, and netting. Ladies' magazines car- **Ladies'**
ried a profusion of patterns for trims, fashion accessories, and **Crafts**
small household items that could be made using these handi-
crafts. Patchwork quilts were another popular activity. Women worked
on quilts alone for their families and in group quilting bees as community activities. Prior to the war, groups of Northern women used their
quilting talents to raise money for the cause of abolition. They renamed
some traditional patchwork patterns to draw attention to the cause. Job's
Tears became known as Slave Chain. Jacob's Ladder became Under-

ground Railway. North Star was so named after the star that guided runaway slaves to freedom. Once the war commenced, Northern women mobilized relief efforts and began to produce quilts to be sent to soldiers in need. U.S. Sanitary Commission records show that an estimated 250,000 quilts were distributed during the war. In Hartford, Connecticut, alone, 5,459 quilts were collected during 1864.[40]

Many of the quilts were more utilitarian than those their makers had created in the past, but it is likely that they were made with no less love. To one quilt was pinned this note: "My son is in the army. Whoever is made warm by this quilt, which I have worked on for six days and most of six nights, let him remember his mother's love." Confederate women also made quilts for soldiers. The Southern blockade, however, severely limited the availability of the requisite materials. Confederate quilts produced during the war were made from whatever makeshift materials were available, including old sheets stuffed with newspaper.[41]

NOTES

1. David Kaser, *Books and Libraries in Camp and Battle: The Civil War Experience* (Westport: Greenwood Press, 1984), 3. In 1830 Alexis de Tocqueville reported that he could not find a man in Connecticut who could not read.

2. Ibid., 14.

3. V. M. Rice, *Code of Public Instruction* (Albany: State Printing Office, 1856), 325.

4. Lydia M. Child, *The Mother's Book* (Boston: Applewood, 1831), 93–94.

5. Stanley J. Kunitz, ed., *British Authors of the Nineteenth Century* (New York: Wilson, 1936), 105–106.

6. See *Antiquarian Books*, http://home.navisoft.com/blackstn/crime.htm; and E. A. Duyckinck, *Cyclopedia of American Literature* (Detroit: Gale Research, 1965).

7. Kunitz, 511–512.

8. Ibid., 383–384.

9. Joel Hawes, *Lectures to Young Men on the Formation of Character* (Hartford: 1835), 144–158.

10. Drew Gilpin Faust, *Mother of Invention: Women of the Slaveholding South in the American Civil War* (Charlotte: University of North Carolina Press, 1996), 154.

11. Tim Halliman, *A Christmas Carol Christmas Book* (New York: IBM, 1984), 111.

12. Ibid.

13. Lewis, 110.

14. "Major General George E. Pickett," *Southern Illustrated News*, August 1, 1863, 26.

15. Alan Taylor, "Fenimore Cooper's America," *History Today* 46, no. 2 (February 1996): 21–27.

16. Croushore, 130–131. See Duyckinck.

17. C. V. Woodward, 245, 307, 381.

18. Kaser, 18, 36.

19. Ibid., 13.

20. Fite, 256n.

21. Kaser, 4, 5; James Morgan, "Send No Trash: Books, Libraries, and Reading During the Civil War," *Camp Chase Gazette*, July 1992, 32.

22. Croushore, vii.

23. Morgan, 32–36.

24. Lawrence A. Cremin, *American Education: The National Experience, 1783–1876* (New York: Harper, 1980), 409.

25. Careful scrutiny of such prints can reveal the boundaries between the individual blocks.

26. Edwin Forbes, *Civil War Etchings* (1876; reprint, New York: Dover, 1994), preface. Forbes may have been the archetype of the young reporter featured in the TV miniseries *The Blue and the Gray.*

27. John E. Stanchak, ed., *Leslie's Illustrated Civil War* (1894; reprint, Jackson: University Press of Mississippi, 1992), v–xii.

28. The lack of widespread circulation of these photographs in newspapers may have been fortunate, as there was no need to add additional fuel to the growing antiwar sentiment in the North.

29. Faust, *Creation of Confederate Nationalism*, 17.

30. Ibid., 8.

31. Ibid., 16.

32. Lewis, 86.

33. *Southern Illustrated News*, August 1, 1863, 28.

34. Faust, *Mothers of Invention*, 168–178.

35. George N. Barnard, *Photographic Views of Sherman's Campaigns* (1866; reprint, New York: Dover, 1977), preface.

36. Andrew J. Russell, *Russell's Civil War Photographs* (New York: Dover, 1982), preface.

37. Francis Trevelyan Miller, ed., *The Photographic History of the Civil War: Soldier Life and the Secret Service* (1911; reprint, New York: Castle, 1957), 30.

38. Alexander Gardner, *Photographic Sketchbook of the Civil War* (1866; New York; reprint, Dover, 1959), preface.

39. Faust, *Mothers of Invention*, 153–154, 156.

40. Roderick Kiracofe, *The American Quilt* (New York: Clarkson Potter, 1993), 109.

41. Ibid., 119.

14

Feast or Famine:
Food and Cooking

"Cold milk, thick with cream, from a dairy on the side of the mountain, fresh venison steaks, the whitest bread and the tenderest broiled chicken reveling in the sweetest butter. No king fared better than that."

—Cornelia Peake McDonald

The Civil War brought developments that would alter the patterns of American eating from home cooking to professional cooking, and from country cooking to city cooking. The seeds of these changes had already been sown as the war approached, but the dynamics of the conflict acted to speed their growth. The war may have retarded the growth of conveniences for civilians, but when it came to providing food for the armies, it drove the technology. Specifically, three major agents of change were at work: improvement in refrigeration, increased speed of transportation, and industrialization of food processing. These served to vastly increase the variety of foods available to Americans.

Food storage in the mid-nineteenth century was a problem **Storage** for everyone, no matter what their economic status. In addition to recipes for preparing food and suggestions on maintaining the household, receipt books like *Miss Beecher's Domestic Receipt Book* customarily contained suggestions on topics such as how to restore the flavor of rancid butter. (Miss Beecher advised using chloride of lime.)[1]

Heat is a great villain when it comes to spoiling food. In the absence of practical mechanical systems for making things cold—which did not arrive until the 1870s—the easiest way to keep food from spoiling during warm weather was to use ice. Freshwater ice was cut from frozen ponds in large blocks and kept in structures called icehouses, which were constructed partially below ground. The temperature a few feet below ground rarely rises above 45° Fahrenheit. The ice was then covered in sawdust to help insulate it. Ice would be gathered when it was thickest, generally late January. Shielded from the heat, ice could theoretically last forever, but practically it could be expected to last through October if conditions were favorable. By the Civil War, the icehouse had become an indispensable component of the farm. Meat, poultry, and perishable fruit could be kept in good condition much longer in the cool temperatures of icehouses or iceboxes.

The icebox also gave individual city homes a means of keeping food fresh. In 1850 *Godey's Lady's Book* called the icebox a "necessity of life." First patented by Thomas Moore in 1803, it consisted of one wooden box inside another, insulated by charcoal or ashes, with a tin container at the top of the interior box for the ice. In 1825 Frederick Tudor and Nathaniel Wyeth solved the problem of preserving ice for long periods and made ice a commercial interest. Just prior to the war, Boston families could obtain fifteen pounds of ice a day from an iceman for two dollars a month. Ice was harvested from New England ponds and shipped to the South or even to the West Indies. New Orleans increased its demand for ice seventyfold between the 1820s and the beginning of the Civil War. Once the war commenced, the South could no longer depend on this improved source of food preservation.[2]

Modern Advancement By mid-century the railroads had become the prime cause of the increasing diversity of food for the American table. Perishables such as milk, oysters, and lobsters were transported by rail to large cities in insulated icecars or packed in barrels of ice. The speed of the railroads not only augmented the diet, it served to improve the quality of the food. Beef was more tender, more tasty, and less expensive. The cattle no longer were driven to market on the hoof, and hence they developed less muscle. The cattle were fed on grain shipped via the railroad, thus improving the flavor of the meat. Finally, meat cost less because less weight was lost between pasture and market. A similar situation arose with pork. Before the railroads were built, long legs were a desirable breeding factor in pigs, as the hog was expected to walk to market. With the advent of rail shipping, breeders began to focus on tastier meats and fatter hogs. The railroads continued to supply the North and Northern troops with fresh meat during the war.

The processing and preservation of food had always been a domestic activity until vacuum-packed, hermetically sealed jars were invented by

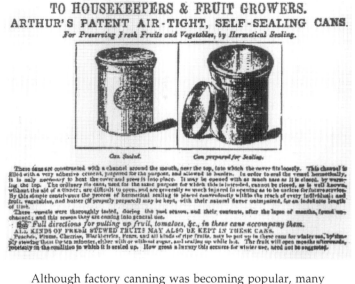

TO HOUSEKEEPERS & FRUIT GROWERS.
ARTHUR'S PATENT AIR-TIGHT, SELF-SEALING CANS.
For Preserving Fresh Fruits and Vegetables, by Hermetical Sealing.

Can Sealed.   *Can prepared for Sealing.*

Although factory canning was becoming popular, many householders still preferred home canning. This advertisement appeared in *Arthur's Home Magazine*, 1855.

a Frenchman named Nicholas Appert early in the nineteenth century. In 1825 the first American patent for tin cans was filed. By 1849 a machine was developed that limited the amount of hand labor needed to produce tin cans, further stimulating commercial food processing. Lobster and salmon were the first foods to be commercially canned, rapidly followed by corn, tomatoes, peas, and additional varieties of fish. By 1860, 5 million cans a year were being produced.

In 1863 the fledgling Great Atlantic Tea Company, destined to become the A&P stores, began to sell a line of canned groceries to supplement their tea business. Two famous brand names emerged from the war— Borden and Van Camp. Gail Borden's first efforts at canned foods met with little success, but his canned condensed milk was extremely popular. Gilbert Van Camp's pork and beans quickly became a best seller, and he was given an army contract to supply the Union troops.

Federal soldiers returning from the war had become so accustomed to canned foods that many insisted that canned foods be served at home so that they could continue to eat out-of-season products with consistent quality. Americans living in isolated western territories particularly welcomed the profusion of canned foods; prices ranged from $1.00 to $2.25 per can by the mid-1860s. A line from the song, "My Darling Clementine" describes Clementine's footwear as "herring boxes without topses," referring to the oval-shaped fish tins plentiful in mining towns.

Despite these movements toward modern food packaging, the single most important controlling factor of the Civil War era diet remained availability. Those who could afford to pay had wider choices, but even these were limited. For most people, the majority of fresh food choices continued to be governed by region and season.

Food Attitudes
Issues of vitamins, salt, fiber, and fat content were virtually nonexistent for most people during the 1860s. *Peterson's* contained the following comment on corpulence: "Dr. Radcliffe recommends that the mouth should be kept shut, and the eyes should be kept open; or, in other words, that corpulent persons should eat little food, and that the quantity of sleep should be diminished. These precautions may be followed with discretion, but it may be dangerous to carry them too far."[3] Most meals at this time contained meat, which was likely to be high in fat content, and bread in one form or another. Frances Trollope, a visitor to the United States in the 1830s, remarked on the extraordinary amount of bacon eaten in American homes. "Ham and beef steaks appear morning, noon, and night." Equally astonishing to her was the way eggs and oysters, ham and applesauce, beefsteak and stewed peaches, salt fish and onion were eaten together.[4]

Common Foods
Pork was the most common kind of meat, particularly in the Southern diet. Pigs are relatively easy to maintain. They required little space and tolerated a wide variety of foodstuffs, including leavings from food preparation. Pigs did not have to be put to pasture and consumed less feed than cattle to add the same amount of weight. Pork could be easily preserved in a number of ways, including pickling, salting, and smoking, without becoming offensive in taste or texture.

Chicken was important in the South, too. Chickens required little space and turned available reserves of corn and meal into meat; but chicken meat was both difficult to preserve and prone to spoil. Like other domesticated fowl, chickens were generally eaten fresh. They had the additional appeal of being egg producers while they lived.

Lamb, or mutton, was not a popular meat in America. Sheep were kept almost exclusively for their wool, and their value as wool producers far outweighed any worth they had as food. Certainly mutton would be eaten in place of other meats in time of scarcity if it were available, but it was not easily preserved. Moreover, the meat of mature sheep had a strong taste that had to be masked by careful preparation.

Supplements to the diet were often regional. In rural areas, hunters would supplement the family larder by bringing home such victuals as geese, rabbits, squirrels, wild turkeys, partridges, pheasants, deer, and reed birds. Contrary to popular belief, Southerners had no particular predisposition for the taste of opossums, snakes, or woodchucks in their diet. Fish and other forms of marine seafood including clams, oysters, mussels, and eels were eaten in shore communities. Freshwater fish included bass, sturgeon, pickerel, perch, pike, whitefish, and catfish. Fish could be salted or smoked, but much of it was eaten fresh. Oysters were extremely popular. They were eaten fresh but were also pickled, smoked, and canned.

Eggs were another good source of protein. Miss Beecher advised homemakers to preserve eggs in the following ways: "Pack them in fine salt, small end down. . . . [or] pack them small end down, and then pour on them a mixture of four quarts of cold water, four quarts of unslacked lime, two ounces of salt, and two ounces of cream-tartar."[5] Hard-boiled eggs were sometimes pickled in vinegar.

Vegetables were eaten fresh in season. Only in the very deep South were they available during the winter. Small amounts of vegetables could be grown in hot frames, which utilized the heat of manure to keep temperatures warm enough to produce year round as far north as Virginia. Vegetables such as beets, cabbage, carrots, cauliflower, onions, parsnips, potatoes, radishes, rutabagas, sweet potatoes, turnips, and winter squash were stored in root cellars where the climate allowed. In other areas they were packed in straw and stored in barrels. The straw acted as a barrier to prevent the spread of spoilage to the entire barrel. Carrots were often buried in sawdust boxes. Other vegetables such as corn, beans and peas were dried and used in cooking. Green corn was preserved by turning back the husk, leaving only the last, very thin layer, and then hanging it in the sun or in a warm room to dry. When it was needed for cooking, it was parboiled and cut from the cob. Sweet corn was parboiled, cut from the cob, dried in the sun, and stored in a bag which was kept in a cool, dry place. Sweet corn was also dried in the husk and then buried in salt. String beans, squash, pumpkin, and, in the South, okra were strung on thread and hung up to dry. String beans were strung whole, while other produce was sliced thinly and dried in strips.

Vegetables could also be preserved by making them into catsups and relishes. Mushroom and tomato catsups were popular. Catsup was the general name given to sauces made from vegetables and fruits. Cabbage was made into sauerkraut. In 1858 John Mason patented the Mason jar with which we are familiar today. These threaded glass jars had zinc lids with threaded ring sealers. They were a welcome improvement for both city and rural homemakers, although many still relied on older methods of sealing jars such as pouring a seal made from molten wax, or tying on leather tops with string.

Food was still accepted in certain areas of the country as payment in kind. An account book from a doctor in Butler, Illinois, showed that accounts for medical service during the war were paid by a variety of items other than cash. The doctor kept spe-

Food Prices

cific records of the amount and price of each item, giving some insight
into prices outside of the South. Accounts were settled by "4 3/4 lbs. of
pork—.20; 16 bushels of corn—8.00; 7 1/2 lbs. meat—10 cts. per—.75;
one bushel of apples—.40; 10 lbs. of beef 4 1/2 cts.—.45; 13 lbs. of honey
15 cts. per lb.—1.95; 50 lbs. flour 4 cts. lb.—2.00; 1/2 bushel potatoes—
.75; 350 pickles—2.10."[6]

The War's Effect

At the commencement of the war, virtually all of the
South's most fertile land was devoted to agriculture. The
North, which relied so much on industrialization, might
thereby be seen to have been at a disadvantage with regard
to food, but the reverse was true. As the war progressed and was continually fought on Southern soil, Southern crops were destroyed. Cornelia Peake McDonald described a visit by federal troops. They "began
to pull up the potatoes ... they did not stop after getting enough for
dinner, but continued amid roars of laughter and defiant looks at me to
pull them till all were lying on the ground ... to wither in the sun. They
were no larger than peas, and the destruction seemed so wanton that I
was provoked beyond enduring."[7]

The North, however, had undeveloped land that it was now able to
put into production to support the war effort. The Homestead Act was
quickly passed in 1862, granting free land to anyone willing to plant it.
This virgin soil produced impressive yields, unlike the overfarmed
Southern soil. Northern industry developed and manufactured machinery that further improved productivity. In 1861 Cyrus McCormick's
reaper was offered for sale at $150 but required only a $30 down payment. The balance was to be paid in six months if the harvest was good,
or longer if it was poor.[8]

The war actually provided an impetus to the development of farming
in the North. Preconceived notions of a rising wartime demand for food
caused farmers to overplant in 1860. Wheat and corn production soared.
Pork preservation for commercial use in 1865 was twice that of 1860. An
additional boon came in the form of good weather, an event not shared
by Europe, which experienced crop shortages during this period. The
North was able to sell surplus wheat and flour to Europe, thus earning
additional funds that could be invested in the war.[9]

Shortages

The war brought about many shortages in the South. A
poor system of transportation prevented the Confederacy's
small resources from being effectively distributed throughout
the South. Furthermore, the blockade of Southern ports caused great
hardship. Blockade runners took tremendous risks and expected tremendous profits. In order to make the risk worthwhile, they tended to carry
luxury items for those who could afford to pay, rather than the staples
of daily life for everyone. Prices soared in proportion. In November 1862

Judith McGuire wrote, "Coffee is $4 per pound, and good tea from $18 to $20; butter ranges from $1.50 to $2 per pound; lard 50 cents; corn $15 per barrel; and wheat $4.50 per bushel."[10] In an April 1863 message to Southerners, President Jefferson Davis urged people to give priority to food crops over cotton and tobacco and to plant corn, peas, and beans.[11]

Receipt books and newspapers carried suggestions for dealing with the food shortages. When successful replacements were discovered, the revelation was readily disclosed to the public in print and by word of mouth. A handwritten receipt book gives the following suggestion for dealing with the unavailability of flour. "Rice Bread, 'Southern Bread'—1 gill of rice boiled very soft, when cold mix in 3/4 lbs. of wheat, 1 teacup of yeast, 1 teacup of milk, salt to taste. Mix and let it stand 3 hours then it must be kneaded in flour enough to render the outside hard enough for the oven. In an hour and a quarter after, bake it."[12]

Additional hardships were caused by raids of Northern troops upon individual homes. Mary S. Mallard recorded the following in her journal:

> About four in the afternoon we heard the clash of arms and noise of horsemen, and by the time Mother and I could get downstairs we saw forty or fifty men in the pantry, flying hither and thither, ripping open the safe with their swords and breaking open the crockery cupboards. Fearing we might not have a chance to cook, Mother had some chickens and ducks roasted and put in the safe for our family. These the men seized whole, tearing them to pieces with their teeth like ravenous beasts. They were clamorous for whiskey, and ordered us to get our keys. One came to Mother to know where her meal and flour were, insisted upon opening her locked pantry, and took every particle. They threw the sacks across their horses. Mother remonstrated and pointed to her helpless family; their only reply was: "We'll take it!"[13]

Coffee was a popular beverage, and the blockade made it very difficult to procure. There are reports of Southern soldiers trading with their Northern counterparts for coffee across the lines during times of truce. Parthenia Hague wrote:

> One of our most difficult tasks was to find a good substitute for coffee. . . . Coffee soon rose to thirty dollars per pound; from that it went to sixty and seventy dollars per pound. Good workmen received thirty dollars per day; so it took two days' hard labor to buy one pound of coffee, and scarcely any could be had at that fabulous price.[14]

The best substitute for coffee was said by some to be okra seeds. This was unfortunate because okra became increasingly difficult to acquire as the war progressed and agricultural output diminished. Other alternatives included yams and carrots, either of which would be peeled, sliced, dried, parched, and ground. Acorns, wheat berries, corn, peanuts, sugar cane seed, chicory, beets, dandelion root, cotton seed, and English peas were also used in various conditions of having been browned, parched, burned, and ground. By 1862 Confederate troops had even embraced peanuts as a coffee substitute. The *Confederate Receipt Book*, which was published in 1863 and is believed to be the only cookbook published in the South during the war, contained the following: "Substitute for Coffee: Take sound ripe acorns, wash them in the shell, dry them, and parch until they open, take the shell off, roast with a little bacon fat, and you will have a splendid cup of coffee."[15]

Tea was also a scarce item, but there have always been many satisfactory herbal substitutes for this mainstay. Tea can be made from a wide variety of leaves, roots, and berries. Some favorites included sassafras root, raspberry, huckleberry, and blackberry. Hague wrote in her memoirs of the war:

> We had several substitutes for tea. . . . Prominent among these substitutes were raspberry leaves. Many during the blockade planted and cultivated the raspberry-vine all around their garden palings as much for tea as the berries for jams or pies; these leaves were considered the best substitutes for tea. The leaves of the holly-tree when dried in the shade, also made a palatable tea.[16]

Butter was also difficult to obtain because it was largely imported from the North. Many Southern dairy cows had been slaughtered for their meat by invading and local armies and even by some civilians. Judith McGuire wrote in March 1863, "Butter was $3.50 per pound in market this morning, and other things in proportion. I am sorry to say that it is true, and that it is evident we must have scarcity, particularly of such things as butter, for cattle must go to feed the army."[17] Sunflower seed oil was often used as a replacement for butter.

A related casualty in this regard was the want of milk and cream. Judith McGuire wrote, "Milk is very scarce and high, so that we have only had it once for many months."[18] The *Confederate Receipt Book* gave this solution for the undersupply of cream: "Beat the white of an egg to a froth, put to it a very small lump of butter, and mix well, then turn the coffee to it gradually, so that it may not curdle. If perfectly done it will be an excellent substitute for cream. For tea omit the butter, using only the egg."[19]

Flour, too, was scarce. Prices continued to escalate throughout the war.

It was reported that in Richmond a barrel of flour sold for $250 during the closing months of the war.[20] Sarah Morgan wrote in August 1862, "I sat on the floor with my plate, and a piece of corn bread (flour not to be bought at any price) and eat with my fingers—a new experience."[21] One month later she wrote again, "If anyone had told me I could have lived off corn bread, a few months ago, I would have been incredulous: now I believe it, and return an inward grace for the blessing, at every mouthful. I have not tasted a piece of wheat bread since I left home, and shall hardly taste it again until the war is over."[22] Parthenia Hague seems less distressed:

> Bolted Meal, when obtainable, made a good substitute for flour, though millers said it injured their bolting cloth to sift the corn meal through it; yet nearly every household, in sending its grist to be ground, would order a portion of the meal to be bolted for use as flour. Such bolted meal when it was sifted through a thin muslin cloth mixed up with scalding water to make it more viscid and adhesive, was as easily molded into pie crust with the aid of the rolling-pin as the pure flour. Nice muffins and waffles were made of bolted meal, and we also made a very nice cake of the same and our home-made brown sugar.[23]

Perhaps the distress over the lack of flour is somehow tied to the American housewife's extreme pride in her bread making. Miss Beecher devoted an entire chapter to bread making. She counseled: "A woman should be *ashamed* to have poor bread, far more so, than to speak bad grammar, or to have a dress out of fashion. . . . When it is very frequently the case that a housekeeper has poor bread, she may set herself down as a *slack baker* and negligent housekeeper."[24] Commercially produced bread was one area in which modern convenience was strongly resisted until the early years of the following century.

Households that did not produce corn, which could be ground into meal, were often at the mercy of the war economy. Judith McGuire lamented that "meal was selling to-day at $16 per bushel. It has been bought up by speculators. Oh, that those hard-hearted creatures could be made to suffer!"[25] Mary A. H. Gray's diary records the lengths to which people would go to obtain, or in this case reclaim, corn: "We spent the preceding day in picking out grains of corn from cracks and crevices in bureau drawers, and other improvised troughs for Federal horses, as well as gathering up what was on the ground . . . about a half bushel was obtained."[26]

Salt became a highly prized commodity. Dolly Sumner Lunt Burge describes disguising a barrel of salt "which had cost me two hundred dollars" as a leaching tub to conceal it from marauders.[27] In 1862 Union forces destroyed a large saltworks on Chesapeake Bay, causing difficulty for individuals and salt pork producers alike.

The obtaining of salt became extremely difficult when the war had cut off our supply. This was true especially in regions remote from the sea-coast and border States, such as the interior of Alabama and Georgia. Here again we were obliged to have recourse to whatever expedient ingenuity suggested. All the brine left in troughs and barrels, where pork had been salted down, were carefully dipped up, boiled down, and converted into salt again. In some cases the salty soil under old smokehouses was dug up and placed in hoppers, which resembled backwoods ash-hoppers, made for leaching ashes in the process of soap-manufacture. Water was then poured upon the soil, the brine of which percolated through the hopper was boiled down to the proper point, poured into vessels, and set in the sun, which by evaporation completed the rude process. Though never of immaculate whiteness, the salt which resulted from these methods served well enough for all our purposes, and we accepted it without complaining.[28]

Resourceful people living near the shore could obtain salt by evaporating ocean water. Sometimes coltsfoot, a wild plant that gave a salt-like flavor to foods, was used in cooking. But lack of salt posed problems other than taste preference. Salt was used extensively as a meat preservative. Parching fish and meat Indian style was only a stopgap expedient. Meat could also be cured in a brine using a lesser amount of salt than other methods. Even the availability of meat to preserve was a problem. Once Vicksburg fell in 1863, Union forces had control of the Mississippi, virtually cutting off the supply of western beef to the Confederacy.

Soda, or baking soda, used as a leavening agent, was also a victim of the blockade. Parthenia Hague wrote, "It was not long 'ere some one found out that the ashes of corncobs possessed the alkaline property essential for raising dough." She noted that it was best "to select all the red cobs as they are thought to contain more carbonate of soda than the white cobs."[29]

Sugar, too, was difficult to acquire. Even though the South possessed its own sugar plantations, most were in federally occupied Louisiana for most of the war. Honey, molasses, and sorghum were used in its stead. Parthenia Hague tells the story of a woman who even used a surplus of watermelon to make sugar and syrup. The deficit of sugar also inhibited the making of jellies, jams, and preserves. Red corncobs were again found to be useful. The cobs were boiled, and the juice was thickened into syrup. The *Confederate Receipt Book* gave this recipe for cider jelly: "Boil cider to the consistency of syrup, and let it cool, and you have a nice jelly."[30]

When apples to make vinegar were in too short supply, Southerners turned to molasses, honey, beets, figs, persimmons, and sorghum. The *Confederate Receipt Book* even had a recipe for "Apple Pie Without Apples": "To one small bowl of crackers, that have been soaked until no hard parts remain, add one teaspoon of tartaric acid, sweeten to your taste, add some butter, and very little nutmeg."[31]

Apparently not all Southerners were subject to deprivations. Mary Chesnut recorded the menu of a "luncheon to ladies" given by Mrs. Jefferson Davis in January 1864 as "gumbo, ducks and olives, supreme de volaille, chickens in jelly, oysters, lettuce salad, chocolate jelly cake, claret soup champagne, &c,&c,&c."[32]

Supplementing the Troops

The Sanitary Commission was a Northern civilian organization that coordinated widespread war relief. "The object of the Sanitary Commission was to do what the government could not," wrote Mary Livermore in her war memoirs.[33] Funds were raised through "Sanitary Fairs," which sold homemade pies and jellies and held raffles for quilts and other homemade crafts, and from direct solicitation. Emma Sargent Barbour received a letter in which her sister remarked, "I had a couple of pamphlets from the Sanitary Commission last week soliciting funds from the Ladies of D. [W]e have about $10 on hand we have been reserving for a fitting occasion, we shall probably send to that object this week."[34]

Children were recruited to solicit funds door to door and to collect nonperishable groceries such as jellies or crackers from merchants to be sent to soldiers at the front. In some farming communities, families set aside portions of their land for the production of easily stored crops, such as potatoes, which were delivered to the Sanitary Commission. Schools held "onion" or "potato" days to collect produce.

Dietary kitchens staffed with dietary nurses were established by the Sanitary Commission in 1862 as a result of the efforts of Annie Wittenmyer. She worked very hard to see that a system was developed to feed wounded soldiers in field hospitals. Women volunteers had been scrounging milk, eggs, and vegetables for the wounded who were too ill to eat the standard pork and beans field ration. Wittenmyer's system established the means for providing appropriate meals for the men.[35]

Similar efforts in Southern communities were unable to match the organization and productivity of the North. Southerners were equally sympathetic to the plight of their soldiers, but the South lacked the efficient transportation and resources necessary for mounting such endeavors.

NOTES

1. Beecher, 286.
2. Waverly Root and Richard de Rouchemont, *Eating in America* (New York: William Morrow, 1976), 148.
3. R. L. Shep, ed., *Civil War Ladies: Fashions and Needle Arts of the Early 1860's* (Mendocino: R. L. Shep, 1987), 155. "Editor's Table," *Peterson's Magazine,* September 1861.
4. Katie Stewart, *Cooking and Eating* (London: Hart-Davis, MacGibbon, 1975), 202.
5. Beecher, 286.
6. Account book of a doctor from Butler, Illinois. 1861–1866 in the authors' collection.
7. Gwin, 58.
8. James Trager, *The Food Chronology* (New York: Henry Holt, 1995), 262.
9. Root and de Rouchemont, 184.
10. Judith McGuire, *Diary of a Southern Refugee During the War by a Lady of Virginia* (Lincoln: University of Nebraska Press, 1995), 173.
11. Trager, 267.
12. Campbell and Rice, 107.
13. Sullivan, 233.
14. Parthenia Antoinette Hague, *A Blockaded Family: Life in Southern Alabama During the Civil War* (Bedford: Applewood Books, 1995), 101.
15. *Confederate Receipt Book: A Compilation of Over One Hundred Receipts, Adapted to the Times* (Richmond: West & Johnson, 1863), 16.
16. Hague, 17.
17. McGuire, 197.
18. Ibid., 257.
19. *Confederate Receipt Book,* 25–26.
20. Trager, 271.
21. East, 242.
22. Ibid., 251.
23. Hague, 25.
24. Beecher, 230–231.
25. McGuire, 203.
26. Harold Elk Straubing, ed., *Civil War Eyewitness Reports* (N.p.: Archon Books, 1985), 204. Quoting Mary A.H. Gay, *Life in Dixie During the War, 1861–1865* (Foote & Davis Co., 1894).
27. Lunt, 30.
28. Hague, 38.
29. Ibid., 48.
30. *Confederate Receipt Book,* 18.
31. Ibid., 16.
32. C. V. Woodward, 551.
33. Mary A. Livermore, *My Story of the War: A Woman's Narrative of Four Years' Personal Experience* (New York: Da Capo Press, 1995), 129.
34. Moskow, 109–110.
35. Trager, 266.

15

The Look: Fashion and Women's Clothing

Dresses for breakfasts, and dinners and balls;
Dresses to sit in, and stand in, and walk in;
Dresses to dance in, and flirt in, and talk in;
Dresses in which to do nothing at all.

—"Nothing at All"

Students of historic fashion find nineteenth-century attire particularly exciting because this is the first period for which widespread photographic documentation of what people actually wore is available. No longer is the study merely subject to interpretations of the hand drawn or engraved fashion plates to which period women may have aspired.

With the ability to print albumen photographs on paper, multiple prints could be made from a single glass negative. This method was inexpensive enough that even those of middle income could afford a photographic portrait. People of the Civil War period ordered multiple copies of these prints to give to friends and family. The prints were mounted on heavy card stock and became known as cartes de visite. Fortunately, these have survived in great numbers and provide tremendous insight into the clothing of the period.

Great care must be taken not to draw overly broad conclusions from these portraits. On the one hand, the photographs are studio portraits, and as such do not provide the informal insight of twentieth-century candid snapshots, which show a variety of attire in numerous settings.

On the other hand, the wardrobes of middle-class Americans of the mid-nineteenth century did not have the breadth of those of today, thus it would be safe to assume in most cases that the clothing worn in a studio photograph was that person's "best dress."

Women's One of the greatest influences on American women's fash-
Clothing ion during the 1860s was *Godey's Lady's Book*, a magazine founded by Louis B. Godey in July 1830. In addition to serials, essays, poems, and craft projects, it featured engraved fashion plates. Each month the magazine depicted morning dresses, walking dresses, seaside costumes, riding habits, dinner dresses, and ball gowns. Such wardrobe depth was seldom needed for the vast majority of the magazine's readers, whose clothes could generally be divided into public or social and domestic or work, with a few seasonal additions for summer and winter. As time passed, *Godey's* began to show fashions better suited to the lifestyle of the American woman. By the 1860s *Godey's* had become a fashion institution, setting the standard for fashion savvy. Other magazines such as *Peterson's, Arthur's, Graham's, Leslie's, and Harper's* began to follow suit or grew in popularity. Parthenia Hague, a woman living in the blockaded South, observed, "Of course we used the same style the whole four years of the war, in our secluded settlement; not a fashion plate or 'ladies' magazine did we see during that entire period, so we were little troubled by the 'latest styles.' "[1]

Whether a woman could afford the extravagances touted by the fashion plates of the day or not, the "look" she was hoping to attain was the same. Women of the Civil War period wanted to create the appearance of a narrow waist. Virtually all lines of garments emphasized the smallness of the waist by creating the illusion of width at the shoulders and hips. This was further accentuated by foundation garments that altered the body's physical appearance.

The Dress The dress bodices during this period can be classified by three basic styles. There was the "O" bodice, distinguished by the fullness of the fabric as it cascaded over the bust and gathered in around the waist. "O" bodices were especially popular prior to the war but continued to be worn throughout the conflict. Period photographs indicate that it was the most common style during the early war. The bodice that was becoming fashionable at this time was the "V" bodice. This very fitted style was characterized by double or triple vertical darts extending from the waist. The darts, as well as the side and back seams, were usually boned. Stays could be made from whalebone, metal, or even wood. By the end of the war this style was most popular. The third bodice style was the "Y." This style has a fanlike appearance. It had been in vogue since the early 1840s and had begun to fall out of favor. Like the "O" bodice, "Y" bodices were relatively loose-fitting.

Regardless of style, bodices ended at the natural waistline. The bodice portion of the dress fastened at the center front by hooks and eyes, while the skirt portion had a side-front closure. This created an awkward opening that extended vertically from the neck, then horizontally along the waist, and then vertically again down a few inches along the left front skirt seam. The armscye, or armhole, was almost always diagonal or horizontal to give the shoulders a sloping and wider appearance.

Sleeves were very full, particularly at the elbow, again imparting the illusion of the slender waist. Sleeves, too, came in three fundamental styles. Straight sleeves were simple and loose-fitting and were gathered together into a cuff at the wrist. Also loose were bishop sleeves, which grew wide at the elbow, causing the sleeve to hang in a curve and creating the appearance of a slightly bent arm. The pagoda sleeve tended to be found on more elaborate dresses. It was a loose sleeve that was widest at its hem and usually of bracelet length. Because of this looseness, undersleeves, which would conceal the forearm from view, were worn for modesty's sake. Undersleeves were separate, straight sleeves that fit closely at the wrist and extended to the upper arm, where they were secured by a drawstring. Most commonly they were white.

Examples of the pagoda and fitted sleeve are clearly
seen in these cartes de visite from the authors'
collection.

Often sleeves had sleeve caps. These were ornamental pieces of fabric
that covered the top few inches of the sleeve, supporting the image of
the wide, sloping shoulder. Sometimes the impression of a sleeve cap
would be created through the use of trim. Short cap sleeves that revealed
a woman's arm could only be found on ball gowns.

The necklines of day dresses usually came to the base of the neck.
Many were trimmed by small, white collars that were sewn flat and met
in the front. Some had very short stand-up collars. Collars were basted
inside to protect the garment from wear and soiling. They could easily
be removed for frequent launderings from which the entire garment
could be saved. The collars would be constructed of sturdy white or very
light-colored fabric which could stand up to the repeated washings this
portion of the garment required. Sometimes these collars had matching
sets of cuffs which were similarly attached and served the same purpose.
Collars were frequently decorated with a brooch at the center of the neck.
If a bow was used, the tails of the bow would extend diagonally away
from the center, continuing to proffer the illusion of the broad upper
torso. Ball gowns often had wide bateau necklines.

Many of the fabrics and dyes used at this time did not hold up to
frequent laundering. Garments were often taken apart and resewn when
cleaned. *The Housekeeper's Encyclopedia* provided nine pages of instructions for washing various fabrics, for example, "Take rice-water, and

wash them quickly, without soap."[2] Other methods included the use of bran, ox-gall, salt, elixir of vitriol, and egg yolk. Most women's dresses were never totally laundered but rather spot cleaned as needed.

Skirts were long but seldom touched the ground. An exception was the elliptical skirt popular during the late war. These skirts were shorter in the front but lengthened in the back to a point where some actually dragged on the ground. Hem tapes were common on skirts. The tapes or trims were wrapped around the finished hem and could be removed for cleaning or replacement. Skirts were very full and were either fully gathered or pleated at the waistline. No effort was made to make the stomach area appear flatter because, once again, the fuller an area away from the waist seemed, the narrower the waist appeared.

Fabrics used for dresses and skirts included silk, linen, wool, and cotton. These were available in an almost infinite variety of weights and weaves, some of which are no longer available today. By far cotton and linen were the most common choices for everyday wear. Silk was expensive. If the average woman owned a silk dress, it would be saved for very special occasions. Linen, because of its extreme durability and ability to be produced at home, was considered frontier or laborer clothing. This was particularly true in the South, where it was in common use among the slave population. Wool continued to have its place because of its warmth and especially because of its fire-retardant qualities. Cotton, a status symbol earlier in the century, had become readily available and affordable for even modest households by the 1830s, thanks to the tremendous development of the textile industry after the invention of the cotton gin. From time to time, there were movements in the North among abolitionist women to avoid the use of cotton due to their belief that it was produced largely as a result of slave activity, but this tended to be confined to relatively small groups.

The blockade and the resulting interruptions in trade caused great hardships for Southern women who had once been the most fashionable element of the population. Parthenia Hague observed, "Every household now became a miniature factory in itself, with its cotton, cards, spinning-wheels, warping-frames, looms, and so on."[3] Mary Chesnut recounted the following exchange after being asked for a bottle of brandy by a visitor. "I replied, 'Whenever you bring me that roll of linen cambric you said you had from a blockade-runner for me.' J.C. said gravely, after Brewster left with the brandy bottle, 'Surely you did not ask that man for a bolt of linen cambric?' Surely I had."[4]

Some Southern ladies continued to dress and to dance in whatever prewar style they could manage as a means of keeping up their courage. With Yankee gunboats anchored off Baton Rouge and Union troops occupying the city, Sarah Morgan made the following entry in her diary:

Suppose we each took a fancy to consider ourselves the most miserable of mortals, and acted accordingly, going about with our eyes streaming, groaning over our troubles, and never cease to mourn. What a jolly world this would be!—And wouldn't my white dress that Tische is ironing for me to wear to church tomorrow get woefully damp!—Ah no! let us all learn to laugh and be happy, and sing "Better days are coming," even if we don't believe it, it will make those around us happy.[5]

Drawing upon their resourcefulness and creativity, Southern women managed to rework prewar finery and to use natural materials. Mary Chesnut wrote: "Went to sell some of my colored dresses. What a scene—such piles of rubbish—and mixed up with it all, such splendid Parisian silks and satins. A mulatto woman kept the shop under the roof of an out of the way old house. The ci-devant rich, the white ladies, sell to, and the Negroes buy of, this woman."[6]

Prices soared. By 1864 Judith McGuire recorded prices that would give a purchaser pause today. "I gave $110 for ladies' Morocco boots; $22 per yard for linen; $5 apiece for spools of cotton; $5 for a paper of pins."[7] Women needing funds to keep their households together often reworked old finery to create collars, undersleeves, neckties, and other items that brought handsome prices in the inflated Confederate currency. In the face of such adversity, Mary Chesnut described the ingenuity she and her friends displayed in preparation for a wedding. "Julia Rutledge was one of the bridesmaids, and we could not for a while imagine what she would do for a dress. Kate remembers some [material] she had in the house for curtains bought before the war and laid aside as not needed now. The stuff was white and sheer, if a little coarse, but we covered it with no end of beautiful lace. It made a beautiful dress."[8] Parthenia Hague remarked, "It was really ridiculous, our way of making raids upon what remained of our fine bed-linen, pillow shams, and slips, for garments of finer texture than our own homewoven cloth."[9]

The color palette available at this time was basically that which could be achieved by natural dyes. While Southern women tended to wear lighter hues, popular colors included browns, soft blues, greens, lavenders, and grays. Yellows and deep berry-toned reds were also in use. Black was a common color for trim and detailing. Even though chemical dyes had been introduced by the end of the 1850s, these colors were mostly found in decorative fabrics for the home. Although some showy young women in the North did wear them, proper ladies did not. *Peterson's* counseled against the use of bright colors: "Though they may gratify the savage, [they] will not please the educated eye." Readers were warned about wearing yellow and yellow-greens. "It is scarcely necessary to observe that, of all complexions, those which turn upon the yellow are the most unpleasant in their effect—and probably for this reason, that in this climate it is always a sign of bad health."[10]

Popular patterns included geometrics such as dots, checks, and stripes. Sometimes these were combined with small floral motifs or grouped into small clusters. Large florals were not in style, nor were very small floral calicoes, which were not popular until later in the century. Patterns were also created by variations in the weave or with the use of shiny and dull threads.

Trim for dresses was generally placed in horizontal or diagonal lines continuing the illusion of the narrow waist. Day dresses had little trim except on the sleeves or bodice. Skirts, if trimmed, were done so near the hemline. The trims used included braid, piping, binding, and ribbon. Ribbons were commonly gathered, pleated, or ruched. Some skirts appeared to be trimmed at the hem but had actually been fitted with a tape wrapped around the hem to protect it from wear. It was much less expensive to replace a worn hem tape than to replace the garment, and the process was less labor-intensive than turning the skirt. Some ball gowns had flounces or even a series of ruffles along the skirt. Trims on gowns tended to be more expensive and elaborate than those on everyday dresses.

Dresses were updated or embellished by the use of accessories. A dress might be given a different look by the addition of a fichu. Fichus were often made of sheer, gauze-like fabrics. They were decorated with ruffles, ribbons, lace, and bows. Fichus were particularly popular in warmer climates at a time when propriety dictated that a lady's shoulders be fully covered until evening. A cooler dress with a scooped neckline could be worn and covered by the lightweight fichu. They were also worn over ball gowns by older women. Once again, practicality dictated that the fichu be a separate piece that could be cleaned more easily than the entire dress. This also allowed dresses to be easily changed to reflect new trends in fashion. There were several styles of fichu, but basically they covered the upper back much like a shawl collar and extended over the front in long tails which either met at the waist or crossed over each other. Some extended down the skirt a foot or so. Berthes served a similar purpose, but were like oversized collars rather than wraparounds.

Sashes and waistbands were made of rich fabrics often embroidered or trimmed. They extended well down the length of the dress. Belts of many different styles were worn. Some were quite elaborate. The Medici belt stands out as perhaps the most notable style. It was several inches wide at the sides and back, but the front flared out into two exaggerated points that extended up to the area between the breasts and down to mid-stomach. The bretelle corset was similarly shaped, with shoulder straps almost like braces.

Ball gowns, naturally, would not have been found in the majority of women's wardrobes, but their splendor and overstated nature demand some comment. Ball gowns had scooped necklines, short sleeves, and extremely full skirts. Silk was the fabric of choice. Ball gowns were elaborately decorated with long sashes, tiers of laced ruffles, flower garlands, or whatever extravagance might have struck the wearer.

Skirts worn with shirts and jackets, or with vests and jackets, were popular among young women in their teens and twenties. It was not until the very end of the war that the skirt and blouse were seen unaccompanied by the jacket. The jackets were similar to what is called the bolero today. Jackets frequently matched the skirt fabric. One of the most popular styles was the Zouave jacket, which was copied from the French military uniform of the same name. As the fashion grew more popular, the jackets became decorated with more and more black braid in increasingly ornate patterns. Vests were generally of a solid fabric.

Blouses were white and generally closed by buttons rather than hooks and eyes. The end of the blouse was sewn into a waistband as opposed to hanging loose. The Garibaldi shirt—based on the unique garment of the freedom fighters who succeeded in uniting Italy in 1860—was a very distinctive style of shirt worn during the Civil War. It was characterized by trim at the center front, the waistband, the shoulders, and the cuffs. As a rule, they were made of colored fabric.

Riding habits consisted of a skirt, jacket, blouse, and occasionally a vest. Hats were small and frequently had a veil. Jackets were decidedly plainer and more masculine during this time than they had been during the previous decade. The fabric was closely woven to withstand snags on branches, and dark colors were preferred for practicality. Of course, not all women rode for exercise. Some rode in parks to "be seen," and these ladies often preferred more elaborately decorated outfits. *Godey's Lady's Book* gives us this description of an illustration: "Riding habit of black cloth with fluted worsted braid and large gilt buttons; white cashmere vest; scarlet cravat; black felt hat with black feather and scarlet bow."[11]

By the 1860s white wedding dresses had come into fashion. However, many women still followed older traditions and were married in their "best" dress. Mary Chesnut wrote: "The bridesmaids were dressed in black and the bride in Confederate gray homespun. She had worn the dress all winter, but it had been washed and turned for the wedding. ... [S]he wore a cameo breastpin. Her bonnet was self-made."[12] Those fortunate enough to be able to afford such a specialized garment tended to choose dresses that might be considered plain by ballroom standards. Expense was more likely to be put into the fabric rather than trim. Generally, weddings were held during the day. Wedding dresses were therefore day dresses with jewel necklines and long sleeves. In keeping with the "look" of the day, headdresses and veils tended to lie flat on the head to avoid adding height. Coronets of real or artificial flowers were arranged so that they framed the face and added width. Mary Chesnut described another bride. "Maggie dressed the bride's hair beautifully, they said, but it was all covered by her veil. Which was blonde lace—and the dress tulle and blond lace."[13] She also recorded the details of a "Negro wedding." "The bride and her bridesmaids in white Swiss muslin, the gayest of sashes—and bonnets too wonderful to be described. They had on red blanket shawls which they removed as they entered the aisle. . . .The bride's gloves were white."[14]

Quite possibly, undergarments reached the highest level of complexity in fashion history during this period. **Undergarments** Undergarments served to protect the outer garment from body soiling, molded the body to create the ideal "look," and served to distribute the weight of the extremely full skirts. Like the previously discussed collars and cuffs, undergarments were constructed of serviceable fabrics that could be laundered. They were usually white.

The garment worn closest to the skin was the chemise—a knee-length, loose-fitting shift. The body was almost triangular in shape due to the gussets on the sides. This basic garment had changed little in the previous 600 years. During this period, the neck was so wide that it was almost off the shoulders, and the sleeves were short, "infant sleeves." Trim, if any, would be found at the neck or sleeve cuff. Sometimes the yoke would be decorated with small tucks. Its prime purpose was to help absorb perspiration and protect outer garments. It was sometimes affectionately called a "shimmy."

A number of garments were worn with the chemise. Drawers, known as pantalettes, were worn beneath the chemise. They were constructed of two independent legs attached to a waistband and extended to just below the knee. Sometimes they were decorated with tucks, fancy stitching, or eyelet.

The corset was worn on top of the chemise. The purpose of this garment was to make the waist look small compared to other parts of the body and to shape the upper portion of the body upward and outward from the waist to the bust. Corsets were lightly boned and usually had steel clasps at the front and lacing up the back to allow for adjustment. Some had laces in the front with a busk inserted for rigidity. Light corsets were introduced to girls around age twelve and certainly by the age of puberty. Over the corset was worn a corset cover or camisole. These were sleeveless and extended to the waist.

The next layer of undergarment is perhaps the single garment most associated with women's clothing during the Civil War, the crinoline or hoop. Crinolines could be covered or caged. Caged crinolines were composed of a series of hoops of varying sizes suspended from strips of tape that descended from the waist. Covered crinolines were fabric petticoats which contained casings to hold the hoops. Crinolines were worn beneath petticoats in order to make the skirt appear more full. They also helped in the practical task of distributing the weight of the skirt, which could become quite oppressive depending on the type and amount of fabric used. Generally, crinolines for day dresses were somewhat smaller than those for evening wear. Atop the crinoline were placed one or more petticoats for added fullness and to soften the ridges that could be created by the hoops. Skirts tended to be so much greater in circumference than the crinolines that they tended to drape over this support in folds.

Even a small sampling of period photographs would indicate that few women actually wore hoops with the extreme proportions depicted in fashion plates of the day. Normally, the diameter of the hoop was approximately 50 to 70 percent of the wearer's height. Women engaged in vigorous work would decline to wear them. Hoops did wear out, posing a great problem for women in the blockaded South. The hoop was often made of a long, thin strip of whalebone, called baleen, turned back on itself in a circle. Baleen was also used to make buggy whips, and since it was generally acquired from New England, it was largely unavailable during the war. The cloth of the hoops also wore. Parthenia Hague recounted the detailed process followed by a resourceful woman who "devised a means of weaving the hoopskirt on the common house-loom."[15]

Peterson's Magazine offers insight into this distinctive fashion component.

> Five years ago when hooped skirts were first introduced, every one predicted for them a speedy decline, and fall; but after encountering the shafts of ridicule and opposition in every conceivable form, they still not only remain a fixed fact, but have become a permanent institution, which no caprice of fashion will be likely wholly to destroy.
>
> The reason of this constant and increased appreciation is found in the acknowledged principle of comfort and utility upon which the idea was based. . . . ladies realized what they needed—something to extend their dresses to proper and becoming dimensions, and save the oppressive weight of a mass of clothing upon the hips.
>
> When a mode, no matter how excellent in itself, becomes a fashion, the tendency is always toward an extreme, and it is not surprising that this was the case with hooped skirts, and that at a certain period the size became absurdly and preposterously large. At the present time a happy medium seems to have been reached.[16]

The nightdress was ankle-length white cotton and approximately two and a half to three yards wide at the hem. The collar, cuffs, and yoke were often decorated with embroidery, lace, ruching, and tucks. Night-

Ladies' outerwear from cartes de visite in the
authors' collection.

caps were still worn and were often decorated with lace and bows. Prior
to dressing, a woman might wear a morning robe over her nightdress.
This was likely to have a shawl or cape collar and wide, loose sleeves.
It was tied at the waist.

When it came to outerwear, women had a wide variety
of options, including capes, cloaks, shawls, jackets, and **Outerwear**
coats. Capes varied in length from just below the hip to just
above the ankle. Consistent with the fashion ideal of sloping shoulders,
they fit the top portion of the torso closely. Some capes had arm slits for
ease of movement. Cloaks were extremely full in order to accommodate
the full sleeves and skirts.

Jackets and coats naturally followed dress lines, making them many
times wider at the hem than at the shoulder. Jackets or paletots, as they
were called, may have been more popular than coats due to the weight

the latter would have added. Even coats tended to be six to ten inches shorter than the hem of the skirt.

Shawls were very popular. They were oversized and extended well down the back of the skirt. Commonly, two yard squares were folded into a triangle. Double square shawls could be 64 inches by 128 inches or more. Some shawls were knitted or crocheted. Others were made from wool or lace. Many were decorated with fringe, ruffles, or lace. Paisley shawls were particularly popular.

"Mantle" was the general term for other outer garments not previously mentioned. Mantles tended to be basically triangular in shape, although the back could easily have a rounded "point." They extended over the shoulders and were slightly shaped at the arms. The long ends in front assumed a variety of shapes. For summer wear the fabrics tended to be light and unlined. Winter mantles were made of heavier, lined fabrics.

Headgear   The bonnet style specific to the 1860s was the spoon bonnet, so named because the brim curved high over the forehead, causing the wearer's face to look as though it was cradled in a large spoon. This style began to be seen in fashion magazines in 1862 to 1863. Some older women still favored the coal scuttle bonnet popular during the 1840s. These bonnets fit the head closely on the sides and extended straight out on all three sides, creating almost a tunnel effect for the wearer. Bonnets were one item of apparel women could constantly update by reworking the trim or decorations to meet the current vogue. Favored decorative features included ribbon, lace, and clusters of silk flowers or berries. These were used on the outside of the bonnet as well as inside the brim to frame the face. Huge ribbons several inches wide were tied in large bows beneath the chin. The outsides of bonnets were covered in silk, or more commonly, polished cotton, which was then pleated, ruched, piped, or quilted. A gathered flounce or skirt was often found attached to the base of the bonnet at the nape of the neck. For summer wear, bonnets were often made of straw.

For country wear, there was the flat-crowned, wide-brimmed "picture" hat made from felt or straw. This often had a lace edging that hung down, almost like a veil. These hats were decorated with materials similar to those used on bonnets, but less elaborately. As the decade progressed, the brim shrank and curved slightly over the eyes, the lace was removed, and the crown became more rounded. Hats continued to shrink as the decade progressed. A popular style was the "pork pie," which resembled a turban in shape with very little space between the brim and the crown. Another type of walking hat had a round crown and a small, rolling brim often decorated by a drooping ostrich feather.

When serious protection from the sun was needed, the slatted bonnet came to the rescue. These work garments were made of cotton or linen and bore neither decorations nor trim. They had long back pieces that extended over the shoulders, and the front could be folded back or fully extended to shade the entire face. Women were seldom photographed in sunbonnets due to their unflattering appearance. During the first federal occupation of Winchester, Laura Lee reported that Master Provost Phileborn opposed the wearing of sunbonnets by women on the street. "Calico and gingham sunbonnets are worn by all the ladies here and styled secession bonnets. They were adopted for their cheapness and for their defense against staring soldiers, but they [the soldiers] resent it and say they are intended as an insult by intimating that we do not care how we dress while they are here."[17]

Indoors, women frequently wore morning caps. These were dainty caps made of muslin, lace tulle, and ribbon. They would never be worn outdoors. Crocheted nets were also worn, but they were generally not considered suitable for dress occasions. Some conservative older women wore more substantial caps, often with lappets, which fully covered the head and were reminiscent of the caps worn during the previous century.

Aprons were an important item in a nineteenth-century wardrobe. Household aprons were extremely large, enveloping almost the entire skirt from front to back and extending **Ancillary Clothing** down to within a few inches of the hem. Often they had rectangular tops, known as pinners because they were held in place by pins rather than a neck strap as we see in the twentieth-century. Aprons would often be made from fabrics with small plaids or checks to help hide stains. While they could be solid, they were seldom white. Aprons were made from linen, flannel, wool, or cotton. Wool was greatly preferred for safety around fires. It does not burn as quickly as linen, and its odor when burning gives fair warning. Burns were the second leading cause of death for women at this time, surpassed only by death during childbirth. Smaller aprons would be worn for mealtimes unless the meals were served by servants. Separate aprons were kept for particularly dirty household chores.

Fancy, decorative aprons were sometimes worn only for show. These were made of fine-quality fabrics and were sometimes decorated with lace, embroidery, or ruffles. *Godey's Lady's Book* illustrates an apron "one breadth of bright plaid silk trimmed with lace and quilled ribbon; black moire d'antique on each side." These aprons would be much shorter than their functional counterparts, extending only two-thirds to three-fourths of the way down to the hem. Light-colored fabrics were often used, and many were made of polished cotton fabric. Ladies' magazines of the period gave patterns for decorative aprons as sewing projects. These aprons would be worn when doing needlework or when receiving guests at home.[18]

Gloves were essential to a nineteenth-century woman's wardrobe. Arthur Martine, in his *Hand-Book of Etiquette, and Guide to True Politeness,* remarks, "When dancing is expected to take place, no one should go without new kid gloves: nothing is so revolting as to see one person in an assembly ungloved, especially where the heat of the room, and the exercise together, are sure to make the hands of the wearer redder than usual. Always wear your gloves in church or in a theater."[19]

Civil War period gloves were short. They extended to the wrist even for evening wear. Commonly, they were joined by a button at the wrist. Some were secured by short lacing. Kid was the most common material, but fabric and lace were also used. For day wear, gloves would be found in a wide variety of colors, but only white was proper for evening and formal wear. Some were embellished with decorative stitching or embroidery. Older women sometimes wore netted, lace, or silk mitts. These fingerless gloves were popular during the 1840s and 1850s and continued to be worn by less fashionable women who perhaps became enamored with this style in their youth.

Footwear Shoes had small heels of one inch or less and flat, square toes. For ordinary wear they were made from leather or cloth and were black, light brown, or gray. Formal day dress shoes would be made of fancier fabrics such as satin. Evening shoes came in a variety of styles. Some had ribbon ties that wrapped around the ankle. Others displayed embroidered tops. Evening shoes were often in bright colors to match the ensemble.

Women's boots were ankle height and laced up the sides at the inside with elastic gussets at each side. Some buttoned at the sides. Dressy boots might be made from kid or satin. Congress gaiters were made of cloth, came in a variety of colors, and were tipped in patent leather. They were a rather low-cut boot and finished with a wide piece of elastic on the side. Balmoral boots were very popular. They laced up the front and were considered very stylish.

House slippers were low-heeled mule-like foot coverings commonly done in Berlin work featured in patterns from ladies' magazines. Slippers were also crocheted in a low, bootie style. *Peterson's Magazine* gave a pattern that directed the maker to finish it in the following manner: "Sew the slipper to a cork-sole, and run an elastic in the top of the slipper."[20]

Accessories As in the previous century, fans were a popular accessory. The traditional semicircular fan was often covered in paper or silk. Some were beautifully painted. A popular style during the 1860s had oval-shaped fabric leaves attached to the sticks. The average fan length of this period was six to ten inches. Circular fans were also fashionable. Their handles, when folded backwards, revealed an accordion-pleated fabric fan. Round or spade-shaped palmetto or straw fans were less expensive and were sometimes homemade.

Umbrellas and parasols were two different accessories, and each served a separate purpose. Umbrellas were for use in inclement weather. They were large and black and were meant to protect the carrier. Parasols were small, ladylike contrivances. Their purpose was to protect the carrier from both the sun and unwanted glances. Frames were made of metal. Handles were ivory or wood. Parasols designed for carriage rides often had a hinge at the top of the stick which allowed the top to tip in order to better fit the confined space. They varied in length from sixteen to twenty-two inches. Parasols used for walking were generally larger, twenty-two to twenty-six inches. Silk was the most common fabric. Trimming was lace or ruching. Oriental-style paper parasols with cane ribs were used at the seaside or for informal occasions.

Purses came in a variety of styles during the 1860s. Some were carried by short handles; others, sometimes referred to as waist pouches, were suspended from the waistband. *Peterson's Magazine* presented two patterns for waist pouches:

> We have just received two patterns from Paris of the little pouches, which still continue to be worn, suspended from the waistband by a chain and hook, and sometimes by a cord. They are made in all kinds of materials, and are embroidered in gold, silver, and jet; or they are made of the same material as the dress with which they are worn, and trimmed in the same manner. Last year, it will be remembered, we gave a pattern of one of those Pouches, when they first came up.[21]

Patterns for crocheted, knitted, or Berlin work purses abound in period ladies' magazines. Purses were decorated with tassels, cording, and embroidery. Shapes were round or rectangular, but the six-inch-square bag was most popular. One of the most interesting kinds of purses was a long, thin knit or netted cylinder closed at both ends with a slit in the center. These were called miser purses or long purses and were quite popular. Formal purses often had beading or were made with metallic thread.

Many photographs from the period show women wearing some jewelry. Popular materials included jet, ivory, bone, onyx, **Jewelry** jade, amber, garnet, and pearl. Still living in the shadow of its discovery in California, gold was the order of the day. Particularly fashionable was the brooch worn at the center of the neckline. Brooches varied in size from large to small and were worn both vertically and horizontally. They closed by simple "C" clasps without safety catches. Cameos were highly favored.They often bore images of mythological figures. The female head, almost synonymous with the modern cameo, was just coming into fashion toward the end of the war. Cameos were made from sardonyx, shell, lava, ivory, and coral.

The mid-nineteenth century was a very romantic and sentimental era.

It was a common practice to have a lock of hair as a keepsake from a loved one. Many period brooches contained a lock of a beloved's under glass in the center of the brooch. Other brooch materials included goldstone, agate, bog oak, enamel, horn, and mosaics. The mosaic pieces were very small and portrayed classical scenes or floral sprays. Enameled pieces were usually blue or black with a gold figure in the center.

Other neckline decorations included short necklaces of single-sized pearls or beads, especially jet. Long chains were popular in the previous decade and were still being worn by some. Both a beaded and a long chain necklace might be worn at the same time.

Other forms of jewelry were prevalent. Bracelets were also stylish and often were worn in pairs, one on each wrist. They tended to be large, almost chunky, bangle style. Serpents were one motif much in vogue. Jet beads strung on wire were also worn. Dangling earrings with long ear wires were worn. These were usually shorter than those worn later in the century. Many earrings were made of hollow wear, an inexpensive rolled gold that appears almost puffed, or formed into hollow tubes. Naturally, this made the earrings very light in weight. Use of acorns as a motif was widespread. Often earrings and brooches came in matched sets.

The wearing of rings was widespread. Unmarried females would wear a ring on the first finger of their left hand, no doubt in hope that they would soon be wearing one on the third digit of that same hand. A simple gold band was the prevalent sign of a married woman. Generally, diamond rings were not worn. The diamond mines of South Africa were not discovered until 1870, and not until then would diamonds become affordable to anyone but the most affluent. Rings were likely to bear garnets, amethysts, pearls, onyx, amber, jade, red coral, or cameos.

Watch ownership was fairly common by this time even for women. Watches were worn on watch chains and were tucked in the belt or carried in a watch pocket at the waist. Patterns for crochet, beaded, and braidwork watch pockets appeared in period ladies' magazines. Watches were hung on a long, fine chain worn around the neck that extended well below the waist. Some were suspended on a short chain from the belt.

Hairstyles   As with other fashion items, hairstyles wanted to emphasize a broad upper body. To that end, the center part is almost universal in period photographs. This allows for a wide, bare forehead, making the face appear broad while adding no height on top. To continue this illusion, the fullest part of the hairstyle was at or below the ears. Some teens wore their hair cut blunt just below the earlobes. Most women, however, had long hair which they wore rolled, braided, or otherwise confined and pulled toward the back of the head. If the hair was not confined, it was generally fixed in long finger

A variety of hairstyles from cartes de visite in the
authors' collection.

curls and pulled to the side of the face. The variety of curls and hair
rolls was as rich as the ingenuity of the women who styled them. As the
war drew to a close, hairstyles were beginning to change to include ten-
drils and greater height.

Ladies' magazines of the period offered many suggestions for elaborate hair dressing for evening wear and suggested incorporating such
items as flower blossoms, pins, combs, chains, feathers, and false curls.
The "Editor's Table" of *Peterson's* offered this counsel to its readers:

Perfect cleanliness is indispensable for the preservation of the
health, beauty, and color of the hair, as well as its duration; this is
attained by frequently washing it in tepid soft water, using those
soaps which have the smallest portion of alkali in their composi-

tion, as this substance renders the hair too dry, and by depriving it of its moist coloring matter, impairs at once its strength and beauty. After washing, the hair should be immediately dried; and when the towel has ceased to imbibe moisture, brushed constantly in the sun or before the fire until its lightness and elasticity are fully restored; and in dressing it, a little marrow pomatum, bear's grease, or fragrant oil should be used. The belief that washing the hair induces catarrh, or headache, or injures the hair is erroneous.[22]

Of course, women's clothing styles changed rapidly during this period; but interest in the Civil War era has frozen many of the archetypes of women's apparel in time. While Civil War era photographs and engravings lock the view of an instant in time, nothing has had greater influence in this regard than the film *Gone With the Wind*. Care must be taken in drawing conclusions from this film, not only about the clothing worn during the period, but also about the lifestyle portrayed and the interpersonal relations among the characters.

NOTES

1. Hague, 81.

2. Mrs. E. F. Haskell, *The Housekeeper's Encyclopedia* (Mendocino: R. L. Shep, 1992), 15–23.

3. Hague, 39.

4. C. V. Woodward, 565.

5. East, 132–133.

6. C. V. Woodward, 588.

7. McGuire, 292.

8. C. V. Woodward, 456.

9. Hague, 115.

10. Shep, 127–129. Mrs. Merrifield, "The Use and Abuse of Colors in Dress," *Peterson's Magazine*, September 1861.

11. From a *Godey's Ladey's Book* print in the authors' collection.

12. C.V. Woodward, 559–560.

13. Ibid., 649.

14. Ibid., 259.

15. Hague, 112.

16. Ann S. Stephens, "Demorest's Prize Medal Hoop Skirts," *Peterson's Magazine*, October 1861. Shep, 184.

17. Campbell and Rice, 83.

18. From a print in the authors' collection taken from *Godey's Ladey's Book*, July 1861.

19. Martine, 55.

20. Shep, 64–65. Jane Weaver, "Crochet Slipper," *Peterson's Magazine*, April 1861.

21. Shep, 151. Jane Weaver, " Waist-Pouches," *Peterson's Magazine*, September, 1861.

22. Shep, 326. "Editor's Table," *Peterson's Magazine*, September 1864.

16

Dressed for the Part: Men's, Children's, and Slaves' Clothing

"Well-bred people do not often dress in what is called the 'height of fashion,' that is generally left to dandies and pretenders."
—*Martine's Hand-Book of Etiquette*

In his handbook of etiquette, Martine remarks, "There are four kinds of coats which a man must have: a business coat, a frock-coat, a dress-coat, and an over-coat. A well dressed man may do well with four of the first, and one each of the others per annum. An economical man can get along with less." Nonetheless, Martine's idea of "getting along" was nowhere near reality. Just as the average woman did not have a specialized outfit for every task of the day, most men did not enjoy the wardrobe depth detailed by Martine. Like women's clothing, men's clothing in practical application tended to fall into formal and informal, summer and winter. New clothes would be considered "best" dress until they became worn, and they would then be relegated to work status.[1] A shirt, vest, and trousers would be the very least in which a man would allow himself to be seen. A man appearing with anything less was considered to be in a state of undress. Even laborers and farmers would not allow themselves to go with less. It was the basest menial or workman who would not be so attired, such as the blacksmith, who would wear a heavy leather apron which covered him above the waist.

Dress shirts were made of white cotton. Longer than the modern shirt, they were pullovers that buttoned from the mid-chest to the neck. Small vertical tucks commonly decorated either side of the buttons, but this became less favored as the 1860s progressed. Shirts had neck bands and detachable collars. For formal day wear, the collar was upright with a gap between the points, which just touched the jaw, allowing for freer movement of the head and neck than had been the style earlier in the century. For informal occasions, men wore either a shallow single collar with sloping points meeting at the center and forming a small inverted "V" opening, or a shallow double collar similar to the modern collar. Work shirts were made in a variety of colors and checks and could be made from cotton or linen.

Cravats, which more closely resemble the earlier neck stock than the modern tie, were worn around the neck. The term "necktie" was just coming into use. The cravat might have been tied in a flat, broad bow with the ends extending across the top of the waistcoat or secured with a pin. Basically, however, it was a band of fabric passed around the neck and tied in either a bow or a knot with hanging ends. Silk was the fabric of choice, and it was one area where a man might be able to display his good taste even if his purse prohibited further extravagances. The decade began with a preference for light-colored cravats, occasionally decorated with embroidery or other fancy work. As the war progressed, however, darker colors became more prominent. Striped, plaid, and dotted cravats were also worn, but with less regularity. Even laborers would simulate the look, although they may only have been able to knot a cotton kerchief around their neck. Ladies' magazines of the period offered patterns for woolen and cotton knitted cravats. A pattern for a striped tie done in brioche knitting in *Peterson's* ended with, "We recommend this for a present for the holidays."[2]

Vests or waistcoats could be made of the same fabric as the suit, or they could be of much finer, dressier fabrics such as silk taffetas, embossed silks, or brocades. Patterns ranged from tone-on-tone to stripes, checks, and paisleys. The neckline cut was moving lower than in the previous decade. Watch pockets became common. Suits were either loose-fitting, almost baggy, or very formal with knee-length frock coats. The fuller suit seems to have been favored by the average man, perhaps because it was more comfortable or needed less skilled tailoring. The formal suit appears to have been the "look" to which men of power aspired. Lapels sported a more modern single notch than earlier in the century. Frock coats sometimes had velvet collars and cuff-link style buttoning. Work trousers had buttoned, full fall fronts, while dress trousers had "French flys," which concealed the buttons.

Wool was the fabric of choice for these items, with linen being popular during the summer, especially in the South. Farmers seemed to favor tweeds and more sturdy woolens. Generally, solids dominated, with

Men's suits from cartes de visite in the authors'
collection.

browns and grays most common. Black was the choice of professionals, who also preferred fine woolen broadcloth, serge, and twill. These fabrics often had a certain amount of silk woven in to give them a finer finish and lighter weight. Martine advises gentlemen:

If a gentleman is able to dress expensively it is very well for him to do so, but if he is not able to wear ten-dollar broadcloth, he may comfort himself with the reflection that cloth, which costs but five dollars a yard will look quite as well when made into a well-fitting coat. With this suit, and well-made shoes, clean gloves, a white pocket-handkerchief, and an easy and graceful deportment withal, he may pass muster as a gentleman.[3]

Hat styles varied. The stovepipe hat favored by Abraham Lincoln also came in a shorter version. Many Southern gentlemen favored what has come to be called the plantation hat. This is a low-crowned, stylish hat with a substantial, but not overstated, brim. The design of the plantation hat may have been brought back from Panama, where a similar hat was seen by travelers crossing the Isthmus to the gold fields of California in the late 1840s and early 1850s. Another hat commonly found had a round crown with a medium brim. The derby was not developed until later in the century. Flat-topped straw hats were worn in summer by many. Rural men often wore wide-brimmed high-crowned hats, which offered less in fashion but more in protection from the elements. In inclement weather, men carried large black umbrellas.

Male jewelry was not as ostentatious as it had been in earlier periods. Rings of all types were popular. They took the form of signet rings, seal rings, mourning rings, and commemorative rings. Smaller neckties made the tiepin unnecessary in most cases. The longer coats of the sixties made the watch chain, which hung below a short waistcoat, impractical. The watch chain was now displayed from the waistcoat pocket to a button at mid-chest.

Braces or suspenders buttoned on to the trousers by means of leather tabs. It was quite the fashion for women to crochet braces or work them in Berlin woolwork. Ladies' magazines featured patterns for this work, but makers were cautioned, "This crochet should not be done too tightly, as a little elasticity is desirable."[4] Elastic, made from natural rubber, had been invented by this time, but its only apparel application was in wide panels in shoes. Men unfortunate enough to have no braces made by an attentive woman may have sported those made of plain or striped linen.

Underwear required two pieces. The undershirt was a long-sleeved pullover that buttoned to mid-chest. The drawers extended down to the ankle and had button fronts. They could be made of silk stockinette, cotton, or linen. One-piece union suits, with or without the "trap door" in the rear, were not developed until the 1890s.

When it came to lounging in the privacy of one's home, gentlemen had several specialized items of attire. Lounging or smoking caps were elaborate items made of rich fabrics and adorned with embroidery, beadwork, or braid. They generally came in three basic styles: the round pillbox style, the fitted six-panel cap, and the teardrop-shaped Scotch style. The first two styles ended with a tassel on top. The last was finished with a narrow ribbon at the back of the cap at the point. Ladies' magazines also carried patterns for making and decorating these caps. *Peterson's* suggests that a hand-made lounging cap "would make a very pretty Christmas, New Year's, or birthday gift for a gentleman."[5] In addition to slippers, which greatly resembled the woman's slipper for relaxed footwear at home, a man might have preferred the dressing, or lounging, boot. *Peterson's* advises, "The Lounging Boot, will almost supersede the slipper, as many gentlemen catch cold by changing from a

The variety of men's hairstyles and facial hair was
almost inexhaustible in this period. This sampling
from cartes de visite in the authors' collection
illustrates some popular styles.

boot to a slipper, even in the house." These boots were made of fabric
and were decorated with elaborate embroidery.[6]

Nightshirts were made of white cotton and extended to the ankle.
They had long sleeves and small turned-down collars. The nightcap was
a bag-shaped item with a tassel on top. Some were knit or crocheted,
but these were going out of style. Over his nightshirt a gentleman may
have worn a wrapper. This was a long, sack-style robe with plain sleeves,
confined by a cord at the waist.

Men wore their hair parted to the side. Facial hair was very stylish.
Men sported beards of all styles, lengths, and degrees. Mustaches were
equally in favor. Period photographs show a tremendous variety of
styles. The names of most of these have become meaningless to modern

observers. The term "sideburns," however, can be traced to General Ambrose Burnside, who sported distinctively bushy whiskers. The size and style of sideburns and beards varied greatly between individuals and over time.

Children's   Children's clothing rivaled women's fashions both in com-
Clothing   plexity and ornateness. Some middle- and upper-class chil-
                      dren were dressed in layers of clothing often constructed of
impractical fabrics. *Godey's Lady's Book* carried the following description, accompanied by a picture: "Child's dress of green silk with narrow pinked ruffles, corselet of green silk, white muslin gimp, white felt hat with white wing." Ornate as it sounds, this outfit is not classified as a party dress. Gauze, silk, wool, and taffeta were common fabric suggestions for children's dress in ladies' magazines. Print fabrics tended to be small geometric or abstract designs. These designs allowed for the economical use of material since it was easier to match such prints, and there was less waste. Braid or ribbon were popular trims even for children.

In rural areas, children's clothing was considerably more practical, much the same as their parents'. Muslin and cotton were the fabrics of choice for country and poorer folk. In order to allow for growth, it was common for seams at the shoulders and under the arms to be folded in an inch each, so that they could be let out as the child grew. Sometimes a waistband was added as the child grew to lengthen skirts and trousers. Several tucks, of an inch or so, were often made near the hems of skirts and trousers. These created an attractive detail and could later be let down to accommodate growth.

Little girls were dressed very much as were their mothers. *Godey's Lady's Book* even contained an illustration for a "corset for a little girl" which laced down the back only. This was not encouraged by everyone, however, as the "Editor's Table" in *Peterson's* points out. "Stays or tight bands about the ribs compress them readily, as these bones are not fully formed, hence readily cause deformities, and alter the natural and healthy position and action of the lungs, heart, liver and stomach, and produce a tendency to disease in these organs."[7]

The main difference between a woman's attire and a girl's was that girls' skirts were considerably shorter, ending about mid-calf. Pantalettes hung just below the edge of the dress. These would be plain for everyday wear and would be adorned with lace or eyelet for dressier occasions. These pantalettes differed from women's in that the crotches were sewn and they buttoned at the sides. Like her mother, a little girl wore a chemise as the basic undergarment. By age seven a girl would have begun to wear a hoop, although it would likely have only one hoop ring at this time. Once again, like an adult woman, she would wear under and over petticoats. One popular style for Sunday and party dresses was

The variety of clothing for girls is exemplified by
these cartes de visite from the authors' collection.
The picture at the lower left illustrates a common
problem with bateau necklines for the very young.

the bateau or "boat" neckline. This extremely wide neckline was another
impractical fashion, and many photographs show one sleeve slipping off
the child's shoulder.

In Margaret Mitchell's book *Gone with the Wind* and in the subsequent
film of the same name, Scarlett O'Hara's dress in the opening scenes was
considered inappropriate by the other characters, not because it was re-
vealing, but rather because it was too juvenile for a young woman of
her age, having an open neckline and a short skirt.

Like their mothers, little girls wore undersleeves and chemisettes. They
also wore tuckers. A tucker was a panel of crimped muslin secured by
a tape and sewn on the inside edge of the neckline and sleeve edge. Its
purpose was to save wear on the fabric, and the tucker could be removed

and laundered separately from the garment. Blouses and skirts were not popular for toddlers but were worn by older girls.

Fancy aprons were popular. They tied around the waist and covered almost the entire skirt portion of a dress. The top covered only part of the dress front and crossed over both shoulders on top. They were commonly decorated with flounces, bows, and other decorative details. Pinafores, which covered almost the entire dress, were more practical and much more common across all economic lines. They were constructed in such fabrics as muslin, calico, or linen. The pinafore fit closely to the chest and hung down loosely to the hem. Another layered style for young girls was the white dress covered by another jumper-like dress.

Children's jewelry tended to be modest and simple. Little girls wore strings of beads, lockets, and chains. Very young girls wore coral necklaces or pairs of coral bracelets. Infants were given elaborate coral rattles mounted in silver or teething rings also made of coral.

Boys wore a series of different types of outfits, each befitting a certain age group. Very young boys often had shirts that buttoned to the waistband of their pants and provided a neater look. From ages one to four, boys wore a nankeen suit. This was a dresslike costume worn over white underdrawers not unlike a girl's pantalettes, although likely to be less fancy. The top portion of the suit was a blousy sack, often with a large sash or a cord tied around the waist.

Between the ages of four and seven, there was the French blouse. Essentially, it was a loose, dresslike tunic secured at the waist by a belt and large buckle or sash. This would have been worn over loose knee pants, although it was also worn over a skirt by very young boys. Boys may also have been attired in a loose jacket and waistcoat, once again with loose knee pants. Boys may also have been clad in a suitlike outfit with a slightly cut-away jacket, gently rounded in front, and very loose trousers which extended to about mid-calf.

From seven to twelve a boy may have worn what would be thought of as a suitlike outfit comprised of loose, ankle-length trousers and waist-length sack coat with a ribbon tie fashioned into a bow. The pants might have "box plaits." Suspenders could be introduced at this point. Sailor suits were also popular for boys seven to fourteen. Some boys in certain areas did not wear long pants until fourteen or fifteen years of age.

It is no wonder that the knickerbocker suit was welcomed by older boys who were as yet considered too young for trousers. Knickerbocker suits consisted of a button-faced jacket fastened merely with a hook and eye at the top; a ten-button waistcoat with small slits at the sides to allow for ease of movement and better fit; and knickerbockers, loose-fitting pants that came tight against the leg just below the knee. Emily May proclaimed in *Peterson's*:

The Knickerbocker costume is now the favorite style of dress for boys, when they are of that awkward age, too young to be breeched, and too old to wear frocks and pinafores. This costume has a great many recommendations: it can be made in almost any material; it always looks neat and tidy; and for the play-ground is particularly suitable, as it leaves boys the free use of their limbs, besides being rather more manly than petticoats, which used to be (particularly at school) a boy's abhorrence.[8]

As older teens, boys dressed much as adult men did. They wore pants, vests, and jackets. Jacket types included sack, frock, and a short, military style. Boys' undergarments included an undershirt and drawers that reached down to the knee. When boys graduated into longer pants, they wore longer, ankle-length drawers that fit the leg more closely.

For outerwear, children often wore coats, jackets, and cloaks similar to those worn by women. They also wore capes secured by buttoned tabs across the chest. Girls generally wore small hats, usually straw for summer and cloth for winter. As with women, slatted bonnets were worn in rural areas. Brims tended to be small, and they were very simply decorated. Boys wore caps and small hats with rounded crowns.

Girls wore leather or canvas short boots for day wear and slippers for dressy occasions. Some of the slippers had ankle straps. The boots either laced up the side or had elastic gussets on the side. Canvas boots often had toe and heel portions covered in leather for added protection and durability. Boys wore similar footwear or short pull-on boots decorated with a tassel on the front.

Girls wore their hair in a short, ear-length blunt cut that was pushed behind the ears. Some wore their hair in long finger curls. The latter style seems to have been more popular among girls of higher economic status. Occasionally ribbons were used to keep the long hair out of the face. Girls of about eight or nine began to wear their hair in hair nets. Sarah Morgan, aged nineteen, wrote in her diary, "The net I had gathered my hair in fell in my descent and my hair swept down half way between my knee and my ankle in one stream."[9] Like their mothers', girls' hair was center parted. Boys parted their hair to the side. The sides and back were usually short. Because fashions for young children were not strongly differentiated by sex, when looking at photographs, the part is often the only clue to the sex of the child.

Finally, the "Editor's Table" of *Peterson's* offers the following advice to mothers about clothing children:

To guard against cold, the child should wear flannel, of varying thickness, according to the season of the year, next to the body, and

All of these cartes de visite show young boys. In
pictures of the young the way the hair is parted is
often the only clue to the child's sex. Boys' hair was
parted on the side.

fitting tolerably close, for, without this protection, the present style
of dress, causing the clothes to project away, leaves the body exposed to sudden chills. The head should be lightly covered, so as
to protect it from the sun, or sudden change of temperature; but it
should never be covered with thick or heavy material. Anything
causing fullness or congestion about the head will very commonly
act by sympathy, as it is called, on the stomach, and cause obstinate
and violent vomiting. . . . A pin should never be used about a
child's clothes at any age; buttons and strings should always be the
modes of fastening.[10]

Infants wore long gowns that were often twice the length of the child.
This was done to keep the child warm. Long gowns could not be cast

off as loose blankets could. The gowns were generally white to withstand the frequent washings infant clothing required and were of "soft material, entirely free from starch."[11] For the first few weeks after birth, infants wore long, narrow strips of fabric known as belly bands. These were several yards long and were designed to protect the navel. In addition to diapers, or napkins, as they were called, infants wore a shirt, a pinner which contained their lower limbs, a skirt or skirts, and a dress. Babies also wore caps, for which women's magazines frequently carried patterns.

The *Housekeeper's Encyclopedia* details the order of operations in dressing a baby:

> The first article put on, after a napkin, should be a flannel band, from four to four and a half inches wide; pin it snugly, but not tight enough to bind, and make the babe uncomfortable; the little shirt is the next article of dress to be put on the child; this should be open at the front, and folded smoothly, so as to leave no wrinkles; the pinner comes next; lay the infant on its stomach, fold the shirt smoothly on its back, fasten the shirt and pinner together with a small pin, leaving the point covered, so as to prick neither child nor nurse; wrap its feet in the pinner, and pin it as close as possible without cramping its limbs; then take the flannel skirt . . . fold the shirt over, and fasten shirt, band pinner, and skirt, together with two pins, near the arms, being sure to have the points hid in the clothing. . . . fasten the dress, and the little one is ready for presentation.[12]

As the child grew older clothing adjustments were made. Mothers were advised, "Keep socks on after the child is two months old; before this, its pinners will be sufficient protection. . . . When a child shows a disposition to creep, shorten its clothes that it may have free use of its limbs, and protect its feet with stockings and shoes."[13]

The clothing of slaves varied with the economic status of the slaveholder and with the tasks the slave was required to do. Slaves who worked in the household, often well dressed in suits, dresses, or "colonial" outfits, were seen by visitors to **Slaves' Clothing** the home, and therefore their appearance would have been a reflection on the slaveholder. Slaves who worked in the fields needed serviceable clothing that would survive the rigors of the work being done. Any benefit that the slave gained in the way of clothing was an accidental advantage of the owner's desire to run an efficient plantation and a model household.

Sarah Stone was the daughter of a Mississippi plantation owner who held 150 slaves. In her diary she described the semiannual process of

A *Godey's* print of a variety of children's fashions (1861).

getting clothes ready for the slaves, which she admits "was no light work."

> When the time would come to have everything cut out; a room would be cleared out and the great bolts of white woolen jeans, Osnabergs, with bolt after bolt of red flannel for the little ones, would be rolled in and the women with great shears would commence their work. There were several sets of patterns with individual ones for the very tall and the very fat, but there was not much attention paid to the fit, I fancy.[14]

Male slaves were furnished with only two or three suits a year. Women were supplied with a calico or linsey dress, head handkerchiefs, and gingham aprons for Christmas. The fabric was sturdy and became as soft as flannel as it was washed. The slaves often dyed the white suits tan or gray with willow bark or sweet gum.

Stone was particularly struck by the shoes the slaves were given.

> And those heavy russet shoes that all clumped about in, the old and the young, men and women . . . so ugly and must have been excessively uncomfortable—about as pliable as wood. After many, many greasings, the poor darkies could at last bend their feet in them.[15]

The quality and quantity of clothing for slaves during the war varied greatly, and generally both suffered as the war continued. These garments often represented white folks' hand-me-downs, remnants, and discards. Slaves, especially those in urban areas, could often be seen in slightly unfashionable, but serviceable, suits of clothing and dresses of cotton and wool. As whites felt the pinch of the blockade, hand-me-downs and discards took on a new value in their eyes and were rarely passed on to slaves. In this manner the slaves were made to bear the worst effects of the shortages.

Plantation slaves were often clothed in coarse but durable "Negro cloth," which was produced from linen in the mills of New England, or in coarse woolen broadcloth. Prior to the opening of hostilities, plantation owners commonly purchased cloth by the yard and allowed the slaves to fashion the clothing on the plantation. This cloth took the form of trousers and shirts for the men and boys, while slave women wore woolen dresses with cotton aprons. The wool helped to prevent the skirts from catching fire and was favored by women, both black and white, who worked near open hearths. Both sexes used straw hats and handkerchiefs in a variety of ways, but generally they were tied to form head coverings or neck cloths.

Shoes were a difficult item to provide for the slave at a reasonable cost, and most ex-slaves complained of rarely having owned shoes that fit well. Unless they owned a slave that was trained in shoemaking from raw leather, plantation owners resorted to buying shoes in bulk. There existed an entire trade in New England dedicated to the manufacture of cheap shoes for slaves. These shoes rarely gave long use without the services of a cobbler. Wooden clogs, a type of sandal with a large wooden sole, often served in place of shoes. Slaves generally preferred to go barefoot in the fields, as did their white farmer counterparts, because shoes do not hold up well in plowed fields. Contemporary illustrations from *Harper's* and *Leslie's* almost always show slaves to be shod. Slaves who were forced to go barefoot in winter greased their feet with tallow to protect the skin, but this circumstance seems to have been rare except in the Deep South. Slaves rarely went unshod in town or in the Northern border states as such a thing would have embarrassed their owners.

NOTES

1. Martine, 49.
2. Shep, 345. Jane Weaver, "Gentleman's Neck-Tye in Brioche Knitting," *Peterson's Magazine*, December 1864.
3. Martine, 49.
4. Shep, 290. Jane Weaver, "Gentlemen's Braces," *Peterson's Magazine*, May 1864.

5. Shep, 344. Jane Weaver, "Imperial Lounging-Cap," *Peterson's Magazine*, December 1864.

6. Shep, 275. Jane Weaver, "Gentleman's Dressing or Lounging Boot," *Peterson's Magazine*, April 1864.

7. Shep, 326. "Editor's Table," *Peterson's Magazine*, September 1864.

8. Shep, 189–190. Mrs. Emily May, "The Knickerbocker Suit," *Peterson's Magazine*, November 1861.

9. East, 102.

10. Shep, 326. "Editor's Table," *Peterson's Magazine*, September 1864.

11. Haskell, 384.

12. Ibid., 383–384.

13. Ibid., 385–386.

14. Sullivan, 6–7. Quoting Sarah Katherine Stone in *Brokenburn: The Journal of Kate Stone, 1861–1868*.

15. Sullivan, 7.

17

Elevating and Expanding the Young Mind

> "If a spirit of inquiry is once aroused, it will, sooner or later, find means to satisfy itself; and thus the inquisitive boy will become an energetic, capable man."—*The Mother's Book*

It was essential that children be prepared for the intellectual and cultural life the nineteenth century valued so highly. A lesson entitled "The Value of Education" in a school reader states, "The highest objects of a good education are, to reverence and obey God, and to love and serve mankind. Every thing that helps in attaining these objects, is of great value, and every thing that hinders us, is comparatively worthless."[1]

The home, of course, was the first place where these foundations were laid. *The Mother's Book* by Lydia Child—the Dr. Spock of her day—advocated the deliberate and early cultivation of a child's intellect. After describing some simple amusements for the small child, Mrs. Child advised, "But something ought to be mixed with these plays to give the child the habits of thought."[2] She then proceeded to describe situations in which basic daily activities could be converted into stimulating intellectual endeavors. She urged that as children grew older they should be told, "The more knowledge you gain, the more useful you can be, when you become a man." Additionally, it was essential that children be fortified with solid moral foundations. Mrs. Child cautioned against selecting readings for children that merely culminated in a moral. "The morality should be in the book, not tacked upon the *end* of it." With such

The little red schoolhouse of Norwalk, Connecticut, was built in 1826. The one-room building served as a grammar school into the twentieth century.

home training, children entered school at age four or five with certain basic moral and cultural understandings upon which would be built a formal education.[3]

In the North and Midwest, schools were community or common schools. These schools would be open to all children from the community. Conditions in common schools varied tremendously not only from north to south but from community to community. School revenue was directly tied to the success or failure of local commerce. In an 1861 report, numerous county superintendents in Pennsylvania reported frosts in June and early July. The resulting loss of the wheat crop caused not only "more than ordinary pecuniary embarrassment"; in addition, teaching time was shortened, and in some communities the wages of the teachers were reduced. More than one superintendent lamented a false system of economy that reduced teachers' wages so much that some of the best teachers left the county or became engaged in "other pursuits." Some districts chose to suspend school for the entire year. Nonetheless, remaining teachers were applauded for their self-denial and the manner in which they bore up during a difficult time. In the same year, where lumbering districts were favored by high water, there was increased prosperity.[4]

School buildings were constructed in a number of ways and might be of brick, frame, log, or stone. In the 1861 state report, 58 percent of the Pennsylvania superintendents who responded used negative terms to describe their schools. It was not unusual to see claims that the schools were "less fit for the purpose of schooling, than would be many modern out houses for sheltering cattle." One schoolhouse was described as "a crumbling, dilapidated, damp, unwholesome stone building with a ceiling eight feet high, room about twenty-six by thirty feet into which one hundred and seventeen are crowded, and placed at long, old fashioned desks, with permanent seats, without backs." One superintendent reported finding "the teacher and pupils huddled together, shivering with cold, and striving to warm themselves by the little heat generated from a quantity of green wood in the stove." Additional complaints included a lack of "out-houses and other appliances necessary for comfort and convenience." Concern was expressed over the fact that schoolhouses were "placed far off the road and buried in the wildest forest."[5]

Yet a number of new schools were described in more favorable terms. One report described a "tasteful brick building 30 x 45 . . . furnished with first class iron frame furniture for 62 pupils." Other new buildings were of wood, and one was "24 x 36 with four tiers of seats for two pupils each accommodating 64 pupils." Another superintendent boasted, "All the rooms are warmed by coal stoves, most of them have ceilings of proper height, windows adapted to ventilation; plenty of black-board surface; and they are tolerably well seated." A new schoolhouse was proudly described as having an "anti-room, closets and platform and in every respect is superior to most of the other houses."[6]

The schools were supervised by a group of designated citizens who oversaw operations. Their duties included "the levying of tax, the location of school houses, the purchase and sale of school property, the appointment and dismissal of teachers, and the selection of studies and textbooks." The dedication and expertise of these directors was, however, often called into question.[7]

Rural districts were often unsuccessful in obtaining a normal school graduate and had to settle for whatever reasonably well educated person they could find. Although both men and women taught, male teachers were preferred. As the war progressed, many young men left the schoolroom to serve in the army or to fill better-paying jobs. This dearth of males opened the doors for women in education. A county superintendent of schools wrote, "The employment of female teachers caused some dissatisfaction, as they were believed inadequate to the task of controlling a winter school. But superior cleanliness and arrangement of their rooms, the effect of their natural gentleness and goodness on the scholars . . . amply compensated for their want of physical force." These qualities were appreciated even more when it was found that the generally younger women could be paid lower salaries than the male teachers. The average salary reported in 1861 for a male teacher was $24.20 per month. Women were paid $18.11.[8]

"The majority of teachers are between eighteen and twenty-five, and are spending a part of the year in attending academies and Normal School," wrote one superintendent.[9] But some of the teachers were little more than children themselves. A superintendent complained:

It is to be regretted, however, that parents will urge their sons and daughters to seek to become teachers at so early an age; and it is a great error in directors, as a general rule, to employ such young persons. Men engage persons of mature age and experience on the farm, in the shop or store, in the kitchen or dairy room; but they hire girls or boys of 15 or 16 to train up and educate their offspring.[10]

School districts established examinations to certify that teachers were competent to assume their duties. Most exams were a combination of written and oral questions. "They were held publicly, and attended by numbers of citizens, who had a desire to see and hear for themselves."[11] Emma Sargent Barbour's sister, Maria, wrote about the examination process in Washington. "[Hattie was] accompanying me as far as City Hall where I was to be examined, when she remarked that she had a good mind to try just for fun. She went in and passed an excellent examination and next Monday will take a position at my school."[12] Not all examinations were quite as simple as Maria implies. Many superintendents in Pennsylvania reported having to turn away applicants who had failed, while others indicated that, considering the rural nature of their district, they were lucky to find teachers at all. "Parents prefer to have there [sic] children work in the mines or learn a trade, and thus but few become qualified to teach school."[13]

Institutes were held periodically to help teachers to improve their skills. Some met only once a year, while others were held semi-monthly on alternate Saturdays. Naturally, not all teachers performed to the satisfaction of the districts. A Wayne County, Pennsylvania, superintendent wrote of his teachers, "Two last winter had the reputation of being of intemperate habits, and some few are rough and rowdyish in their manner."[14]

About 50 percent of children outside the South attended school with some regularity. Some areas of the Midwest and New England had enrollments as high as 90 percent. Attendance in rural areas still suffered from the fact that many parents "task their children heavily with farm labor, and [not] until such tasks are finished are they allowed to start school."[15] Not everyone was convinced that public education was beneficial, but public sentiment was gradually becoming more favorable to the system. "People are beginning to see that their children can get a sound practical . . . education in our common schools."[16]

A *Harper's Weekly* conception of a mid-century
schoolroom.

Most Southerners were opposed to tax-supported education. The
school reformers and educational advocates of the 1840s were mostly
Northerners. This contributed to a certain skepticism on the part of
Southerners, who felt that the school systems were at least partially responsible for Northern attitudes in the decade preceding the war. Most
Southerners preferred to send their children to private institutions. By
1860 only four Southern states and a few isolated communities had common school systems.

Popular instructional materials included *McGuffey's Eclectic Reader*,
Ray's Arithmetic, and Webster's "blue back" *Speller*. Spelling was just
becoming standardized. *Leach's Complete Spelling Book* of 1859 contained
a "Collection of Words of Various Orthography," which included words
of "common use, which are spelled differently by the three most eminent
Lexicographers . . . Webster, Worcester and Smart."[17] Emma Sargent Barbour's letter from her young cousin Mary gives additional insight into
period texts: "I am getting along first rate, at school. I don't always get
10 tough by any means. I always get 9 in writing. I study Robinson's
Arithmetic, it is a very hard one. Frost's United States History, Towen's

speller, Weld's Grammar, the same almost exactly like the one I studied on east, but the Grammar is not at all like it. I read out of Sargent's Reader."[18] Students were graded by the reader from which they read. Many schools suffered from a lack of uniform class sets of texts, although the adoption of this practice was frequently a goal. "In time, however, as the old books, (some of which, carefully preserved, have descended from grand-fathers) are worn out, uniform class-books will be used, much to the advantage of teachers and pupils."[19]

In many schools sufficient blackboards were also wanting. Blackboards were made by taking smooth boards—painted black—and covering them with a chalk dust, which provided the erasable surface. Well-supported schools not only had blackboards but also outline maps, spelling and reading cards, charts, and globes. The average school had only one or two of these instructional materials. Paper was scarce in rural schools. Students commonly wrote on wood frame slates, although these were initially "confined to such as had made advancement in arithmetic; but now we find the smallest scholars engaged with their slates."[20]

Furniture was, at best, sparse in most classrooms. "It is useless to complain of school furniture," lamented one superintendent. "It seems that people would sooner see their children have spinal or pulmonary affliction, than furnish the school room with proper desks and seats." A York County, Pennsylvania, superintendent noted, "I witnessed a great deal of uneasiness, amounting in many instances to intense suffering, among the small children, from . . . being seated too high. In some instances, the desks are still attached to the wall, the scholars with their backs to the teacher."[21]

There were few, if any, educational standards at this time. The length of the school day and year varied as the individual community saw fit. The average length of the school term in 1860 was five months and five and one-half days. A typical school day ran from nine to four with an hour for recess and dinner at noon. The day often commenced with a scripture reading followed by a patriotic song. Emma Sargent Barbour received a letter from her sister, Maria, addressing her teaching duties. "I am a regular schoolmarm. School commences every day at nine o'clock when they write a half hour and the lessons follow."[22] A subsequent letter provides more details of a teacher's day. "School! School!—is the cry, my daily life may almost be embraced in the following programme; rise at seven, breakfast at half past, practice my little singing lesson and ready to start for school at half past eight. Direct the youths how to behave and hear lessons until twelve, then from twenty minutes to a half an hour, hear missed lessons and eat lunch, chat with the boys until one o'clock, then proceed as before until three; prepare for dinner and sometimes attend receptions or receive company in the evening."[23]

Most learning was done via rote memorization and recitation. To motivate the students, less interesting material, such as geographic facts, was sung to popular tunes. Multiplication tables were often taught in verse; for example, "Twice 11 are 22. Mister can you mend my shoe?" or "9 times 12 are 108. See what I've drawn upon my slate." Mental arithmetic was still an innovative technique, and more than one district reveled in the fact that it was taught in their schools. "Mental arithmetic has been extensively introduced during the past two years and will soon be considered an indispensable item even in our primary schools."[24]

In Connecticut, towns with eighty families were required to have a single school for young children that taught English grammar, reading, writing, geography, and arithmetic. Towns with 500 families added a school for older students that offered algebra, American history, geometry, and surveying. Places with larger populations offered study of the physical sciences—sometimes referred to as natural or revealed philosophy—and Greek and Latin. The subjects taught depended on the competency of the teacher and varied greatly from school to school. In the annual report of Armstrong County, Pennsylvania, the superintendent boasted: "The number of schools in which geography and grammar are not taught is steadily diminishing. There is a considerable increase in the number in which mental arithmetic is taught. Algebra was taught in 11 schools; history in 4; natural philosophy in 2; Latin in 1; composition in 5 and in several there were exercises in declamation and vocal music."[25]

In the same report, Beaver County noted, "The Bible is read in 140 schools; not read in 17. I trust that all our teachers may become so deeply impressed with a sense of their duty, in the moral education of their pupils, that we may soon report the Bible read in every school."[26] In addition to the three R's, schools were expected to infuse a strong moral sense, foster polite behavior, and inspire good character. Another instructional objective, presented in a reading text, was "a desire to improve the literary taste of the learner, to impress correct moral principles, and augment his fund of knowledge."[27] An introductory geography book contained the following extraordinary attestation in its preface: "The introduction of moral and religious sentiments into books designed for the instruction of young persons, is calculated to improve the heart, and elevate and expand the youthful mind; accordingly, whenever the subject has admitted of it, such observations have been made as tend to illustrate the excellence of Christian religion, the advantages of correct moral principles, and the superiority of enlightened institutions."[28]

Readers contained lessons entitled "The First Falsehood," "Effects of Evil Company," "Contrast Between Industry and Idleness," and "Dialogue between Mr. Punctual and Mr. Tardy." Stories, poems, and essays used in instruction drilled the message that good triumphed over evil, frugality surpassed extravagance, obedience superseded willfulness, and family always came first. This can be seen even in brief multiplication rhymes—"5 times 10 are 50. My Rose is very thrifty"[29] or "4 times 10 are 40. Those boys are very naughty." The last was inscribed beneath a picture of two boys fighting.[30]

Some texts published in the North during the war contained distinctly pro-Union sentiments. *Hillard's Fifth Reader,* printed in 1863, contained such readings as "Liberty and Union" and "The Religious Character of President Lincoln," as well as "Song of the Union," the poem " Barbara Frietchie," and an essay on the "Duty of American Citizens" among many similar patriotic themes. Caroline Cowles Richards wrote in her 1861 diary, "I recited 'Scott and the Veteran' today at school, and Mary Field recited, 'To Drum Beat and Heart Beat a Soldier Marches By.' Anna recited 'The Virginia Mother.' Everyone learns war poems now-a-days."[31]

Rural schools were often ungraded and had no standard final examinations or report cards. Scholastic success was still given a showcase via exhibition bees and quizzes held for parents. Students demonstrated their expertise in spelling, arithmetic, geography, and history. In addition to praise, winners were given certificates and prizes such as books or prints. Gifted students could pass through the entire local system of schools by age fourteen or fifteen, but only the most affluent could move on to college or university. A foreign visitor to New England found that most men had a basic education that stressed reading and writing, but that few exhibited the fine formal education available in Europe.

Southern teachers were even more challenged by the need for educational materials than their Northern counterparts. The South had depended on the North and Europe for texts prior to the war. Once the war began, Northern publications were held in contempt and the blockade curtailed European imports. A movement commenced in the South to produce its own texts, but shortages of materials and the destruction of printing equipment impeded implementation of the plan. What texts were published tended to be extremely propagandistic and of low quality. Marinda Branson Moore of North Carolina was probably the most audacious of Southern authors in this regard. She published *Dixie Primer for Little Folks* and *Dixie Speller,* which was "revised from Webster and adapted for Southern schools . . . leaving out all Yankee phrases and allusions." Her geography addressed the issues of slavery and secession and laid blame for the war on the North.[32]

Southerners regretted having allowed Northerners to teach their children prior to the war. Teaching was a respectable vocation, but women who taught in the South were often pitied for their obvious dire financial situation. With the outbreak of hostilities, the distaste for Northern teachers spread rapidly. Advertisements for teachers soon came to request that applicants be natives of Dixie or from Europe. Wartime dangers eventually suspended many Southern schools, and the task of educating youngsters fell to the mothers.

While common schools were well established by this time, and enrollments grew throughout the war in Northern cities, the development of high schools, slow before the war, faced even more obstacles. The lure of the military, or opportunities made available by army enlistments, siphoned off many would-be students. High schools were essentially an urban institution, founded with the intention of providing opportunity for boys who wished to become merchants or mechanics. Such an education was seen as terminal. Boston, a leader in educational matters, did not open a high school for girls until 1855. Although some Northern areas required larger cities to establish high schools, most people felt that this was a form of higher education and should not be part of the legal public school system. By 1860 there were 300 high schools in the United States, 100 of which were in Massachusetts.

College enrollments also suffered as idealistic young men rushed to join the forces of their cause. Caroline Cowles Richards listed in her diary a number of young men who "talk of leaving college and going to war."[33] She described a rally at the Canandaigua Academy and detailed how "Capt. Barry drills the Academy boys in military tactics on the campus every day. Men are constantly enlisting." Southern colleges had the additional complications of the loss of funding, physical destruction from battle, and conversion to hospitals, barracks, and headquarters.[34]

College studies were heavily classical. Students read Latin and Greek from Livy, Cicero, Homer, Plato, and others. As in primary school, recitation was the most common form of instruction. Work in the sciences, which covered physics and astronomy, with some chemistry and geology, consisted mostly of lectures along with occasional laboratory demonstrations. Mathematics explored geometry, trigonometry, and calculus and encompassed memorization of rules with some effort to apply them to problems. Rhetoric students studied composition as well as speaking. Other studies included philosophy and logic.

The year 1862 was an important one for education. The Morrill Act passed through the federal Congress, establishing the land grant colleges. It was also the year in which Washington, D.C., made the first provisions for Negro schooling. While the effects of both of these events may have been felt more after the war, they nonetheless show an extremely positive federal attitude toward education, even amid the turmoil of war.

At the outbreak of the war only about 5 percent of slaves could read. As federal troops occupied an area and set the slaves free, many former slaves established schools to help others prepare for freedom. Often Union commanders occupying an area mandated the creation of such schools or allowed their creation by Northern missionaries. These practices led to the creation of the Freedmen's Bureau in 1865, through which the federal government took a formal stance toward the education of former slaves. Northern teachers who traveled to the South during the war suffered tremendous hardships. They were deeply resented by Southerners, who commonly refused them any accommodations, and overworked by the Northern agencies that sent them. What passed for schoolrooms were often worse than the most desolate of Northern facilities.

While the North provided for the education of some free blacks, the idea of racially integrated schools was vehemently opposed. When Prudence Crandall attempted to integrate her fashionable Connecticut school for girls, the white students were quickly withdrawn by outraged parents. Crandall herself was insulted, threatened, and stoned. In the interest of the safety of her students, she was forced to acquiesce. Some common school systems established schools for minority groups such as Amerindians and free blacks. Considering the inadequate support many regular schools were given, one can imagine the facilities that would have been provided when a separate school was established for a minority group. An observer of a "Colored School" remarked that although the Black pupils "were not so far advanced . . . if the same facilities be afforded to them, which are given to the children in other schools in the borough, they will soon compare favorably with them, not only in the lower branches, but also in the more advanced departments."[35]

NOTES

1. Charles W. Sanders, *The School Reader Third Book* (New York: Sower, Barnes & Potts, 1860), 185–186.

2. Child, 11.

3. Ibid., 90.

4. Thomas H. Burrowes, *Report of the Superintendent of Common Schools of Pennsylvania* (Harrisburg: A. Boyd Hamilton, 1861), 20, 24.

5. Ibid., 20–97.

6. Ibid.

7. Ibid., 14.

8. Ibid., 4, 32.

9. Ibid., 43.

10. Ibid., 27.

11. Ibid., 40.

12. Moskow, 193.

13. Burrowes, 83.

14. Ibid., 91.

15. Ibid., 27.

16. Ibid., 51–52.

17. Daniel Leach, *Leach's Complete Spelling Book* (Philadelphia: H. Cowperthwait & Co., 1859), 140.

18. Moskow, 99.

19. Burrowes, 36.

20. Ibid., 80.

21. Ibid., 81, 97.

22. Moskow, 122.

23. Ibid., 139.

24. *Marmaduke Multiply's Merry Method of Making Minor Mathematicians* (1841; New York: Dover, 1971), 13, 65. Hereafter cited as *Marmaduke*; Burrowes, 42.

25. Burrowes, 21.

26. Ibid., 22.

27. Salem Town, *The Fourth Reader, or Exercises in Reading and Speaking* (Cooperstown: H. & E. Phinney, 1849), IV.

28. S. A. Mitchell. 5.

29. *Marmaduke*, 41.

30. Ibid., 33.

31. Richards, 132.

32. Mary Elizabeth Massey, *Women in the Civil War* (Lincoln: University of Nebraska Press, 1966), 119.

33. Richards, 143.

34. Ibid., 136.

35. Burrowes, 67.

18

Till the Mournful Night Is Gone: Death and Dying

The sorrow for the dead is the only sorrow from which we refuse to be divorced. Every other wound we seek to heal, every other affliction to forget; but this wound we consider it a duty to keep open; this affliction we cherish and brood over in solitude.

—Town's *Fourth Reader*

Amid the romanticism and sentimentalism of the nineteenth century, death was viewed from a different perspective than in earlier times, or even than it is today. High infant mortality and the tragic loss of 600,000 soldiers in war made death a part of daily living. Accidents were common in a society that had few safety regulations for industry and public transportation. Charles Baldwin of Catskill, New York, kept an 1860s diary that contained a special section headed "Accidents, Catastrophes, Etc." Some of his entries involving fatalities included the following:

Explosion of Powder Mills at High Falls; Wesley Sitser severely injured by machinery at Broom Corn Factory; explosion of the boiler on the "Isaac Newton." Honora Barrigan horribly crushed in machinery in Woolen Mills at Leeds; explosion of locomotive at Catskill Station, fireman died; fall at a span of the old bridge; a drowning in a bleach-vat at the paper mill; an explosion of the soda water generator at Smith's Drug Store.[1]

Death simply was not the taboo topic it is in modern society. Children's stories and poems contained references to death. Battlefield deaths provided inspiration for songwriters. Numerous examples of then popular piano sheet music detail and sentimentalize the final moments of dying heroes. "Comrades, I Am Dying", contains the following lines:

> Comrades, comrades, I am dying! I see my mother now:
> See her coming down from heaven with a wreath upon her brow.
> God has sent her to the soldier, she will teach him how to die;
> And when He has called my spirit, she will bear it to the sky.[2]

It is difficult to imagine a family wanting to gather around the piano in the parlor to sing about a soldier's final moments with "The Drummer Boy of Shiloh" or "Little Major," but to the nineteenth-century mind this was not the morbid activity it would be labeled today. Death was the final scene of life's drama as written by God.

Following the Great Awakening of the late eighteenth century, religious belief allowed man to anticipate his salvation with pleasure. In the short story "The Star Vision" a dying boy describes a dream foretelling his death. He says, "Then I wished to be a star, Mother."[3] Death was, in a certain way, a joyous occasion, an opportunity to be joined once again to family who had already passed on to their reward. Following the untimely death of her brother, Hal, in a duel, nineteen-year-old Sarah Morgan recorded these thoughts:

> There is no disappointment in the tomb . . . better to be laying in your grave, Hal, with all your noble longings unsatisfied, than to have your heart filled with bitterness as it would have been. . . .Those glorious eyes, with God's truth sparkling in them, are now dimmed forever, Hal. Yet, *not* forever; I shall see them at the Last Day; bury me where I may see them again. O please God, let me die as calmly as he. And let Hal be the first to welcome me, and lead me before Thee.[4]

Attitudes toward cemeteries changed. Even nomenclature began to change. Romanticism, with its emphasis on the boundary between life and death, found the location of the grave profoundly symbolic. The term "cemetery," from the Greek for "sleeping chamber," replaced the earlier phrase, "burying ground." During the 1830s a phenomenon known as the rural cemetery movement emerged. The deplorable conditions in crowded and neglected city cemeteries created a desolate setting for loved ones making their final farewells. This coincided with a general concern that society was changing too rapidly. The once almost inseparable concepts of family, community, and church were being torn asunder. Urbanization was pulling men away from a home that was becoming an isolated and romanticized refuge from society's tumult. The church was increasingly the province of women. Domestic tranquility was closely identified with agriculture and horticulture, in reaction to the urbanization that was taking place. The rural cemetery created an idyllic place where peace and calm would reign and the family bond could remain forever unbroken. The layout created a sort of garden of graves. Cemetery paths meandered over landscaped hills and valleys. Benches were placed at grave sites, providing an inviting place for contemplation. The landscape offered air and light, safety and nature, joy and optimism. It facilitated acceptance of the physical separation of the dead from the living. In the rural cemetery death had been transformed from grotesque to beautiful.

Mary Chesnut's diary records this exchange between two women following the death of Rebecca Haskell: "[Annie said] 'This is the saddest thing for Alex.' 'No,' said his mother, 'death is never the saddest thing. If he were not a good man, that would be a far worse thing.' Annie, in utter amazement, whimpered, 'But Alex is so good already.' 'Yes—seven years ago the death of one of his sisters that he dearly loved made him a Christian. That death in our family was worth a thousand lives.' "[5] Death could indeed be a cause for somber celebration.

Rural cemeteries continued to expand into the 1850s. By the time of the Civil War, virtually every sizable city in both the North and South had its own rural cemetery. The primary focus of the rural cemetery was the family plot. It provided a safe, secure resting place where the remains of loved ones would not be moved, abandoned, or vandalized. Sections in cemeteries were designed to highlight family plots. The winding roads, constructed so that many family plots would be able to have highly desired roadside locations, were built wide enough to accommodate carriages. Grave site visitations were akin to afternoons in the park. "But the grave of those we loved, what a place for meditation!"[6]

The entire institution was designed to honor, strengthen, and maintain the family. *Frank Leslie's Illustrated Newspaper* carried a lead story in the April 25, 1863 issue on the increasing volume of mourners at cemeteries. "The cemeteries of New Orleans are very interesting places, for almost every day may be seen parties of mourning relatives and friends decking the grave of some loved one, who, by an early death, has been spared the pangs of regret."[7]

Family monuments were the most obvious man-made structures in the designed landscapes. They were a physical manifestation of the philosophical shift in attitudes toward death from the eighteenth to the nineteenth century. The tombstone skeletons and death's-heads of previous times, meant to instill fear in the living, were replaced with angels and cherubs who would lead the departed to heaven. Charlotte Selleck's gravestone bears a common eighteenth-century epitaph, found in several variations into the first third of the following century.

Behold and see as you pass by
As you are now so once was I
As I am now you soon shall be
Prepare for death and follow me.[8]

It was not uncommon for nineteenth-century tombstones to bear more reassuring epitaphs, such as the following:

Harriet Miles
Fell asleep in Jesus
January 16, 1857
Aged 15 years
Her last word was HAPPY[9]

Following the death of Mary Barnwell, Mary Chesnut wrote the following in her diary: "Not in anger—not in wrath—came the angel of death that day. He came to set her free from a world grown too hard to bear." Earlier grave markers had elaborate epitaphs and flat carvings. Mid-century monuments were three-dimensional works carved in imitation of the work of European sculptors, creating a virtual museum of memorials. The new monuments depicted symbols of hope, immortality, and life. Ivy was used to symbolize memory, an important component of mid-nineteenth-century mourning. The poppy represented sleep. The anchor symbolized hope. Oak denoted immortality, and the acorn was life. This symbolic language became so complex that writers even interpreted their meanings.

A book on rural cemeteries by Edward Fitzgerald included an "Appendix on Emblems" that detailed the significance of twenty-six such symbols, much like the more popular "language of flowers." Equally common were representations of the trappings of home and family. Books, hats, dogs, chairs, even home facades, were carved in loving memory of the departed. "The world outside was changing, and seemed to be turning upside down. But at least in the permanence of graveyard, traditions could be maintained—indeed maintained, exaggerated, and sentimentalized—if not for those still living, at least for posterity, and for posterity's remembrance of the dead, and preserved, and sentimentalized."[10]

Children's graves received unprecedented attention. Popular literature such as Harriet Beecher Stowe's *Uncle Tom's Cabin* celebrated the passing of young innocents. Early death provided the assurance of being "free from the sin and stain of this low earth."[11] Children's brief existence protected them from corruption. Upon the passing of her infant child, Cornelia Peake McDonald recalled her friend's words, "You may live to thank Him for taking your precious little babe from the sorrow and evil to come."[12]

Rural cemeteries provided separate sections in which young families not yet able to afford a family plot would bury their children. These young or stillborn children could later be reinterred when the family was more established and could afford a family plot. Families that could afford it, however, often created gravestone markers steeped in sentiment and imagery. The most common image was that of the sleeping child. Sleep as a tie between life and death was a recurring theme of the period. The image makes a connection back to the home where the youth once slept. It brought to mind the comforting picture of a child safely tucked away in his bed. The child with a lamb was another recurring image that reinforced the belief in the closeness of children and nature. Empty furniture was also depicted on memorials. An unfilled chair or bed was commonly used to symbolize the child's unfilled life. The song "The Vacant Chair" reinforces this graveyard imagery, as does "Sleep today, O early fallen, In thy green and narrow bed."[13] Judith McGuire reflected, "In all the broad South there will scarcely be a fold without its missing lamb, a fireside without its vacant chair."[14]

Other items appearing on memorials included rattles, dolls, or favorite playthings. The use of toys in such a permanent form reflects the period's recognition of the naturalness of play and was a lasting reminder of the separate worlds of children and adults. Sculptural portrayals of children and their belongings ensured that they would remain forever one with the goodness of the home. They would be undisturbed and constant, forever innocent in the world.

Months after the loss of her own child, Cornelia Peake McDonald recorded an incident wherein she was told that she should be thankful that her babe had been taken. "I thought of that when I looked at old Mrs. Dailey's face when she stood by her son's corpse. Would my darling's forehead ever have looked so dim and weary? Her work was finished, and she went to rest 'while yet 'twas early day.' I would not bring her back if I could to resume the burden her Savior removed that day when she fled from my arms as the sun was setting."[15]

Such thoughts must have been a great consolation to the parents who lost child after child to sickness and accidents. Both Abraham Lincoln and Jefferson Davis had to cope with the devastation of the loss of a child while dealing with the complex issues of the Civil War. Lincoln lost his youngest son, Willie, to a fever on February 20, 1862. Willie was the second of the Lincoln children to succumb to sickness. Twelve years earlier the Lincolns had lost four-year-old Eddy to diphtheria. Davis lost his "Little Joe" when the boy fell from the north piazza of the Southern

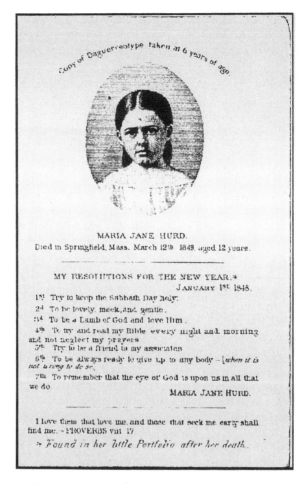

Copy of Daguerreotype taken at 6 years of age.

MARIA JANE HURD.

Died in Springfield, Mass. March 12th 1849, aged 12 years.

MY RESOLUTIONS FOR THE NEW YEAR.*
JANUARY 1st 1848.

1st Try to keep the Sabbath Day holy.

2d To be lovely, meek, and gentle.

3d To be a Lamb of God and love Him.

4th To try and read my Bible every night and morning and not neglect my prayers

5th Try to be a friend to my associates

6th To be always ready to give up to any body — [when it is not wrong to do so.]

7th To remember that the eye of God is upon us in all that we do

MARIA JANE HURD.

I love them that love me, and those that seek me early shall find me. - PROVERBS VIII 17

* Found in her little Portfolio after her death.

This touching memorial carte de visite from the
authors' collection may seem extremely morbid to
the modern eye, but in its time it was a lasting
memorial devotion to the deceased.

White House on April 30, 1864. When a child died, the family felt the loss deeply. The death rate among the young remained relatively high throughout the war years. Family separation and a lower birth rate during the conflict led people to value surviving children all the more.

The fear death held was less for the ending of life and more that of never having been loved or lamented. When asked by a surviving soldier to see to the proper care of a dead companion whom she had never known, Cornelia Peake McDonald wrote, "Betty and I wept over him tears of sincere sorrow, the more so as we thought that perhaps ours and those of the poor soldier would be all that would fall on his lonely bier." Mourners of the 1860s went to great lengths to demonstrate their love and devotion to the deceased. The loss of family members and the personal trauma of death became the focus of mourning and ritual. To this end, mourning became an extended, almost institutionalized process.[16]

Writing elegies for departed friends was popular. Sometimes these black-bordered tributes were attached to the coffin or to the hearse. Other times, they were decorated with designs abundant with death imagery and distributed as souvenirs to the mourners. It was not uncommon for them to be printed in local newspapers.

Widows were expected to remain in mourning for two and a half years. This time was divided into three segments. During heavy mourning the widow wore only black, with collars and cuffs of folded untrimmed black crepe. No other trim was used. She might wear a simple bonnet but never a hat. Her face would be covered entirely in a long, heavy black crepe veil whenever she left home. Silk fabrics used for dresses, bonnets, or capes had to have matte finishes. Not even ribbons were allowed to have a gloss. Kid gloves were not permitted. Gloves had to be made from cotton or silk, or crocheted or knit from thread. Handkerchiefs were made of the sheerest white linen with a broad, deep border. Jewelry was restricted to black jet—usually unpolished—and even that would not be worn during the initial months. Dark furs were permitted in cold weather. Throughout the entire mourning period a widow's hair had to be worn simply.

This period was followed by full mourning, which still required the wearing of black, but permitted black lace collars and cuffs. Veils were permitted to be shortened and could be made of net or tulle. Lighter veils were also allowed. Handkerchiefs needed only to have a narrow black band border. Polished jet jewelry was allowed as well as some gold or glass beads.

Half mourning was the final stage. During this period, print and solid-colored dresses of gray or lavender were permitted. A bonnet might be trimmed with lace and adorned with white or violet flowers. Emma Sargent Barbour received a letter with the following comment about a dress: "Mrs. Hutchens bought her a purple and black [half mourning] mohair."[17] *Godey's Lady's Book* carried a literary selection that contained a scene where a young woman was preparing to attend her first party since the death of her father. Her mother "opened a jewel case . . . and taking from the velvet cushion a necklace and bracelets of pearl, she clasped them around the throat and wrists of her daughter. 'Oh, Mother! Your bridal jewels?' 'They are not misplaced here, I think, Ellen, for your dress is simple; and these will be a happy relief.' " The young woman declined to wear the pearls, fearing she would be too conspicuous. Although fiction, the story illustrates the strong sense of fashion propriety.[18]

Some women, of course, chose to remain in mourning for longer periods, even the rest of their lives. For a woman who wanted to remarry in a period of less than two and a half years, an accommodation was made. She was permitted to be married in a conservative gray dress. However, she was expected to complete the period of mourning following the new union out of respect for the first husband. If a woman married a widower, she was expected to dress in half mourning for the remainder of her husband's mourning period.

Not so surprisingly, men were not as restricted as women. Their period of mourning lasted as little as three months to a year. Fashion required them to wear a plain white shirt with black clothes, shoes, gloves, and hat. This differed little from what the properly dressed businessman would wear in any case. Some men followed this with a period of gray. The only distinguishing additions would be a black crepe band on their hat or black-bordered cuffs. Widowers were encouraged to remarry following a respectable period, particularly if they had young children. Mourning attire was suspended for the wedding day but reestablished immediately thereafter.

Children were not sheltered from death and mourning. In *The Mother's Book*, Lydia Child advises mothers not to allow their children to be frightened by death. She encourages them to share the beautiful imagery of returning to heaven to be with the angels with even very young children. Older children wore black and crepe upon the death of a parent for six months, followed by three months each of full and half mourning with lessening degrees of black. Children in mourning under the age of twelve wore white in the summer and gray in the winter. Suits were trimmed with black buttons, belts, and ribbons. Even infant robes were trimmed in black. Often, out of practicality, children's regular clothing was dyed for mourning rather than purchased new.

A woman mourning the death of her father, mother, or child wore black for a period of one year. For grandparents, siblings, or someone having left the mourner an inheritance, the proper period was six months. The obligation for an aunt, uncle, niece, or nephew extended for only three months, and white trim was allowed throughout this time. Families in mourning often restricted their contacts with the outside world. Following the death of her mother-in-law, Mary Chesnut made the following diary entry: "Mr. Chesnut being in such deep mourning for his mother, we see no company."[19]

Martine's Hand-Book of Etiquette, and Guide to True Politeness details the proper protocol for condolence visitation:

Visits of condolence should be paid within a week after the event which occasions them; but if the acquaintance be slight, immediately after the family appear at public worship. A card should be sent up; and if your friends are able to receive you, let your manners and conversation be in harmony with the character of your visit. It is courteous to send up a mourning card; and for ladies to make their call in black silk or plain-colored apparel. It denotes that they sympathize with the afflictions of the family; and such attentions are always pleasing.[20]

Mourning dress was one of the first areas where mass-produced clothing gained acceptance. The need for the proper attire to conform to the rigid rules regarding dress often came unexpectedly. There were many people who felt that it was unlucky to keep black crepe in the home between deaths. Surviving items from previous losses were often discarded when no longer required. Providing mourning attire and accessories became a worthwhile commercial endeavor. Some retailers, such as J. S. Chase and Company of Boston, dealt exclusively in mourning goods. There was a great demand for black crepe for veils, collars, cuffs, skirt trim, and armbands. Other needed items included black hat pins, straight pins, and buttons. Millinery and jewelry that met the expectations of society were equally in demand. Mourning caps were such a common item, with virtually no design differences for age or demand for customization, that milliners commonly made them when they had nothing else to do. Those in mourning also required stationery and calling cards bordered in black. Many companies made fortunes on mourning clothing and related ancillary materials.

Perhaps the most favored of these goods was mourning jewelry. Sentimental melancholy for its own sake was a hallmark of gentility and refinement. The simple wearing of mourning jewelry transferred virtue to the wearer. Mourning pins and rings were given to mourners as keepsakes. Frequently, in the interest of economy, the gifts were of two price levels. The more expensive gifts were given to close friends and family, while less expensive items could be more widely distributed.

Jet, onyx, and black glass or "French jet" were extensively used, but it was jet that reached an unprecedented popularity. While French jet is black glass, true jet is fossilized driftwood formed, like coal, by decaying vegetation over hundreds of thousands of years. Jet is found in stagnant water—often seawater—and the greater the depth of the water, the harder the jet. Jet was made into carved beads for necklaces, brooches, bracelets, and earrings. Its inherent lightness allowed for the creation of pieces that would have been impractical had they been made from another material. Additionally, jet was relatively inexpensive, yet it was attractive and properly somber.

Another jewelry trend that came into full flower in this period was "hair work." This was not a new fashion. To some degree, hair jewelry had been popular since the beginning of the century, but during the

An advertisement from the *Boston Directory*
particularizes a wide selection of mourning attire.

war it reached new heights. Rings, lockets, brooches, bracelets, watch chains—almost any kind of jewelry was likely to include human hair in one way or another. Sometimes the hair was that of a living person, but more often it was from a departed loved one. The period song "Bear Gently, So Gently, Roughly Made Bier," subtitled "Burial at Camp," contains the following line: "From the damp clotted hair sever one precious tress."[21] Judith McGuire concluded her tale of the burial of a Confederate soldier thus: "We cut a lock of his hair, as the only thing we could do for his mother."[22]

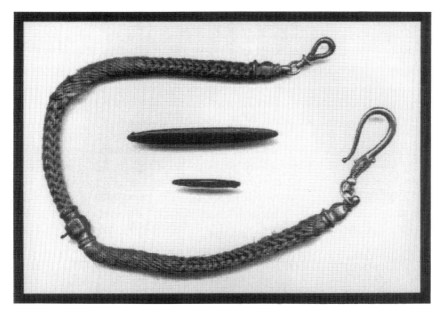

A hair watch fob and jet mourning pins on black-bordered mourning stationery. From the authors' collection.

Godey's Lady's Book championed the use of hair jewelry, quoting an English writer, Leigh Hunt, in saying, "Hair is at once the most delicate and lasting of our materials, and survives us, like love. It is so light, so gentle, so escaping from the idea of death, that with a lock of hair belonging to a child or friend, we may almost look up to heaven and compare notes with the angelic nature—may almost say: 'I have a piece of thee here, not unworthy of thy being now.' "[23]

The simplest way to prepare such a relic was to encase a lock of hair under a crystal which would be mounted in a ring, brooch, or locket. More elaborate pieces contained miniature allegories of grief. Often parts of designs, or their entirety, were made of human hair. Sometimes the miniatures were portraits of the deceased mounted on a background of their hair. Another variation of this form was "hair painting." This lost art appears to have used finely chopped hair mixed into the pigments of the paint, but no description of the exact process seems to have survived. Finally, hair was sometimes plaited in many strands and then formed into watch chains, fobs, brooches, rings, necklaces, earrings, and bracelets. These items might have been made for oneself from the hair of a loved one or made as a gift using the giver's hair.

Pattern books like Campbell's *Self-Instructor* contained numerous patterns for incredibly intricate hair jewelry designs. *Godey's Lady's Book* offered designs, instructions, and even finished pieces. If a woman lacked the talent to create a piece herself, she could give the hair to a jeweler who would then create the desired item based on hundreds of available designs.

Some photographers specialized in posthumous photographs. Period advertisements carried the names of many photographers who offered this specialty. The photographer normally came to the home, but it was not unusual for the deceased to be taken to the studio. Future president James Garfield, as a soldier in the Civil War, hurried home to have a picture taken with his dead infant in his arms. Infants were the most common subject of this type of photograph. Perhaps this was because there had been little opportunity to capture the child's likeness in life. Perhaps it provided a concrete reminder of a life that had passed too quickly. Sometimes the deceased child would be posed cradled in the mother's arms. Other poses might show the child resting on a pillow. Photographers sometimes borrowed from the imagery of portrait painters and included a cut rose in the picture, symbolizing a bloom cut early—the death of a child. The family of Maria Jane Hurd created a memorial card for the deceased twelve-year-old. Beneath her portrait, copied from a daguerreotype taken at age six, were enumerated her "Resolutions for the New Year," which were "found in her little portfolio after her death."[24]

A woman in mourning often occupied herself with stitchery, paperwork, or other memorial projects. Memorial work abounded with symbolism. A butterfly symbolized the passing from this world to the next. A sheaf of wheat denoted the passing of an elderly person. Pansies, in the language of flowers, meant "Think of me." The most persistent symbol by far was the weeping willow. The very shape of the willow brought to mind the image of a mourner bent over with grief. Willow branches were often carried by mourners at funerals as symbols of resurrection. Personalized items such as pets, ships, churches, and distant towns were also memorialized.

Memorial pictures worked in silk embroidery were most common. A typical scene contained black-clad mourners beside an urn-topped gravestone beneath the hanging boughs of a weeping willow tree. Some memorial pictures were painted, frequently by young girls still in school. These could be for a relative long deceased or could be kept and then completed by inscribing the name of that person on the waiting tomb at a later date. Occasionally, they were used for the painter herself. During the late 1830s memorial pictures published by Nathaniel Currier could be purchased as lithographs. A mourning card could then be pasted on to complete the scene. Another form of memorial, although less popular, was cut paperwork. The cut paperwork contained similar imagery, and the contrast of white against black was stark and visually effective. These

A period postmortem memorial card of a young child from Hopkinsville, Kentucky. From the authors' collection.

items could either be done by the mourner or purchased and personalized by inserting a memorial card identifying the deceased.

Theorem paintings, oils, and pen and ink sketches were also done as memorials, but less frequently. Watercolors were also used to create memorials. These tended to be gayer than some other kinds of works due to the colors. Watercolors were even used in conjunction with other forms of artwork. Some embroidered pictures contained watercolor skies or had watercolor faces pasted or sewn on to the needlework. As many as four different media could be used in the creation of a single work.

Immortals were fairly large, ornate floral arrangements made from wax, cloth, beads, or hair and were covered by tall glass cases. The complex designs incorporated flowers, often made by weaving or braiding the hair of the deceased over wire. Wreaths might also include yarn, seeds, berries, feathers, or dried flowers; they were later framed in shadowboxes to be displayed in parlors. Sheaves of wheat used to decorate the casket were often preserved in a similar fashion.

Death rituals among slaves and Southern free blacks still retained their African meanings. In dying, one "went home." To a slave, this was a reason to celebrate, for it meant freedom. Graves were decorated, as they were in Africa, with the last items that the deceased had used. The most common articles were pottery or glass containers, but medicine bottles, toys, dolls, and quilts were also found. It was essential that the items be broken in order to break the tie to the living. Failure to do so was believed to invite a similar fate for the surviving family. Some slaveowners gave a portion of the day off for the funeral of a departed slave and even allotted food for the following celebration. Others required that the funeral be held at night. Mourning clothing restrictions were not likely a part of slave mourning traditions; however, some slaves were known to have had mourning clothing. It is very likely that these items were initially purchased for them following the death of "the master" and could later be used for their own personal losses.

As the war progressed, the Union blockade made the acquisition of manufactured mourning goods in the South difficult, if not impossible. Women had to borrow from one another; but, as so many were in need of mourning attire themselves, availability was limited. Many women had to resort to dying fabrics in order to be properly outfitted.

Battlefield casualties brought about altered mourning practices. Families were accustomed to living and dying in close proximity, and this was the first time many experienced the loss of someone far away from home. The horrendous numbers of deceased soldiers involved affected almost every family. The inability to recover loved one's remains after a battle, a frequent occurence, presented a kind of eternal separation that compounded the sense of loss. Soldiers went to great lengths to identify themselves so that their remains could be returned to their loved ones at home. In a time before "dog tags," some soldiers purchased brass or wooden identity discs to wear around their necks. Others attached slips of paper to their backs. However, many soldiers were interred in mass graves. Others were left in shallow pits near where they fell. Some families traveled to battle sites in the vain hope of being able to retrieve their loved one's remains. Few were successful.

Getting the remains home presented other problems. Although the process of embalming had long been known, the effort to preserve physical remains had not been practiced beyond the needs of medical research. During the Civil War, however, a new market was opened. Itinerant embalmers, mostly doctors, traveled to battlefields and used arterial embalming to preserve bodies for shipment home. In some instances, these embalmers contracted their services to soldiers prior to battle in the event of their demise. This process created a professionalism not found in "undertaking" before the war. Undertakers now required a special skill that set them apart from the carpenters and casket makers who preceded them. It was no longer enough to provide a coffin, a horse, and a special carriage.

Perhaps the most famous battlefield identification of a departed soldier was that of Amos Humiston, a sergeant in the 154th New York Volunteers. Humiston's body was found on the battlefield, following the Battle of Gettysburg, clutching in his hand an ambrotype of his three little children. His name remained a mystery for months. Francis Bourns, a physician, obtained the picture, had it copied on an engraving plate so that it could be circulated in the hope of learning the identity of the fallen soldier, and set up a fund for the orphaned children. Many newspapers across the country supported the effort. Finally, it was learned that a woman in western New York had read the account in the religious newspaper *American Presbyterian*. She had sent her husband a picture of their three small children and had not heard from him since July. A copy of the picture was sent, and her worst fears came to fruition. James G. Clark wrote a poem set to music based on the story, called "The Children of the Battlefield." The net proceeds of the sales of the music, which contained an introductory sketch melodramatically detailing the entire incident, were "reserved for the support and education of the Orphan Children," Frank, Frederick, and Alice.[25]

The Civil War also created a new category of sacred ground, the national cemetery. Congress authorized the first nationally managed cemetery as early as 1862. Former army post cemeteries were rededicated for the use of the increasing number of Union army dead. As early as 1863, the battle sites of Gettysburg and Antietam were named national cemeteries for the Union dead. Battlefield cemeteries continued to grow as the war progressed. The earliest burials were quick and rough, but as casualties escalated an attempt was made to provide each grave with a wooden marker. After the conflict, the War Department set out upon a campaign to reinter the dead in appropriate locations and to formalize the markers. This striking act of democracy, where men of varied backgrounds and means were memorialized side by side with uniform markers, set these areas very much apart from secular cemeteries of the day.

The death of President Lincoln in April 1865 sent the Union into the deepest mourning. As Washington prepared for a state funeral, citizens streamed to the capital. Extra trains had to be added to accommodate the mourners. Reportedly, 100,000 people came to bid the president farewell. Mourning decorations quickly sold out, and residents combed ever widening areas to find sufficient amounts of black crepe. Even the poorest families gathered what bits of black cloth they could to drape their homes. Tens of thousands of people lined the trackside as the president's body was carried by train back to Springfield, Illinois.

Mrs. Alexander Major left a rare insight to the reaction of Southerners in the hours following the news of the president's death:

The stores were ransacked for black material to hang forth as symbols of mourning. Every house was ordered to be draped in black, and where the rebel inmates refused, it was done for them by the Union boys. . . . We had nothing black whatever in our possession except my husband's coat, and as he had to wear that, I asked him to go down the street to buy a few yards of some black goods, which I intended to hang out from our bedroom window as a token that we grieved at the terrible calamity that had befallen a great and good man.[26]

This compassion was not shared by all Southerners. Mrs. Major continues to relate how the woman in whose house she resided as a boarder refused to comply with the directive. When a committee of soldiers came by to ensure that the order was being observed, an ugly scene ensued. Angry soldiers ransacked the landlady's belongings, searching for something black. When they emerged with the mourning veil she had worn for her husband and son, both of whom had perished in the Confederate cause, she determined that she had endured too much. Asking that she be left alone to acquiesce, she carried the veil to her veranda and mounted a chair so that she could reach the fretwork above. Only then was it noticed that she had changed her clothes and was now dressed all in black. With deliberate action and to the horror of those watching, she pushed away the chair and hanged herself. The dictate had been satisfied.[27]

NOTES

1. Margaret M. Coffin, *Death in Early America* (New York: Thomas Nelson, 1976), 19.

2. Thomas Manahan, "Comrades, I Am Dying" (Boston: Henry Talman & Co., 1864). A sheet music cover.

3. Charley Hunt, "The Star Vision," *Christian Parlor Magazine* 9, no. 12 (1852), 370.

4. East, 11.

5. C. V. Woodward, 397.

6. Town, 218.

7. "Mourners Strewing Flowers on the Graves of the Slain," *Frank Leslie's Illustrated Newspaper*, April 25, 1863, 1.

8. The gravestone of Charlotte Selleck, who died on January 1,1806, stands in the cemetery at Mill Hill Historic Complex in Norwalk, Connecticut.

9. Coffin, 183.

10. David Stannard, "Calm Dwellings," *American Heritage*, September 1979, 47.

11. Mrs. L. G. Abell, "The Dying Girl," *Christian Parlor Magazine* 9, no. 12 (1852): 274.

12. Gwin, 72.

13. George F. Root, "The Vacant Chair (or We Shall Meet but We Shall Miss Him)" (Chicago: Root & Cady, 1862). A sheet music cover.

14. McGuire, 250.

15. Gwin, 91.

16. Ibid., 53.

17. Moskow, 163.

18. Martha Gandy Fales, *Jewelry in America* (London: Antique Collector's Club, 1995), 211. Quoting *Godey's Lady's Book*, Book 54, 1857.

19. C. V. Woodward, 589.

20. Martine, 122.

21. E.A.B. Mitchell, "Bear Gently, So Gently, Roughly Made Bier" (Louisville: Wm. McCaroll, 1864). A sheet music cover.

22. McGuire, 143.

23. Fales, 215.

24. From a memorial card in the authors' collection of twelve-year-old Maria Jane Hurd, who died in Springfield, Massachusetts, on March 12, 1848.

25. James G. Clark, "The Children of the Battlefield" (Philadelphia: Lee & Walker, 1864). A sheet music cover.

26. Sullivan, 274.

27. Ibid., 275–276.

Bibliography

Abell, Mrs. L. G. "The Dying Girl," *Christian Parlor Magazine* 9, no. 12 (1852).

Adams, Alice Dana. *The Neglected Period of Anti-slavery in America*. Boston: Corner House, 1973.

Albree, John, ed. *Whittier's Correspondence*. Privately published, 1911.

Anderson, Patricia. "Romantic Strains of the Parlor Piano." *Victorian* 3, no. 3 (1997).

Armstrong, Richard. *Seventh Virginia Cavalry*. Lynchburg: H. E. Howard, 1992.

Ashby, Thomas A. *The Life of Turner Ashby*. New York: Neal Publishing, 1914.

Barnard, George N. *Photographic Views of Sherman's Campaigns*. 1866. Reprint, New York: Dover, 1977.

Bauer, K. Jack, ed. *Soldiering: The Civil War Diary of Rice C. Bull*. Novato: Presidio, 1977.

Beecher, Catherine E. *Miss Beecher's Domestic Receipt Book*. New York: Harper & Brothers, 1850.

Berry, Harrison. *Slavery and Abolitionism, as Viewed by a Georgia Slave*. Atlanta: M. Lynch, 1861.

Billings, John D. *Hardtack and Coffee*. Boston: G. M. Smith, 1887.

Blassingame, John W. *Black New Orleans*. Chicago: Chicago University Press, 1973.

———. *The Clarion Voice*. Washington: National Parks Service, 1976.

Bowman, John S., ed. *The Civil War Almanac*. New York: Bison Books, 1983.

Burrowes, Thomas H. *Report of the Superintendent of Common Schools of Pennsylvania*. Harrisburg: A. Boyd Hamilton, 1861.

Bushrod, Millard K. *Old Jube: A Biography of General Jubal A. Early*. Shippensburg, PA: Beidel, 1955.

Byrne, Frank L., and Jean Powers Soman, eds. *A Jewish Colonel in the Civil War:*

Marcus M. Spiegel of the Ohio Volunteers. Lincoln: University of Nebraska Press, 1994.

Campbell, Edward D.C. Jr., and Kym S. Rice, eds. *A Woman's War: Southern Women, Civil War and the Confederate Legacy.* Charlottesville: University Press of Virginia, 1996.

Catton, Bruce. *The Picture History of the Civil War.* New York: American Heritage, 1960.

Child, Lydia M. *The Mother's Book.* Boston: Applewood, 1831.

Clinton, Catherine. *The Plantation Mistress: Woman's World in the Old South.* New York: Pantheon Books, 1982.

Coco, Gregory A. *The Civil War Infantryman: In Camp, on the March, and in Battle.* Gettysburg: Thomas, 1996.

Coffin, Margaret M. *Death in Early America.* New York: Thomas Nelson, 1976.

Colton, Calvin, ed. *The Private Correspondence of Henry Clay.* Cincinnati: N.p., 1856.

Confederate Receipt Book: A Compilation of Over One Hundred Receipts, Adapted to the Times. Richmond: West & Johnson, 1863.

Cook, Fred J. "The Slave Ship Rebellion." *American Heritage,* February 1957.

Cornish, Dudley T. *The Sable Arm: Black Troops in the Union Army, 1861–1865.* New York: Longmans, 1956.

Cozzens, Peter. *No Better Place to Die: The Battle of Stones River.* Urbana: University of Illinois Press, 1990.

Crawford, Richard. *The Civil War Storybook.* New York: Dover, 1977.

Cremin, Lawrence A. *American Education: The National Experience, 1783–1876.* New York: Harper, 1980.

Croushore, James H., ed. *A Volunteer's Adventure,* by Captain John W. De Forest. New Haven: Yale University Press, 1949.

Davis, David Brion. *Slavery in the Colonial Chesapeake.* Williamsburg: Colonial Williamsburg Foundation, 1994.

Davis, William C., ed. *Diary of a Confederate Soldier,* by John S. Jackman. Columbia: University of South Carolina Press, 1990.

Denny, Robert E. *Civil War Medicine: Care and Comfort for the Wounded.* New York: Sterling, 1995.

DeRosa, Marshall L. *The Confederate Constitution of 1861.* Columbia: University of Missouri Press, 1991.

Dictionary of American Biography. Edited by Dumas Malone. New York: Scribner's Sons, 1943.

Donald, David. *The Civil War and Reconstruction.* Boston: Heath, 1961.

Douglass, Frederick. *Narrative of the Life of an American Slave, Written by Himself.* 1845. Reprint, New York: Penguin, 1968.

Dowdey, Clifford. *The Great Plantation.* Charles City, VA: Berkeley Plantation Press, 1957.

Duyckinck, E. A. *Cyclopedia of American Literature.* Detroit: Gale Research, 1965.

East, Charles, ed. *Sarah Morgan: The Civil War Diary of a Southern Woman.* New York: Touchstone, 1991.

Editors of Time-Life. *Voices of the Civil War.* New York: Time-Life, 1995.

Eggleston, George C. *A Rebel's Recollections.* 1874. Reprint, Bloomington: Indiana University Press, 1959.

Fales, Martha Gandy. *Jewelry in America*. London: Antique Collector's Club, 1995.

Faust, Drew Gilpin. *The Creation of Confederate Nationalism: Ideology and Identity in the Civil War South*. Baton Rouge: Louisiana State University Press, 1988.

————. *Mothers of Invention: Women of the Slaveholding South in the American Civil War*. Charlotte: University of North Carolina Press, 1996.

Fehrenbacher, Don E. *The Era of Expansion, 1800–1848*. New York: John Wiley & Sons, 1969.

Fite, Emerson David. *Social and Industrial Conditions in the North During the Civil War*. Williamstown: Corner House, 1976.

Fitzpatrick, Michael F. "The Mercy Brigade." *Civil War Times Illustrated*, October 1997.

Fletcher, William A. *Rebel Private: Front and Rear*. 1908. New York: Meridian, 1997.

Foote, Shelby. *The Civil War: A Narrative. Fort Sumter to Perryville*. New York: Vintage, 1986.

————. *The Civil War: A Narrative. Fredericksburg to Meridian*. New York: Vintage, 1986.

————. *The Civil War: A Narrative. Red River to Appomattox*. New York: Vintage, 1986.

Frederickson, George M., ed. *Great Lives Observed: William Lloyd Garrison*. Englewood Cliffs: Prentice-Hall, 1968.

Gardner, Alexander. *Photographic Sketchbook of the Civil War*. 1866. Reprint, New York: Dover, 1959.

Garrison, William Lloyd. *Thoughts on African Colonization*. Boston: N.p., 1832.

Genovese, Eugene D. *Roll, Jordan, Roll: The World the Slaves Made*. New York: Pantheon Books, 1976.

Grimsley, Mark. *The Hard Hand of War: Union Military Policy Toward Southern Civilians, 1861–1865*. Cambridge: Cambridge University Press, 1995.

Guernsey, Alfred H., and Henry M. Alden, eds. *Harper's History of the Great Rebellion*. New York: Gramercy Books, 1866.

Gwin, Minrose C., ed. *Cornelia Peake McDonald: A Woman's Civil War. A Diary with Reminiscences of the War from March 1862*. Madison: University of Wisconsin, 1992.

Hague, Parthenia Antoinette. *A Blockaded Family: Life in Southern Alabama During the Civil War*. Reprint. Bedford, TX: Applewood Books, 1995.

Halliman, Tim. *A Christmas Carol Christmas Book*. New York: IBM, 1984.

Halsey, Francis W., ed. "The Disbanding of the Northern Army, 1865, by James G. Blaine." In *Great Epochs in American History*. New York: Funk & Wagnalls, 1884.

Handlin, Oscar, and Lilian Handlin. *Liberty and Expansion, 1760–1850*. New York: Harper & Row, 1989.

Hannaford, Ebenezer. *The Story of a Regiment: A History of the Campaigns, and Associations in the Field of the Sixth Regiment Ohio Volunteer Infantry*. Cincinnati: Privately printed, 1868.

Haskell, E. F. *The Housekeeper's Encyclopedia*. Mendocino: R. L. Shep, 1992.

Hawes, Joel. *Lectures to Young Men on the Formation of Character*. Hartford: 1835.

Hunt, Charley. "The Star Vision." *Christian Parlor Magazine* 9, no. 12 (1852).

Johnson, Robert U., and Clarence Clough Buel, eds. *Battles and Leaders of the Civil War*, 4 vols. Edison: Castle, 1887.

Jones, Archer. *The Art of War in the Western World*. New York: Oxford University Press, 1987.

————. *Confederate Strategy from Shiloh to Vicksburg*. Baton Rouge: Louisiana State University Press, 1991.

Jones, Howard. *Mutiny on the "Amistad."* New York: Oxford University Press, 1987.

Jones, Terry L., ed. *The Civil War Memoirs of Captain William J. Seymour*. Baton Rouge: Louisiana State University Press, 1991.

Jones, Virgil Carrington. *Gray Ghosts and Rebel Raiders*. New York: Galahad, 1956.

Jordan, Ervin L., Jr. *Black Confederates and Afro-Yankees in Civil War Virginia*. Charlottesville: University Press of Virginia, 1995.

Kaser, David. *Books and Libraries in Camp and Battle: The Civil War Experience*. Westport: Greenwood Press, 1984.

Keegan, John. *The Mask of Command*. New York: Vintage, 1987.

Kellar, Herbert A., ed. "The Diary of James D. Davidson," *Journal of Southern History* 1 (1935).

Kennedy, James R., and Walter D. Kennedy. *The South Was Right*. Gretna, LA: Pelican, 1995.

Kiracofe, Roderick. *The American Quilt*. New York: Clarkson Potter, 1993.

Kunitz, Stanley J., ed. *British Authors of the Nineteenth Century*. New York: Wilson, 1936.

Laas, Virginia Jeans, ed. *Wartime Washington: Letters of Elizabeth Blair Lee*. Chicago: University of Illinois Press, 1991.

Leach, Daniel. *Leach's Complete Spelling Book*. Philadelphia: H. Cowperthwait & Co., 1859.

Leech, Margaret. *Reveille in Washington*. New York: Harper & Brothers, 1941.

Lewis, Thomas A. *The Guns of Cedar Creek*. New York: Bantam, 1991.

Livermore, Mary A. *My Story of the War: A Woman's Narrative of Four Years' Personal Experience*. New York: Da Capo Press, 1995.

Lord, Francis A. *Civil War Collector's Encyclopedia*. 5 vols. Edison: Blue & Gray Press, 1995.

————. "The United States Military Railroad Service: Vehicle to Victory," *Civil War Times Illustrated*, October 1962.

Loving, Jerome M., ed. *Civil War Letters of George Washington Whitman*. Durham: Duke University Press, 1975.

Lunt, Dolly Sumner. *A Woman's Wartime Journal*. Atlanta: Cherokee, 1994.

Mallinson, David. "Armed with Only Their Drums." *America's Civil War*. November 1992.

Marmaduke Multiply's Merry Method of Making Minor Mathematicians. 1841. New York: Dover, 1971.

Martine, Arthur. *Martine's Hand-Book of Etiquette, and Guide to True Politeness*. New York: Dick & Fitzgerald, 1866.

Massey, Mary Elizabeth. *Women in the Civil War*. Lincoln: University of Nebraska Press, 1966.

Mayer, J. P., ed. *Journey to America*, by Alexis de Tocqueville. Translated by George Lawrence. New Haven: Yale University Press, 1960.

McCarthy, Carlton. *Detailed Minutiae of Soldier Life in the Army of Northern Virginia, 1861–1865*. 1882. Reprint, Lincoln: University of Nebraska Press, 1993.

McGuire, Judith W. *Diary of a Southern Refugee During the War by a Lady of Virginia*. Lincoln: University of Nebraska Press, 1995.

McPherson, James M. *Battle Cry of Freedom*. New York: Oxford University Press, 1988.

———. *For Cause and Comrades: Why Men Fought in the Civil War*. New York: Oxford University Press, 1997.

Menge, W. Springer, and J. August Shimrak, eds. *The Civil War Notebook of Daniel Chisholm*. New York: Ballantine, 1989.

Miers, Earl Schenck, ed. *A Rebel War Clerk's Diary, by John B. Jones, 1861–1865*. New York: Sagamore Press, 1958.

Miller, Francis Trevelyan, ed. *The Photographic History of the Civil War: Soldier Life and the Secret Service*. 1911. Reprint, New York: Castle, 1957.

Mitchell, Joseph B. *Decisive Battles of the Civil War*. New York: Fawcett, 1955.

Mitchell, S. Augustus. *An Easy Introduction to the Study of Geography*. Philadelphia: Thomas, Cowperthwait & Co., 1853.

Morgan, James. "Send No Trash: Books, Libraries, and Reading During the Civil War." *Camp Chase Gazette*, July 1992, 32.

Mosby, John S. *Stuart's Cavalry in the Gettysburg Campaign*. New York: Moffat, Yard & Co., 1908.

Moskow, Shirley Blotnick. *Emma's World: An Intimate Look at Lives Touched by the Civil War Era*. Far Hills, NJ: New Horizon Press, 1990.

Nesbit, Mark. *Saber and Scapegoat: J.E.B. Stuart and the Gettysburg Controversy*. Mechanicsburg: Stackpole, 1994.

New Orleans as It Is. New Orleans: N.p., 1850.

Nye, Wilbur S. "The U.S. Military Telegraph Services." *Civil War Times Illustrated*, November 1968: 28–34.

Parkhurst, Clinton. "Corinth: Tenting on the Old Camp Ground." *Civil War Times Illustrated*, January 1987, 30–35.

Rhodes, Robert Hunt, ed. *All for the Union*, by Col. Elisha Hunt Rhodes. 1985. Reprint, New York: Random House, 1995.

Rice, V. M. *Code of Public Instruction*. Albany: State Printing Office, 1856.

Richards, Caroline C. *Village Life in America, 1852–1872*. Gansevoort, NY: Corner House, 1997.

Robertson, James I. Jr., ed. *One of Jackson's Foot Cavalry*. Wilmington, NC: Broadfoot Reprints, 1987.

Root, Waverly, and Richard de Rouchemont. *Eating in America*. New York: William Morrow, 1976.

Rose, Anne C. *Victorian America and the Civil War*. Cambridge: Cambridge University Press, 1994.

Rothman, David J. "Our Brother's Keepers." *American Heritage*, December 1972, 38–42, 100–105.

Russell, Andrew J. *Russell's Civil War Photographs*. New York: Dover, 1982.

Sabine, David B. "Resources Compared: North Versus South," *Civil War Times Illustrated*, February 1968, 5–15.

Sanders, Charles W. *The School Reader Third Book*. New York: Sower, Barnes & Potts, 1860.

Scott, Sir Walter. *The Fair Maid of Perth*. New York: Harper, 1831.

Scroggs, J. J. "A Tour of a Hardtack Factory: Diary of J. J. Scroggs 5th US Colored Infantry." *Civil War Times Illustrated*, October 1972.

Sewell, Richard H. *A House Divided: Sectionalism and the Civil War, 1848–1865*. Baltimore: Johns Hopkins University Press, 1988.

Shep, R. L., ed. *Civil War Ladies: Fashions and Needle Arts of the Early 1860's*. Mendocino: R. L. Shep, 1987.

Smith, James West. "A Confederate Soldier's Diary: Vicksburg in 1863." *Southwest Review* 28 (1943): 304, 312.

Smith, Raymond W. "Don't Cut! Signal Telegraph." *Civil War Times Illustrated*, May 1976, 18–28.

Stampp, Kenneth M. *The Imperiled Union*. New York: Oxford University Press, 1980.

————. *The Peculiar Institution*. New York: Vintage, 1956.

Stanchak, John E., ed. *Leslie's Illustrated Civil War*. 1894. Reprint, Jackson: University Press of Mississippi, 1992.

Stannard, David. "Calm Dwellings." *American Heritage*, September 1979, 47.

Stevens, George T. *Three Years in the Sixth Corps*. Albany: S. R. Gray, 1866.

Stewart, Katie. *Cooking and Eating*. London: Hart-Davis, MacGibbon, 1975.

Stinson, Byron. "The Invalid Corps." *Civil War Times Illustrated*, May 1971, 20–27.

Straubing, Harold Elk, ed. *Civil War Eyewitness Reports*. N.p.: Archon Books, 1985.

Strother, Horatio T. *The Underground Railroad in Connecticut*. Middletown: Wesleyan University Press, 1962.

Sullivan, Walter. *The War the Women Lived: Female Voices from the Confederate South*. Nashville: J. S. Sanders, 1995.

Swartwelder, A. C. "This Invaluable Beverage: The Recollections of Dr. A. C. Swartwelder." *Civil War Times Illustrated*, October 1975, 10–11.

Taylor, Alan. "Fenimore Cooper's America." *History Today* 46, no. 2 (February 1996): 21–27.

Thayer, John A. *The Practical Expedite or Time-Book Companion*. Stoughton, MA: Privately printed, 1847.

Thomas, Emory M. *The Confederacy as a Revolutionary Experience*. Columbia: University of South Carolina Press, 1991.

Tice, Douglas O. "Bread or Blood: The Richmond Bread Riot," *Civil War Times Illustrated*, February 1974, 12.

Tosh, John. "New Men? The Bourgeois Cult of Home." *History Today* 46 (December 1996).

Town, Salem. *The Fourth Reader, or Exercises in Reading and Speaking*. Cooperstown: H. & E. Phinney, 1849.

Trager, James. *The Food Chronology*. New York: Henry Holt, 1995.

Walton, William, ed. *A Civil War Courtship: The Letters of Edwin Weller from Antietam to Atlanta*. New York: Doubleday, 1980.

Weigley, Russell F. *The Age of Battles: The Quest for Decisive Warfare from Breitenfeld to Waterloo*. Bloomington: Indiana University Press, 1991.

Weld, Theodore. *American Slavery as It Is*. New York: N.p., 1839.

White, David O. *Connecticut's Black Soldiers*. Chester: Pequot Press, 1973.

Wills, Brian Steel. *A Battle from the Start: The Life of Nathan Bedford Forrest*. New York: HarperCollins, 1992.

Wise, Stephen R. *Lifeline of the Confederacy: Blockade Running During the Civil War.* Columbia: University of South Carolina Press, 1988.

Woodward, C. Vann. *Mary Chesnut's Civil War.* New Haven: Yale University Press, 1981.

Woodward, George E. *Woodward's Architecture and Rural Art.* 2 vols. New York: Privately printed, 1867–1868.

Woodward, John H. "Herding Beef for the Union Army." *Civil War Times Illustrated*, December 1970, 28–39.

WARTIME PERIODICALS

Frank Leslie's Illustrated Newspaper January 31, 1863; April 17, 1863; June 6, 1863; April 9, 1864; May 28, 1864; August 6, 1864.

Harper's Weekly, October 4, 1862; October 11, 1862; December 27, 1862; May 23, 1863; July 2, 1864.

New York Times, April 15, 1861; September 23, 1862; December 17, 1862; July 6, 1863; April 10,1865; April 15, 1865.

New York Tribune, May 1–May 9, 1863; May 16, 1864.

Southern Illustrated News, February 21, 1863; March 28, 1863; August 1, 1863; October 17, 1863.

SHEET MUSIC

Clark, James G. "The Children of the Battlefield." Philadelphia: Lee & Walker, 1864.

Manahan, Thomas. "Comrades, I Am Dying." Boston: Henry Talman & Co., 1864.

Mitchell, E.A.B. "Bear Gently, So Gently, Roughly Made Bier." Louisville: Wm. McCaroll, 1864.

Root, George F. "The Vacant Chair (or We Shall Meet but We Shall Miss Him)." Chicago: Root & Cady, 1862.

Index

Abbott, Henry L., soldier, 187
Abolition: allied with other social issues, 41–42; Emancipation Proclamation, 5, 105; as a political issue, xvi, 7–8, 20–21; as a war aim, 5
Abolitionists: Black moderates among, 88–89; espousal of violence by, 88; ethnic prejudice among, 9; radical rhetoric of, 85–88; religious affiliation of, 85–86; slave narratives published by, 66–68, 209; Southern attitudes towards, 25, 84, 88
Accidents, 32, 283
Agriculture, 8–10, 63–65
Aiken, David W., soldier and diarist, on marching, 176
Alexandria, VA, xi, 169
American Anti-Slavery Society, xv, 41, 86, 91
American Bible Society, 169
American Colonization Society, 81–85; berated by abolitionists, 84–85; Black members, 84; formed in 1817, 83; politically popular, 84
American Party. *See* Nativists

American Revolution: Founding Fathers, 10; as a source of Southern nationalism, 53–54
American Unitarian Association, 86
American Tract Society, 169
Amistad case, xv, 91–92
Amusements and diversions, 146–147, 194, 210, 218–222. *See also* Games; Literature; Reading
Anti-Semitism, 105–106
Appert, Nicholas, inventor, 227
Armies, 160–163; ancillary units, 163, 165–167, 174; artillery, 174, 177, 179; cavalry, 4, 148, 154–155, 163–164, 174; headquarters, 163; infantry, 179–181; officers and staff, 106, 115, 163, 177; organization, 98, 161–165
Army of Northern Virginia, 162. *See also* Confederate armies
Army of the Potomac, 162. *See also* Federal armies
Arthur's Home Magazine, 238; illustrations from, 192, 194, 196, 227
Ashby, Turner, Confederate officer and hero, 154
Avery, Isaac E., soldier, 187

Bacon and salt pork, 69, 124–126
Baldwin, Charles, diarist, quoted on accidents, 283
Baldwin, Roger S., abolitionist lawyer involved in the *Amistad* case, 91
Barbour, Emma Sargent, diarist, quoted on: carpets, 198; mourning, 289; Sanitary Commission, 235; schoolroom routine, 276; textbooks, 275
Barclay, Alexander T., soldier and diarist, on breaking camp, 175
Barkesdale, William, radical secessionist, 23
Barnum, P. T., publisher and showman, 212
Battle experiences, 173–187; battlefields described, 173, 179; behavior of troops, 173–174, 177–178, 180, 184; bloodiest battles, 99; care of wounded and dead, 167–168, 174, 181–187; climax, 174, 184–185; column of march, 164–165, 174, 175–177; disengagement, 174, 186; engagement of forces, 174, 178–181; major battles and campaigns, xvii-xviii, 13, 151; planning, 174; prisoners, 177, 187; skirmishing, xvii, 174, 177–178; theaters of war, 151–153; truces, 185–186
Battlefields listed by date, 151–154; Antietam, xviii, 99; Cold Harbor, xviii, 99; 1862 Valley Campaign, xvii, 159; Fort Sumter, xvii, 26; Gettysburg, xviii, 99, 132, 165; Shiloh, xviii, 99
Bayly, William H., diarist and Gettysburg witness, 179
Beadle, Irwin P., publisher of dime novels, 210
Beauregard, P.G.T., Confederate General, 106, 160
Beecher, Catherine E., author of *Miss Beecher's Domestic Receipt Book*, 200, 225; quoted, 225, 229, 233
Bell, John, southern politician and presidential candidate, 21

Benjamin, Judah P., member of Confederate cabinet, 27, 55
Benson, Eugene, sketch artist, 213
Berghaus, A., sketch artist, 143
Bernard, George N., war photographer, 216–217
Billings, John D., soldier and diarist, quoted, 81–82, 130
Billy Yank and Johnny Reb, 97–112
Black anti-slavery activists, 88–89
Black Codes, 70
"Black Republicanism," 21
Blaine, James G., politician and Speaker of the House, 112–113
"Bleeding Kansas," xvi, 19, 25
Blockade and blockade runners, 57–58, shortages created by, 230–235
Books: about the War, xii, 4; specific titles mentioned, 205–211, 215–216. *See also* Literature; Reading
Booth, John Wilkes, Lincoln's assassin, xviii
Borden, Gail, merchant, 227
Border states, 25, 215
Boston, MA, 31, 35–36, 40
Bourns, Francis, doctor, 296–297
Bowen, Edward R., soldier and diarist: on being wounded, 182; on graves, 186
Brady, Matthew, photographer, 216
Breckinridge, John C., Confederate General and presidential candidate, 21, 170
Brooks, Preston, politician, xvi
Brown, John, radical abolitionist, xvi, 19, 25, 85
Browne, H. K., illustrator, 205
Buchanan, James, President, 19, 22
Buglers, 107
Bull, Rice C., soldier and diarist, quoted on: army food, 115, being wounded, 183–184, 186–187
Bull Run (Manassas, VA): first battle, xvii, 151, 160; photographs taken of, 216; railway, 155–156, 159; second battle, 151; supplies captured at, 121

Burnside, Ambrose, Federal General, 162, 262

Butler, Benjamin, Federal General, 170

Butler, Jay, soldier and diarist, on value of rubber blanket, 144

Byron, George Gordon (Lord), author, 205

Calhoun, John C., southern politician, 22

Calling cards, 192–193

Campbell's *Self-Instructor*, on hair jewelry designs, 293

Camp life and recreation, 145–147. *See also* Games

Camps, 133–139; arrangement by regiment, 133–134; barracks, 134; company streets, 134, 137; furnishings, 134–135; innovations created by the troops, 138–139; lack of shelter for Southern troops, 139; latrines, 134; officers' and NCO's quarters, 134–135; types of tents, 135–139

Cartes de visite, 197–198; illustration of a period album, 197; popularity, 216

Catholics, 9, 39–40, 168

Chaplains, 169

Chestnut, Mary, diarist, quoted on: death and mourning, 285–286, 290; fabric shortages, 241–242; Mrs. Jefferson Davis' luncheon menu, 235; wedding dresses, 244–245

Child, Lydia, author of *The Mother's Book* and moralist, on the dangers of romantic literature, 204–206; death and children, 290; moral education, 271

Children: attitude toward slaves, 78; chivalry toward, 10; death, 286–288, 290; entrusted to slaves, 72; enlisted in armed forces, 106–108; estrangement of fathers from, 10, 41; gradual emancipation of slave children, 81–82; illustrations of, 44, 263, 266, 268; of mixed race, 77–78; photographs taken, 197; poverty among,

41, 44–45; and the war effort, 235; war orphan's 296. *See also* Education; Fashion (children's)

Chisholm, Daniel, soldier and diarist: on the experiences of battle, 184–185; on battle deaths, 186

Clarke, James G., poet, 297

Clay, Cassius, abolitionist, lecturer, and Federal General, 220

Cleburne, Patrick, Confederate General, 106

Clem, John Lincoln, drummer boy, 108

Clothing: children's, 107, 262–267; men's 257–266; slaves', 267–269; women's, 237–255. *See also* Fashion

Code of Public Instruction for the State of New York (1856), on the dangers of romantic literature, 204

Commissary. *See* Confederate armies; Federal armies

Compromise of 1850, xvi

Confederacy: constitution of, 54–55; establishment of, xvii, 26; need for popular consensus, 51, 57; as a unique Southern identity, 59, 150–151

Confederate armies: command structure, 151, 163–165; communications, 107, 165–166; mail services, 214; medical services, 167–168; names of units, 162; organization, 151, 160–162; Quartermaster's Department, 170; raiders and partisans, 154–155, 171; Subsistence Department, 117–118, 131

Conscription, 72, 108–111

Constitutional Convention of 1787, 6–7, 32

Cook, George S., war photographer, 217

Cooper, James Fenimore, author, 208, 215

Corinth, MS, heart of western railway system, 157–158

Corn and cornmeal, 8, 70, 128, 230

Cotton, 8–9, 57, 64
Cotton gin, 64
Crandall, Prudence, educator and reformer, 280
Crane, W. T., sketch artist, 83
Custer, George Armstrong, Federal General, 154, 215
Currier, Nathaniel, memorial pictures by, 294

Davis, Jefferson, President, CSA: on the Confederate Constitution, 54–55; first president of Confederacy, 26; on food shortages, 231; leader of Southern Democrats, 16; loss of his child, 287; overall commander of Confederate forces, 162; reaction to Bread Riots, 59; Secretary of War, 41
Davis, Theodore, sketch artist, 213
Dawson, F. W., soldier and diarist, on civilian support for the war, 175
Death. *See* Mourning
Democratic Party, xvi, 16–21
DeForest, John W., Federal officer: as author and war reporter, 208–209, 211; quoted on battlefield death, 181; quoted on black troops, 104; quoted on fear in battle, 178, 180; quoted on morale, 169–170; quoted on skirmishing, 174; quoted on tactics, 97
DeLancey, Martin R., moderate black abolitionist, 84
Dickens, Charles: popularity of, 205, 206–207, 215; as a social reformer, 207; works mentioned, 207, 210
Dix, Dorothea, nurse, 167
Dooley, John E., soldier and diarist, on marching, 176–177
Douglas, Stephen A., politician and presidential candidate, xvi, 16, 18, 21
Douglass, Frederick, author, former slave, and radical abolitionist, 67–68
Draft riots, 72–73
Drummers, 107, 166

Dwellings, 191–202; floor plans, 192; lack of bathrooms and closets, 202; types, 191

Early, Jubal, Confederate General, 160, 170
Education, 271–282; acceptance of public education, 45–46, 206, 274–275, 278–279; Black education, 67–68, 279–280; Catholic schools, 40, 45–46; conditions in common schools, 272–273, 275–276; curriculum, 274–275, 277–278; enrollment and student body, 274, 279; extent of public education, 273, 277, 279; higher education, 40, 279; moral education, 271–272, 277–278; private education, 45–46, 201; punishment, 273; "ragged schools," 206; school buildings, 272–273; school day and routine, 276–278; slates, 276; southern distaste of northern teachers, 278–279; standards, 274, 276, 278; teachers, 272–274; textbooks, 275–276, 278
Edwards, J. D., war photographer, 217
Elections and voting: election of 1856, 18–19; election of 1860, 20–22; election of 1864, xviii; expansion of franchise, 33; local, 19–20, 32–35; national, 2–22; rotation in office, 33
Emancipation Proclamation, xviii, 5, 105
Equipment for the individual soldier: bayonet, 142; blankets, 138, 142; canteen, 145; cartridge box, 145; greatcoats, 142–144; hats, 139; haversacks, 139, 145; as an impediment, 139, 143; knapsacks, 143–144; oilcloths, 143; rubber blanket, 138, 143–144; shelter (dog) tent, 137–139; shoes, 140–141; uniform allowance for one year, 141; uniforms, 139–140, 144–145; weapons, 141–142, 148, 163
Etiquette: condolence, 290–291; dining, 200; gloves, 250; men's suits, 257, 259; visitations, 193
Evans, Augusta Jane, author, 215

Evans, Susan, 198
Extension of slavery into the territories, 20

Family farming. *See* Agriculture
Fashion (children's): boy's, 107, 264–265, 268; color and dyes, 262; fabrics and pattern, 262, 265–266; girl's, 262–264, 268; hairstyles, 265; infant's, 266–267; Knickerbockers, 264–265; mourning clothes, 290; outerwear, 265; styling, 262; suspenders, 264
Fashion (for civilian men): coats, 257; collars, 258; colors and dyes, 258–259; cravats and neckties, 258; fabrics and patterns, 258–259; facial hair and hairstyles, 261–262; frock coats, 259; hats, 259–260; jewelry and watches, 10–11, 258, 260; mourning clothes, 290; nightdress and lounging attire, 260–261; shirts, 257; styling, 258; suits, 259; suspenders, 260; trousers, 257–258; undergarments, 260; waistcoats or vests, 258; work clothing, 257–258
Fashion (for women): accessories and trim, 240–241, 243, 245, 250–251; aprons, 249; ball gowns, 243–244; blouses and shirts, 244; bodice, 238–239; bonnets and hats, 244, 248–249; capes, coats, and outerwear, 245, 247–248; care and cleaning, 240–241; collars and cuffs, 240, 246; colors and dyes, 240, 242–243; dresses and skirts, 238–245; effect of blockade on, 241–242; fabrics and patterns, 241–244, 249–250; footwear, 250; gloves, 245, 250; hairstyles, 244–245, 252–254; hemlines, 241; hoops, 245–246; jackets and vests, 244; jewelry, 251–252, 254, 264, 291–294; magazines and fashion plates, 238, 246, 250, 252; mourning clothes, 289–290; neckline, 240, 244, 252; petticoats, 245–246; photographic record, 237–238, 251, 254; prices, 242; riding habit, 244; sleeves, 239–240, 244; styling, 238–239, 241–242; types of garments, 238; undergarments, 245–247; waistline, 239, 241; wedding dresses, 217, 242, 244–245
Federal armies: command structure, 150; communications, 107, 165–167; corps and divisions, 163–165; medical services, 167; names, 162; organization, 160–162; Quartermaster's Department, 118, 170; raiders and partisans, 3, 217; Subsistence Department, 117
Field fortifications, described, 142, 180, 184
Fire-eaters, 22–23, 26
Fitzgerald, Edward, author, on rural cemeteries, 286
Flags and flag bearers: Confederate battle flag, 26; Federal and regimental flags displayed, 28, 166; first national flag, 56; importance of, 165–166; secession flags, 52
Fletcher, William A., soldier and diarist, quoted on: being wounded, 181; politics 12
Food: advertisements, 227; bacon and salt pork, 124–126; bread, fresh baked, 126–127; canning and canned foods, 226–228; coffee and coffee substitutes, 115, 129–130, 231–232; common diet, 228–229; cornbread, 128, 233; dairy products, 232; flour, 232–233; foraging, 122–124, 132, 164; hardtack, 115, 127–128; meat, 124–126; officers' mess, 121; preparation, 116–117; preservation, 119, 225–226; prices, 57, 229–230; quality and nutritional value, 118–119, 131, 228; rations, 115–120; salt and salted foods, 70, 130–131, 233–234; shortages, 58, 115, 124, 132, 230–235; storage, 225–226; sutlers, 120–121
Forbes, Edwin, sketch artist, 69, 213, 223
Force Bill, xv, 22
Forrest, Nathan Bedford, Confederate General, 154

Fort Sumter, xvii, 26
Foster, Abby K., abolitionist and feminist, 86
Free Blacks (Freeman). *See* Slavery
Freedmen's Bureau, 66–67; 280
Fremont, John C., Federal General and presidential candidate, 18
Fuller, Charles A., soldier and diarist, on being wounded, 182

Games, 70, 146–147, 220. *See also* Amusements and diversions
Gardner, Alexander, photographer, 216
Garfield, James, U.S. President, death of his child during the war, 294
Garibaldi, Giuseppe, Italian freedom fighter, 49, 103
Garnet, Henry H., moderate black abolitionist, 84
Garrison, William Lloyd, radical abolitionist and publisher, xv, 31, 40, 88; attacks "pro-slavery" churches, 88; berates gradual emancipation, 84; taken seriously by the South, 88; violent rhetoric of, 84–85
Gay, Sidney H., abolitionist, 86
Gearhart, Edwin A., soldier and diarist, on linear tactics, 179
Gedney, T. R., U.S. Naval Officer, 91–92
Geography, 55–56, 151–154
General Order No. 11, anti-Semitic order issued by U. S. Grant in 1862, 106
General Order No. 28, insulting to southern women, issued by Benjamin Butler in 1862, 170
German immigrants, 37–38, 104
Gettysburg, xviii, 132, 165
Godey, Louis B., publisher, 238
Godey's Ladies Book, 238; fashion illustrations from, 239, 268; quoted on aprons, 249; quoted on children's dresses and corsets, 262; quoted on hair jewelry, 293–294; quoted on iceboxes 226; quoted on mourning

etiquette, 289–290; quoted on riding habit, 244
Gone with the Wind (motion picture), 254. *See also* Mitchell, Margaret
Gordon, John B., Confederate General, 170, 207
Graham's Magazine, 238
Grant, Ulysses S., Federal General, xviii, 99, 106, 167
Gray, Mary A. H., diarist, 233
Grierson, Benjamin, Federal officer, 217
Grimke, Angelina and Sarah, abolitionist sisters, 86–88

Hague, Parthenia, diarist, quoted on: coffee substitutes, 231; fashion during blockade, 238; hoopskirts, 246; sugar and sugar substitutes, 234
Hall, C. S., sketch artist, 213
Halleck, Henry W., Federal General and Chief of Staff, 150, 162
Hampton, Wade, Confederate General, "Beef Steak Raid," 125
Hannaford, Ebenezer, soldier and diarist, on preparations for battle, 177
Harper, Fletcher, publisher, 213–214
Harper's Ferry, VA, 25, 85, 152, 211–214
Harper's Weekly, 41, 238, 269, 275
Hawes, Joel, author and moralist, 203, 206
Hawthorne, Nathaniel, author, 209
Hazen, William B., soldier and diarist, on the description of battles, 173–174
Health: ambulances, 167, 169; bathing, 202; diet, 69–70, 118–119, 131, 228–230; lack of first aid kits, 188; medical stores, 177; military hospitals, 167–168; organization of medical services, 163, 167–168; wounded quoted, 182–185
Henry, Patrick, politician, quoted, 7
Heth, Henry, Confederate General, 178
Hillen, C.E.F., sketch artist, 213

Homestead Act of 1862, 230
Honor and duty, 27, 101–103
Hood, John B., Confederate General, 104
Hooker, Joseph, Federal General, 170
Hoops. *See* Undergarments
"House Divided" speech, xvi, 19–20
Household furnishings: advertisements for, 194, 196; art and prints, 198; beds, 201; books, 199; cardholders, 193; chairs, 192, 195; chamber pots, 202; desks and writing tables, 199; draperies, 199; floor coverings, 193, 198–200; lighting, 193, 200, 202; mirrors, 192; musical instruments and sheet music, 195–197, 284; natural objects, 194–195, 199; prices, 199, 201; sofas, 195; tables, 192, 193, 197, 200; upholstery materials, 195; utensils, 200–201; wall treatments, 198
Housekeeper's Encyclopedia, quoted on: fabric care, 240–241; infant care, 267
Howard, David R., soldier and diarist, on being wounded, 184
Humiston, Amos, departed soldier and father, 296
Hunter, David, Federal General, 160
Hurd, Maria Jane, memorial card of, 288, 294
Hyde, John H., abolitionist editor, 91

Ice and iceboxes, 226
Illiteracy, 100, 203
Immigration and its effects, 9, 35–41
Inflation, 57. *See also* Food; Household furnishings
Irish immigrants: attitude toward Blacks, 72–73, 104–105; involvement in the war, 104, 191; treatment of, 9, 37–38
Irrepressible conflict, 3–4, 13
Italian immigrants, 37, 103–104

Jackman, John S., soldier and diarist, on the experiences of battle, 180–181

Jackson, Mary, leader of Bread Riots, 58–59
Jackson, Thomas J. "Stonewall," Confederate General and hero: attacks railways, 156; corps commander, 163; religious fervor, 169; seizes Harper's Ferry arsenal, xvii; as southern hero, 55; Valley Campaign of 1862, xvii, 159
James, John T., soldier and diarist, on the experiences of battle, 179
Jefferson, Thomas, President: concern over growing size of government, 33; on equality of races, 6–7, 81; as a Southern icon, 54
Jewelry, effect of California gold strike on availability and style, 251, 260. *See also* Fashion; Mourning
Jewish immigrants, 37–39
Johnson, Andrew, Vice-president, xviii
Johnston, David E., soldier and diarist, on being wounded, 182
Johnston, Joseph E., Confederate General, 160
Jones, John B., Confederate war clerk and diarist, quoted, 24, 27, 57
Judson, Andrew T., judge, 91

Kansas-Nebraska Act, xvi, 16–19
Know-Nothings, 19. *See also* Nativists

Ladies' craft projects, 221–222, 251, 260
Lectures, 219–220
Lee, Elizabeth Blair, diarist, quoted on prices, 199–201
Lee, Henry "Light Horse Harry," Revolutionary hero and father of R. E. Lee, 53–54
Lee, Laura, diarist, quoted on secession bonnets, 249
Lee, Robert E., Confederate General: captures John Brown, xvi; commands Army of Northern Virginia, 162; on honor, 27; references to opponents, 187; releases northern

artists, 213; sanctions killing of prisoners, 154; on supplies, 32, 157
Lemmon Case, 92–93
Leslie, Frank (Henry Carter), publisher, 211–214
Leslie's Illustrated Magazine: development of, 211–214; illustrations from, 26, 28, 56, 101, 123, 143; on mourning, 285; popularity of, 238; on slave shoes, 269
Lewis, Matthew G., author, 205–206
Lincoln, Abraham, President, xvi–xviii; assassinated, xviii; on boys in war, 107; calls for volunteers, xvii, 26; cancels General Order No. 11, 106; death of child, 287; directing military strategy, 149–150; escaping cares of office, 167; favors colonization, 84; mentioned in textbook, 278; mourning the death of, 297–298; photographs of, 216; as a politician, 19–22; resigned to loss of 1864 election, 3; stovepipe hat, 259
Lincoln, Mary Todd, 198
Lind, Jenny, singer, 198
Literature, 203–211; adventure stories, 209–210; American and foreign authors, 205–206; book publishing, 210; classics, 205; influence on readers, 203–211; instructive reading, 204, 215; novels, 203–205; popular works, 207; religious reading, 211, 215; tales of terror, 205; women authors, 215–216. *See also* Books; Reading
Livermore, Mary, diarist, quoted on a "Sanitary Fair," 235
Longstreet, James, Confederate General, 162–163
Louisiana, 25, 89
Lovejoy, Elijah P., murdered abolitionist, 86
Lovie, Henry, sketch artist, 5, 213
Lumbard, Joseph A., soldier and diarist, on fear in battle, 177
Lumley, Arthur, sketch artist, 213

Lunt, Dolly Sumner (Burge), diarist, 233
Lytle, A. D., photographer, 217

Madison, James, President, 7
Major, (Mrs.) Alexander, quoted on Lincoln's death, 297–298
Mallard, Mary S., diarist, 231
Manifest Destiny, 31
Maps: of Northern Virginia, 152; of Railways in the Western Theater, 158
Martine's Hand-Book of Etiquette, and Guide to True Politeness. See Etiquette
Mason, John, inventor, 229
Mason-Dixon line, 54
Maturin, Edward, author, 205
May, Emily, quoted, 264–265
McCarthy, Carlton, soldier and diarist: on honor, 27–28; on skirmishing, 177
McClellan, George B., Federal General and presidential candidate, xvii, xviii, 125, 213
McCormick, Cyrus, inventor, 230
McDonald, Cornelia Peake, diarist, quoted on: burial and mourning, 144, 287–288; food, 255
McDowell, Irvin, Federal General, 160
McQuire, Judith, diarist, quoted on: burial and mourning, 287, 292; prices, 231–233, 242
Medicine. *See* Health
Mexican War of 1846, xvi
Miles, Harriet, gravestone inscription, 286
Military education, 51
Military strategy and tactics, 150–151; Anaconda Plan, 149; concentration in space and time, 164–165; drill, 145–146; interior lines, 165; linear tactics, 165, 177, 179–180; Napoleonic influence, 163–164; pickets and outposts, 145, 163; railroads, 155–158; sharpshooting, 142; turning movements, 165, 174; weapons, 141–142

Military supplies: and the blockade, 57; massive support of Federal troops, 118; need to defend supply lines, 150, 154; Quartermaster General and, 163; Southern lack of, 120, 144; U.S. Navy and, 153–154

Miscegenation: Black females as victims of, 77–80; persons of mixed race, 75

Missouri Compromise, xv, xvi

Mitchell, Margaret, author of *Gone with the Wind*, 263; clothing described by, 254

Mobile, AL, 56

Moore, Marinda Branson, Southern textbook author, 278

Moore, Thomas, inventor, 226

Morgan, John Hunt, Confederate partisan, 154

Morgan, Sarah, diarist, quoted on: food, 233; hairstyles, 265; sacrifices brought on by war, 241–242; Southern uniforms, 144–145

Morrill Act of 1862, 279

Mosby, John Singleton, Confederate partisan, 154, 171

Mourning: attitudes toward death, 284–289; battlefield deaths, 216, 296–297; businesses dedicated to, 291–292; children's deaths, 286–288; death of Lincoln, 297–298; deaths among presidential children, 287, 294; dress, 291–292; effect of Blockade on, 296; embalming, 296; etiquette, 290; fear of unlamented death, 288–289, 296; hair memorials, 293–294; jewelry, 291–294; memorials, 285, 294–295; posthumous photographs, 216, 288, 294–295; rural cemeteries, 284–285, 297; among slaves, 295–296; suppliers, 292; symbols, 286–287; widows and widowers, 289–290

Music: military, 107; patriotic, 28; popularity with soldiers, 147; sheet music industry, 195–196; somber, 284, 292

National cemeteries, 297

Nationalism, 49–59; blockade runners and, 57; in Europe, 49; failures of, 59; as a motive for soldiers, 52–53; in the North, 31–32; support for, among common citizens, 52; unique Southern characteristics, 50–53, 55; ties to American Revolution, 53–54

Native Americans, 106

Nativists, 16–21

Naval operations, 153–154

New Orleans, xviii, 9, 56, 66, 170

Newspapers, 211–214; Black newspapers, 89; illustrated press, 212; southern radical press, 23–25; Unionist papers destroyed, 24

New York City, 9, 36

Non-commissioned officers (NCO's), 134–135

Norfolk, VA, 56

Northern attitudes toward Blacks, 72–73, 82, 105–106

Northern attitudes toward the South, 11, 36, 51, 76

Northern society, 9–10, 17–18

Norwalk, CT: 1826 schoolhouse, 272; gravestone from, 298

Nullification, xv, 22

Nuns and sisters as hospital workers, 168

Office Holding, 32–35

Oligarchy. *See* Planter aristocracy

O'Niell, James, sketch artist, 213

Optical novelties, 218–219

Overseer, 64, 71

Parkhurst, Clinton, soldier and diarist, 120

Partisan Warfare, 3

Pelham, Camden, author, 205

Petersburg, VA, 4

Peterson's Magazine, 238; illustration from, 221; quoted on children's clothing, 265–266; quoted on corsets, 262; quoted on cravats, 258; quoted on hair care, 253–254; quoted on hoops, 246; quoted on

Knickerbockers, 264–265; quoted on men's lounge wear, 260–261; quoted on waist pouches, 251

Phillips, Wendell, abolitionist and lecturer, 84, 220

Photography: collecting, 197–198; limitations on, 183, 216–218, 237; photographers, 216–217

Pianos and organs, 195; advertisement for, 196

Pickett, George, Confederate General, 165, 207

Pierce, Tilly, diarist and witness to Gettysburg, 181, 188

Plantation Economy, 8–9, 63–65

Plantations. *See* Corn and cornmeal; Cotton; Rice; Sugar; Tobacco

Planter aristocracy: equality among, 63; firm hold on social structure, 33, 50; kinship, 10–11; as a percentage of population, 63; weakened by secession, 55

Poe, Edgar Allan, author, 208; former editor of *Southern Literary Messenger*, 24

Politics: lack of restraint in, 12, 15; as a popular pastime, 15–16

Polk, Leonidas, Confederate General and Bishop, 169

Poor whites, 11, 44, 72

Popular sovereignty, xvi, 16–18

Ports, importance to the South, 56

Poverty, 43–46

Prostitution, 76–77, 170, 172

Protestants, 9, 17, 38–40, 74, 85–86

Pryor, Roger A., editor, 24

Quakers, 39, 85

Race relations. *See* Northern attitudes toward Blacks; Southern attitudes toward Blacks

Radcliffe, Ann, author, 205

Railroads, 32, 143, 155–158; charters, 34; differences in gauge, 157; effect on lifestyle, 226; lack of maintenance, 157–158; locomotives, 156;

map of railways in the Western Theater, 158

Reading: availability of reading materials, 204–205, 214–215; danger of escapist literature, 203–206; dime novels, 204, 210–211; four categories of reading material, 203; illustrated magazines and newspapers, 211–214, 238; libraries, 199, 204, 211; low quality materials, 210; popular titles listed, 210; reading groups, 219

Receipt books: cider jelly, 235; coffee and flour substitutes, 231–232; defined, 225; illustration of cover, 204

Recreation, 145–147

Reenactors of Civil War: artillery, 183; cavalry, 164; encampments, 137; in reenactments, 166, 176, 178, 183; uniforms of, 98

Reform movements: controversy over, 50; failures, 42–43, 45–46; major movements, 40–46; moral basis, 40–41, 83–84; need for, 35, 41, 49; Northern reaction to Southern lifestyle, 11, 51; reaction to radical reform, 33–35, 87–88; shift from symbolic to conclusive goals, 41, 43

Reformers: characteristics of 40–41, 84; optimistic views of, 31–33, 35, 46; public rejection of methods used by, 12, 35, 81, 86, 87–88

Reid, Mayne, author, 208

Religion and religious revivalism: among abolitionists, 85–86; Black churches, 73–74; Catholics, 9, 39–40, 168; change of traditional emphasis, 35, 39; Judaism, 37–39; on plantations, 69; Protestant crusade, 9, 17, 40; Protestant sects, 38–40, 85–86, 169, 284–285; Quakers, 39, 85; slaves and, 73–74, 79–80

Religious tracts, 169, 199, 211

Report of the Superintendent of Common Schools of Pennsylvania (1861), quoted on: the abilities of men and women as teachers, 273–274; "Colored Schools," 280; enrollment of rural students, 274; lack of funds and materials, 272, 276; moral education, 277; school board, 273; school buildings, 273, 276; teacher salaries, 273; textbooks, 277–278

Republican Party, xvi–xvii, 16–21

Rhett, Robert B., radical secessionist and publisher, 23–24

Rhodes, Elisha Hunt, soldier and diarist, on the experiences of battle, 179

Rice, 8, 63

Richmond, VA, 152; Bread Riots, xviii, 58–59; city changed by secession, xii, 27; Confederate government, xii, 126, 157; Confederate White House, 288; hospitals in, 168; objective of Federal strategy, 150; War office at, 27, 157, 160

Rivers: ability of Federal Navy to control, 154; as natural obstacle to invasion, 152–153

Roads, 158–160; corduroy, 159; Macadam, 159–160, 171; mud, 149, 159; plank roads, 159

Romanticism, 205–206, 284–285

Rosser, Thomas, Confederate General, 170

Ruffin, Edmund, radical secessionist, 23, 54

Russell, Andrew J., Federal officer and photographer, 217

Salt, 130–131, 233–234

Schell, F. B., sketch artist, 62, 156, 213

Schell, F. H., sketch artist, 213

Scott, Dred, xvi, 19, 91, 93

Scott, Walter, author, 10, 208, 215

Scott, Winfield, Federal General, xvii, 149

Secession, xvii, 5, 21–28; Ordinance of Secession (Dec. 20, 1860), 25; secession congress, 26

Selleck, Charlotte, gravestone inscription, 285–286

Seward, William H., 3–4

Sexual relations outside marriage, 76–78, 80

Shakespeare, William, author, 205, 215

Shenandoah Valley, xvii, as a battlefield, 151–153; Valley Campaigns, 156, 159–160

Sheridan, Philip, Federal General, 103, 160

Sherman, William T., Federal General, 214

Sibley, Henry, Confederate General and inventor, 135–136

Sigel, Franz, Federal General, 160

Signal Corps, 166

Sketch artists and reporters, 211–214

Slave aristocracy. *See* Planter aristocracy

Slave power conspiracy, 21

Slaveowners, 89–91

Slavery and slaves, 61–75; abolition of slavery, 5, 20, 85–88; anti-slavery groups in the south, 81–83; Atlantic slave trade, 61, 63–64, 83, 91; Black slave owners, 66; children of slaves, 75–76; clothing, 68, 267–269; congressional power to control, 6–8; contraband, 69; death, 295–296; effect of *Uncle Tom's Cabin*, 209–210; election issue, 20; emancipation, xviii, 171; entertainment, 70; fear of slave revolts, xv, 85; female slaves, 75–78; food, 69–70; free blacks, 61–62, 90, 93, 104; hardships, 65, 68–69; health, 63; hired out to others, 72; legal rights, 70–73; literacy, 279–280, manumission, 65; marriage, 74–75, 79, 245; narratives, 66–67; plantation records, 67; plantation slavery, 65–68; punishment, 70–71; religion, 73–74, 88; sale of, 90; schools for, 279–280; skills, 61, 66; slave patrols, 62; slaves as tradesmen, 65–66; value of slaves, 63–64, 71, 77

Small, Abner, soldier and diarist, on flags, 179

Society for the Prevention of Pauperism, 43–44
Soldiers, 97–112; age, 99; Black soldiers, 55, 93, 104; boys in the ranks, 106–108; casualties among, 99, 283; civilian occupations, 100, 109–110; composition of opposing forces, 98; conscripts vs. volunteers, 98, 101–103, 108–111; deserters and skulkers, 161; disbanded at the end of the war, 111–112; education of, 99–100; fear of unlamented death, 288–289, 296; fighting style, 97; foreign born, 103–104; health, 109; height, 99; illiteracy among, 100, 203; Irish soldiers, 104; Jewish soldiers, 104, 106; marital status, 99; messmates, 160; Native Americans, 106; partisans and irregulars, 108, 154–155; prisoners, 105, 111; statistics regarding, 97–100; weight, 99
South Carolina, 22, 89
South Carolina Convention, xvii, 25–26
Southern attitudes toward Blacks, 11, 65, 71–72, 105–106
Southern attitudes toward Northern society, 11, 19, 37, 53–54
Southern society, 10, 49–52
Spiegel, Marcus, M., Federal officer, 106
Stanton, Edwin M., Federal Secretary of War, 150, 167
State sovereignty, 6
States' rights, 6–7, 55
Steinway, Henry, piano maker, 195
Stephens, Alexander, Vice-President, CSA, 26, 55
Stevens, George T., army surgeon and diarist, on the experiences of battle, 180
Stone, Kate, diarist, 85
Stone, Margie, cartes de visite collection of, 140, 197
Stone, Sarah, diarist, on slave clothing, 267–268
Stowe, Harriet Beecher, author, xvi, 199, 209–210, 215, 286

Stuart, James E. B., Confederate General, 171
Sugar, 9, 63
Sumner, Charles, abolitionist and politician, xvi, 220
Supreme Court, xv–xvi, 8, 91–93

Taliaferro, William B., Confederate General, 106
Tappan, Louis, abolitionist, 86, 91
Taylor, William B., soldier and diarist, on marching, 175
Teachers. *See* Education
Telegraphy, 32, 166–167
Temperance, 37–38, 41–43
Tennessee: as a breadbasket for the South, 150; as a provider of troops, 153; as a rail center, 156; as the western theater of war, 153
Tennyson, Alfred, poet, *Enoch Arden*, 107
Texas, xvi, 25, 31, 89, 149
Thayer, John A., author, 11
Theories of war causation, 8–13
Tilton, Theodore, abolitionist, 86, 220
Time. *See* Watches
Tobacco, 9, 63
Trent Affair, xvii
Trollope, Frances, foreign visitor, 228
Tucker, Nathaniel B., secessionist author, 215
Tudor, Frederick, inventor, 226
Turner, Nat, Black leader, xv, 85

Uncle Tom's Cabin, xvi, 25, 209, 286
Undergarments, 245–246; camisole, 245; chemise, 245; corset, 245; crinolines, 245–246; hoops, 245–246; nightdress, 246; petticoats, 245
Underground Railroad, 86
Uniforms, 28, 139–140; color and material, 144–145; photographs of, 140; similarity between opponents, 144
Unionism, 24–25
Unitarians, 85–86
Urbanization, 9, 35–38, 285
Utopian views of society, 31–32, 49

U.S. Christian Commission, 130, 169, 211

U.S. Military Rail Road, 156

U.S. Military Telegraph Service, 166

U.S. Sanitary Commission, 168–169, 222, 235

Van Camp, Gilbert, merchant, 227

Vesey, Denmark, Black leader, xv, 85

Vicksburg, 4

Victorian home, 191–202; bedrooms, 191, 201; dining room, 191, 200; front hall, 191–193; kitchen, 191, 200–201; library, 191, 199; necessary, 202; nursery, 191, 201; parlor, 191, 193–199; stoves and fireplaces, 194, 200–201

Victorianism, 10

Virginia, 22, 25–26, 150–151

Volunteers, 26, 27–28, 52–53, 100–101; draft substitutes, 110; enlistment bounties, 101, 110; euphoric response to mobilization, xvii, 143; recruiting offices, 101

War weariness, 3, 122, 223

Washington, D.C.: the Capitol, xi, 41; threatened, 152; troops defending, 150; War Department, 28

Washington, George, President, 53–54

Watches, 10–11, 252

Wati, Stand, Native American and last Confederate General to surrender, xviii, 106

Waud, Alfred and William, sketch artists and brothers, 56, 213

Weld, Theodore D., abolitionist and author, 87, 209

Weller, Edwin, soldier and diarist, on the rigors of marching, 147, 176

West Virginia, xvii

Wheat, 230, 272

Whigs, 15–16

White supremacy, 72, 76

Whitfield, James M., moderate black abolitionist, 84

Whitman, George Washington, soldier and diarist, on battle deaths, 186

Wilmington, NC, 56

Winchester, VA, 122, 144, 156, 249

Winthrope, Theodore, author and diarist, 211

Wise, Henry A., editor of the *Enquirer*, 24

Wittenmyer, Annie, establishes dietary kitchens, 235

Women: female-dominated household, 10; filling cartridges, 170; as nurses, 167; supporting the war effort, 27; traveling with the army, 170

Women's American Association for Relief, 168

Women's rights and feminism, 41, 86–88

Woodward, John H., Federal officer, 124–125

Work for wage economy, 11

Worsham, J. H., soldier and diarist, on marching, 175

Wounded and killed: ambulances and Invalid Corps, 167–169; burial of the dead, 186, 296–297; number of deaths, xii, 186; nurses, 168; photographs of battlefield dead, 216; treatment, 168–169, 183–184; types of wounds, 142; wounded quoted, 182–185

Wyeth, Nathaniel, inventor, 226

Wyndham, Percy, soldier, 103

Yancey, William L., radical secessionist, 23, 54

YMCA(Young Men's Christian Association), 58, 169

About the Authors

DOROTHY DENNEEN VOLO is a teacher and historian. She has been an active living history reenactor for twenty years and has been involved in numerous community historical education projects.

JAMES M. VOLO is a teacher, historian, and living history enthusiast. He has been an active historic reenactor for more than two decades, participating in a wide range of living history events, including television and screen performance.